T0131769

PULP VIETNAM

In this compelling evaluation of Cold War popular culture, *Pulp Vietnam* explores how men's adventure magazines helped shape the attitudes of young, working-class Americans, the same men who fought and served in the long and bitter war in Vietnam.

The "macho pulps" – boasting titles like *Man's Conquest, Battle Cry,* and *Adventure Life* – portrayed men courageously defeating their enemies in battle, while women were reduced to sexual objects, either trivialized as erotic trophies or depicted as sexualized villains using their bodies to prey on unsuspecting, innocent men. The result was the crafting and dissemination of a particular version of martial masculinity that helped establish GIs' expectations and perceptions of war in Vietnam.

By examining the role that popular culture can play in normalizing wartime sexual violence and challenging readers to consider how American society should move beyond pulp conceptions of "normal" male behavior, Daddis convincingly argues that how we construct popular tales of masculinity matters in both peace and war.

Gregory A. Daddis is a professor of history and the USS Midway Chair in Modern US Military History at San Diego State University. A retired US Army colonel, he has served in both Operations Desert Storm and Iraqi Freedom. He has authored four books, including *Withdrawal: Reassessing America's Final Years in Vietnam.*

MILITARY, WAR, AND SOCIETY IN MODERN AMERICAN HISTORY

Series Editors
Beth Bailey, University of Kansas
Andrew Preston, Cambridge University

Military, War, and Society in Modern American History is a new series that showcases original scholarship on the military, war, and society in modern U.S. history. The series builds on recent innovations in the fields of military and diplomatic history and includes historical works on a broad range of topics, including civil-military relations and the militarization of culture and society; the military's influence on policy, power, politics, and political economy; the military as a key institution in managing and shaping social change, both within the military and in broader American society; the effect the military has had on American political and economic development, whether in wartime or peacetime; and the military as a leading edge of American engagement with the wider world, including forms of soft power as well as the use of force.

PULP VIETNAM

War and Gender in Cold War Men's Adventure Magazines

Gregory A. Daddis

San Diego State University, California

CAMBRIDGE
UNIVERSITY PRESS

CAMBRIDGE
UNIVERSITY PRESS

Shaftesbury Road, Cambridge CB2 8EA, United Kingdom

One Liberty Plaza, 20th Floor, New York, NY 10006, USA

477 Williamstown Road, Port Melbourne, VIC 3207, Australia

314–321, 3rd Floor, Plot 3, Splendor Forum, Jasola District Centre, New Delhi – 110025, India

103 Penang Road, #05–06/07, Visioncrest Commercial, Singapore 238467

Cambridge University Press is part of Cambridge University Press & Assessment, a department of the University of Cambridge.

We share the University's mission to contribute to society through the pursuit of education, learning and research at the highest international levels of excellence.

www.cambridge.org
Information on this title: www.cambridge.org/9781108737302

DOI: 10.1017/9781108655774

First published 2021
First paperback edition 2022

A catalogue record for this publication is available from the British Library

ISBN   978-1-108-49350-5   Hardback
ISBN   978-1-108-73730-2   Paperback

For Susan,
who deserves one all her own

Contents

Acknowledgments

There's an adage among academics that teaching and scholarship should reinforce one another. This work is proverb in practice, as the central idea for *Pulp Vietnam* first took root in an undergraduate course at West Point. In the spring of 2015, my colleague Jen Kiesling and I co-taught an elective titled "War and Gender in Modern America." We had discussed the idea for years and after wrangling over course goals, readings, and writing requirements – mostly while swimming laps in Crandall Pool – we started on an intellectual journey that was one of the most satisfying teaching assignments during my entire tenure at the US Military Academy. Jen and I learned as much from our discussions in class with a group of phenomenal cadets as we did from lesson planning with each other.

As we read K. A. Cuordileone's *Manhood and American Political Culture in the Cold War*, I started searching for pop culture images of American soldiers in the 1950s and 1960s. It was then that I came across the January 1953 cover of *American Manhood* magazine. A barrel-chested GI, whose bare pectoral muscles rivaled Arnold Schwarzenegger's in his prime, stands upon a tank while holding a semi-automatic rifle, unsubtly extending forward from his hips. The cover teased some of the exhilarating articles within: "Hell's Hill in Korea" and "What You Should Know About Sex." Clearly, this was not the GI Joe I had played with as a child. My interest was piqued.

From West Point, I moved to Chapman University, directing a graduate program in War and Society Studies and eventually procuring funding to purchase a collection of some 250 men's adventure magazines, now housed in Chapman's Leatherby Library. I integrated the magazines into our graduate course on war and gender and, once more, benefited from my students' insightful reflections on how these postwar "macho pulps" were illustrating a conception of militarized masculinity that suggested something rather profound about the Cold War era.

And, because timing is everything, I had the good fortune to share my ideas on a book project with Beth Bailey, one of my real-life heroes in the historical profession. Along with Andrew Preston, Beth was starting a new series on war and society with Cambridge University Press. Beth invited me to the University of Kansas to hone my ideas with some superb historians and gender scholars before I had the chance to pitch my idea to Cambridge's Debbie Gershenowitz. Thankfully, all three saw merit in pursuing this project, Debbie more than matching her reputation as one of the finest editors in business. To work with these amazing professionals has been a dream come true. I admire each of them and am so grateful to have had this opportunity to work with the very best of the best.

At Cambridge University Press, I also want to thank Cecelia Cancellaro, Thomas Haynes, Steven Holt, and Michael Watson for seeing *Pulp Vietnam* across the finish line. Special thanks go to Rachel Blaifeder, a spectacular senior editorial assistant, for all her hard work that too often goes unnoticed. Truth be told, Rachel did far more work getting this book to print than the Jonas Brothers ever did!

I also have been incredibly fortunate to share ideas with an immensely talented group of graduate students at Chapman University. Spenser Carroll-Johnson and Robbie Del Toro were instrumental in helping collect research materials, even if Robbie is still scarred by a certain copy machine incident. Cameron Carlomagno deserves special recognition for her careful reading of every draft chapter and for providing exceptional feedback along the way. All three went above and beyond. So too did Sarah "Eagle Eye" Markowitz, whose perceptive advice and stunning attention to detail I greatly appreciated as the final manuscript took form. Each represents a wonderful graduate program in War and Society Studies at Chapman, and I can't thank these four young scholars enough for their first-class assistance.

Just as helpful were my Chapman colleagues, who graciously endured my incessant talk of the macho pulps and offered insightful recommendations, even as they winced at some of the more outrageous stories and artwork I shared with them. First and foremost, Bob Slayton solidified himself as "mentor supreme" in the Chapman history department, guiding me through Cold War-era social and cultural history with a scholarly eye and the experience of a true Bronx native. Alex Bay provided wonderful counsel as perceptive historian, talented department chair, Foucault–Danzig lover, and my favorite beer aficionado. Charissa Threat was a phenomenal sounding board from her very first day joining Chapman's faculty, as were Marilyn Harran, Jeff Koerber, Erin Mosely, Bill Cumiford, and Mateo Jarquin. Shira Klein put together a marvelous reading group in our department, whose members offered sensible and practical feedback in the draft's final stages. I could not ask for better friends who, luckily, are also my colleagues.

Thanks also to other Chapman University faculty and staff who proved instrumental to this work: our extraordinary college dean Jennifer Keene, whom I admire greatly, by far leads the list; and to art historian Denise Johnson and special collections and archives librarian Rand Boyd for all their remarkable assistance. Leatherby Library's Robert Ferrari and Catalina Lopez were amazing resources, helping me manage what I'm sure was an overload on the interlibrary loan system. Special thanks go to Allison Devries, Stacy Laird, and Mary Shockey, without whom our graduate program and history department would not function.

I have benefited from the generosity of a terrific group of enthusiasts and scholars. Robert Deis was an early supporter, helping me collect magazines and, more importantly, providing me with expert advice at critical moments. Bob is a wealth of knowledge on the genre and a charitable collaborator. Amber Batura, whose work on *Playboy* in Vietnam inspired me to think more deeply about the consequences of popular culture on American soldiers serving overseas, was a superb partner in crime. Kara Dixon Vuic, one of the nation's finest gender military historians, helped with far more than just "blahahahaha," even if this was some of the very best feedback I received along the way! Another stellar historian, Meredith Lair, generously shared her research notes on the post exchange system in Vietnam and conversed with me on a number of vital topics. I could not have made sense of this complex topic without their assistance.

I also have relied on the scholarship – and, much more importantly, friendship – of some of the most accomplished historians in the business. Bob Brigham, Jim Willbanks, and Ron Milam deserve special mention.

I cherish time spent with each of them. They are like family to me. Thanks also go to Bill Allison, Christian Appy, Pierre Asselin, Larry Berman, Martin Clemis, Andrew Huebner, David Kieran, Mark Lawrence, Kyle Longley, Hang Nguyen, Heather Stur, Jackie Whitt, and Andy Wiest. Whether in the classroom or in my research, their scholarship and advice have been indispensable to the foundations of this book. And, from the beginning, Jen Kiesling helped propel *Pulp Vietnam* into motion. She remains a dear, dear friend – even though she never sends chocolate-chip cookies to the left coast!

Special mention, once again, goes to Paul Miles. As in my past explorations of the American experience in Vietnam, Paul read draft portions of this book, bringing his expertise to bear and offering perceptive recommendations to improve my writing and key arguments. Generous does not begin to fully describe this wonderful mentor and friend.

My family continues to be an integral part of my scholarship because they are an integral part of my life. Thanks, as always, to my mom for our regular calls and far too infrequent visits and shared glasses of wine. (We need to move Florida closer to California!) Jim and Judy, Carol, Jill, and Paul were amazing supporters these past few years, to me as much as to Susan. My feline writing assistants George and Beatrice regularly checked in on my progress. Any mistakes in this work can be attributed to their stepping on or lounging about my computer keyboard. And what dad could be more proud of his daughter – and benefit from her professional editorial "skillz" – than I am of Cameron? Cam read nearly the entire manuscript and offered fabulous advice … in between the "eeewws" that these men's magazines so often prompted.

Finally, this book is dedicated to my best friend. For the last three years, I have been immersed in pulp stories of heroism and courage, of bravery and determination that, to be frank, always seemed just a bit unbelievable to me. No one could be *that* tough, *that* resilient, *that* formidable. As this book was being written, however, I watched my wife battle breast cancer in a way that made the pulp heroes look downright fragile and weak by comparison. Every single day, I was so humbly fortunate to stand next to a companion who showed me the true definition of courage and bravery. I knew long ago I had been lucky in marrying a strong woman. I never fully realized how strong.

Introduction: Warrior Heroes and Sexual Conquerors

J OHN WAYNE. For so many men that came of age during the Cold War era, he was, with Hollywood's blessing, the epitome of the ideal self-made man who proved his masculinity with cool-headed courage under fire.[1] More than anyone else, the "Duke" set male expectations for intrepid wartime behavior at the midpoint of the twentieth century – when the United States, fresh from a victorious "hot war," faced a far vaguer cold one with indistinct combatants and fuzzy boundaries. Wayne's breakthrough performance in *Sands of Iwo Jima* (1949) was a defining role for the actor, if not a generation of young men who felt they had missed out on their chance for heroism in World War II. Wayne's Sergeant Stryker was tough, disciplined, a "clear-cut hero." The imitation seemed so authentic that one young marine lieutenant heading to Vietnam in 1968 contrasted his own "self-doubt and insecurity" with the imagined bravery of the Hollywood star.[2]

The male ideal embodied by Wayne and created by Hollywood replicated itself in many facets of American popular culture during the Cold War, perhaps most pervasively on magazine racks across the country and in the post exchanges on military bases around the globe, nestled within the pages of men's adventure magazines. These "macho pulps" trumpeted the exploits of larger-than-life, self-satisfied men, valiant on the battlefield and accomplished in the bedroom. These warrior heroes were physically fit, mentally strong, and resolutely heterosexual. At the same time, men's adventure magazines alternatively portrayed women as threat or spoil, exotic temptresses who were as dangerous as they were desirous.[3]

1

How the Vietnam generation attempted to make sense of these some-times contradictory and often unattainable roles when they found them-selves in Vietnam is the subject of this book. Unlike previous wars fought by American soldiers and depicted in graphic and gaudy detail in the pulps, GIs arriving in Southeast Asia with John Wayne fantasies in their heads found an environment starkly different than the theaters of World War II and, to a lesser degree, Korea. How, then, did soldiers reconcile their frustrated expectations with the reality of Vietnam?

A *Male* story from January 1964 illustrates the sort of adventures that some GIs in Vietnam might have hoped to encounter there, or at least a variation of the sort. The tale features a downed US Army pilot in World War II working behind enemy lines with Kiev "love gang girls" and "outcast gypsy dancers."[4] The accompanying artwork showcased a buxom brunette in a low-cut red top, carrying a rifle next to our "concrete-nerved" hero as they eluded chasing Nazi soldiers. *Stag*'s February 1967 "Nude Tribe Caper" equally contained many of these magazines' clichés. Artist Earl Norem's enticing illustration displays our champion held at gunpoint while surrounded by bare-breasted local Chilean women. "Peacetime in suburbia had no charms" for this marine veteran turned contract intelligence officer. After brawling his way through most of the plot, he has sex with a "gorgeous blonde" before story's end. There we find the enemy is none other than Nazi doctor Kurt Mengel – clearly, a reference to "Angel of Death" Josef Mengele – who is raising Adolf Hitler's son, the product of artificial insemination. The blonde, of course, proves to be a Nazi spy and is killed off "without compassion."[5]

Considered by the era's cultural critics as disposable consumer kitsch, perhaps because of their formulaic writing and flamboyant artwork, these magazines' impact on the mass culture of the Cold War mostly has been discounted. Never mind that United States senators, like New York's Jacob K. Javits, were writing letters to magazine editors, or, that by the mid 1960s, they had a collective circulation of roughly twelve million copies a month. Too easily dismissed as low-brow art or "throwaway, hardboiled writing," men's postwar pulps offer deep insights into an overlooked source of how American masculinity was broadcast during the Cold War era.[6]

Fig. I.1 *Stag*, February 1967

In fact, gritty adventure stories that were the lifeblood of postwar macho pulps struck a chord with many American men seeking inspiration, stability, and identity in an uncertain postwar world. Despite having rescued the globe from totalitarianism during World War II, Americans entered the postwar period with shaky confidence. The first two decades of the Cold War was a period of immense change – socially, culturally, and politically. The September 1952 issue of *Male*, for example, included an exposé on "How Stalin Stole Our B-29," followed immediately by a story from Dr. Shailer Lawton on the "million marriages ... in constant jeopardy because of deep-seated, sexual inferiority complexes." Men's adventure magazines both manifested these popular fears and offered an antidote for men struggling to prove their manhood. In short, the construction of warrior heroes in the pages of macho pulps was a response to many Americans' fears inspired by the twin forces of international communism and a postwar consumer culture at home.[7]

As a corrective, adventure magazines in the 1950s and into the mid 1960s depicted the ideal man as both heroic warrior and sexual conqueror. War stories illustrated the exploits of courageous soldiers, fighting against the "savage" enemy in foreign lands, and defending democracy in a harsh world where the threat from evil actors always seemed lurking. Sex underscored nearly all of these tales, with pulp heroes rewarded with beautiful, seductive women as a kind of payoff for their combat victories. Within these popular magazines – boasting titles like *Man's Conquest, For Men Only,* and *Man's Epic* – men courageously defeated their enemies in battle, while women were reduced to sexual objects, either trivialized as erotic trophies or depicted as sexualized villains using their bodies to prey on unsuspecting, innocent men.[8]

Adventure mags also sought to strike a chord with their primary readership: working-class young men, the same demographic that disproportionately fought a long and bloody war in South Vietnam. Working-class males read flashy stories of their fathers' generation who, during World War II, conquered not only their enemies but women as well.[9] These men, then, consumed a form of masculinity that was tough, rebellious, and decidedly anti-feminine. Read a different way, however, these magazines might also be seen as a form of entertainment and escapism from deep class anxieties and fears about not measuring up in a rapidly changing postwar society.[10]

Yet it was the hypermasculine narratives, not the subtext of anxiety, that helped shape the attitudes of young men who went to war in Southeast Asia during the mid to late 1960s. One lieutenant recalled how "men's magazines were associated with home, and we read them, owned them, and traded them as if they were gold." Another veteran remembered that the "most widely-read literature among the guys" was "comic books and adventure stories," filled with pictures of "some guy killing somebody and the bare-breasted, Vietnamese-type, Asian-looking woman."[11] In fact, men's adventure magazines regularly appeared on the list of top sales in the post exchange (PX) system in Vietnam. Thus, we might think of these magazines as both cultural text and cultural phenomenon. Not only did they foster ideas about what it meant to be a man, but they also helped their readers negotiate those meanings within their daily lives, both at home and abroad.[12]

Indeed, in many of these magazines, letters to the editor contained feedback from soldiers deployed overseas, including those serving in Vietnam. The May 1968 issue of *Man's Illustrated* included three letters from soldiers deployed to Vietnam, all serving in different provinces. One noted how "We grunts don't have much to look forward to by way of pretty faces." Luckily for the young private, the March issue included a pictorial of Joan Brennan, the "prettiest Irish lass" he had seen and over whom his squad mates "flipped."[13]

Moreover, many veterans themselves wrote stories for these magazines, suggesting important linkages between war and society during the 1950s and 1960s, and as such they were one of the few venues that specifically connected martial valor with sexual entitlement and violence with virility.[14] Neither comics nor television shows nor John Wayne movies so purposefully melded war with sex. If there was a dominant narrative at play in these magazines, that paradigm unabashedly fused together violence and sexuality.[15]

Pulp Vietnam thus explores how men's adventure magazines defined masculinity during two crucial decades of the Cold War era and suggests how that definition may have helped shape American soldiers' expectations in Vietnam – expectations that were in stark contrast to what GIs found in Southeast Asia. These magazines offered young men a model of masculinity that was physically powerful, emotionally shallow, and sexually aggressive. By the time soldiers arrived in Vietnam, many had an explicit, albeit constructed, vision of how a conquering warrior should behave. Did realities in Vietnam enable these men to act on their expectations when confronted with Vietnamese people, friend or foe, and especially women?[16]

At its core then, *Pulp Vietnam* argues that men's adventure magazines from the post-World War II era crafted a particular version of martial masculinity that helped establish and then normalize GIs' expectations and perceptions of war in Vietnam. Cold War men's magazines, like no other medium in contemporary popular culture, inundated American adolescents and men with idealized storylines of wartime heroism coupled with the sexual conquest of women. Such magazines correlated a kind of sexual prerogative with military service, making one the reward for the other.[17]

By comparing the stories and imagery in men's adventure magazines with soldiers' memoirs, oral histories, and court-martial proceeding testimonies, *Pulp Vietnam* asks whether male soldiers in Vietnam described their actions and experiences in language similar to the tales that filled the pulps, and focuses particularly on whether these adventure magazines may have shaped the ways that some soldiers thought of war and of women.[18] Such an undertaking ultimately emphasizes the broader connections between war and society, appraising the role of popular culture at home with soldiers' actions overseas. Historians commonly claim that basic training provoked an aggressive heterosexuality in young men, and it is likely that drill instructor outbursts of "you dirty faggot" or "can't hack it little girls" engendered attitudes that contributed to violence or hostility against women. Yet it seems just as important, if not more so, to examine the preexisting sociocultural dynamics that prepared GIs to think and perform in certain, violent ways. How the home front affected soldiers' behaviors in Vietnam is key to my analysis.[19]

In large part, *Pulp Vietnam* rests on the notion that popular representations of war often entice young men by relying on heroic language and imagery. They help to define certain expectations, even those that view exaggerated, militarized masculinity and sexual conquest as a natural component of war.[20] The September 1966 issue of *Stag*, for example, published a letter in its "Male Call" section from a sergeant stationed on a California base. Along with other non-commissioned officers, he was preparing for deployment to Vietnam and had enjoyed an article on "Bachelor Girls Who Prey on Married Men." Most of the NCOs in the unit, in fact, were married but stationed too far from home for weekend visits. "When you're in the field 72 hours at a time, a man needs some relaxation," the sergeant confessed. "If it wasn't for the chicks around here who overlook the fact we're married, I think we'd all go off our rockers." Military service as stereotyped in men's adventure magazines promised heroism and sexual satisfaction, unabashedly linking them together in a symbiotic relationship.[21]

These same magazines, however, were poor preparation for actual war. They left readers with a distorted view of battle and often unprepared to deal with the realities GIs faced. Combat wasn't adventurous. It was deadly, impersonal, and corrupting. The warrior hero illusion never emerged as a tangible reality.[22] What men's adventure magazines did, then, was create a narrative framework that bestowed upon young men a warped knowledge of war and sex, one that helped make violence against the Vietnamese population seem acceptable, if not a routine feature of overseas military service. War might have been alien to working-class American teens in the 1950s and early 1960s, but its portrayal in the postwar "macho pulps" proved immensely alluring to many young boys who believed combat would help make them into men.[23]

Fig. I.2 *Men,* January 1962

On one hand, the experience of combat in Vietnam was far different than the pulp stories, and that gulf between expectation and reality left soldiers with little reassurance they were doing the right thing. The magazines presented a scenario of heroic battlefield exploits that rarely, if ever, were realized in the largely unconventional fighting of Vietnam. The "man triumphant" never emerged. As one veteran recalled, his "romantic notions of war began to dull as the exhausting, frustrating months passed with nothing but a few snipers' bullets and the shells of mortarmen to break the tedium." Slowly he began to suspect that his "pursuit of glory was a hopeless task."[24] Of course, many American GIs who fought in World War II and Korea also found that they had little control over events that might determine life or death. The murky political–military struggle in Vietnam, though, seemed only to exacerbate the disconnects between anticipated heroic deeds and genuinely brutal wartime acts, while the gradual loss of public support for the war further challenged the notion that combat heroism would be the man-making experience that the magazines had promised.[25]

If the pulps' combat narratives differed so much from reality, then perhaps, on the other hand, American soldiers' relations with local women might align more closely with the sexual champion depicted in the magazines. Frustrated that combat in Vietnam had left them few opportunities to "prove" their manhood, soldiers who sought to establish their dominance in relations with the population could find convenient examples in men's adventure magazines. As one writer has suggested, "carnal conquest" was a way for soldiers to compensate for "military impotence in fighting an unwinnable war."[26] Via sexual conquest or violence, GIs could still measure up to the myths being propagated within the magazines. Surely, this redirection of hostility was made easier by the tactic of dehumanizing the enemy that was so central to contemporary basic training methods. Yet the pulps' basic depictions of women – as sexually promiscuous and available, if not rightful objects of conquest – must be considered if we are to better understand the sexual violence in Vietnam committed by American soldiers.[27]

Accounts from veterans in combat suggest these men had few opportunities for heroic acts on the battlefields of Vietnam; they had little chance to resemble the warriors of pulp magazines. But when dealing with the population, GIs were in positions of relative power. They could control decisions of whether or not a hut was burned, a woman raped, or, in lesser ways, treated as a "spoil" of war. As one veteran recalled, "I had a sense of power. A sense of destruction ... in the Nam you realized you had the power to take a life. You had the power to rape a woman and nobody could say nothing to you ... It was like I was a god. I could take a life. I could screw a woman."[28]

It's important to make clear that I am not accusing all or most US servicemembers in Vietnam of committing rape or sexual violence. This is not a detailed study of the actual sexual atrocities committed by ordinary GIs in Vietnam. Rather, *Pulp Vietnam* focuses more on culturally constructed expectations, and a main expectation derived from men's magazines was that soldiers could – and, perhaps, should – conquer the local female population while serving overseas. Stories that portrayed "warrior heroes" exerting their dominance over seemingly threatening yet desirous women helped to normalize wartime interactions based largely on accepted notions of power disparities between men and women during the 1950s and 1960s.[29]

Pulp Vietnam, therefore, is as much about Cold War gender conceptions as it is about pulp narratives of wartime heroism and sexual conquest. In truth, they are intimately connected. If soldiers did make the choice to engage in sexual conquest in Vietnam – which was without consent and by force in many instances – men's magazines provided a graphic framework rarely, if ever, found in other forms of popular media. They alone established perceptual norms that suggested aggressive behavior in wartime, against both the enemy and women, was not just acceptable, but admirable.[30] And while none of this is to argue for direct causality – reading macho pulps did not lead men inevitably to rape – we still must consider the role socialization plays in male soldiers' wartime behavior. If young GIs were going to act out their frustrations in Vietnam, men's adventure magazines offered a graphic instruction manual.[31]

Young, naïve, and idealistic Americans went off to Vietnam expecting an affirmation of their manhood in the cauldron of war. When their experiences in combat or in rear areas did not match the pulp magazine stories of wartime heroism and triumphalism, many of these young men were left searching for some form of compensation or for connection between fantasyland and reality. Some found it in the realm of sex. Having grown up with tales that coupled martial valor to sexual conquest, the connection would not have been difficult to make.[32]

Yet as alluring as the macho pulp fantasies were, they fabricated a world for young readers that veered widely from actual wartime experiences. That the knowledge gained from these magazines was so flawed helps explain, in part, the vast discord between the imagined war in Vietnam and the real one fought by American soldiers far from the world of pulp fiction.[33]

PULP FICTIONS: MEN'S MAGAZINES IN COLD WAR AMERICA

In their depictions of wartime heroism and sexual conquest, Cold War men's adventure magazines were not just pop culture products representative of their era, but rather drew upon a decades-long expansion of a market that reached into millions of American homes after World War II. We tend to forget the presence of a print magazine culture at the midpoint of the twentieth century and how much it contributed to popular ideas on masculinity and femininity. Betty Friedan's *The Feminine Mystique* (1963), for example, is largely a reaction to the images of domesticated women emerging from popular magazines like *Ladies' Home Journal* and *Good Housekeeping*.[34] In order to fully grasp the significance of mid-century adventure magazines, we need to understand their origins and the development of a market for contemporary ideas on militarized masculinity, a key theme that defined the Cold War macho pulps.

By the mid 1950s, men's adventure pulps had evolved from earlier forms of magazine publishing while maintaining many of their forerunners' core themes. Though national magazines dated back to the middle of the nineteenth century – *Harper's*, for example, was founded in 1850 – technological advances in the late 1800s allowed publishers to produce and distribute higher quantities at lower prices for a wider readership. Frank Munsey's *The Argosy* illustratively cost only fifteen cents in 1912, a full twenty cents cheaper than *Harper's*. The latter fell in the category of "slicks," so named for their higher-quality (and costly) paper and, thus, more middle-class readership.[35] "Pulps," however, were produced from a wood-fiber base and quickly earned a poor reputation for "crudely written stories [and] embarrassingly garish covers" that "generally contained little to attract intelligent readers."[36]

With their emphasis on formulaic fiction stories, though, pulps held broad appeal. *Argosy* alone reached a circulation of half a million by 1907. Moreover, in the early twentieth century, the price of all magazines became even more affordable thanks to advertising revenue, a key innovation of national periodicals.[37] Before long, all-fiction periodicals – *Popular, Blue Book, Adventure* – were being eagerly consumed by an enthusiastic market. Collections of crime stories, such as *Black Mask*, and other detective and western "hero pulps" soon followed, magazines that were purposefully sensational in title and content. And within this newer "hard-boiled" adventure fiction emerged an aggressive form of American masculinity.[38]

To be sure, some magazines like *Esquire*, founded in 1933, cultivated an upper-middle-class male audience. Within the pulps, though, the heroic male icon represented something more visceral. Whether a hard-boiled detective fighting back against the social and economic conditions of the Depression era or Tarzan of the Apes carving out space in a savage, primitive jungle, these men were autonomous, physically powerful, sexually potent, and interminably courageous. These were manly men. In large sense, the depictions of manliness advanced by the pulps idealized what their readers already considered to be real men. If magazines themselves were exemplars of modern mass production, then the champions within their covers gave hope that the mythic "frontier hero" was alive and well in contemporary American society.[39]

The relationship between the pulps and gender conventions became more pronounced during the Great War (1914–1918), inspiring a particular brand of pulps highlighting the exploits of men in combat. During the mid to late 1920s, nearly fifty new pulp titles hit the market, dedicated in part or whole to war. *Battle Stories, War Aces,* and *Under Fire* all recounted stories of Yanks in the American Expeditionary Force (AEF), many written by veterans themselves, who interestingly tended to steer clear of heroic self-description.[40] When young Americans went off to fight in the next world war, comic books, paperbacks, and magazines followed them across the globe, setting the stage for the postwar macho pulps. In one strand, comic books, like those featuring the heroic *Flying Tigers*, constructed the Japanese enemy as "dirty, buck-toothed ... savages" who were little more than "rising sons of Satan."[41] In another strand, popular magazines like *Esquire* deployed images of sexually suggestive pin-up girls overseas to aid in the fight for freedom. Indeed, the US Army accorded *Esquire* special mailing privileges based on the magazine's supposed ability to sustain GI morale. By war's close, one could readily discern the links between war, masculinity, and sexuality in the most popular forms of reading materials.[42]

With the end of wartime paper quotas, and a ready-made market of primed readers, the popular fiction industry boomed. Postwar men's adventure magazines, though, carved out a special place by consolidating rugged machismo, battlefield heroism, and over-the-top, aggressive heterosexuality into single tales. Scores of titles flooded newsstands – *Saga* (1947), *Stag* (1950), *Man's Conquest* (1956), and *Man's Book* (1962) to name but a few.[43] At times referred to as "sweats" or "armpit magazines," these newer versions of the classic pulps seemed a corrective to fears that American masculinity was under siege in a postwar, consumer-oriented society. Within their covers, stories of "real-life" adventures might remedy the boredom that was ostensibly gripping the thousands of suburban communities springing up across the United States. In fact, many of these pulps' readers, like their World War I predecessors, were veterans not only trying to make sense of their wartime experiences, but seeking a return to the supposed glory days of their youth.[44]

How was a reader supposed to distinguish between such a glut of magazines? According to editor Bruce Friedman, a clear-cut hierarchy reigned in this genre. At the top stood *True* and *Argosy*, men's true adventure magazines for the "hunting, beer, and poker set." Next were titles published by the likes of Martin Goodman's Magazine Management Company, the same house that would publish Marvel Comics. Here, one could find *Stag, For Men Only, Man's World*, and *Action for Men*. On the lowest rungs, according to Friedman, were the "legions of other titles that generally featured Gestapo women prancing around captive Yanks in leg shackles."[45] If *True* and *Argosy* seemed more intended for middle-class men with disposable income – the quality of goods advertised suggested so – a clear misogyny still ran through all three tiers of these men's magazines. Moreover, because most of these magazines were published in New York City, pulp stories and illustrations had to rely on the active imaginations of writers and artists who had little practical experience with the exotic locales they were portraying.[46]

Fig. I.3 *Stag*, January 1961

Indeed, it was this very exoticism that drew many readers to the macho pulps. The stories were intended, in short, to stimulate. They attracted veterans returning from World War II or Korea seeking ties to a significant experience in their lives, perhaps countering the much-heralded "crisis of masculinity" that seemed so credible in the 1950s. They invited patriotic anti-communists who believed "effete" cosmopolitans were actively undermining the nation's security. They drew in nervous traditionalists hoping to fight back against an onslaught of feminists apparently intent on usurping men's roles as patriarchal leaders.[47] They enticed teens seeking examples of what it meant to be a "real" man. And, in the early and mid 1960s, they appealed to men combating a sense of isolation from a changing culture in which old verities seemed to have lost public approval and support. As in earlier pulps, men's adventure magazines spoke to the discontented man with an "infinite capacity for wishing." And what better wish than to escape from the uncertainties of a rapidly changing postwar American society?[48]

Of course, readers of varying ages and socioeconomic positions likely consumed these magazines in different ways. One pulp writer believed the "average reader" to be "a mature man and an immature boy." For the older reader, here was an opportunity "to escape into the literature of actions instead of ideas." For the adolescent, however, pulps had the ability to influence "an immature mind which has not had, or has not profited by experience."[49] Thus, as boys were conceiving their future identities as men, the macho pulps boldly presented them with attractive images of "gritty action and tawdry sex."[50]

If such popular depictions of masculinity now seem cheap and vulgar, it would be inappropriate to simply dismiss pulp writers as "penny-a-line scribblers." True, many of their stories were mechanical and clichéd. One writer shared how he simply divided his tales into three natural parts: "characters, setting and problem; problem gets worse; problem still gets worse – and then is solved." But behind the colorful heroes and dastardly villains were some notable authors, including Mario Puzo and Andy Rooney.[51] Classic hard-boiled authors Mickey Spillane and Raymond Chandler also contributed the occasional murder mystery. And there were those well acquainted with war. Vietnam journalist Malcolm Browne penned combat stories, as did Robert F. Dorr, an Air Force veteran who would go on to complete a twenty-five-year career with the US Foreign Service.[52]

While battlefield exploits proved popular article entries, so too did the "hotsie-totsies." In the early Cold War years, male consumers could find few sexual stimulants in popular culture, especially before the publication of *Playboy* in 1953. In fact, Hugh Hefner's first choice for his new magazine's title was *Stag Party*. Only after attorneys representing *Stag* magazine's publisher complained did Hefner decide upon *Playboy*.[53]

Without question, *Playboy* was different than the macho pulps, intentionally so. From his Chicago office, Hefner wanted to offer something more refined than the "hairy-chested editorial emphasis" he found in adventure magazines. The ideal man who read *Playboy* was less about hunting and fishing and more about "inviting in a female for a quiet discussion on Picasso, Nietzsche, jazz, sex." Of course, Hefner's supposedly progressive views, targeting the single middle-class consumer with an interest in sports, clothes, and liquor, conveniently obscured a gender hostility toward the very female bodies he was promoting.[54] True, the women in *Playboy* were depicted more as girls next door than as sexual temptresses. Yet an editorial in the June 1953 issue suggested these women were not just the stuff of erotic fantasy, but of suburban, domestic oppression as well. "All woman wants is security. And she's perfectly willing to crush man's adventurous, freedom-loving spirit to get it." The booming circulation numbers of *Playboy* verified that Hefner had tapped into the cultural zeitgeist of the early Cold War era.[55]

To be sure, however, only manly men graced the pages of the postwar pulps. *Cavalcade*, for example, advertised that its magazine contained "96 pages of real man's reading," while others, like *Male*, regularly included western yarns, literary spotlights on the rugged individualism so crucial to the narrative of American independence.[56] Yet, not far below the surface, one could discern an uneasiness pervading men's sense of social power. If masculinity, like gender, is a social construction, then in the 1950s and early 1960s, it also was a reaction to fears that passivity and femininity in an age of capitalist consumerism might be undermining traditional definitions of manhood. Take, for instance, the March 1960 *Battle Cry* article "Are You Yellow?" The story begins with World War II hero Audie Murphy fighting off elite Nazi troops before asking the reader if he can measure up to such feats of courage. After drawing upon psychological studies and historical examples, the author offers thin encouragement despite a confident tone: you, too, young reader can "make calls upon bravery no matter what your field of work, your age, or your place of residence."[57]

As noted, that residence, for most pulp consumers, likely would have been found in America's working-class neighborhoods. Both articles and advertisements catered to the "low brow" who, according to *Life*, drank beer, played craps, and spent time in his local lodge.[58] Ads similarly indicated the targeting of working-class audiences. "Is there an 'education barrier' between you and promotion?" asked one company. "Are young college graduates being brought in to fill positions above you?" Other ads offered work clothes bargains, while still others promised that the "trained man" would have "no trouble passing the genius who hasn't improved his talents." Indeed, advanced education was hardly a guarantee of success. "You don't need a college diploma but you do need plenty of common sense and you've got to like people," trumpeted one personality self-help advertisement.[59]

More than a few blue-collar Vietnam veterans recalled growing up and being intrigued by their fathers' war stories that were a mainstay of these macho pulps. "It seemed so exciting and exotic," one infantryman remembered. And yet despite wartime evidence of class inequities in draft policies, the adventure mags pushed back against any perceived injustices. Veteran Micheal Clodfelter noted that the men "with whom I shared the Vietnam War were overwhelmingly the sons of steelworkers, truck drivers, mechanics, small farmers and sharecroppers, men from small towns and rural routes in the South and Midwest or from big city ghettoes."[60] A *Stag* offering from July 1966, however, argued that men like Clodfelter were mistaken and the army was "almost a perfect cross-section of U.S. population, with people from every walk of life in just about the same proportion as they are in civilian population."[61]

Perhaps because of adventure magazines' popularity among veterans and in working-class neighborhoods, they also were rabidly patriotic. Pulp writers did not simply defend Cold War policies, they trumpeted nationalism through a military lens, often decrying America's weak-kneed response to the glaring threat of communism. In a precursor to Vietnam-era criticisms of civilian interference in military affairs, one author asked why the Pentagon was "keeping handcuffs on our jet fighters" in the skies over East Germany.[62] Another, deriding US social policies overseas, demanded "It's Time for America to Get Tough!" In many ways, a sense of militarized masculinity thus became embedded into the nationalist rhetoric emblazoned on the pages of the pulps.[63]

Such a linking should not surprise. In large part, ideas about power stood at the core of conceptualizations on both nationalism and masculinity. After all, gender – of which masculinity is a part – is as much a political system as a symbolic one. The macho pulps clearly illustrated a preference for male social domination, one that could be extrapolated outward to Cold War America.[64] Manly adventure stories within these magazines symbolized an idealized gender structure that no doubt

resonated with many male readers. Here, historian Joan Scott's definition of gender seems most useful. To Scott, gender is a "primary way of
signifying relationships of power." How pulp readers viewed and went on
to enact their understandings of gender and masculinity in Vietnam will
become an important part of this story.[65]

Of course, these magazines competed with other forms of popular
culture, such as comics and television, offering a wide range of popular
masculine images. By the end of 1952, there were more than nineteen
million television sets in American households. Young and old alike
could watch heroic gunslingers in scores of westerns, either on TV or
in local movie theaters.[66] And, perhaps just as importantly, young readers
doubtlessly compared the pulps' "true adventures" with tales they heard
from World War II and Korea veterans who were family and friends, even
if those vets might be reticent to share the more unpleasant aspects of
their wartime experiences. Yet, despite the fact that several vying
mediums were competing for audiences, the circulation of all magazines
increased by more than twenty percent between 1950 and 1960. Television may have been seeping into the "nation's bloodstream," but the
publishing industry was still clearly holding its own.[67]

Without question, assessing how a masculine ethos and its values are
carried on to younger generations defies precision. Yet men's adventure
magazines clearly evinced an established male culture that relied heavily
on patriarchal notions of society. And it did so in a fashion that was both
compelling and alluring, since the stories highlighted both war *and* sex.
At least some part of this philosophy was transmitted to, and internalized
by, the Vietnam draft generation.[68] Surely, marine veteran Philip Caputo
wasn't alone in sharing that "the heroic experience I sought was war; war,
the ultimate adventure; war, the ordinary man's most convenient means
of escaping from the ordinary." It seems probable that certain key aspects
of adventure magazines became embedded in male culture, socializing
young men how to think about war and women. In this way, magazines
were one manifestation of popular culture shaping broader Cold War
stereotypes and public opinions.[69]

By the early 1970s, men's adventure magazines had fallen out of favor,
ultimately left behind by a generation willing to reject many of their
elders' traditional cultural assumptions. But it was the war in Vietnam

that rang the macho pulps' death knell. The long, unsatisfying conflict had yielded few heroes, leaving little incentive for readers to view military service as a rite of passage to manhood.[70] A decade earlier, though, as Americans went off to war in Southeast Asia, the elements of male culture depicted in adventure magazines were clearly identifiable in the language of those slogging their way through the rice paddies and jungles of Vietnam. As one war correspondent shared, "Young men court danger as they court women, and for much the same reasons . . . secretly each wants to be a hero, in the finest and best sense of the word, and there's nothing wrong with that, because quiet heroism is the stuff of war."[71] Or so young boys were told in Cold War America.

MILITARIZING MANHOOD

"We are a nation at war," boomed Pennsylvania State Senator Albert R. Pechan in 1953. Never mind that World War II had ended almost a decade earlier, or that the fighting on the Korean peninsula was coming to a close. For Pechan, the distinction between war fronts and home fronts made little sense in this new era. "The force that is killing our loved ones, the power that is fighting against our democracy, is Communist, Godless Russia. It is fantastic," Pechan argued, "to fight Communism with all our strength abroad and to ignore it at home."[72]

By 1953, the nascent ideas of persistent war and a national security state in constant need of maintenance were taking hold in communities across America. Everywhere Americans turned, they saw an international crisis – in Korea, Chile, Algeria, Iran, and Indochina to name but a few. Worse, clandestine communist forces and Soviet spies seemed to lurk behind every corner right here at home. The very idea of peace seemed dangerous. Though the public might recoil at the thought of an American empire, surely a robust, global military machine was necessary to keep these evil forces at bay.[73]

This inability to fully demobilize after World War II led to vast increases in defense spending, the re-installment of a peacetime draft, and the notion of continuous "wartime" mobilization. The outbreak of fighting in Korea in July 1950 only reified worries that global communists were on the march. In the process, conceptions of military service,

Fig. I.4 *American Manhood*, January 1953

citizenship, and masculinity all became tightly intertwined.[74] The February 1953 issue of *American Manhood*, for instance, offered advice on the prospects of a military career. Being drafted could "pay off big dividends," as "you can come out a far better man than when you entered the armed forces." Four years later, *Saga* was extolling the men of the US Air Force's Strategic Air Command (SAC) as "real pros" who were members of an "elite corps. If there was ever a more self-confident outfit in military service, history does not record it."[75]

Such applause proved useful for US military leaders who, competing with civilian businesses for talent, needed to retain young men's attraction to war. Selling the "soldier" as the best venue for becoming a "man" clearly helped with recruiting efforts. And while the macho pulps were far from a government mouthpiece, they nonetheless were energetic promoters of the armed forces. "You're a Marine," declared one article, "then mister, you're a man. There's no two ways about it." To uphold the traditions of the Marine Corps' "brilliant service" to the country took "a lot of man." Another on marine boot camp claimed that when a recruit completed his training, "he knows he's proved himself a first-rate fighting man."[76] A full decade later, such storylines had hardly changed. "Combat commanders in Viet Nam," *Male* declared in 1967, "are sending back reports that younger men still make the best fighters – that means 18–20 in age."[77]

So too could social critics exploit the macho pulps' depiction of masculinity which, to them, was under assault from overprotective mothers. This threat of "momism" suggested to commentators like Myron Brenton that an overinvolved mother might "devour her sons emotionally," leading to "mama's boys," an epidemic of homosexual children, and, ultimately, a feminized society. As early as 1945, *Ladies' Home Journal* had published an article asking "Are American Moms a Menace?"[78] Luckily, postwar men's magazines offered an answer. If the mother could not teach her son to be a man, then the armed forces would. Take, for instance, a *Stag* "confidential" from March 1966. "Lots of mothers who cry 'hardship' when their sons are being drafted are actually interested in smother-loving the son to death than in protecting him. Draft Board is actually doing these boys a favor by putting them in uniform." That child rearing and national security remained so interconnected for so long surely implies deep anxieties about gender conceptions in the Cold War era.[79]

Given the weighty implications of defining the military as a wellspring of American masculinity, what better way to attract men to war than by linking it to sexual rewards? Here the macho pulps enhanced the myth-making power of cultural stories by claiming that women were naturally attracted to men in uniform. Adventure magazines were rife with tales of the military man's sexual virility and exploits, such as when *American Manhood* told readers that the US Air Force not only offered "unlimited career opportunities," but the cut of a uniform "with its attractiveness to the opposite sex."[80]

This conflation of military and sexual power was on full display on pulps' cover images, which regularly displayed courageous men dealing with danger, overcoming adversity, and usually winning sexual rewards for their heroics. The cover for the October 1957 issue of *Battle Cry* flaunted several GIs being kissed by Parisian women, offering chocolate to a small child, and astride a tank firing at an unseen enemy. Rifles unsubtly protruded in all their phallic grandeur. A story in *Big Adventure* described postwar Parisian girls – "thousands of them" – as "literally fighting each other off in an attempt to capture the GI's interest." In this way, according to historian Mary Louise Roberts, the American knight could be "duly awarded" for protecting not only the French nation, but its women as well.[81]

Fig. I.5 *Battle Cry*, October 1957

The pulps' flattering representations of the American soldier allowed civilians (and noncombat veterans) to live vicariously through warriors' experiences, to read stories where anyone could be a hero. For boys of the "boomer" generation, many of whom admired their fathers' triumphant return from World War II, magazines helped validate a concept of manliness embedded in martial valor. In the process, according to one military psychiatrist, masculinity became "an essential measure of capability," wherein "the maleness of an act is the measure of its worth and thus a measure of one's ability."[82] Nowhere were masculine acts more viscerally portrayed than in the macho pulps. They offered a world where young men could assert their manhood by defeating the enemy.[83]

In feting these American heroes, adventure stories clearly oversimplified, crafting a reductive narrative of good versus evil that was readily transferable to and consumed by their readers. Here were villains easy to understand. In the pulps, only the Nazis or "commies" – "the Red legions" according to *Saga* – were interested in taking over the world. And even if racialized enemy foes, like the Japanese, were "worthy of hate," they did not reach the level of condemnation reserved for Hitler's murderers or communist sympathizers. In a pinch, Nazis always could serve as a pulp writer's villainous nemesis.[84] Thus, throughout the Cold War, Nazi henchmen, "merely following orders" in their prosecution of mass murder, easily could be contrasted to the just American warriors defending against the red hordes in far-off places like Korea.[85]

Such a simplified version of the enemy would have severe ramifications when young men were exposed to a much more complicated enemy situation in South Vietnam. The fighting there, in one accounting, tended to render World War II "heroism unattainable." Surely, the depictions within adventure magazines were neither completely manipulative nor fully authentic.[86] Yet the storylines just as surely painted a world view in which the United States was a bastion of freedom defending against the evils of a barbarous, godless communism. It is plausible that such simplistic renderings helped persuade more than a few young Americans off to war in the early to mid 1950s. As historian Christian Appy has argued, the boys "who would be sent to fight a war of counterinsurgency in Vietnam grew up fighting an imaginary version of

World War II." Many would be sorely disappointed that reality hardly matched the pulp magazines' fantasies.[87]

And yet we – like those young men – want certain narrative arcs when it comes to war. We are inspired by stories of young men's perseverance in combat, of their ability to withstand both imprisonment and even abuse. We are heartened by tales linking national will and security to the resolve of hearty individuals willing to sacrifice for the greater good. And, in the same vein, we are disappointed when soldiers, like one Vietnam veteran, return home and share that they "felt it was all so futile." In short, we want to find meaning in war, a sense of purpose that makes us feel better about ourselves and our nation.[88]

Indeed, the very success of the macho pulps rested upon the notion that real men still mattered, both at home and abroad. And these adventure magazines not only adopted models of contemporary gender differences, but exploited the fantasy that battlefield heroism legitimized sexual conquest. One army medical corps physician suggested as much as the conflict in Vietnam was coming to a close for weary Americans. To him, war historically had conferred upon soldiers "complete sexual license," with sex itself often viewed as an "allowable excess of battle and particularly a reward for victory."[89] Pulp writers couldn't have agreed more.

WAR AS SEXUAL CONQUEST

John Wayne may have been the epitome of the postwar generation's "manly man," but we tend to forget that throughout his movie career, the "Duke" largely remained an asexual figure.[90] Post-World War II men's adventure magazines, however, departed from such chaste depictions, instead constructing the "noble" warrior as a sexually charged male seeking release and reward. And perhaps here, the pulps, in a narrow sense, accorded more with reality. Both military commanders and GIs of the era worried about sexual deprivation on the battlefield. Indeed, one senior US officer held that "male sexual activity was healthy for battle."[91] Soldiers imparted similar beliefs. War, popular notions held, seemed to increase the GI's sexual appetite. What better place to satiate these cravings than in a combat zone? As one American soldier serving in

Europe noted, war "offers us an opportunity to return to nature and to look upon every member of the opposite sex as a possible conquest, to be wooed or forced."[92]

The covers and artwork of men's adventure magazines purposefully exploited these convictions, intertwining war and sex in enticing images that might draw hungry eyes to newsstands. The cover for the September 1957 issue of *Man's World*, for example, shows a tough GI straddling a .50 caliber machine gun, its barrel jutting out toward the reader while spewing bullets. Next to the soldier, in bold white letters, is a teaser for one of the articles inside, "Sex Life of the American Woman." (Rifles and machine guns as phallic stand-ins seemed an artistic requirement.) One *Battle Cry* illustration depicted an American GI evading Nazis through a burning European village. His M1 Garand extends out from his waist, while a local red-headed woman – with bright red lips and a low-cut white top – stands behind the American, her hand gently resting near his trigger finger.[93]

The rhetoric of these gendered images suggested a hardening of the post-World War II patriarchal structure. In the pulps, women were to be subservient in American society. Take, for instance, one *All Man* article targeting "sex shy men," which offered advice on how to "make every woman your slave." Surely, such articles predisposed men toward seeing sexual conquest in war as the norm.[94] Veteran J. Glenn Gray spoke in similar terms. In his World War II memoir, Gray argued that for the "sensualist as soldier," war was a "convenient opportunity for new and wider fields of erotic conquest."[95] Might it be that young soldiers in Vietnam reading articles about forced sexual conquest of enemy women believed that such behavior was well within the normal boundaries of war?

It must be emphasized, and strongly, that reading men's adventure magazines did not result in a chemical reaction ensuring America's youth would mindlessly commit sexual violence overseas. Yet, if the articles were not prescriptive, they still normalized or at least familiarized a certain type of behavior in their storylines and opened up a narrative space for what some American soldiers deemed acceptable in their contacts with the Vietnamese population.[96] One Vietnam-era offering highlights how popular culture may well support sexual violence.

Fig. I.6 *Man's World*, September 1957

In September 1966, *Male* ran an exclusive that clearly promoted rape. "Many women, young ones in particular, are 'sexually reversed' in their actions, that is whatever they say can be taken to mean the opposite. 'I absolutely don't want to sleep with you' for example, means precisely the opposite."[97]

If, in Vietnam, adventure stories ranked among the "most widely read literature among the guys," then it is worthwhile to assess how they connected militarized masculinity to sexual conquest by force. Without question, cultural products like the macho pulps were read in diverse ways, often unanticipated by their authors."[98] Individuals make sense of images and texts differently. Still, these magazines embraced misogyny in their portrayals of American soldiers and their place in wartime societies and, as such, may have primed aggressive behavior once those soldiers arrived in South Vietnam. Given their alluring artwork and persuasive stories, adventure magazines resonated with young Americans seeking validation of their manhood in the early and mid 1960s. For some, the fantasy must have been irresistible. And, in far too many ways, utterly disappointing.[99]

In the chapters that follow, we will witness deeply disturbing images and storylines that appeared in the pulps and search for links between GIs' frustrations over the reality of combat in Vietnam and the messages espoused by such cultural products. Our exploration will begin by placing men's adventure magazines within their Cold War context before examining how they constructed a version of World War II and Korea that depicted heroic men as warriors, protectors, and sexual conquerors. The narrative then moves to the macho pulps' portrayal of women, especially non-European, non-white women, and suggests that such representations left young male readers with the impression that American dominance overseas allowed them to engage in a form of sexual oppression there. We end in Southeast Asia, comparing the fantasy of war as depicted in the magazines with the reality of Vietnam, considering ways in which the pulps contributed to a culture which found it acceptable to engage in violence against the Vietnamese population, especially its women.

Several studies have identified a relationship between aggression levels in previously angered men and an exposure to pornographic images.[100] In a similar way, I suggest that men's adventure magazines fostered an implicit consent of sexual subjugation by defining militarized masculinity as embodied in both the battlefield hero *and* the sexual conqueror. For some, theory became practice, violence a sort of male wish-fulfillment already whetted by Cold War culture. As one veteran laconically recalled, in war, GIs and women were "almost always the two main classes of people getting fucked."[101]

With this in mind, *Pulp Vietnam* should be read as a purposeful melding of popular cultural, social, and military history, one that asks serious questions about the connections between these three fields. How much of sexual conquest is part of war in general and how much is due to a particular set of historical circumstances? How widespread and influential were images of American warriors that equated military masculinity to the sexual domination of women? And how, in the end, do we measure the cultural and individual impacts of men's adventure magazines, their power to reinforce certain ideas about Cold War manhood that may have reaped horrific rewards on the battlefields of Southeast Asia?[102]

CHAPTER 1

Macho Pulp and the American Cold War Man

I F AMERICANS HAD FOUGHT IN WORLD WAR II to achieve a sense of security, to be free from fear, such peace dividends did not last long. By the late 1940s, the United States once more seemed under assault, from threats both foreign and domestic. As Cold War political lines hardened, the distinction between external and internal menaces became ever more difficult to perceive. Not only was the globe under threat from a vast communist conspiracy – all ostensibly controlled by Moscow, many believed – but the tentacles of communism apparently were reaching deep into American society. Just as threatening, the postwar consumer society appeared to be enfeebling an entire generation of men. It was no coincidence that contemporary social critics spoke of "proletarianized" white-collar workers who were losing their individuality in corporate America. How would such men defend the nation? How could they at once counter communist aggression, at home and overseas, while resisting pressures to conform to a society seemingly intent on emasculating them?[1]

While communist conspirators posed a threat, so too did women. Indeed, American women appeared more menacing than Stalin's red henchmen. It looked as if female antagonists were attacking men from all sides. Suburban wives and mothers were exercising a "suffocating control" over sons and husbands. *Femmes fatales* stood ready to pounce on unsuspecting men, exploiting female sexual wares to deceive and demoralize.[2] Call girls and mistresses chipped away at the moral integrity of American society. And, in this era of persistent war, female "camp followers" preyed on decent servicemen, a "sinister force" which threatened the nation's "entire defense programs." As one account in

Real Combat Stories warned, becoming involved with these "harlots" was to "engage in a game of Russian roulette."[3]

This general atmosphere of persecution, fear, and distrust of women and other forces that might weaken the World War II-era military man intimated larger anxieties gripping American society. The designs of global containment, aimed at preventing communist expansion overseas, rested on accepting a healthy dose of fear at home. Fear of nuclear Armageddon. Fear of communist subversion. Fear of men not measuring up in an apocalyptic battle pitting good against evil.[4] Such worries ran deep enough for historian Richard Hofstadter to argue in 1964 that a "paranoid style" in American politics had created a central image in which a "vast and sinister conspiracy" had been "set in motion to undermine and destroy a way of life." Yet these same anxieties – domestic, ideological, geopolitical – were essential to pulp culture writing.[5]

In this era of Cold War anxieties, adventure magazines helped shape young male readers' world views, driving home an alternative version of masculinity for a mass society seemingly bent on weakening American manhood. They imparted hope for rehabilitation, a way to meet the contemporary challenges besetting the nation's men.[6] Moreover, the pulps' message was timely. In terms of expectations about sex, gender roles, and the societal responsibilities of both men and women, the period from World War II through the late 1960s saw a great deal of upheaval. The postwar macho pulps thus offered a paradigm for men to embrace, a way to exemplify a traditional sense of masculinity in an uncertain time. Within the magazines, men were once more the unencumbered protector and provider. There, they could bask in gallant stories of the glorified male warrior. And, as one Vietnam veteran recalled, they could return to a heroic time, "before America became a land of salesmen and shopping centers."[7]

COLD WAR ANXIETIES

Despite the unconditional surrender of their enemies in World War II, Americans could not shake a deep sense of insecurity as they entered the postwar years. They worryingly faced new villains. Indeed, they helped to create them. Communist devils conveniently replaced sadistic Nazis and savage Japanese as the new foe.[8] The 1950 McCarran Act, for example, declared that the world communist movement posed a "clear and present danger to the security of the United States and to the existence of free American institutions." In the process, the bill limited civil liberties, requiring all communist organizations to register with the attorney general and authorized the president to proclaim the existence of an "Internal Security Emergency."[9] Apparently, the nation once more was at war.

Yet what if American men, feminized by the postwar consumer society, could not meet the demands of this new war? What if they had become too soft? These were hardly new questions and, in truth, reflected prevalent concerns over "modern manliness" at the opening of the twentieth century. Then too, men seemed under siege. They were becoming "overcivilized" in this new industrial age, soft and flabby, all while American society was being "womanized" by first-wave feminists demanding political emancipation.[10] This obsession over masculinity, and the challenges to it, may not have reached a crisis, but clearly the opportunities to prove one's manhood seemed ever more constricted in a decadent, modern society.[11]

The antidote came from the likes of Teddy Roosevelt, charismatic men who advocated living a "strenuous life." To be sure, only traditional gender relations supported such a rejuvenation. As Roosevelt pronounced in 1899, "When men fear work or fear righteous war, when women fear motherhood, they tremble on the brink of doom."[12] Men's magazines of the day took notice, selling the ideals of a physical culture based on sport and outdoor adventure. Such newly reinvigorated men then could transfer their prowess to arenas where it mattered. As *Century Magazine* put it, strong men would no longer fight "in the fields or forests," but rather "in the battles of life where they must now be fought, in the markets of the world." It took few steps to marshal this philosophy in support of an expansionistic, if not imperialistic, US foreign policy. Only virile, vigorous men could lead the nation – and the world.[13]

Such gendered language reemerged during the Cold War. Only strong men could steer and protect a strong nation. George F. Kennan, the author of containment doctrine, evocatively portrayed the Soviet government "as a rapist exerting 'insistent, unceasing pressure for penetration and command' over Western societies."[14] By the 1960s, Lyndon B. Johnson was using far less subtle language when it came to US foreign policy. The president derided one administration official for "going soft" on the war in Vietnam, scornfully asserting "he has to squat to piss." Reacting to the late 1966 bombing of North Vietnam, LBJ proudly declared, "I didn't just screw Ho Chi Minh. I cut his pecker off." Yet behind this bravado lurked a chronic anxiety. Biographer Doris Kearns shared with her readers Johnson's fears of being regarded as a "coward" and an "appeaser." To journalist David Halberstam, the president desperately wanted "to be seen as a man... he wanted the respect of men who were tough, real men, and they would turn out to be hawks."[15]

To help combat these anxieties, many Americans during the Cold War era turned inward to the family, the "cornerstone of our society" in Johnson's words, which would help promote civic values, morals, and patriotism.[16] Yet men's adventure magazines alluded to problems with such conceptions. Apparently, all was not well at home. The November 1959 issue of *Cavalcade*, for example, ran a story on the "recent revolution in sex customs" that was causing a spike in extramarital relations. Changing mores – "largely in the matter of the woman's behavior" – implied that the traditional American family might be breaking down. Worse, it seemed, men were bearing the brunt of these changes. That same autumn, *Challenge* printed a story on the "millions of anxiety-ridden American men" who faced "serious mental illness" because they could not cope with numerous "upsetting sex problems." According to the article, these men were "deeply troubled because they feel sexually inadequate, abnormal or guilty."[17]

Not surprisingly, the macho pulps spoke little of the costs endured by women who were forced to subordinate their own desires to reinforce traditional values. Not all freely chose the postwar "retreat to housewifery." In the pulps, though, it was men who suffered as a result. As women increasingly controlled the domestic sphere, so a popular narrative went, they became an "idle class, a spending class, a candy-craving class."[18] In social critic Philip Wylie's eyes, men were spending most of their time supplying "whatever women have defined as their necessities, comforts, and luxuries." No wonder then, as the editors of *Look* magazine argued, women's new "economic and sexual demands" were "fatiguing American husbands." Of course, where fears lurked, so too did opportunities exist. Thus, thumbing through adventure magazine ads, readers might remedy their ailments by sending in for a guide explaining "How to double your energy and live without fatigue."[19]

Surely, not all men lived in panic during the 1950s, but the pulps did reflect widespread gender anxieties of the day. The domestic costs of containing communism at home, coupled with concerns about the dampening effect of women's desires for affluence and security, suggested that suburban life might be corrupting real men. Certainly, popular novels like *Revolutionary Road* and *The Man in the Gray Flannel Suit* spoke to these anxieties, as did pulp articles like "Why Do We Have to Marry Women?"[20] Men's adventure magazines thus might be seen as an outlet for the frustrations of living in a conformity-inducing society. If Betty Friedan correctly surmised that male outrage was the result of an "implacable hatred for the parasitic women who keep their husbands and sons from growing up," then the macho pulps offered a wish fulfillment for those fantasizing about reaching their full potential as manly men.[21]

The corporatization of America further fanned male anxieties. Arthur Miller's Willy Lohman and William Whyte's "Organization Man" both illustrated the decline of individuality, if not spirit, in an era of consumer capitalism where mass corporations seemingly reigned supreme. Moreover, these works suggested that World War II veterans were having a difficult time reintegrating into a society that did not fully appreciate their sacrifices. In the 1956 film version of *The Man in the Gray Flannel Suit*, Betsy Rath accosts her husband Tom for being more cautious since returning home from war: "You've lost your guts and all of a sudden I'm ashamed of you."[22] Two years later, an *Esquire* essay by Arthur Schlesinger, Jr. argued that men had retreated "into the womblike security of the group" and that mass democratic society itself constituted an "assault on individual identity." "The frontiersmen of James Fenimore Cooper," Schlesinger lamented, "never had any concern about masculinity; they were men, and it did not occur to them to think twice about it."[23]

But how to maintain a sense of self-reliance when you were accepting government handouts? Take, for instance, the GI Bill which expanded access to education for an entire generation of American veterans yet clearly fell within the realm of social welfare expenditures. Some eight

million World War II vets, just under fifty percent of the eligible population, received training benefits from the program. Roughly two million
Korean War veterans did the same.[24] In addition, federal housing loans
enabled young families, many for the first time, to purchase their own
homes. Might it be that such welfare programs offering education and
advancement came at a cost? Didn't white-collar jobs stimulate fears of
feminization? Perhaps this is why the most common reason veterans
cited for not using the GI Bill was that they "preferred work to school."
Indeed, men's adventure magazines walked a fine line when it came to
questions that were so intertwined with class conceptions. The pulps
extolled the benefits of military service, and how it could promote social
advancement, yet openly venerated working-class ideals and their value
to proving one's manhood.[25]

Thus, it seems likely that many white, middle-aged men, bored or
frustrated with their postwar lives, read men's magazines to regain a sense
of what the periodicals were selling most – adventure. As historian Heather
Marie Stur argues, the pulps "glorified the outdoorsman and the warrior as
the antidote to stifling wives and domestic responsibilities."[26] According to
Stag, the US Navy held "that exactly half the guys who volunteer for and go
on Antarctic duty are there to escape women. If they're married, then
Antarctica represents a cooling-off period." *Men* magazine went further.
A July 1964 article, "A Young Legal Mistress for Every Man," asked readers if
they were "plagued by a nagging wife" and if their jobs were driving them
crazy. The "natural solution"? A *querida* who could serve as the "married
male's last link with his romantic bachelor past." On the word of *Men*, the
system worked so well that "even wives are for it."[27]

Despite these potential solutions, in numerous magazines – from
Cosmopolitan to *Playboy* to *Man's Action* – it appeared as if wives were
gaining the upper hand to "dominate" the American male. Modern mass
society supposedly had feminized men. *Cosmopolitan* argued that "a boy
growing up today has little chance to observe his father in strictly masculine pursuits." Writing for *Playboy* in 1958, critic Philip Wylie decried the
"womanization of America," a "sad condition" in which women had
secured dominance over men. The article's tagline left no doubt where
Wylie stood: "an embattled male takes a look at what was once a man's
world."[28]

Adventure magazines went a step further: men weren't just being emasculated by the domestication process, they were being fully "castrated" by women in the home. *Sir!* offered a 1962 contribution titled "The Mental Castration of Husbands." Author Joe Pearson argued that "frustrated females" were waging "an all-out campaign against their mates." The goal, apparently, was to turn the man into a "converted housemaid." One year later, *Brigade* followed suit with "Castration of the American Male." A photograph of a sullen husband, in floral apron doing the dishes, accompanied the article. In it, Andrew Petersen claimed that the "manly virtues – strength, courage, virility – are becoming rarer every day... Femininity is on the march, rendering American men less manly." By mid 1966, the process of emasculation seemed complete as *Man's Action* asked if men's "sex guilts" were making them impotent.[29]

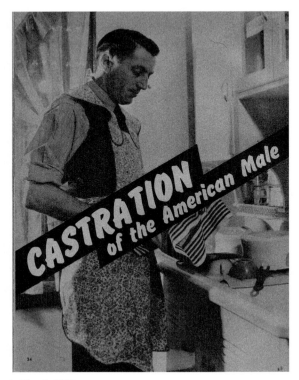

Fig. 1.1 *Brigade*, March 1963

In an era of endless war against communism, concerns abounded that this emasculation of the American man might undermine military readiness. One periodical worried that if men were "denied a sphere of vigorous action," they could lose their "chance of heroism." The macho pulps, though, took the matter head on, especially in the immediate aftermath of the Korean War. Famed aviator Alexander P. de Seversky, writing for *Man's Day* in 1953, pushed back against impressions that "American boys have suddenly become 'afraid to fly.'" To Seversky, there was "nothing wrong with our young manhood." Yet doubts persisted. In 1955, Senator Estes Kefauver (Democrat, Tennessee, a member of the Senate Armed Services committee) penned an essay for *Real Adventure* on the problems of American men being rejected for military service. Kefauver found that one of every ten men would be unqualified for service because they were "emotionally unfit or sexual deviants or unable to stand up mentally under the strain of army life and combat." The problem had left the United States "shockingly, dangerously vulnerable," so much so that the senator asked his young readers, "Are you the ninth man?"[30]

While fears of military unpreparedness reflected broader social anxieties, such concerns did not extend to matters of race in Cold War America. Men's adventure magazines were written by and for white men. Rarely did African Americans appear in the pulps' pages. Occasionally, men's magazines would focus on contemporary racism, such as a 1952 *Stag* article highlighting a black World War II army air corps veteran who tried to move into a Chicago suburb.[31] A few pulp stories drew attention to the 1963 assassination of civil rights activist Medgar Evers, and *True* published an essay on "The Klansman." But nowhere could readers listen to the stories of Ralph Ellison, James Baldwin, or even Louis Armstrong.[32] Only in periodicals like *Ebony* and *Duke* could black men find similar treatments on masculinity and the challenges and opportunities of the Cold War consumer culture.[33]

Catering to a white male audience meant that men in minority groups – blacks, Latinos, Asian and Native Americans – were not recognized in the pulps as "real" or "full" men. This, despite the US armed forces becoming increasingly diverse in the 1950s and 1960s. Mexican American Raymond Buriel, for example, believed that if he and his peers "went into the military and served, nobody could question ... our place here."[34] Yet such aspirations seldom made it into the macho pulps. In large sense, adventure magazines not only deprived minority men of a place within the dominant narrative of masculinity enjoyed by fellow white soldiers – a kind of "sexual camaraderie" – but also implied that these men were not truly part of the heroic warrior–sexual conqueror paradigm. The "All-American" melting pot infantry squad, so popular in wartime movies, rarely saw action in pulp adventure stories.[35]

In other endeavors like sports – baseball and boxing, in particular – white Americans might allow some form of racial integration. Within the postwar pulps, blacks almost always were portrayed as athletes. Stories ran on boxers Jack Johnson, Floyd Patterson, and Sam Langford, "The Boston Tar Baby," or on African American weightlifters like George Paine.[36] Racial fears and sexual anxieties, however, proscribed black men from being more. If their heroes were white, pulp writers could combine martial exploits with sexual conquest. An African American man, though, could never be linked to such sexual fantasies, especially those involving the taking of a white German Fräulein, a popular target of pulp heroes. White sexual champions, even predators, were acceptable, not black ones. In this vein, *American Manhood* published an article on venereal diseases and covered only syphilis and gonorrhea, because other STDs did "not occur too often among white people" and thus did not warrant discussion.[37]

Sporadic storylines did emerge of minority soldiers performing acts of heroism. *Stag* ran a few paragraphs on Private First Class Milton Olive, the first African American to earn the Medal of Honor in Vietnam, while *Male* featured Sioux Indian athlete and US marine lieutenant Billy Mills, who won a gold medal at the 1964 Olympics.[38] But in these stories, the hero never attained the sexual rewards reserved for his white compatriots. Or, in many cases, the recognition. As one civil rights leader, quoted in *Stag*'s piece on Olive, shared, "Men who have won our country's greatest honor have become, in a sense, unknown soldiers."[39]

Of course, men engrossed in these magazines may have been less apt to think about the state of racial inequality in 1950s America. Still, not all seemed right with the world. A host of Cold War anxieties – racial, gendered, social, domestic – intimated that working-class men were somehow not reaping the full rewards of a mass, consumer-based society. Despite the sense of a growing middle class, many Americans still felt they were being left behind, still confronted with the realities of social and economic inequality. Perhaps this explains why men's adventure magazines promised quick fixes to life's daily problems. One advertisement declared that you could "achieve more social and economic success" by developing a "stronger he-man voice." Here was your chance to "Be a 'Somebody,'" the ad proclaimed. An essay in *Real* assured readers that "Your Screwy Idea Can Make You a Million," the money-making brainstorms including whiskey-flavored toothpaste, do-it-yourself voodoo kits, and wax for "butch" haircuts.[40]

These strange ideas vowing profitable businesses, laughable in retrospect, illustrated genuine worries that men weren't measuring up in the aftermath of World War II. They also underscored the class component of men's adventure magazines. A sense of fiscal insecurity permeated ads and storylines of working-class men unable to take full advantage of the postwar consumer culture. One correspondence school advertisement, for instance, asked, "Are you expendable?" Another queried readers on whether they were "standing still" on their jobs. "Will recognition come?"[41] And as the nation inched closer to full-scale war in Vietnam, *Male* offered an exposé on why work pensions might not be "worth a red cent." So distressing were these economic hardships that *Saga* found it necessary to publish an article on men who, "working overtime, commuting to the suburbs, [and] taking care of a lawn," could no longer even afford a mistress.[42]

For pulp readers, though, an alternative to these frustrations existed. Adventure magazines promised untapped resources to achieve or regain one's masculinity. Pay raises, promotions, women, heroism, and success in life all lay within reach. Or so the pulps implied.

SELLING A NEW AMERICAN MAN

Despite magazines' promises of advancement and security, working-class anxieties never seemed to subside during the years leading up to America's war in Vietnam. While the nation's gross national product grew by over $200 billion between 1950 and 1960, many male workers felt increasingly overworked and underpaid. Studies showed that "disposable time" dropped for working-class men, while the income inequality gap grew between them and the middle class.[43] Moreover, job attitude surveys suggested a widely held dissatisfaction with work. Sociologist C. Wright Mills even claimed there was a "fatalistic feeling that work *per se* is unpleasant." Men's magazines might have revered working-class ideals of the "self-made man," but such notions increasingly appeared more myth than reality. Could it be that World War II had also failed in delivering "freedom from want"?[44]

Worries over being unable to provide for one's family reintroduced fears from the Great Depression, when high unemployment rates undermined men's identities as breadwinners. This relationship between work and masculinity remained strong well into the 1960s, and pulp adverts were sure to exploit these associations.[45] In *Battlefield*, the Commercial Trades Institute ran an ad on training to become a skilled auto mechanic. Here was an opportunity to "make your income grow with family needs." International Correspondence Schools, though, put shame at the center of its advertising campaign. "I saw my job failure in my family's eyes," declared a man looking into the disappointed faces of his wife and three children. Needless to say, such gendered conceptions of work ignored women's economic dependence on men. But compassion wasn't necessary in the pulps' definition of manhood. Real husbands and fathers were providers, plain and simple.[46]

One remedy to this occupational angst was to focus on the male body. Certainly, there was a military component at play. In early 1953, for example, *American Manhood*, a muscle-building and physical culture magazine, paid tribute to the burly men of the US Army's tank corps who stood "ready to hold the forces of Repression at bay."[47] Yet class further layered martial images of the body. *Male* published "College Men Are Sexually Inferior" in July 1954. According to the author, Dr. James Bender, not getting into college may have left some men with "an uneasy sense of inferiority."[48] Nevertheless, the strong, "average" man could still discern an attainable path toward masculine fulfillment, simply by following ostensibly proven methods. Pulp ads sold strength and vitality as key components of success, and by the 1950s, magazine adverts were commanding a hefty percentage of advertising revenue within the

Fig. 1.2 *Man's Magazine,* April 1957

United States, as companies purposefully linked consumption with the achievement of status.[49] But these ads were not just selling goods and services. Advertisements, targeting working-class men, were also promoting and reinforcing a conception of manhood that paralleled magazine

storylines and artwork. Masculine dominance, in a sense, could be purchased (and, thus, validated), through new job opportunities, "how-to"
sex manuals, or products enhancing one's physical stature and looks.[50]

Towering above the mail-order business stood Charles Atlas, an Italian American bodybuilder who titled himself "The World's Most Perfectly Developed Man." Atlas left little ambiguity in arguing that real men
could "just pick the kind of body" they wanted, amass bulging muscles,
and go on to perform heroic acts of strength, either on the beach or in
the boardroom. Yet male anxieties never lurked far below the surface.
"Don't Be Half A Man!" exclaimed one popular ad. "Don't Spend Your
Life on the Sidelines" decried another.[51] In these adverts, "real he-men"
were not "held back by a half-a-man body." Instead, they had chosen to
attain their "dream build" which brought them success in everything they
did. And, of course, women were "naturally attracted to the strong, red-
blooded man who radiates magnetism." Thus, getting "power-packed
shoulders" would "make girls go 'Ga-Ga' on the beach." Atlas's version
of manhood rested on the assumption that "big brawny he-men grab the
most attention, the best jobs, [and] the prettiest girls."[52]

Joe Weider, editor-in-chief of *American Manhood*, replicated this connection between men's bodies, sexual attractiveness, and hoped-for
sexual conquest. The magazine's editorial policy noted that bodybuilding would lead to "impressive muscular development," "strong character," and one's place in society as a "respected citizen." In many ways,
Weider's magazines were little more than eighty pages of ads for his
system of muscle building. He exhorted his readers to be proud of their
bodies and "Stop Being a Weakling Today!" To Weider, "millions of
boys" were "underdeveloped and weak," being bullied and "pushed to
the side." But, like Atlas, he had the solution. Hardened bodies could
propel young boys into manhood.[53]

Yet these bodies were an idealized version of masculinity that may
have seemed improbable for the average reader to attain. Consumption
thus became a way to assuage male insecurities, a chance to transform
one's self and remake one's body. As one pulp editor recalled, virility was
a "subject close to the male fiction reader's heart." Both stories and
advertisements therefore played on these fears of being an imperfect,
even deficient man.[54] *Challenge*, for instance, noted that "Americans

Fig. 1.3 *Battle Cry*, August 1962

spent $167 million in 1957 for non-prescription 'quick pills' to sooth minor disturbances." Meanwhile, ads stoked men's anxieties over their loss of virility – and their hair. Most pulp magazines included at least one advert on "the miracle of hair regrowth." Taylor Topper told prospective customers there was no need to be bald and that they could "feel better" and do their jobs better. "Don't be ignored," the ad declared,"because you look older than you are."[55]

In the Cold War era, moreover, any loss of virility could have stark military consequences. When American POWs in the Korean War refused repatriation, ostensibly because they had succumbed to communist brainwashing, critics worried that soft, flabby American men were not strong enough to endure "advanced new techniques of psychological torture and mind control."[56] President-elect John F. Kennedy, writing on the "Soft American" for *Sports Illustrated* in 1960, argued that the "first inclination of a decline in the physical strength and ability of young Americans became apparent among United States soldiers in the early stages of the Korean War." Military officers shared Kennedy's concern. The head of physical education at West Point, Colonel Frank J. Kones, feared that without a vigorous fitness program, "our children will certainly become a race of eggheads walking around on bird-legs."[57]

This decline in "moxie," according to one army general, not only placed the nation at risk in an ideological war with the communists, but also informed popular attitudes about the country's enemies. Russian soldiers were hearty. Chinese and Vietnamese troops lived and fought on a bowl of rice a day. The Korean War images of brainwashing, in comparison, depicted American GIs as weak, succumbing to the greater strength of the Reds. In the 1956 film *The Rack*, for example, Paul Newman plays a former POW from Korea on trial for treason. At movie's end, he is convicted, despite the many tortures he experienced while a prisoner.[58] Arguably, *The Rack* spoke to American weaknesses far more powerfully than *The Manchurian Candidate* (1962), in which the target of Chinese subversion was a spineless politician. That Paul Newman could succumb to torture suggested the nation might not be producing men worthy of military service. Marine Colonel Lewis "Chesty" Puller went further, linking indulgent American lifestyles to an existential threat. As he declared to his troops in Korea, "Our country won't go on forever, if we stay as soft as we are now. There won't be an America – because some foreign soldiers will invade us and take our women and breed a hardier race."[59]

Following Puller's logic, for the United States to survive the Cold War, strong American men also needed to procreate. Here, the macho pulps stood ready with advice columns and advertisements for readers who hoped to "banish sex ignorance" and avoid "shameful errors" that might ruin their lives. An ad for the book *Sex and Exercise* listed a host of potential sexual pitfalls. "Keep your virile powers healthy and strong. Protect yourself against impotency. Conquer weakening habits. Night losses. Sex fatigue." Indeed, as one article on "Sex Knowledge for Young Men" warned, there were "beautiful aspects of sex," but also a dangerous, "gloomy side." Thus, "heavy petting" – kissing and "handling and fondling of more intimate parts of the body" – could lead to unwanted pregnancies or, apparently worse, venereal disease.[60]

While women might be toxic vehicles carrying gonorrhea and syphilis, "well hidden in the vulva or vagina," they also generated fears that men might underperform in marriage. *Challenge* offered advice for the "many men [who] stumble through the crisis of the wedding night like bulls in heat." *Stag* ran a similar ad counseling "the bewildered groom" on the "hazards of the first night." "How Much Is 'Too Much Sex?'" asked yet another report from *Showdown*. The possible nightmares piled up from story to story. Virginity could cause cancer. Infertility was normally the husband's fault. Emotional, psychic, and physical deficiencies kept men from an "ideal sexual union." Frigidity and differences in age undermined happy marriages. No wonder young pulp readers might be anxious about their sexual performance. As *Battle Cry* proclaimed, "Ignorance Can Ruin Your Sex Life." The answer, "according to prominent authorities," was that "book learning is no substitute for actual, practical experience."[61]

Recommending that men be more promiscuous surely increased the prospects of young pulp readers developing or reinforcing sexist attitudes toward women. Constantly proving one's manhood required testimonials that men were not, in fact, inferior. "Sex guides" consequently offered advice on the "causes and cures of female frigidity," how "techniques of seduction" could open up new worlds for readers, and the need to be persistent when one's sexual advances were discouraged. If glamour girls were a "pain in the boudoir" – the pulps regularly used the term "girls" over "women" when discussing sex – men still could gaze upon them without repercussion. As *Men* declared, "Ogling girls is the God-given prerogative of any male with corpuscles in his veins and hormones that aren't completely atrophied."[62]

Cartoons similarly reinforced these attitudes. In one sketch, a naked male doctor, with only a stethoscope draped around his neck, exposes himself to a female patient in a low-cut black dress. Entering the waiting room, he asks "Who's next?" In another, a male executive is seen tape measuring a female job applicant's chest. "I don't mean to pry, sir," she queries, "but what has this to do with typing 120 words a minute?" Apparently, professional men in positions of power could act without any fear of consequences.[63]

These depictions surely left their mark on young men, especially those with limited sexual experiences. As one Vietnam veteran recalled of his childhood, the erotic content of men's magazines "held the promise of wonderful possibilities for the future and was for years as close as I would come to the forbidden pleasures of the opposite sex." Yet the tensions between desire and fear promoted an underlying sexism pitting man against woman. Ads ran on how men could achieve the "ultimate conquest," while advice columns told readers how to avoid "bedroom barracudas."[64] A *Men* story from 1961 on boosting one's "sexual batting average" noted how the "male–female relationship is a highly competitive one." Consequently, numerous pulp offerings instructed men on how best to find "tramps" and "all-out love kittens" or how to turn "temporary virgins" into "eager, passion-starved women who'll 'swing' with the first man available." *Male* even promoted emotional manipulation, arguing that the best time "to finesse a girl into the hay is when she's just been jilted by a guy. She'll be out to prove her 'femininity,' that she's really an effective sex partner, and will often go on a wild bedroom fling to prove this."[65]

This Cold War sexism advanced in the macho pulps could be found in the 1940s armed forces as well, especially targeting women who served in uniform. Those who volunteered in World War II were met with disdain, condescension, or outright hostility. As one advisor on wartime women's units found, "If the Navy could possibly have used dogs or ducks or monkeys, certain of the older admirals would probably have greatly preferred them to women." Many male GIs saw their female counterparts as whores, lesbians, or "confused women who think they want to be men." Moreover, a number of these women suffered intense slander campaigns aimed at demonstrating their unworthiness to wear the uniform.[66] Similar attitudes persisted after the war. Male recruits in basic training were called "ladies" by overbearing drill instructors, while *Battlefield* published a 1959 cartoon that reeked of outright sexism. In it, a curvaceous WAC stands in front of a male officer's desk, her uniform outlandishly tight-fitting. "You said no to my pass yesterday, Corporal, so I'm doing the same to your request for a furlough." The double-meaning of "pass" underpinned the joke, but the quid pro quo clearly qualified as sexual harassment.[67]

While popular images both scorned and eroticized women in uniform, men's adventure magazines picked up on the realization that army training was not providing basic information on wartime sex to new recruits. Sex education within the military ranks had never embodied sound pedagogical practices, but the World War II experience seemed to demand a reconsideration of training methods.[68] The pulps lambasted the army's "Mickey Mouse" training films for not being more honest, thereby inadvertently promoting venereal disease within the ranks. Apparently, these movies fell into two ineffective categories – the "shocker" and the "preacher." To *Battle Cry*, the "shocker" proved particularly futile since "bleeding canker sores were too much to take for some of the weaker stomachs." The problem seemingly stemmed from the "American attitude toward sex – a guiltiness and a sense of shame, perhaps – which makes it impossible even for grown-up Army strategists to face the facts of life without fear and trembling."[69]

Though the pulps suggested that Army films might be too "straightlaced," the magazines themselves contributed to a stilted sense of what was acceptable, if not normal, for how young men should view women. Ads for lingerie products, stag movies, and pornographic photos all depicted women as objects to be consumed or controlled. Readers, for instance, could purchase glossy photos of Brigitte Bardot, "that delectable piece of French pastry," for only one dollar. Or they could order *The Pleasure Primer*, which ran under the tagline "No woman is safe (or really wants to be) when a man's mind is in the bedroom." Might such language leave a young man with the impression that women didn't really mean it if they spurned his sexual advances?[70]

Of course, an unskilled "cog in the machine" likely had little chance of wooing someone like Brigitte Bardot. Men's magazines therefore offered opportunities to achieve status and financial security. Advertisements ran the gamut, from jobs in meat cutting, which offered "success and security," to training as auto mechanics, plumbers, steamfitters, and welders. One man "hit his stride" by becoming a locksmith, while others found "profits hidden in broken electrical appliances."[71] Striving for status took center stage in these ads. "Be a Clerk all my life? Not Me!" declared one advert. "Don't Stay Just a 'Name' on the Payroll," proclaimed another. By the mid 1960s, ads spoke of "unlimited opportunities . . . in programming IBM computers" where the "prospects for high pay and professional standing" were "unlimited." In a sense, these careers offered opportunities to embrace the ideal of becoming a skilled artisan, a highly trained worker whose talents were admired and valued. As one advertisement pledged, "Here is your chance for action and real job security."[72]

Once more, though, anxieties lingered. What if these trade jobs did not offer higher status as promised? What if pulp readers were falling behind their more educated peers? Advertisements thus pushed self-help booklets aimed at personal growth. Or at least the impression of growth. "Everyone takes Bill for a college man," began one ad, "until he starts to speak. Then the blunders he makes in English reveal his lack of education." Because these mistakes were holding men back, correspondence courses vowed to help them "Speak and Write Like a College Graduate."[73] If they had been barred from better jobs because of a lack of education – "Sorry, we hire only high school graduates" ran one advert – then there were plenty of chances to finish high school at home. As the Wayne School in Illinois encouraged, men who had "had enough of just working in a rut," who wanted to "make up rapidly for lost time," could "know the feeling of pride and confidence that comes with saying, 'Of course, I'm a high school graduate.'"[74]

This selling of a new American man, however, had its limits. A young working-class male might improve his vocabulary or earn a few extra dollars a month, but how much adventure came with packing meat or repairing electronics? Though several ads promised "Exciting Outdoor Careers of Adventure," becoming a game warden or fish hatcheryman hardly garnered as much respect as a combat veteran with rows of medals on his chest.[75] Perhaps unsurprisingly then, many young men who

Fig. 1.4 *Big Adventure*, June 1961

ultimately went to Vietnam recalled seeking a sense of adventure there. One recalled, while driving a delivery truck at home, that "the bug hit me to try something different." Another remembered that he "burned for a new adventure," while still another admitted being afraid to serve but also realizing that joining the army "was probably the greatest adventure I was going to have in my life."[76] Especially if such service could be linked to larger notions of defending the nation against an enemy threatening freedom across the globe.

THE RED MENACE

Men's adventure magazines from the 1950s and 1960s made it clear that World War II had spawned a new threat, not just overseas, but at home as well. Pulp writers shared the fears of US foreign policy experts who believed that Soviet communists had transformed the whole world into a massive battlefield. To them, the Cold War had become a "titanic contest" between good and evil.[77] If Wisconsin Senator Joseph McCarthy was correct in arguing that Americans had become apathetic to evil in the aftermath of World War II, that there was an "emotional hangover and a temporary moral lapse which follows every war," then the pulps offered a tangible reminder that the communist threat was authentic.[78]

Articles abounded of "fanatical communists" bent on world domination. Soviet agents murdered US diplomats in Europe, while others trained "fake Americans" in the Ukraine who then would live in the United States and steal state secrets. Russian spy fleets, posing as "oceanic expeditions," trawled along US coastlines, setting up a "high seas espionage network capable of everything from stealing the results of our latest missile test to sneaking Red agents into America!"[79] Another report focused on a huge "Russian undersea armada" and questioned if the Soviet navy was planning a "submarine Pearl Harbor." "The danger is *now*," declared the piece. So pressing had the threat become that the head of the KGB apparently held so much power, he could "tip it to total annihilation of the world any time he chooses."[80]

Making matters worse, the threat came not only from the Soviets, but from the Chinese as well. In the aftermath of the 1949 communist victory in the Chinese civil war, many Americans mistakenly deemed Mao's China merely a puppet of Moscow.[81] Pulp writers thus spoke of Chinese brainwashing and torture and of the "million-man Chicom horde" and its plans for a "merciless 'blitzkrieg' that would gut free Asia." One author described Peking as the "capital of a slave-state where 'brainwashed' millions toe the line." Additionally, an exposé on the Cultural Revolution described Chinese Red Guards, unleashing an "orgy of death," as "murder monsters who may be America's front-line enemies in World War III."[82]

In fact, the global communist threat appeared so dangerous that perhaps the United States was being harmed in playing by the rules. *Battle Cry* published a 1957 screed titled "Let's Scrap the Geneva Convention." According to the author, the "terrorists of the Kremlin must be made to realize that their soldiers will suffer the same fate they mete out to others if they are captured."[83] This view of the enemy, that savages only responded to force, permeated into the highest levels of government. During the Eisenhower presidency, General James Doolittle, hero of the first air raid over Tokyo in World War II, conducted a review of CIA activities. In his report, Doolittle painted communists as an "implacable enemy" pursuing global supremacy. "There are no rules in such a game," the general argued. "Hitherto acceptable norms of human conduct do not apply." Thus, covert operations aimed at regime change could be seen as legitimate foreign policy tools, leading to American-inspired coups from Guatemala to Iran.[84]

Such moral relativism appeared to make sense, especially since communists were engaging in unconventional warfare across the globe. In Southeast Asia, North Africa, and Latin America, revolutionaries were avoiding decisive encounters with their enemies and relying on "indirect, irregular, unconventional strategies."[85] Their challenges, however, usually were local. Not so for the United States. Locked in a global contest to contain communism, nearly every spot on the map could be judged vital to US national security, thereby justifying almost any military means. And because the threat had materialized on America's doorstep – *Fury* described "Crazy Ché" Guevara as the "toughest guy in the Western Hemisphere" – there seemed little alternative but to engage the enemy on his terms.[86]

But what if the threat was domestic as well? What if communist subversives, from Latin America and beyond, had infiltrated the United States and were planning to conquer the nation? Without question, men's adventure magazines contributed to Cold War hysteria over this threat of domestic communism. *Male*, for instance, wrote of secret Red "subversion clubs" that were popping up in every American town, while

For Men Only believed that communists had a "carefully built espionage setup in America." South of the border, insurgents were attempting to build a "new Red dominion" in the Western Hemisphere and "take control of the Panama Canal." These fears of communist subversion reached ludicrous heights. One *Stag* confidential from 1964 linked the ideological threat to what would soon become a national debate over reproductive rights. "Many of Cuba's abortionists, refugees from Castro, are on the loose now in our southern states, giving America a whole flock of abortion centers."[87]

Such irrational fears, present long after the political demise of Wisconsin's infamous senator, were emblematic of Cold War McCarthyism. The constant dread of imminent war allowed political opportunists the chance to strike out at "Communists, near-Communists, and nowhere-near-Communists" with little concern for social injustices. Thus, equating the Communist Party with a "huge iceberg," as did McCarthy, where the most dangerous part was "under water and invisible" made sense.[88] Who had evidence to credibly question how deep the true threat went? In line with the macho pulps, wily politicians saw merit in conflating contemporary political issues with sexual anxieties. As "Tailgunner Joe" told reporters at an impromptu press conference, "If you want to be against McCarthy, boys, you've got to be a Communist or a cocksucker."[89]

Even military men were not immune from castigation and charges of conspiracy. McCarthy undoubtedly overreached by accusing former five-star general and Secretary of State George C. Marshall of betraying American interests, but genuine fears endured that GIs might be susceptible to communist infection. Vietnam veteran Ron Kovic recalled his childhood certainties that communists "were infiltrating our schools, trying to take over our classes and control our minds."[90] In the January 1957 issue of *Real Men*, Mark Davis shared "The Red Plan to Conquer America," in which a "weird Soviet-supported dope ring" was attempting to "sap the strength of American fighting forces." This it did by turning thousands of GIs into "sick, helpless and almost insane dope addicts." *Man's Adventure* followed with a story on a US Army private who deserted during the Korean War, improbably catching the eye of Mao himself and becoming a "commander of the Communist Chinese terror-troops in Mongolia!"[91]

Overshadowing all these anxieties, the fear of nuclear Armageddon became part of daily conversations across Cold War America. In military circles, scientific laboratories, and popular media outlets, the possible end of civilization pervaded the cultural landscape. Naturally, the pulps contributed to what one anthropologist called a "fear psychosis" by asking frightful questions. "Can the Hell Bomb Destroy the World?" "What Are Your Chances for Survival?"[92] Yet even here, men's magazines could incorporate sexual innuendo into the mix. The "Barracks Beauty" for the September 1957 issue of *True War*, Marley Sanderson, was described as "radioactive" and an "experiment in atomic energy." *Sir!* introduced Iris Bristol, a popular pin-up model, as a "Fallout Shelter Girl," meaning "the girl we'd most like to come up out of the fallout shelter with." In one 1958 account, which estimated more than fifty million dead from a nuclear war, *Real War* predicted "Women will be selling themselves for an apple – if it isn't radioactive." For young readers, would it not later be unsurprising that in war-torn Vietnam, women also would be offering themselves to American GIs for a morsel of food?[93]

Despite the awesome destructive power of nuclear weapons, adventure magazines ensured these soldiers remained central to the nation's security. While nuclear war might be an "atomic-hot nightmare haunting every battle-tough pro in our armed forces," courageous boys still could find a man-making experience in uniform.[94] One pulp story from 1958 imagined an apocalyptic global struggle ten years into the future, "The Last War on Earth." After Russian divisions crashed into Germany, the world plunged into war. In North Africa and the Middle East, Arab forces harassed their enemies but "lacked the courage or ability to overrun the 'hated Americans.'" Meanwhile, back in Europe, the Russians "spent human lives with a callousness that shocked even hardened veterans." While all sides employed new armaments, they were "only an adjunct to the basic and age-old weapon – *the foot soldier.*" Of course, the Americans prevailed because "in the last analysis it was the clash of men against men that tipped the scales. As in every war, the great ultimate weapon was man. To nobody's surprise, G.I. Joe turned out to be far better than Commie Ivan."[95]

Perhaps as a corrective to the potentially emasculating reliance on technology, the macho pulps drove home storylines in which real men protected the nation's security. *Stag*, for example, ran a 1961 cover story on US Air Force Chief of Staff Curtis LeMay, "The American General Russia Fears Most." While the article gushed over the Strategic Air Command's bomber fleet, LeMay's grit took center stage. "The way to win a war," the general sparingly briefed his men, "is to hit the enemy hard and keep right on slugging him." Not surprisingly, a few years later LeMay would be recommending to President Johnson that the US Air Force bomb North Vietnam back "into the Stone Age."[96]

Only true heroes, warriors with the requisite "balls," were capable of defending the nation – not just from communists, but from women right here at home.[97]

THE SEXUAL MENACE

In line with many contemporary depictions in popular culture, men's adventure magazines presented multiple constructions of women. Some were decorative status symbols, akin to men's private property that could be flaunted in public. Some were sexualized objects to be sought after. Others were damsels in distress, oftentimes innocent victims of war, "helpless, passive creatures who could only be saved by the heroic actions of brave men."[98] Still others were sexual predators, tramps, and *femmes fatales* who graced the pages of *noir* thrillers or, in the pulps, seduced Nazi counterintelligence agents and by morning had become their "willing slave." As Woody Haut observes, regardless of how "they were described, women in pulp fiction culture were objects of male fantasy and obsession."[99]

Photographic spreads of scantily clad women surely propelled many male fantasies. Taking their cue from World War II-era pin-ups, men's adventure magazines regularly included photos of "cheesecakes," women in seductive poses and various stages of undress. The pulps, though, portrayed their models differently than pin-up icons like Betty Grable or *Playboy* centerfolds. Hefner's Playmates, for example, were crafted as sensual yet "sexually naïve," provocative yet sweet, if not innocent-looking girls next door.[100] While World War II pin-up Rita Hayworth might be seen as more erotic than wholesome, she still offered American soldiers a vision of romantic escape rather than cheap sex.

In either case, these women were highly sexualized models fashioned for male gratification.[101]

The pulps' cheesecake girls, however, appeared far more lascivious. Alluring, "racetrack-curved" women promised both pleasure and sexual knowledge to the voyeuristic male reader. In "Recipe for Cheesecake," *Man's Day* laid out how a "persuasive lensman" could induce a girl to show "more legs and/or bosom" and how "professional clothes-shedders" made the "most willing subjects." It apparently took little encouragement to get these women to strip off their brassieres or undress completely. "An amazing number of women," the story recounted, "don't wear panties, and it is even more amazing how many women who don't wear panties forget that they are not wearing them when posing for pictures." The pulps may not have explicitly represented the sexual act, but these pin-ups appeared to be offering a clear invitation.[102]

Fig. 1.5 *Man's Day*, March 1953

Body measurements almost always accompanied these pictorial spreads, a way for men to rank order their "pulse-stimulating" pin-ups on an inch-by-inch basis. Moreover, the women were presented as one-dimensional, almost vacuous, sex objects. Cheesecake "comes naturally to Karen" read one spread in *Man's Magazine*.[103] In an interview with

Real, model Lisa Varga was asked why she posed for cheesecake. "Because the photographers want me to," she responded. After noting Lisa's measurements, the interviewer queried, "Do most men try to seduce you soon after you meet?" He then asked if her build developed by itself or if she helped it along with "bust exercises." By the late 1960s, *Stag* and *Man's Epic* were sharing their first exposures of fully naked breasts, even as one model noted that "ninety percent of the men I've met were real wolves."[104]

If men were wolves, then women must be damsels in distress in need of a savior. Of course, the pulps never wrestled with the contradiction that men needed to protect women from other men. Instead, damsels craving rescue advanced plotlines wherein the hero could prove his courage and generosity, and, if all went well, be sexually rewarded for his troubles. In such stories, Nazis proved a customary villain. American protagonists saved French girls from Nazi raiders, repatriated female nurses who unknowingly crossed over enemy lines, or ferried the "wives and daughters of local French politicos to safety in England."[105] In one tale, the hero bursts into a "pest-ridden female penal castle" to rescue "dozens of young, golden-bodied girls [who] were held in helpless bondage by sadistic, lust-crazed male guards."[106]

Yet, even while being portrayed as helpless victims, women could not be trusted. Fears of social degeneracy and juvenile delinquency ran rampant throughout much of the 1950s, feeding anxieties that women in the postwar era were not meeting their societal obligations. J. Edgar Hoover, for instance, blamed moms' "absenteeism" for the spike in postwar juvenile delinquency. War-worker mothers, the argument went, had fallen down on the job by not providing a decent home for their children, instead tempted to escape their household routines and earn a little spending money in war jobs. As the FBI Director claimed, the "lack of wholesome influences at home are contributing factors to youthful misbehavior."[107]

These fear-mongers maintained that women exhibited the most alarming social misbehavior, especially young, single ones deemed to be from the lower class. Just as it underpinned discussions of martial masculinity, class loomed large in these debates. Women from "delinquent subcultures" often were portrayed as excessively independent and mature, the product of a "permissive" social climate that failed to set proper boundaries.[108] They were rebellious troublemakers living outside of accepted sexual norms, painted as "loose" girls at the center of a teen pregnancy "epidemic." In such popular narratives, women were not supporting their men as they should, but rather contributing to a society that seemed intent on undermining the traditional male role. In short, they posed a danger not only to men, but to society as a whole.[109]

Women supporting the war industry during the 1940s no doubt contributed to these worries. Yet it is important to note that Rosie the Riveter never truly upended larger social norms. Historian D'Ann Campbell concludes that "while the war certainly caused an increase in the average number of women employed, it did not mark a drastic break with traditional working patterns or sex roles."[110] True, the number of women working outside the home rose in the first decade of the Cold War, confusing conventional definitions of gender roles and challenging many women to rethink their identities in relation to their supposedly proper roles as wives and mothers. But, for the most part, traditional, patriarchal norms remained in place after World War II.[111]

In men's adventure magazines, however, women of the postwar era apparently had shed their inhibitions and were creating sexual havoc across America. Throughout the 1950s and 1960s, the macho pulps tended to depict women as sexually liberated death merchants. *Men* wrote of "Young Girl Wolfpacks" who were "utterly nonchalant about sex," terrorizing US cities, and making "male gangs look like Little Leaguers." Clearly, a double standard was at play here. The pulps were offering men advice on how to get women to have sex with them, yet apparently many of those same women were vicious predators. Thus, in "Death Wore a Tight Bikini," author William Ard described his female antagonist as an "undressed, murdering kitten."[112] Another tale on housing development sex parties blamed "destitute young Mothers" for turning public housing projects into "vice ridden jungles devoted to booze, brawls and alarmingly casual sex." To ensure readers understood the class component, the author quoted a Washington psychologist who maintained that the "poor often have sex as their only pleasure. But they have it in abundance."[113]

Even into the mid to late 1960s, as cultural norms already were shifting, the pulps remained wedded to storylines where "Beatnik Girls" and "Cycle Girl Gangs" thumbed their noses at society by "living for speed, sex, and violence." In the 1966 "Sex Revolt of Young Society Girls," Barry Jamieson wrote of the unconventional behavior from a "new breed" of good-time girls who could beat out "hardened sex pros in talent for far-out bedroom capers."[114] The list of hedonists ran long. Nymphomaniacs, "calldoll bait" bleeding soft-hearted Americans, lustful madams engaging in "all sexual activity" where nothing was barred. These women were as tantalizing as they were dangerous. "All-or-Nothing Girls" illustrates how generational changes seemingly were challenging traditional gender roles. "Throwing out the old belief that the male takes the lead in the act of lovemaking," the article claimed, "this new breed of passion-starved young woman is re-writing the bedroom rules to satisfy her own, newly-liberated cravings – and the guy who doesn't understand her needs would be better off living in a monastery."[115]

Men might benefit from this sexual liberation, but the pulps left readers with the impression that women still threatened good social order. Worse, "tramps" were preying upon the armed forces, a phenomenon popularized in World War II by "Victory Girls" who notoriously swarmed around military bases in search of easy sex. (Congress passed the May Act in 1941 which made prostitution near these bases a federal offense.) Such "sex happy dames" remained after the Korean War, "parasites and vultures that feast on the loneliness of the Serviceman." Of course, while female "scum" preyed upon "unsuspecting" soldiers, the GIs themselves were just on "the harmless prowl."[116]

In 1960, *Man's Magazine* presented a disturbing piece on sex and the armed forces. According to the story, "the uniform doesn't corrupt the boy," a clear intimation that it was the women in town who did. And yet, away from home, these poor, corruptible soldiers "often felt free to patronize floozies and brothels." In one scenario, the "virginal" eighteen-year-old Bart, drafted and sent to Fort Bliss, is pressured by other GIs to go to Juarez, Mexico. Bart is "appalled by the bare-breasted whores" but is afraid to "seem chicken" in front of his comrades. When he finally accepts a Mexican prostitute's offer, he not only remembers the army doctor's warning that Juarez is a "venereal hotspot," but also is "frightened of the brazen whore who attempted to force his sexual ardor." In the end, poor Bart "simply could not arouse himself, and remained impotent," leaving as "virginal as when he'd entered" the brothel.[117]

The contradictions in Bart's story clearly escalate upon closer inspection. If American GIs were so moral, why were they actively seeking out prostitutes? Were the Mexican women taking advantage of the US soldiers or vice versa? And if sex was intended to be a man-making experience, what did Bart's inability to perform say about his masculinity? (Of course, when he rejoins his pals he pretends to "have enjoyed the whore's favors.") Such incongruities also could be seen in portrayals of women not being loyal to their soldier. In a story on "Dear John" letters, *Battle Cry* derided female backstabbers for kicking a soldier "in the seat of his pants when he is most helpless." Naturally, it was acceptable for the GI to play "'housey-housey' with fraulein or mama-san" overseas – at least the "woeful little women" at home had "family and friends to soften the blow." Given that wives and girlfriends were expected to be obediently supportive while their men were away defending democracy, such sexual double standards hardly required further explanation by male pulp writers.[118]

Worse, female culprits could be operating from within the armed forces. One 1956 pulp story asked if army nurses were "saints or sinners," suggesting that at least some were taking sexual advantage of combat GIs. The fact that white women were rare in World War II combat zones like New Guinea – the "native belles were hardly alluring by American standards of feminine beauty" – only heightened men's temptations. Furthering sexual contradictions, *Battle Cry* even admitted that nurses required armed escorts at all times. "The plain truth was that the nurses were being protected from their own sex-starved countrymen."[119] Still, most narratives placed blame on promiscuous women. Thus, tramps disguised as nurses also competed with wartime American Red Cross volunteers and USO girls for men's favors. *Real War* exposed these "bawds for the brass," highlighting the girls "who drank the Scotch, played pound-the-pillow with the officers and often cleaned up big dough." To ensure class issues remained in close view, the article reminded readers that these "dames . . . were all from well down the ladder."[120]

Condemning lower-class "harlots" – they were "ubiquitous" in America, according to Philip Wylie – conveniently redirected male anxieties of women purposefully upending traditional sexual norms. Seductresses were not moral anchors of society. In subverting their femininity, they were chipping away at family and social stabilities so necessary to men dominating contemporary gender roles. Thus, even while men were out "doll-hunting," they castigated "sexually reckless females" and "abandoned, man-destroying" women.[121] In the process, even class issues could be overturned, as in one story where a twenty-nine-year-old socialite was "able to enjoy herself sexually only with men who are socially inferior to her." According to *Stag*, she was one of "many thousands of 'troubled women.'" Occasionally, men also could misstep in the sands of these shifting sexual norms. *Real Adventure*, for example, reported a doctor's prognosis that increasing rates of vasectomies were leading to "more venereal disease, more illegitimacy among the young and more wife-swapping among the middle-aged." So portentous had "that operation" become, that the physician wondered "where the next generation of children will come from?"[122]

Still, men's adventure magazines reflected a widespread male unease that women were articulating themselves in ways that challenged prevailing sexual conceptualizations. Perhaps no better example could be found than in Betty Friedan's 1963 *The Feminine Mystique*. Author and activist Friedan argued that women could no longer ignore that inner voice saying "I want something more than my husband and my children and my home." Fulfillment as a woman meant more than just becoming a "housewife-mother." The task was to move beyond the public images of housewives buying "washing machines, cake mixes, deodorants, detergents, rejuvenating face creams, [and] hair tints." Instead, Friedan called for women to "accept or gratify their basic need to grow and fulfill their potentialities as human beings, a need which is not solely defined by their sexual role."[123]

Such appeals for greater social and sexual freedoms sat uneasily alongside yet another challenge to Cold War gender norms. "The pill," which was first approved for contraceptive use in the early 1960s, promised further shifts in the balance of sexual power and independence. If women could more freely choose when and how often to have sex, how could certain men not feel threatened? Indeed, many pulp writers were. One article on "sexually aggressive women" lamented how oral contraceptives had given the "American girl a sexual freedom she never had before ... A great many women are so highly-sexed they insist on calling all the shots in the bedroom."[124] *Man's Magazine* bemoaned the fact that men's "dominant role is being challenged as more and more wives use oral contraceptives." So confusing had this sexual state of affairs become that pulp writers were showcasing single "bachelor girls" who now were preying on married men. By 1967, a *True Action* story on the "new morality" demonstrated the outcome of women's sexual independence – "quickie love affair girls" had made the "double standard ... as outdated as grandma's whale-bone corset."[125]

Of course, gendered double standards never quite extinguished themselves. Real men could keep them alive and, if properly approached, benefit from these changing sexual norms. The challenge, for critics like Norman Mailer, was to fight against the "built-in tendency to destroy masculinity in American men." By winning "small battles" in the bedroom or in combat – performance in one augured well for performance in the other – men could contest and even reverse their supposed decline.[126] Take, for instance, Ian Fleming's *Goldfinger*, in which James Bond is able to bed the "psycho-pathological" lesbian Pussy Galore. When Bond comments "They told me you only liked women," she replies, "I never met a man before." This penetrating masculinity surely served as an example for embattled men, a reassuring fictional release from the domination of the "new" American woman.[127]

Without question, men's adventure magazines contributed to these misogynistic imaginings. Several articles highlighted the rewards of wife swapping, while *Man's Magazine* posited that "outrageous sex demands" from husbands were often "harmless, healthy, legitimate desires."[128] In "How to Handle Those New Free Love Girls," *Men* offered readers thirteen hints on handling "the astonishingly liberal-minded sexual behavior of many of today's women." Dr. Efrem Schoenhild began by arguing that women were never liberated from sex and that even "Man-hating women are by no means free of the attachment to the male." To the doctor, women needed the "male influence" and a "man's strength and solidarity." After offering advice on arousing a woman's curiosity and not getting "hung up" on her body, Schoenhild left men with an important message: "Remember, your role is to lead."[129]

The pulps frequently intimated that well-to-do men held certain advantages in leading and, notably, in profiting from women's sexual liberation. Just like *Playboy*, men's magazines presented affluent masculine role models to whom working-class readers could aspire. Modern executives flew on private company jets and enjoyed mid-air orgies with "airborne vice girls."[130] For those who could afford a Caribbean cruise, they might catch a single woman like the one showcased in *Man's Illustrated*. "When a girl like me goes on vacation, she wants to let off steam. That may mean a little drinking, a lot of laughs with good company and a liberal sprinkling of sack time with the right partner." (There was nothing to worry about if this vacationer became "hot and bothered" since she was on the pill.) In fact, according to the pulps, it appeared as if "mod-affluents" had time for little else besides sexual tourism on the high seas. *Bluebook* noted that the liquor bill alone on one "pleasure craft bash" rivaled "better than a month's pay for the average working stiff." Apparently, this new version of freedom of the seas came with a hefty price tag.[131]

As young draftee Bart's Mexican misadventure implied, though, keeping up with liberated women evoked plenty of sexual anxieties. Men now had to gratify themselves *and* their sexual partners. What if they failed to assert their virility? What if they disappointed in bed? The pulps tackled these fears in numerous ways. In one cartoon from *Stag*, a bride, still in her wedding dress, returns home to her parents carrying two suitcases. "Then, about four in the morning, Albert lost his luster," she complains.[132] An advertisement from the Vitasafe corporation hit upon a similar theme. A frustrated wife wearing lingerie and dark lipstick sits up in bed next to her sleeping husband. As she stares directly into the camera lens, the ad cries out "He Didn't Even Kiss Me Goodnight!" Lastly, in "The Failure," readers confront a man who has left his wife but cannot perform with his newfound mistress, silently "raging helplessly at this stupid, worthless body." The article failed to mention what this impotence may have suggested, though by story's end our adulterer has little remorse for cheating on his wife.[133]

Fears of not being able to perform sexually in this new age engendered one final anxiety, perhaps the most disquieting of all. If men could not derive pleasure from or provide pleasure to women, might it be possible they were gay? The 1948 and 1953 release of the sexual behavior studies collectively known as the "Kinsey Reports" left in their wake a frenzied debate over how Americans should define "normal" sexual conduct.[134] Alfred Kinsey, a biologist by training, revealed a wide range and variation of sexual activity – some eighty-five percent of his subjects admitted to premarital intercourse and sixty-nine percent had sex, at least once, with a prostitute. For the pulps, though, Kinsey's finding that thirty-seven percent of adult men had engaged in homosexual activity to orgasm presented a troubling conclusion. In Barbara Ehrenreich's words, gay men could be viewed as "failed" heterosexuals, an admission of "defeat" on the part of American manhood. While the macho pulps openly repudiated those in the gay community, the disquieting fact remained that impressionable young men might be vulnerable to the contagion of homosexuality.[135]

This homophobia ran rampant in the macho pulps. To *American Manhood*, homosexuals were "simply mentally sick people and should be regarded as such." Apparently, though, young men constantly needed to guard their masculinity as some boys became gay after "being taught by older persons while they were in their formative years before puberty. This is one danger all young boys are subject to." *Man's Magazine* published an exposé on "New York's Homosexual Underground," written by a reporter who posed as a gay man for twenty-four hours. In imparting what he saw – "the pathetic, the bizarre, the sick" – the author admitted that most of it "would make a normal person want to vomit." When the intrepid reporter, for instance, meets Billi, a "queen's queen," it is clear that the nightclub inhabitant isn't a real man. "I shook hands with him. It was like grasping a limp piece of putty."[136]

In other stories, wives could "go lesbian" or men might unsuspectingly marry one since "scientific investigators [had] discovered that better than 50% of all women have some lesbian tendencies." Perhaps unsurprisingly, the pulps ran more than a few accounts on electric shock therapy to treat this alleged ailment. So alarming had the threat become that Americans considered adopting methods of relief from foreign enemies. As *Male* related, the "Russians may have come up with a surefire way to cure homosexuals. They've been using electric shock treatments ... After 28 horrible treatments most of the deviates wind up cured and get married to girls."[137] Some men and women went further, electing for sex change operations that left even sympathetic pulp writers astonished. One author deemed transgender people a "true legion of the damned ... incredible victims of a colossal blunder by Nature." Through the "wizardry of modern medicine," one former GI, George Jorgensen, Jr., transformed into a "beautiful woman" and could "now look forward to a happy and a normal marriage."[138]

Jorgensen's reassignment surgery, which garnered national attention at the time, incited further unease that the homosexual menace might undermine military readiness. Sexual perverts might infect straight soldiers, resulting in sissified armed forces unable to defend against the communist threat. Popular conceptions held that homosexuals were emotionally unstable, prone to panic, and filled with neuroses – hardly traits needed to win on the modern battlefield. In fact, *True War* shared an ex-Stuka pilot's tale of how high-strung, hysterical "perverts" had ruined Hitler's air force. Misconstruing T. E. Lawrence's sexual orientation, *Sir!* described Lawrence of Arabia as both desert fighter and woman hater. "Captured and tortured by a homo caliph, he may have come to believe he was a homo, too." Under the strain of combat, even the most celebrated western guerilla fighter might be turned into a homosexual.[139]

If Lawrence of Arabia was vulnerable to infection, how could the US armed forces inure their own draftees from homosexual contamination? At induction centers across the country, the threat seemed real enough. Gay men might blend unnoticed into the military ranks, causing unseen havoc, or, if discovered, bring discredit to the armed forces. The toughest "thing a psychiatrist at an induction center has to determine," *Stag* declared, "is whether a man is homosexual. Some homosexuals try to pass as heterosexuals in order to get in. Some try opposite tack – play being 'queer' in order to stay out." *Male* was certain there were "high ranking military men hiding homosexual pasts," thus "easy marks for strong-arm extortionists." The macho pulps made it adamantly clear to their readers. Homosexual men and women posed a clear and present threat to Cold War society and, in particular, the US armed forces.[140]

And yet gay men ranked among adventure and muscle magazine consumers. George Takei, Star Trek's Sulu, was one of them. Growing up in a Japanese American internment camp as a young gay man, he

Fig. 1.6 *True War*, September 1957

later recounted reading these magazines because they offered a way to look at strong, attractive men in slinky bathing suits while keeping his own sexual preferences hidden. In fact, some of the earliest American homoerotic photographers – Bruce of Los Angeles and Lon of New York – ran ads selling "Dramatic Dual Photos" where the "physiques emphasize the dramatic impact of the pose." Bruce marketed "Cowboys of the West," glossies of ruggedly handsome young men in cowboy hats, hyped as "distinctly different source material on the man of the range." These appeared in the same magazines where writers declared homosexuality a mental illness or a "maladjustment of glands" that could be cured by heavy physical exercise.[141]

Of course, magazine editors had to navigate these waters carefully. At the height of the "lavender scare," sexual inquisitions had been swept into the larger anti-communist crusade. Publishing homosexually oriented material came with the risk of censorship or, worse, indictment for obscenity. By the mid 1950s, as Andrea Friedman notes, most commentators "understood homosexuality and Communism to flow from like sources – moral corruption, psychological immaturity, sex-role confusion – and to pose similar dangers to the nation."[142] Perhaps in this way, pulp readers saw themselves as righteous citizens, protecting American masculinity while safeguarding the United States from threats at home and abroad. In an ironic twist, though, World War II itself had contributed to the rise of "homophile" organizations intent on discreetly but more successfully integrating gay men and women into American society.[143]

All told, the multitude of Cold War anxieties left many men in an uneasy state. Fears over sexual performance and inability to provide for one's family. Fears of communist subversives and of nuclear Armageddon. Fears that women were emasculating men and "taking charge of sex relations." Of course, not all men shared these concerns. It seems probable, though, that pulp readers more intimately felt the weight of these uncertainties. They might have been more inclined to suffer from economic disparities in the 1950s and 1960s. They likely were in the position to be more frustrated when the women in adventure magazines – so desirable yet so dangerous – never materialized in real life. They may have been more predisposed to accept the pulp narrative that communist women and "savage" locals were far different from the pretty cheesecake fantasy living in Hometown, USA. Or worse, readers worried that when American women rated their "menfolk," they were not measuring up to the idealized sexual conquerors inside the pages of the macho pulps.[144]

If pulp definitions of masculinity emerged as fragile in relation to women, then perhaps one's manhood could better be demonstrated on the field of battle. There, at least, men could be liberated from the "castrating scissors" of female thighs. What better way to transmit these martial virtues to young men than through the shining example of their fathers who had served so valiantly in World War II?[145]

CHAPTER 2

My Father's War: The Allure of World War II and Korea

"IKE FATHER, LIKE SON." In March 1968, *Stag* ran a short yet tragic piece on a World War II and Korea veteran whose son had a choice between college or Vietnam. The nineteen-year-old "naturally" opted for the Marine Corps and was assigned to a combat unit in Quang Tri, "right in the heart of the action." His father worried for his son's safety, though, and after finding a loophole in military regulations, pulled some strings, reenlisted, and headed to Vietnam, joining the same outfit as his boy. "He made it up to the battalion command post," *Stag* reported, "just as remnants of a patrol were straggling in. Cornering one of the surviving Marines, the uneasy father asked if the soldier knew his son. 'Oh, yeah,' came the weary reply. 'He got killed.'"[1]

Published as the 1968 Tet offensive was still raging across much of South Vietnam and domestic support for the war appeared to be fracturing, *Stag*'s terse homage left a clear message. This patriotic family was serving its nation, even at great personal cost. The article ended by noting how the father flew back home with his son's body to attend the funeral, but was "still eligible to return to his unit on the line in the Far East."

Pulp stories like this highlighted how gendered codes of conduct helped reinforce child rearing during the Cold War era. Fathers raised their sons to value service in uniform. They transmitted the valorization of manhood and encouraged behavior that reflected these ideals. In the process, boys hardly questioned the manner in which their own definitions of masculinity were being militarized.[2] To one Vietnam veteran, his dad "was a hero. As kids growing up in the fifties, we used to play army all the time, and we'd talk about what our dads had done." Another, Bill

Ehrhart, similarly recalled sneaking into the bedroom of a friend's father and stealing a look at his Silver Star. "When we finally screwed up enough courage to ask him how he'd earned it," Ehrhart remembered, "his modestly vague response fired our ten-year-old imaginations to act out the most daring and heroic deeds."[3]

In many ways, men's adventure magazines helped young boys emulate their World War II and Korean War fathers. However, the pulps also offered appealing narratives for the veterans themselves. Within these magazines, men could find multiple versions of masculine citizen-soldiers – just and moral warriors, youthful combatants, heroic protectors, and sexual conquerors.[4] Here was an escape from overbearing wives and domineering bosses, perhaps even an antidote for those veterans who felt emasculated by their post-traumatic stress and were reluctant to share their pain. In pulp war stories, the heroes never suffered such frustrations. They shone in a wartime environment and passed the test of manhood with flying colors. As the nation's protectors, they made the difference between survival and extinction. In short, the macho pulps reinforced the overarching narrative of war as a masculine sphere of influence.[5]

This narrative construction seemed particularly important given the transition from the unconditional victory of World War II to the indecisiveness of Cold War era conflict. With the termination of hostilities on the Korean peninsula in 1953, Americans confronted the possibility there might be limits to US military power overseas. How was it possible, many wondered, that more than 33,000 American GIs had died in combat for a negotiated settlement that left the communist enemy still standing? If men were expected to serve and protect the nation, did such an unsatisfying conclusion portend a coming crisis, not only in American masculinity but in national security as well? A more positive view of battlefield exploits might ameliorate such worries. Men's magazines thus carved out space for accounts remembering and celebrating a more "heroic" period of war, tales no doubt desired by their readers, young and old alike.[6]

Indeed, the macho pulps courted two audiences. They sold themselves as both a friendly genre for veterans and a way for curious young teens to get a glimpse of what war might be like. Men's magazines tended to humanize American GIs, showing unvarnished respect for their service and sacrifices. One *Stag* author, for example, denounced what he saw as the "unfair or unrealistic treatment" of men in uniform. "If we want the security provided by a dedicated military, then it's time we level with our GIs and started giving them the fair shake they deserve." Just like popular 1950s television series such as *Crusade in Europe* and *Victory at Sea*, the pulps also presented virtuous Americans clashing dramatically with savage Nazis and fascists. "Singular bravery" could be found in the pages of almost any adventure mag. Along the way, military service became the embodiment of a masculine ethos.[7]

Fig. 2.1 *Stag*, July 1966

Just as importantly, the pulps also seduced younger readers with an opportunity to learn about the man-making experience of combat. These would-be soldiers, already imagining fighting in their own wars, proved a receptive audience. War permeated American youth culture in

the 1950s and early 1960s. Boys built models of Spitfire and Messersch-
mitt airplanes while devouring books like *The Desert Fox* and *Thirty Seconds
over Tokyo*. In New Jersey, Bruce Springsteen remembered passing after-
noons as "Hannibal crossing the Alps" or "GIs locked in vicious mountain
combat."[8] A recently graduated lieutenant from the Virginia Military
Institute wrote an approving letter to *Saga* about its story "The Day the
Kids Went to War," a rousing tale of the 1864 Civil War battle of New
Market. Most likely, more than a few teens attentively read through
Climax's "Baptism of Fire." The magazine wanted to know what it felt
like "the first time under fire," so it dispatched photographer Bob
Schwalberg to Fort Dix, New Jersey so he could go through the infil-
tration course for GI trainees. At story's end, with the reader in tow,
Schwalberg proclaims, "You're a 'veteran,' now. You've had your baptism
of fire and you're ready for the Real Thing – you hope!"[9]

Yet for veterans to wax nostalgic over their wartime experiences and
for young boys to remain hopeful war would make them into men, the
pulps had to accentuate the positive aspects of American GIs in battle.
Myths had to be constructed and framed in such a way that the needs of
Cold War society could be fulfilled by a "good war" narrative. In this way,
as pulp writer Mario Puzo maintained, World War II was a "gold mine."
Properly fabricated, the memory of the Second World War might guide
new recruits as they deployed to Southeast Asia in search of martial glory.
At very least, pulps like *Man's Epic* could showcase the heroism of those
courageous GIs who "smashed open the door to France" in the summer
of 1944. Even when it was becoming clear the war in Vietnam might be
mired in a stalemate, men's adventure magazines still emphasized the
very best of Americans at war.[10]

VETERANS REMEMBER

Much of what American society read about combat in World War II was a
sanitized version of reality. Advertisements, film, and even letters home
rarely shared the dark side of war. Indeed, watching war films could lead
some viewers to believe ground combat looked something akin to a
"choreographed football scrimmage." Despite this often rosy outlook, it
would be wrong to assume that all Cold War teens regarded military

service as a highly prestigious profession. A 1955 Gallup poll suggested that many teenagers thought enlisted soldiers remained in uniform because they were "either unable or unwilling to make a civilian living." Two years later, a *Harper's Magazine* correspondent found that armed forces recruiting ads targeted "a young but relatively sophisticated audience which feels little romantic enchantment about wars or about the men who fight them." If Americans increasingly were seeing World War II as a "good war," clearly not all were convinced.[11]

Men's adventure magazines, however, carved out a pop culture space where the "good war" narrative flourished. The pulps feted GIs and their individual heroism, for these citizen-soldiers exemplified the best of American grit and spirit. Within the magazines' covers, war-related storylines were neither complex nor ambiguous. Good triumphed over evil. Soldiers proved themselves as men. Moreover, because so many veterans remained hesitant to share their personal stories with family and friends, romanticized interpretations of the Second World War more easily took hold in 1950s society. As such, the lack of honest conversation from World War II and Korea veterans may have indirectly legitimized the pulps. Without dissenting voices to contest or provide nuance to the prominent narrative, adventure magazines could lay claim that they were offering the "real" or "hidden" history of America's greatest war.[12]

Of course, veterans themselves contributed to the pulps. *Stag*'s editorial director, Noah Sarlat, was a World War II vet. So too was Walter Kaylin, one of the most prolific writers of the genre. Kaylin, a graduate of William and Mary College, served as a radioman in the Philippines with the Army Signal Corps and no doubt relied on his experiences when crafting pulp sagas. Like so many of his peers, he also could be prone to hyperbole. In his 1964 account of the Burma campaign, published in *Male*, Kaylin lauded the "towering heroes" who led a handful of allied troops to become "the savage pliers that pulled the Japanese army's teeth out of Asia's throat and turned the Burma Road into a four-lane highway straight to Tokyo."[13]

As a former radioman, though, was Kaylin living vicariously through the tales of men braver than he? Communication equipment operators never rated as lead protagonists in adventure tales. Pulp illustrator Norman Saunders believed these magazines were geared to the majority of men who had served in the war, but not in actual combat. As his son revealed, "He felt that men who saw action never wanted to think about it again, while most servicemen who never reached a front line were doomed to a life of wondering about their manhood in the face of battle." Surely many teens also speculated about their battle worthiness. In fact, Kaylin recalled that his primary audience was young men "who wanted stories with action, violence and ridiculous sex."[14]

While boredom proved a common experience for many World War II veterans, those who did see combat often repressed their struggles to cope with the horrors of war. A late 1945 study of those soldiers still in the army found that most had felt the "experience had done them more harm than good." Over forty percent of those surveyed said they were more nervous, high-strung, and tense after their service. Few of these veterans, however, shared their pain. One Vietnam vet noted how his father never talked much about World War II "except for the usual glorious things, about service to the country and becoming a man." When the son returned home from Vietnam, only then did his dad start talking about "the killing and the death." Another veteran of the fighting in Europe admitted that his children did "not know all the things that happened in the World War. I prefer that they don't." Additionally, Korea vets found their war had been little more than a distraction to those back home, likely adding further impediments to recounting any horrors they had seen.[15]

The pulps, though, served as a unique venue for veterans to unburden themselves by offering a safe space where wartime stories nearly always left an inspiring message. In the process, the magazines helped to democratize war. Everyone had potential to tell their story, even the lowliest private. Writing could become a form of catharsis, especially for those unwilling to reveal the ugliness of war with their own families.[16]

One young paratrooper recounted the perils of a night jump over the island of Sicily in 1943, the whole world "screaming" in his ears as he exited the transport plane. Kaylin wrote on the 1942 invasion of Guadalcanal and its subsequent defense by marines who bravely withstood an "avalanche of booming destruction" that had burst down on them. In its February 1956 issue, *Battle Cry* ran a story on invasion planning by Major Howard L. Oleck. Oleck detailed the logistical requirements of assaulting an island like Iwo Jima or Guam, the air support needed to cover the landings, and the role of the intelligence staff in estimating enemy troop dispositions. Yet the author knew success depended on more than just moving pins on a war map – "when the men hit the beaches and the first shot is fired, you can forget about the plans and the schemes. Now it is up to the GIs and the Marines who will try to carry it out. And they always do."[17]

Such a tribute hinted at another role the macho pulps played by publishing war stories. They allowed senior officers to extol the bravery and heroism of those men who fought below them in critical battles. (Might they share in the subordinates' gallantry?) Former Marine Corps commandant Lemuel C. Sheperd, Jr. opened his account of the fighting on Okinawa with a plucky corporal who cracked jokes "in the face of withering fire." Writing in 1959, Sheperd dismissed atomic age "push-button-war" advocates and recounted what he saw as the "good old days" of World War II. "When the chips were down man met man in mortal combat."[18]

Heroic and congratulatory accounts alluded to something more private – war was an experience to look back upon fondly, even for veterans who spent World War II wishing it to be over so they could return home. Such "sentimental militarism" found a welcome place in the adventure mags. Myths could be constructed and recycled wherein patriotic citizen-soldiers sacrificed for the nation, proved their manhood, and then returned to raise boys capable of following in their footsteps. One veteran wrote to *Battlefield* that after reading a story on the 3rd Armored Division in Europe, the "memories came flooding back" of the "great bunch of fighting men" with whom the author had served. "The fierce determination of the tankers as they led the charge into Germany will always be remembered by me with pride," he shared.[19]

Of course, such sentiments rested uneasily alongside the 1945 survey data suggesting that "more men reported undesirable than desirable changes" immediately after being discharged from the army. Might it be that over time veterans were privileging wartime myths and fantasies over their own experiences? In retrospect, how many men agreed with their comrades who professed that their wartime service was the time they felt the most "manly" or "rugged," "the way a man ought to feel"?[20]

Fig. 2.2 *Real Men*, December 1960

After deploying overseas and fighting in a global war, how many returned to suburbia and found their civilian lives monotonous, if not somehow inconsequential? To these men, it seems likely that the macho pulps may have resonated more deeply. There they could find electrifying stories of rugged World War II bomber pilots crash-landing behind enemy lines, and then joining the French Resistance to sabotage a key bridge over which the Nazis were planning to send reinforcements to pinch off the D-Day beachheads in Normandy. In the pulps, men mattered.[21]

If the magazines inspired a sense of nostalgia while also allowing men to reaffirm their masculinity, they equally gave readers a chance to engage with pulp writers and editors. In an important way, letter sections allowed veterans to participate in a larger, albeit sometimes mundane, dialogue about war. Readers certainly were not shy. One "critical paratrooper" cried foul about a story in which a ripcord got tangled up, while *Real* was taken to task for getting the details of war medals wrong.[22]

Besides offering technical critiques – Mario Puzo recalled getting scolded for "incorrectly identifying a tank tread or rifle designation" – veterans responded to pulp stories with their own anecdotal accounts. After reading "First GIs on Omaha Beach," as an example, one shared how his unit was ambushed by Germans near the town of Longville, France. "I am not much of a writer or story teller," he admitted; "the ambush was only a matter of three minutes, but it would take three hours to tell. I will never forget it as long as I live."[23]

This engagement with the pulps created, in David Earle's words, a "symbiotic supply-and-demand relationship between reader and magazine." It was a tradition that carried on into the 1960s. Soldiers wrote in to ask if they could meet a certain cheesecake girl, one sharing that *Bluebook*'s photos of model Diane Dexter were tacked to the barracks wall, making "this army grunt stuff easier to take." A marine corporal in South Vietnam shared how he was "out here fighting 'Charlie' for eight months without the sight of a decent chick." Along the same sex-hungry lines, an airman with the 18th Tactical Fighter Wing in Okinawa disappointedly wrote to *Real*'s editors: "I'd try your J.B. (James Bond) approach to women, but over here, for some reason, they don't talk like you say. So solly, have to wait'til I get home."[24]

While the pulps most certainly contributed to this racialized sexism – clearly a product of the Cold War era – many letters from GIs in Vietnam attended to more banal topics. One reader complained about the South Vietnamese censors, while a lieutenant stationed in Saigon cleared up a few missteps made by *Saga* in a recent story about comic books. Additionally, a marine stationed in Vietnam blasted a fellow letter writer who argued that older men in their late thirties or early forties were just as capable as the young men serving in Southeast Asia. "I have news for him," the marine declared. "It has been proved that the young can withstand more hardships than the old . . . We are a new breed of fighting man, the finest the world has ever seen."[25]

Editors surely presented veterans' letters in such a way as to make the most impact on their readership. Yet they also took it upon themselves to advocate for vets and help educate them on their rights. *True War*, for example, advised readers in 1957 to pressure their congressional representatives on what it saw as a "serious GI housing loan bottleneck." That same year, *Adventure* responded to a Camp Pendleton marine asking for advice on using the GI Bill, even offering to send the young man a booklet on careers in forestry.[26] In the same vein, *Real War* included a department called "The Service Bureau," which aimed to answer questions on government benefits and veterans' rights. Topics ranged from civil service careers to discharge paperwork to working through the VA system. In *Battle Cry*, old soldiers could turn to the "Whatever Happened to—?" section in hopes of reconnecting with lost buddies. Meanwhile, other magazines, like *Stag*, regularly ran articles warning servicemen of corrupt civilian businesses looking to take advantage of the gullible GI.[27]

Of course, it did not hurt that vets could rely upon advocates outside their formal ranks who helped tell their stories. Men's adventure magazines regularly showcased nationally renowned authors and historians who wrote sympathetic treatments of the American wartime experience. In many ways, the values of GIs in battle – tenaciousness, courage, rugged individualism – came to symbolize an idealized version of larger American values. In commemorating these GIs, the pulps featured pieces from famed novelists like Norman Mailer and respected military historians such as Richard Tregaskis and Robert Leckie. In the November 1963 issue of *Man's Illustrated*, Leckie combined stirring prose with dramatic photos of the US Marines' "savage attack" on the island of Saipan in World War II. The brutal fighting left little room for quarter. As the article noted, the "last ditch effort by [the] Japs, who preferred to die rather than surrender, left Marines no choice but to fight to the bitter end." And, because this was a men's mag, Leckie's story immediately was followed by a photo spread of a nude Las Vegas showgirl tantalizingly swimming in a pool.[28]

In addition to offering memories from "ordinary" veterans, the magazines also excerpted storylines from celebrated authors like war correspondent Ernie Pyle and offered a "book-length adventure" pulling from James Clavell's *King Rat*. Retired brigadier general and military historian S.L.A. Marshall contributed several tributes, most notably on the twentieth anniversary of D-Day, where his oral histories focusing on the individual combatant brought readers down to the lowest levels of the tactical battlefield. If "God helps the bold," as Marshall claimed, then the almighty could find no better candidates for assistance than those daring Americans assaulting the Normandy beachheads on 6 June 1944.[29]

Such narratives contained little subtlety lest readers miss the point. War was a contest between good and evil, and Americans always wore white hats. This plot point certainly helped set the foundation for the "greatest generation" myth, advanced by such nationalistic historians as Stephen Ambrose, who argued that democracies produced better soldiers than totalitarian regimes. As Ambrose claimed in his popular work *Band of Brothers*, the United States won in World War II because "Americans established a moral superiority over the Germans." The less complicated the narrative, the more likely the war could be used, in Michael Dolski's words, as an "instructional tool to guide younger generations."[30] Thus, young *Fury* readers could aspire to be like Jimmy Doolittle, the legendary pilot who led the first air raid over Japan after Pearl Harbor. "The United States was fighting for its life in the greatest war in all history," the *Fury* article declared. "His country needed him, and he was still to give her all the brilliant leadership and fighting fury he could command."[31]

The stark comparisons between American democratic values and Japanese militarism or German Nazism likely help explain why infiltration into or escape from Nazi prison camps became such a popular entry in the macho pulps. Yet the traditional captivity narrative also allowed men's magazines to feature the best of military masculinity. In these stories, men may have been captured, but they hardly were submissive "captives." In fact, the drama built from their ability to resist their captors, to mine the best qualities of human nature for survival, and, ultimately, to escape back to freedom. Along the way, in the pulps at least, bikinied women often entered the story so they could properly demonstrate their gratitude to the self-assured hero.[32]

World War II escape-from-captivity narratives proved an adventure mainstay in the late 1950s and early 1960s. Air Force prisoners of war, as one example, were able to flee from "escape-proof stalags," while in its very first issue *War* showcased "Breakout King" Jerry Sage, a "strapping, blond giant" and innovative US Army officer who apparently came to the attention of Hitler himself. "They chained him to walls, threw him into

Fig. 2.3 *Male*, January 1964

'steel coffin' cells, buried him in underground 'mole holes' – but always this indomitable Houdini of a Yank POW found a way out." *Stag* ran a similar piece on pilot Larry Haber, dubbed "Capt. 'Bustout.'"[33]

Not to be outdone, Mario Puzo penned a "complete book bonus" for *Male* in early 1965. The story centered on Bax Durkin, a "stubborn stallion-muscled ex-football player" leading a band of allies out of war-torn Singapore in 1942. In the yarn, Durkin is an American architect who, after the Japanese invade, voluntarily joins an Australian infantry battalion and is in disbelief that "these puny Japs were beating the hell out of the armies opposing them." After helping four other civilians escape imprisonment, it is Durkin who leads the party – including, of course, two attractive women – pushing them "mercilessly" through the jungle. (Apparently American architects are far better navigators than any Australian infantryman.) On the third night, Durkin wrestles with a bout of food poisoning but is "cured" by nurse Kay Medford, who once was told that "sexual release can act as a sedative in place of drugs." Back on his feet the next morning, our hero guides the ragtag group on an adventure-packed trek for another 1,000 miles before ultimately leading them "home, safe again in the Free World."[34]

Rambo himself could not have performed better. Indeed, the pulps arguably had established a prototype of hypermasculinity for future action heroes to emulate long before Rambo ever first set foot in Vietnam.

COLD WAR "RAMBO"

War stories tend to focus attention on elite units or tales of personal heroism rather than on the average soldier who often suffers most, and the postwar pulps took a keen interest in army rangers, commandos, and airborne paratroopers, who were indisputable warriors. These men stood apart, winning their battles – and their manhood – on an individual basis. In small-unit combat, men controlled their own destinies. They retained their distinctiveness on the mass industrial battlefield. Through acts of near-superhuman strength, they could right wrongs, as in *True Action*'s "The Ranger Raid to Save 512 Dying Yanks." In a storyline comparable to *Rambo: First Blood Part II*, elite US Army soldiers, a "handful of the toughest, deadliest knife-fighters in the Sixth Ranger Battalion," break into a Japanese prisoner camp to save survivors of the Bataan Death March. These saviors are "mean, tough, gutty daredevils, and ... best of all, smart and disciplined." Unsurprisingly, every prisoner makes it back alive. Readers thus could share in the triumph and courage of such an elite unit, making possible a sense of "collective glory" felt by all Americans.[35]

This focus on individual and small unit actions allowed pulp writers to rejuvenate those self-reliant pioneers who had carved out civilized spaces on the edge of the North American wilderness. *Male*, for instance, harkened back to the colonial era in its chronicle of Sergeant Alvin York, a "war-hating Tennessee backwoodsman" who fought in World War I and became the "deadliest Yank rifleman of all time." The article described York as a "latter day descendant of the American frontier, a plain-talking, no-nonsense sharpshooter," a "striking-looking man with a body hardened by years of physical labor, hunting and hiking, and a natural leader." As the body count escalated, the Tennessean won praise from his commanders and became a national sensation. General John J. Pershing called York the "greatest civilian soldier of the war," while *Male* linked his stunning war record to the "old-fashioned virtues of pride and patriotism."[36]

Luckily for the nation, citizen-soldiers of the "greatest generation" were more than capable of following in York's footsteps. A 1957 account in *True War* focused on the men of the 101st Airborne Division, a popular unit among pulp writers. Cut off and surrounded during the World War II Battle of the Bulge, determined paratroopers "held out against a total of 12 savage attacks" as the Germans continued "plastering the defenders with tons of shrieking high explosives." *Guy* likewise highlighted the saga of "Slim" Jim Gavin, who had risen from private to major general and wartime commander of the famed 82nd Airborne Division. The magazine pointed out that Gavin had made more than 200 parachute jumps, a "rare kind of fighting man" who "took on the Nazis and ripped them apart." That both York and Gavin came from humble origins implied that becoming a wartime legend might be in the grasp of any pulp reader.[37]

This focus on elite units also foreshadowed the near-cult status achieved by the US Army's Special Forces in the early 1960s. The Green Berets, a favorite of President John F. Kennedy, not only fought along the Cold War frontiers, but also served as advisers and "bolsterers of democracy." While regular army commanders looked warily upon their special-operations brethren, pop culture fawned over these heroic warriors who seemed equally capable in hand-to-hand combat and cultural sensitivities.[38] A post-Vietnam War study comparing men in the Special Forces with war resisters even claimed a heightened sexuality among these elite soldiers. They first experienced sex at the average age of fifteen, far younger than civilian doves, and notched up a remarkable "28.5 contacts with prostitutes per man." In yet another arena, young boys could find a distinct relationship between martial masculinity and sexual prowess.[39]

On rare occasions, antimilitarism would crop up to contest these heroic exploits of intrepid warriors. In its inaugural issue, *Battle Cry* ran a comedic piece titled "I Was a Filing Tiger," an obvious play on Claire

Chennault's famed "Flying Tiger" volunteers of World War II. Written by a quartermaster corps clerk who dismissed frontline "glory-hounds," the article noted that it was "pretty hard to dig up dames if you're living in a fox hole or pup tent." Away from the shooting, rear-echelon troops could take advantage of the supply system, and the black market, all while staying warm and well-fed. An accompanying photo shows a bespectacled, lean private sitting behind a typewriter as a curvaceous female secretary bends over him. Thanks to her low-cut blouse, he is able to stare directly at her breasts, the sidebar text blatantly sexist. "A GI can get shellshocked at a job like this," the private declares, "did you ever see such artillery!" Turn the page, however, and battlefield bravery returns in a tale about the World War II fighting in New Guinea. Apparently, working deals to stay out of harm's way had its limits. What young man would want to read a magazine called *Coward* anyway?[40]

Rather, men's magazines churned out tales where heroism stood at the center of "adventure." The "Filing Tiger" may have avoided derring-do, but the pulps situated him in stark comparison with men who displayed masculine qualities so desired by military leaders – physical fitness, mental and emotional strength, and an ability to perform as an individual or member of a hard-hitting team. Adventure mags frequently intensified these traits to near-superhuman levels. In "I Was a Commando Raider!" a World War II veteran recalled being a twenty-year-old US Army ranger charged with sneaking through enemy fortifications, locating a train-load of naval mines, and blowing them up before they could be emplaced in a strategic harbor. A similar entry from *Valor* magazine detailed the exploits of the men spearheading the 9th Armored Division as it raced toward the Remagen bridgehead in Germany's Rhine province. The "men-in-battle" feature spotlighted a young lieutenant leading the bridge crossing and promised readers "a first-hand account of gallantry and valor toward which all armies strive but few attain."[41]

Without question, the best way for men's magazines to highlight singular acts of bravery was to run stories on recipients of the Medal of Honor, the nation's highest award for valor in combat. This they did regularly.[42] *Stag* trumpeted the "beyond-human-courage" of Sergeant Roy Harmon who served in the 91st Infantry Division during the allied offensive in Italy. In tough fighting against German forces, Harmon's unit became pinned down by enemy fire. Though wounded, the sergeant continued a one-man assault against three enemy positions, successfully destroying them before being riddled by German bullets.[43]

Though Harmon was awarded his Medal of Honor posthumously, one Korean War recipient lived through his own battlefield ordeal. Operating south of Seoul in early 1951, Captain Lewis L. Millett led his marine infantry company in what S.L.A. Marshall characterized as "the most complete bayonet charge since Cold Harbor in the Civil War." In its first issue, *War* gushed over the "muscular New Englander" who made all the marines in his unit "cold steel conscious" by issuing them brand new bayonets. When Millett and his men confronted enemy troops in February, they were ready. Attacking a North Korean defensive position, Millett screamed with "wild defiance" as he slashed and jabbed his way forward. To *War*, there was "something primitive and personal in that gleaming pointed bayonet. There was something animal and lethal in the American officer's ear-splitting shouts." Of course, the Americans took their objective, "wrecking" the enemy. Just as importantly, though, Millett proved that he had not forgotten "old fashioned Dan'l Boone tactics."[44]

The warriors highlighted in men's adventure magazines also proved that Americans were the real heroes of World War II and, to a lesser extent, Korea. Harmon and his brother warriors helped lead the larger cultural shift that ultimately bequeathed the "greatest generation" narrative to a grateful nation. According to the now legendary tale, shared by Robert McDowell, these Americans transcended "motivations of self-interest" and pulled together to "do uncommon, extraordinary things." In full agreement, one newspaper account declared that these "citizen heroes" – and occasional heroines – "put themselves on the line" and "saved the world." They became symbols of all that was good in America, an example for future generations to follow in a world reengaged in a global struggle of good versus evil.[45]

This militarized glorification of masculinity served as an essential antidote to the presumed emasculating influences of Cold War America. Across the globe, tough men had survived the worst of war. Individual, virile warriors were in control of war's chaos. Perhaps, then, their example could remedy the influence of smothering moms who apparently were raising a generation of "sissies." The pulps' conceptions of military masculinity might prod young ones into developing themselves physically for service to a nation at war. Clearly, their country needed them. According to *Stag*, by late 1968 more than "40,000 GIs were drafted into the armed forces over the last two years who were later found physically unfit." The magazine, however, failed to mention that in World War II, senior military officials similarly worried about the physical condition of America's youth. As one colonel serving in the War Department reported, "Many young men are entering the army today totally unprepared for military life."[46]

Not so in men's adventure magazines. There, young American men were hardy, resilient, and physically powerful. In *Stag*'s account of the 1942 Battle of Midway, the heroic Ensign George H. Gay is described as a "lean, hard-muscled flyer." Across the globe, fighting in Italy, Maurice Britt's heroism earned him the Bronze Star, the Silver Star, the Distinguished Service Cross, and the Medal of Honor. *Men* detailed this "One-Man Army" who had played football at the University of Arkansas as having "tremendous speed," "remarkable stamina," and "massive power."[47] Likewise, the adventure magazine highlighted US Navy Lieutenant Hugh Barr Miller, a "shrapnel-torn phantom who wouldn't die." Operating in the British Solomon Islands, Miller's destroyer was sunk by a Japanese torpedo. After leading a survivor party ashore, the former Crimson Tide quarterback, seriously wounded and lacking strength, ordered his men to leave him behind. Astoundingly, Miller recovered. For the next thirty-nine days, *Men* regaled, he operated behind Japanese lines, "his insides torn, infected feet, almost half-starved, [and] his left arm badly shattered." All the while, Miller had "killed more than two dozen of the enemy and secured invaluable data for Army and Navy intelligence." The Japanese, *Men* intimated, never stood a chance.[48]

For sure, Miller's story, and those like it, built upon a narrative of racial hatreds that seemed so very commonplace in the World War II Pacific theater. American veterans' memoirs are replete with a visceral animosity toward their Asian foes. "Yellow bastards" and "yellow monkeys" were familiar epithets both during and immediately after the Second World War. In his classic *With the Old Breed*, as an example, Eugene B. Sledge shared his "rage and hatred for the Japanese beyond

He grabbed the cockpit cushion floating past, pulled it over his head as the Japanese started sniping at him.
Art by James Bama

HELL-AND-BACK AIR HERO OF MIDWAY ISLAND

"If there is only one plane left to make the run, I want that man to go in—get a hit..." His CO's order echoing in his ears, Tex Gay went in—alone—and lived to see the suicide run of the 15 Devastators turn the tide of the war in the Pacific.

by GLENN INFIELD

ENSIGN George H. Gay could barely see the Japanese carrier *Kaga* through the black curtain of antiaircraft fire coming at him. At a near hit rocked his slow-flying Devastator torpedo bomber he called Torpedo 8's squadron commander, Lieutenant Commander John C. Waldron: "Do you see the carrier? Is it straight ahead?"
There was no answer. Gay glanced to his right and saw immediately that Waldron was in trouble. The left gas tank of his Devastator had taken a direct hit. As the ensign watched, the torpedo bomber burst into flames.
"My God, Waldron, jump!"
Gay saw him stand up and try to force his head and shoulders through the canopy, but it was useless. Just as his flying suit began to burn the Devastator nosed over, splashed into the Pacific and disappeared.
Radioman Bob Huntington in the back of Gay's plane called, "Let's go back and help him, sir."
"It's too late now," Gay said, *(Continued on page 54)*

Fig. 2.4 *Stag,* July 1961

anything I ever had experienced." After a fellow marine had been mutilated following one fierce battle, Sledge seemed to lose part of his humanity. "From that moment on," he recalled, "I never felt the least pity or compassion for them no matter what the circumstances."[49] Another veteran of the Pacific shared Sledge's hardheartedness. Herchel McFadden of the American Division noted how he and his fellow soldiers were "motivated to a high degree of anger and hate toward the Japanese... They placed no value on human life... They were not people."[50]

Perhaps such depictions of the enemy made it easier to validate the battlefield worthiness of American GIs. If the "Japs" were to be killed "as if they were animals," according to one vet, then it was far simpler for adventure magazines to focus on the "self-respect and dignity" of patriotic citizen-soldiers who "choke down their fear, and go forward, because a free man must."[51] Had not these warriors' frontier forebears also fought against ruthless savages on the edges of civilization?

This hero-versus-savage narrative would need to be re-engineered after World War II as the Japanese transformed into a Cold War Asian ally. The adventure magazines proved equal to the task. Rather than fighting Japanese brutes, real men serving in Korea and Vietnam could employ their manhood to spur on reluctant Asian allies. *Action* related how a grisly American marine taunted his South Korean counterpart into action, ultimately creating a "deep comradeship" that was "fostered by mutual interest of two peoples seeking democratic freedom." So influential had the Americans become that within Korean frontline bunkers, visitors could find pin-ups of "Liz Taylor, Esther Williams and other shapely Hollywood lovelies."[52] The next war found GIs similarly guiding their South Vietnamese charges. In one fantastical story from *Male*, an American sergeant even recruits a leper colony – their bodies "hideously eaten away by the rot of their disease" – and molds them into a "ferocious brigade of the damned" that bests the local Vietcong insurgency. Even the weakest raw material could be cast into an aggressive fighting force under American tutelage.[53]

In fact, given the right training and opportunities, any young man could become a hero. The pulps may have emphasized a kind of Cold War Rambo within their pages, the muscle-bound warrior who seemed more suited to war than peace. But men's magazines also offered the hope and possibility that heroism lay within reach of most any working-class teen.

THE MERITOCRACY OF WAR

In men's adventure magazines, war appeared as one of the most meritocratic endeavors young men undertook. Regardless of class, social status, or, on very rare occasions, race, anyone could be a battlefield hero. The pulps fashioned manhood as a wartime accomplishment, a triumph of courage over fear, of self-sacrifice over personal interests. War became a solution to fears of effeminacy, a way to prove that nagging insecurities were wildly misplaced. Veteran Robert Rasmus illustratively recalled being a teen when the Germans invaded Poland in 1939 and looking forward to the glamour and excitement of war. As Rasmus, who served as an infantryman in World War II, shared with oral historian Studs Terkel, "I was a skinny, gaunt kind of mama's boy. I was going to gain my manhood then. I would forever be liberated from the sense of inferiority that I wasn't rugged. I would prove that I had the guts and the manhood to stand up to these things." In short, boys could *achieve* their manhood by participating in war.[54]

With brave individuals at the center of pulp war stories, adventure mags presented clear examples wherein even the weakest boys could aspire to become "real men." In 1956, *Saga* included a story on "frail" Rodger Young, the most "unwarlike a guy as ever won the Congressional Medal of Honor." Only 5'3" tall and weighing 137 pounds, it went without saying, according to *Saga*, that Young "would not have been cast as the hero." Yet Young did become a hero in 1943, assaulting a Japanese machine gun emplacement on New Georgia island in the Solomons after his patrol had been pinned down. Despite numerous wounds, the Ohio native attacked the enemy with hand grenades and allowed his comrades to safely withdraw before himself being killed. Two years later, songwriter Frank Loesser penned "The Ballad of Rodger Young," an elegy quoted heavily not just in *Saga*, but in *Life* magazine as well.[55]

The same year *Saga* featured Rodger Young, another Medal of Honor recipient hit the pages of *Battle Cry*. This time, however, the story was autobiographical and intimated that even those who survived the test of battle did not return home unscathed. In "The Day I Cried," national hero Audie Murphy recounted the emotional and psychological costs of fighting German troops in the European Theater of Operations (ETO) and losing a close friend. Only two inches taller than Young, Murphy also appeared an unlikely hero before the war. Yet his experiences suggested that physical size and strength mattered less on the modern battlefield than automatic weapons or field artillery. The account in *Battle Cry*, though, offered readers another often unexpressed lesson of war – the horrors of combat left long-standing emotional scars that needed as much attention as broken or amputated limbs. Murphy hoped that by being more honest with the public, he might help close the "great gap between those who fought and those who didn't."[56]

Such honesty likely did not register fully with anxious young readers who may have felt vulnerable to charges of being a "wimp" or a "sissy." In most pulp stories, skinny intelligence officers from the US Navy performed miracles behind enemy lines, gaining valuable information on the Japanese for MacArthur's headquarters.[57] Or the hero might be a "freckle-faced kid" who won three Navy Crosses before receiving a Medal of Honor for leading his submarine to a record of tonnage sunk by a US naval commander in World War II. *Guy* magazine even showcased an

American adventurer who "conquered China" in the early 1900s. While the article declared Homer Lea as "one of the bravest fighting soldiers the world has ever known," his body clearly did not hold him back. "Physically, he was a skinny, nearsighted little man with a hunched back." How many teen readers took heart that they too had Lea's boldness stored deep inside them as well?[58]

Overcoming one's physical traits clearly mattered in pulp storylines. *For Men Only* went so far as to share military doctors' claims that men "most capable of heroics and winning medals sometime are also the ones most likely to show feminine traits." Yet war also could resolve social shortcomings as well. In *Saga*, US Air Force Brigadier General Monro MacCloskey wrote about a "crew of misfits" in his squadron, some of whom had been "tagged 'yellow' by their comrades because they couldn't brave dangerous combat missions." Despite being called "cowards" – perhaps because of it – the men took on a dangerous mission over Italy which made heroes out of these "Gutless GIs." Even a stateside KP potato-peeler, "and a poor one at that," could go on to become one of America's deadliest commandos in World War II. War apparently could solve any man's defects.[59]

Not surprisingly, such aspirational stories did not include women, even though they were still serving on active duty in the Second World War's aftermath. (The pulps also largely ignored the exploits of African American soldiers.) WACs and army nurses operated near the front lines in Korea, with a total of 48,700 women serving in the US armed forces by October 1952. The macho pulps, though, rarely incorporated these women's voices. The same might be said for American culture writ large. True, the armed forces did target women in some of their recruiting ads, one navy poster declaring "Serve with Pride and Patriotism" as it showed an officer, nurse, and enlisted sailor, all three in uniform, all three slender and attractive. Yet, as Lisa Mundey demonstrates, most recruiting materials designed for women "downplayed the masculine aspects of military service." Women thus were expected to retain their femininity in uniform while simultaneously not posing a threat to men seeking military service as a path toward manhood.[60]

Of course, there were costs to heroism in battle, and the pulps regularly heralded the soldier who gave his life in an attempt to save a buddy. *Man's Magazine* showcased two downed pilots in the Korean War, Captain Wayne Sawyer and Lieutenant Clinton Summersill, who crashed behind enemy lines in January 1951. Both wounded, Summersill severely, neither officer gave up on the other. After an arduous trek through the worst of weather, they fended off hunger and enemy patrols before making it back to friendly lines. The effort, though, proved costly. Sawyer lost part of his left big toe, while Summersill, after returning to Walter Reed Hospital in Washington, DC, had both of his feet amputated at the ankles. Loyalty and sacrifice went hand-in-hand.[61]

It was in these stories of self-sacrifice that the band of brothers myth took full form. Separated from society and women – there were no sisters in this martial family – male soldiers supposedly bonded together in ways unknown to the civilian world. Take, for instance, Staff Sergeant George Peterson, who died near Eisern, Germany saving his company from a relentless enemy attack. To *Battle Cry*, Peterson had "made his rendez-vous with destiny" and proved "that the supreme, most perfect sacrifice is one of love, not hate; of life not death."[62] Such a fidelity to one's soldierly brothers clearly touched an emotional chord with many future Vietnam veterans. John Ketwig knew his wartime friendships were special, just "as the strongest steel is tempered by fire." Likewise, Phil Caputo believed that comradeship "was the war's only redeeming quality," even while acknowledging that it "caused some of its worst crimes – acts of retribution for friends who had been killed." Might it be that despite claims otherwise, wartime kinship was, in fact, subject to impeachment?[63]

It seems feasible that perceptive readers may have seen something less than heroic in these stories. Without question, the band of brothers allowed men to share their fears and anxieties as long as they continued to perform in combat. Yet sanitized versions often omitted the less humane aspects of combat. Far from celebrating war, famed correspond-ent Ernie Pyle instead wrote sympathetically of "men at the front suffering and wishing they were somewhere else." Medal of Honor recipi-ent Audie Murphy felt "burnt out, emotionally and physically exhausted" after the loss of a close buddy. Rather than encouraging deep friendships or offering the chance to become a popular combat hero, war ended up depersonalizing many of those who fought, through either sheer terror or abject boredom.[64]

Moreover, a far less appealing attribute lurked just below the surface of popular storylines. What if war traumatized the soldier, disturbed his moral sense of right and wrong? In its tribute to Private First Class Patrick L. Kessler, who received the Medal of Honor for his actions in Italy, *Bluebook* lavished praise on this seemingly average GI Joe. The article described Kessler as "sociable with a liking for almost everyone without aggressive instincts." Coming under fire near Ponte Rotto, Italy, though, the young Ohioan transformed – "he suddenly became a killer. Cold, calculating, implacable." According to *Bluebook*, "White-hot fury burned in Kessler as he saw [his] platoon being decimated." And while Jack Lasco described him as the Sergeant York of World War II, the pulp author also noted that Kessler went "battle mad" as he killed a number of German soldiers. If war had the capacity to turn any young boy into a heroic man, *Bluebook* implied war might also turn them into psychotic killers.[65]

Indeed, at the tail ends of both World War II and Vietnam, civilian anxieties arose over reintegrating broken soldiers back into society. One sociology professor even worried that World War II vets could become a "threat to society" if they were not properly "renaturalized." William Wyler's *The Best Years of Our Lives*, which won the Academy Award for best film in 1946, equally dramatized the challenges of wartime veterans assimilating into families and small towns that appeared to have moved on without them during the war. All the while, women's magazines urged their readers to be more supportive at home, "to return to a docile domesticity to placate their wounded men."[66]

Men's adventure magazines, however, rarely touched upon the returning veteran. Rather, the major theme in wartime stories – "I was somebody" – allowed men to retain their individuality and to be inspired by acts of heroism on the modern battlefield. As one infantry lieutenant serving in Korea shared with *Man's Life*, "There is no other job in the world that can give a man the type and degree of satisfaction that a man gets when he knows the outfit is depending on him to protect it."[67]

Such tales certainly contested the reality of industrial, mass warfare as a dehumanizing experience. In truth, war proved far less ennobling than young boys anticipated. Replacements came into units and were killed before anyone knew their names. Frontline soldiers often felt expendable. Killing and dying extracted a heavy emotional toll. As the first major psychological study of the World War II soldier found, a "fundamental source of strain was the sheer impersonality of combat." Any young man might become a hero. But plenty more saw only the very worst war had to offer.[68]

THE UGLY FACE OF WAR

When American soldiers and marines died in war movies throughout the 1950s and early 1960s, their deaths were quick, painless, and often bloodless. Their bodies remained clean and whole. Harold Russell's character in *The Best Years of Our Lives* may have lost both of his hands in war, but we never see Homer's devastating injury take place, only his painful reintegration back home in Boone City.[69]

Men's adventure magazines similarly focused on the individual triumphs of war, rather than its bloody costs. Such narratives arguably held deep consequences for young recruits conditioned to think about war in idealized ways. When fighting failed to live up to their lofty expectations, when the shock of combat impacted soldiers unexpectedly, the results easily could manifest as post-traumatic stress (PTS). Although PTS was not part of the contemporary medical lexicon – physicians and commanders generally used the term "battle fatigue" – its symptoms were readily identifiable to doctors and more than a few pulp writers.[70]

The May 1953 issue of *Action*, for example, featured a look at GI marriage problems from psychologist R.C. Channon. The piece noted that "Often the hell of war causes soldiers to change their personalities." To Channon, if the wife was "not as meticulous in the execution of her household chores," she might exacerbate her husband's mental problems. Even worse, however, Channon found that some Korean War veterans had experienced impotency, a "delayed reaction" to being on the battlefield. Surely quite a few young readers were taken aback in learning that this "sexual maladjustment" was part of war's supposed man-making experience.[71] They likely wondered if they too were susceptible to the "silent killer" of "war neurosis," as detailed in a full-length essay in *Real Combat Stories*. *Battle Attack* went so far as to publish a piece titled "Are Heroes Psycho?" The article quoted one psychologist who found outstanding

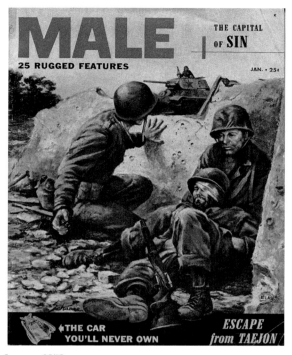

Fig. 2.5 *Male*, January 1952

combat soldiers to be "hostile, emotionally insecure, extremely unstable personalities who might well be termed clinical psychopaths."[72]

Clearly, something was amiss. John Wayne did not act in such anti-social ways. He was a hero, not a psycho. The dissonance must have been unnerving for teens brought up on more romantic versions of war in popular movies and comic books. Occasionally, though,the macho pulps did run stories sharing the ugliness of war, setting them apart from other pop culture venues. Despite the predominant themes of individual hero-ism and triumph, men's magazines did shed light on both the moral and the physical injuries sustained in combat. For veterans dealing with their own PTS or loss of limbs, such articles may well have let them know they were not alone. Other veterans also felt vulnerable, bore wounds, or found war less dignified than advertised.[73]

In some cases, the pulps highlighted physical injuries. *Male*, for instance, published a photographic essay of a World War II soldier with a shrapnel wound in his left eye. The grisly photos included doctors probing and saving the eye, as well as bloody bandages and "dead flesh" on the operating room floor. In other cases, as in a *Saga* essay on Medal of Honor "heroes," the magazines briefly alluded to the emotional damage suffered by veterans. One medal recipient acknowledged an often unspoken aspect of the military valor so romanticized in the macho pulps. As Cecil Bolton shared, "I hate to recount the action because I still have bad dreams about it." If *Saga* was correct in arguing that a "genuine act of courage is an act of giving, not taking," then these men seemed to have surrendered a permanent part of themselves on the field of battle. Surely marine E. B. Sledge would have agreed, recounting in his memoirs that "something in me died" on Peleliu island during the Pacific War fighting.[74]

While *Fury*'s 1959 account of Peleliu hardly captured the same horrors as did Sledge, other tales contested the notion that Americans always defeated their enemies in battle. A story on one of the US Army's first World War II battles at the North African Kasserine Pass noted bitterly how "green, inexperienced" GIs were "blooded," "mauled," and "slaughtered" by Erwin Rommel's Afrika Korps.[75] Two separate articles on the "blunder at Anzio beachhead" in Italy were even less complimentary. One, from *Battle Cry*, stressed the futility of one of the war's biggest stalemates. Miserable soldiers "griped and complained, went on dirty little patrols that accomplished nothing, and tried to make themselves a little less uncomfortable." In its Anzio account, *Men* resentfully asked who was responsible for throwing 40,000 GIs "down the drain." There seemed plenty of blame to go around. On these nightmarish battlefields, few heroes arose for the pulps to valorize, leaving behind an awkward evaluation of war as a man-making endeavor.[76]

Not surprisingly, the stalemated fighting in Korea offered further examples of war's ugliness. The legacy of America's first "limited war" sits uncomfortably beside that of World War II, for the Asian conflict left behind no clear winners, a host of GIs wondering why they were fighting, and a swath of destruction across South Korean society. To pulp writer Mario Puzo, Korea was "the non-fun war."[77] It certainly seemed that way in many magazine articles. According to one story on combat there, "It's rain and mud, cold and misery. It's blood on your bayonet and murder in your heart. It's a lousy way to live – and a hell of a way to die." Accompanying photographs displayed bearded GIs with sunken eyes: "always there is the face of pain and grief." Another autobiographical story from *Real Men,* where soldiers fought off enemy troops with their fists, spoke of "kids who bled from ugly wounds," the veteran-author sharing that he was haunted by "bloody nightmares."[78]

If young boys aimed to spy a glance at war's heroism or veterans sought to alleviate their own postwar anxieties, more than a few Korean War stories surely left them wanting. *Battlefield* published an essay on how North Korean captors massacred American prisoners of war, the GIs suffering from infected wounds, dropping from lack of food, the victims of bullets and bayonets. The magazine also ran a photo essay on "the look." The sullen, dark-eyed faces of GIs stare out to the reader in images far different than the bold illustrations adorning the magazines' covers. With the "look" came "Exhaustion. Sheer, utter, complete exhaustion. And bitterness. Always bitterness." *Battlefield* told its readers not to pity these men because they were heroes, "every mother's son of them," but the price for that heroism seemed steep indeed.[79]

Utter exhaustion, however, was one thing. Losing one's genitals was quite another. While the macho pulps heightened men's fears of being emasculated at home, they also ran stories of soldiers literally being castrated in war. *Challenge* shared the frightening tale of Sergeant Wally Smith, who was wounded on D-Day, the "spurting blood vessels in his groin" clamped and tied off before his "organ had to be amputated." After six operations, doctors had created a "*neo-penis*" for Wally, and eighteen months later, he left the military "with his virility fully restored." To demonstrate the sergeant was no different from any other husband, the article made sure to point out that he was happily married with two normal, healthy children.[80]

Of course, men's magazines likely would have sold few copies if editors had placed graphic and candid images on their covers. Rather, they marketed sensationalist modern artwork from what one cultural commentator described as "geniuses of a populist hyperrealist style." In these artists' hands, illustrations depicted war as dramatic and compelling, with battlefields frequented by beautiful women eager to please the male protagonist. Mort Künstler, for example, helped pulp writers tell their stories with striking cover paintings and alluring interior illustrations. Trained at Brooklyn's Pratt Institute, Künstler highlighted both the warrior hero and the sexual conqueror. The cover of *Male*'s January 1964 issue shows a muscular, cigar-chomping American POW leaning over his diminutive Japanese captor, leaving little doubt who holds real power in this prisoner camp. To accentuate Richard Gallagher's "The Island of Sea Nymphs Who Lived with PT-Boat 629," Künstler brought eye-catching sexuality to the forefront of his work. As an enemy ship sinks in the background, a young naval lieutenant pulls aboard two bare-breasted natives, their "honey-skinned" torsos glistening from the ocean water.[81]

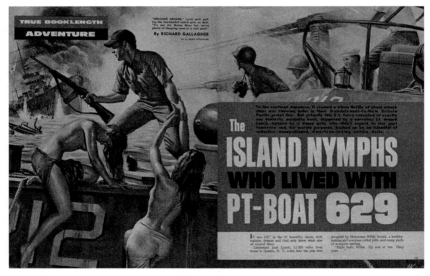

Fig. 2.6 *Male*, December 1962

Another popular artist, Bruce Minney, graduated from the California School of Arts and Crafts before packing up for New York to make his way as a freelance illustrator. Like Künstler, he contributed artwork that now seems indispensable to the pulp genre. For one Vietnam-era story, Minney drew a lone American GI attacking a Vietcong anti-aircraft gun pit. With grenade in one hand and bayonet in the other, our hero straddles the gun's tube, eliciting visions of Slim Pickens riding an atomic bomb in the penultimate scene of *Dr. Strangelove*, while the guerrilla fighters cower below, intimidated by the GI's audacity. In another example, Minney teamed with Mario Puzo for a *Male* book bonus on a jungle breakout from the "Amazon's Captive Girl Pen." Here, "lush, silken-bodied females" are rescued from a "lust-crazed" South American warlord. In the story's illustration, Yank adventurers save bikinied women from the back of a truck-bed cage, the driver riddled with American bullets. Minney's visual suggested the heroes would be justly rewarded not long after they make their escape.[82]

Still other artists brought a wealth of talent and experience to the pulps. Norman Saunders began illustrating back in the 1930s, often serving as his own model for Nazi commanders or frontier cowboys. Of note, Saunders also drew the "Mars Attacks" trading cards released in 1962 by Topps Bubblegum Company. Rudy Nappi illustrated covers for the Nancy Drew and Hardy Boys books, while also contributing interior work for *Male* stories on World War II GIs in luscious Pacific settings. Artist Charles Waterhouse served as a marine and was wounded during the battle for Iwo Jima before attending classes at the Newark School of Fine and Industrial Arts. Finally, Samson Pollen had spent time in the Coast Guard Reserve and painted in genres ranging from adventure magazines to teen books and romance novels. In one illustration for a *Male* adventure story on the Korea War, Pollen's white t-shirted hero breaks into a Chinese bunker, three undersized soldiers trembling in the corner. A nude woman with Eurasian features, only slightly covered by bedsheets, fills the entire left side of the magazine.[83]

It seems doubtful many Korean War bunkers were occupied by such beautiful women, and perhaps that was the point. Dramatic artwork could serve as a useful counterpoint to those pulp stories honest enough to share the ugliness of war. Paired with stirring first-person accounts, the artists might also help pulp readers deal with the larger strategic impasse in Korea. Focusing on beautiful women or battlefield successes allowed men's magazines to shift the narrative away from what had clearly turned into a stalemated war. Foreshadowing later disappointments in Vietnam, the "limited" Asian conflict left Americans wondering why they could not translate all their massive power into a clear-cut strategic victory. Thus, as the deadlock in Korea became increasingly unpopular, the pulps centered their attention on satisfying heroism at the tactical level, even

Fig. 2.7 *Male*, February 1962

as they occasionally revealed the darker side of war. Heroic tales might contest claims, like those from one US senator, that Korea had "shown us how weak we are, and how strong the enemy is."[84]

While the pulps did not shy away from the hard fighting in Korea, they nonetheless flaunted the common soldier's bravery. In "Hell on No-Name Hill," American grunts stave off Soviet-made T-34 tanks, Korean snipers, and hordes of enemy infantry to protect a major road running into Seoul.[85] *Male*'s account of Captain Bill Barber surely disputed allegations that American men had turned soft. Fighting near the Chosin Reservoir in North Korea, Barber "engineered the greatest no-surrender stand since Valley Forge." With temperatures well below zero and surrounded by more than 1,000 Chinese troops, Barber led his marines with unflappable determination, even refusing to be evacuated after being shot in the legs. When a lieutenant requested Barber head back with the wounded, the captain replied, "Listen, kid, I came to fight." By story's conclusion, *Male* ensured its readers knew who had come out of the battle victorious. "Everywhere the enemy was dying, fleeing, surrendering. . ."[86]

The heroism of men like Barber, for which he received the Medal of Honor, surfaced in other Korean War stories as well. The weather always seemed bone-chillingly cold. Americans almost always found themselves surrounded by a greater number of "Chicom" forces. Stalwart GIs and their officers never failed to hold their positions. When one veteran-author detailed the fighting at Chipyong-ni, he shared how the "cries of the wounded and dying rose above the battle noises." A GI next to him took a rocket fragment to the belly. Another was blown off a tank by a mortar shell. Yet there is little emotional distress in his tale, except an admission that his unit had taken "heavy causalities – very heavy casualties."[87]

Such stoic heroism appeared in more than a few contemporary books on Korea, if not as much in combat films. Movies like *Pork Chop Hill* (1959) proved far less celebratory than Wayne's *The Sands of Iwo Jima*. The Gregory Peck drama of GIs holding a worthless piece of terrain against repeated Chinese attacks suggested that the ugliness of war could not so easily be dismissed. But other venues could supplement the dominant narrative within the pulps. S.L.A. Marshall's 1953 *The River and the Gauntlet*, for example, valorized the GI, even as the author maintained that the theme of his book was "not one of tactical victory, but of adversity." Still, Marshall lavished praise on those who served as "an example of courage, unity of action in the face of terrible odds, and the ability of native Americans to survive calamitous losses and give back hard blows to their enemies."[88]

Marshall's unforgiving nativism equally was reflected in Andrew Geer's *The New Breed* from 1952. This thrilling account of marines in Korea surely would have made many a pulp writer envious. In one episode, an infantry battalion suffers fifteen killed, thirty-three wounded, and eight missing in action after a hard battle. Far from being weakened by the ordeal, the unit comes out "physically tough and psychologically hard." Moreover, Geer's depiction of the enemy ensures his American heroes are battling a worthy, if not wicked, foe. The Chinese soldier has the "Asian stamina and mental fortitude to withstand the harshest demands of command, conditions and climate." And because he has a low standard of education and has been taught "blind obedience," he will follow his commanders to the death. Thus, there is much to cheer when, in I.F. Stone's "hidden history" of the war, we read of this heartless enemy being "slaughtered in astronomical numbers." Yes, fighting conditions in Korea might be horrendous. But how many young readers aspired to be just like the brave American marine who yelled "Let the bastards have it" as he opened fire with his heavy machine gun on the communist monsters?[89]

In the end, how young teens imagined their fathers' wars depended in large part on how pop cultural mediums and veterans themselves relayed America's wartime experiences to the next generation. Men's adventure magazines most certainly helped transmit certain values from fathers to sons. As one advertisement declared, "A Boy Needs a Dad He Can Brag About!" In the postwar era, it seems plausible that many working-class kids saw their fathers as "the strongest, smartest, bravest guy in the world" because of their military service in World War II or Korea.[90] There, they had affirmed their manhood as patriotic citizen-soldiers. Sons no doubt built expectations based on these gendered codes so artfully displayed in the pulps. And while adventure magazines clearly targeted men, the number of interior ads selling rocket ships, flying helicopters, plastic toy cars, and "monster-size monsters" suggested that pulp editors knew younger readers were consuming their products, perhaps just as much as their dads.[91]

The depiction of war within men's adventure magazines ultimately might be seen as both a product of and a contributor to how fathers taught their sons the value of uniformed service in making them men. Surely, not all working-class families subscribed to such notions of martial glory. Yet in the Cold War era, many fathers did worry about making men out of their boys, some compulsively so. The social reality in the macho pulps thus not only helped establish the collective memory of the "greatest generation," but also influenced how Vietnam-era soldiers defined their own brand of masculinity thanks to what was passed down to them. As one West Point graduate recalled, "we were taught and mentored by an exceptional cadre of seasoned veterans who fought in World War II or Korea... These great men molded our characters, shared their wisdom, and taught us the hard lessons of warfighting paid for by the blood of their fellow soldiers."[92]

These same great men, however, far too often avoided the truths of war's uglier side. So too did men's adventure magazines. The pulps constructed a battlefield memory that relied mostly on an imagined reality. Death was clean. Men overseas rarely if ever took out their frustrations on the civilian population. Americans never shrank under the pressures of combat, no matter how much the odds were stacked against them. But, as Steven Dillon suggests, what "looks like hard-minded heroism might be an anxious shield flung up against female sexuality." With American women seemingly on the warpath to oppress men at home, perhaps these allegedly embattled males could look elsewhere for sexual satisfaction and domination. Viewing the macho pulps from this angle reveals how young men in the Cold War era fantasized not just about heroic combat, but also about sex and the availability of the erotic, sensual "Oriental" woman.[93]

CHAPTER 3

The Imagined "Savage" Woman

ON A FUNDAMENTAL LEVEL, war is about power. Battlefield victors impose their will over the enemy, while states reap the rewards of hardy soldiers fighting successfully on their behalf. Men's adventure magazines relied on this narrative construction wherein both individual combatants and the country as a whole profited from the experience of war. War made men, while also making America a more powerful, if not indispensable, nation.

In a similar arc, the macho pulps crafted a discourse in which gender and sexuality also hinged on power relations. Readers' knowledge of "normal" sexual relations rested, in part, on how the pulps reinforced prevailing social relations while simultaneously offering images and storylines that editors deemed most desirable to their core audience, of which the working-class market occupied a significant portion. As with narratives on war, adventure magazines depended upon a set of simplified dualisms: good versus evil, masculine versus feminine, primitive versus civilized, and white versus dark. Such storylines might then fuel men to perform in ways they reasoned were socially acceptable. Thus, as Judith Butler has argued, we might consider discourse not only by its intellectual origins but also as a "condition and occasion for further action."[1]

The discourse of gender and sexuality in the macho pulps clearly placed men in a dominant role. If overbearing women at home were aiming to reign supreme over the domestic sphere, men could retaliate by objectifying the very thing they feared. Exotic locales proved particularly inviting for pulp writers who responded to these social anxieties. Whether on a Polynesian island or in the enticing "Orient," adventurers could wield their power over the allegedly untamed and sexually liberated native. Boys transformed into men not only by physically conquering these natives, but by exhibiting their sexual power over "savage" beauties. In the process, the man-making experience of both war and sexual conquest might seem more meaningful to young readers aspiring to break free from the seemingly oppressive atmosphere of Cold War culture.[2]

Typical of mid-century sexism, the pulps' construction of gender reinforced images and practices whereby men controlled women. Adventure magazines surely were not alone in their paradoxical storylines both praising and condemning women for taking charge at home in the 1950s. Yet the macho pulps assertively led their readers across the boundaries of outright misogyny. The July 1959 edition of *Battle Cry*, for example, included an advert hawking "'Stuffed' Girl's Heads." For only $2.98, men could purchase a woman's plastic head – with "saucy glittering eyes, full sensuous mouth and liquid satin complexion" – mounted on a genuine mahogany plaque. Here was a "unique trophy" that offered the chance for "every man to boast of his conquests." While the ad drew attention to the heads' life-like appearance, it also bragged that "one of the nicest qualities is that they don't talk back."[3]

Sexist representations of women as objects filled the pages of adventure magazines. *Stag* noted how the Russians had given up the idea of female astronauts since their first space woman "broke down in hysterics" during a secret flight. *Male* featured a photograph of a topless dancer performing at the annual meeting of the National Wholesale Furniture Salesmen. Finally, *Man's Illustrated* included an article titled "Women – Which Nationality Is Best?" This "guide to the world's greatest mistresses" opened with its author grumbling that American men were suffering in a "matriarchal society," barely surviving against a "gigantic conspiracy to keep our women dominant." Luckily, foreign women all had the same ambition – to snag a Yank husband. The article then took its reader on a world tour comparing "Malayan beauties" with Asian "bombshells" and "abnormally oversexed" Polynesians. Incredulously, the piece also offered insights into the "secret-flesh markets" of Singapore and Macao where "even the slave girls prefer American owners." If conflict and struggle informed men's understanding of domestic gender relations,

Fig. 3.1 *Battle Cry,* July 1959

at least overseas they could exhibit power in unabashed fashion, if the pulps could be trusted.[4]

The imagined foreigner thus became a mainstay in men's adventure magazines. The pulps' multiple constructions of women, however, surely left some readers dubious of their own prospects. While depicting women as dangerous, authors and illustrators demonstrated that, in the right locales abroad, they were also sexually available. Magazine articles spanned the globe exposing the best "sin-filled" places where women supposedly threw themselves at American men. In the "sensual city" of Rome, readers could delight in the ease of organizing an orgy given so many "wild playdolls." In the "swinging land" of Sweden, US visitors could savor the "lovely lasses" who were "as broad minded and uninhibited as every man wants them to be." Unsurprisingly, Rio – "Sexville of the Americas" – proved a popular destination for "fun-hungry guys on the loose."[5] The challenge, though, was how to differentiate between the good and the bad. Were women devious vamps or sensual playthings? Should men hate women or desire them? Perhaps the safest bet was to do both.

Throughout the years leading to America's involvement in Vietnam, adventure magazines reinforced mythical notions of "racialized sexuality." White foreign women, mainly communist or Nazi *femmes fatales*, might be packaged as passionate seductresses, alluringly dangerous (yet typically surmountable) to the heroic male protagonist. But the pulps seemed to take special pleasure in fetishizing the more mysterious, perhaps more desirous, darker "Oriental" woman. In Edward Said's estimation, Western conceptions of the Orient long have suggested not only "sexual promise (and threat)" and an "untiring sensuality," but also "unlimited desire" and "deep generative energies." This sense of "unbounded sexuality" pervaded adventure magazines. In short, women of other races invited sexual conquest.[6]

For younger working-class readers, many of whom likely had yet to travel overseas, the idea of beautifully exotic and sexually subservient women must have held great appeal. Pulp heroes engaged in sex without emotion or consequence. In the process, they could reinforce unequal power relationships that seemed so fragile to men in the 1950s and early 1960s. The pulps' message about gender and sex, however, held ominous implications. Fears of sexually enticing women, the desire to control them, and the failure to do so seemed only to inspire more fear. Such narratives ultimately would send a powerful message to young American boys, one that seemingly endorsed soldiers' sexual violence against native women in far-off places like South Vietnam.[7]

THE RED SEDUCTRESS

Stories on alluring yet treacherous female spies were a Cold War mainstay in adventure mags. In "Sex Is Their Secret Weapon," *Battle Cry* highlighted how an "unusual number of prostitutes" were communist agents or associating with known communists. The magazine discerned a clear pattern, surely directed by the Kremlin. "Using sex, along with other weapons of the cold war, the Reds are actually committing themselves to warfare." Such a metaphor proved immensely popular in the early 1960s. The communists were using "sex as a weapon in espionage," and, according to *Man's Illustrated*, "sexological warfare, as practiced by the Russians, has been alarmingly successful against the West." Worse, these tactics seemed to pose an existential threat to the United States. "Sex harnessed to politics, either local or global, can be a force as destructive as a nuclear bomb."[8]

With every page turned by pulp readers, ex-Nazi or communist maneaters waited to pounce on American men and turn the tide of the Cold War. Russia apparently maintained a spy fleet of "lush honey-blondes from the Ukraine" and "satin-bodied Oriental girls from Azerbaijan" who traveled on luxury liners in hopes of blackmailing Western travelers and gaining vital intelligence for Moscow. All-action book bonuses featured German Fräuleins selling information to the Reds from within the CIA's West Berlin office.[9] An article by Mario Puzo even showcased how the allies could use sex as a weapon, highlighting "four Free World spy dolls whose lush, exciting bodies had ferreted out dozens of Russian top secrets." Of course, these women could not be trusted, evidenced by one "Judas joy girl" who had "traitorously sold out to the Reds." The hero's assignment? "Bed-hop from one wanton to another" until he uncovered the turncoat and brought her to justice.[10]

The frequency of pulp storylines in which women used their bodies to deceive suggests these *femmes fatales* were symbolic of larger male

Fig. 3.2 *Man's Illustrated*, November 1963

anxieties during the Cold War. Women might offer love, but also deception and humiliation. Certainly, some young readers must have judged sex as both alluring and precarious. In this regard, prostitutes served as a vivid demonstration of male fears. *Stag* illustratively noted how pretty European communists filtered through Castro's Cuba before arriving in America as part of a massive "sex-spying" ring. Targeting defense officials and US servicemen, these "prostitute-spies" then filtered their secrets back to Russia and China. Moreover, such duplicity threatened the burgeoning American effort in South Vietnam. One popular account revealed how the Vietcong were employing, "with considerable success, young beauties who pose as bar-girls and prostitutes and worm military information out of relaxed and trusting Americans they dance, drink, and sleep with."[11] The message for pulp readers seemed obvious: women could not be trusted.

This woman-as-seductress image resonated with pulp readers at the same time Americans in the 1950s and early 1960s were coming to grips with an increasing openness on individual sexuality and a surge in academic sexual studies. If some women seemed to be rejecting their femininity and traditional role as child-rearing caregivers, critics more easily could argue that they posed a danger to predominant social, economic, and political conditions. Additionally, these shifts in sexual attitudes occurred when Cold War fears of communism echoed throughout American society. It was only a small step for detractors to link sexually liberated women to communist subversives. Both, in their own way, threatened the male-dominated status quo.[12]

Adventure magazines made sure their readers understood that deceitful women were not simply a sexualized byproduct of the Cold War. Vamps also had used their bodies to lure good men astray during World War II. Propagandist Tokyo Rose may have captured America's attention in the 1940s, but the pulps left little question that seductresses were operating in boudoirs across the globe during the war. *Brigade*'s "The Passionate Widow Who Seduced a B-17 Pilot" presented a brave American flyer stationed in London. In between bombing runs over Germany, he meets Celeste, "a woman who could blot out with the ravishing flesh of her body all thoughts, all remembrances of war's mayhem and madness." Though Pete professes his love for her, by story's end we find that Celeste had been married to a Luftwaffe pilot killed in the blitz over London. To avenge his death, she leaves her children behind in Germany to become an undercover agent and report on British and American air movements. As Pete's commander tells the heartbroken airman, "You were her pigeon. And don't feel badly, you weren't the first."[13]

While beautiful Hungarians and Poles engaged in "bedroom espionage" against American servicemen and their allies, even the Nazis were not safe from scheming women who hoped to change the course of history thanks to their sexual intrigue. In one story from *Fury*, Ilse Stöbe, who supposedly looked like a "blonde *houri* from a sultan's harem," bedded SS General Reinhard Heydrich in an attempt to keep the allies informed of German war plans. Her dual role as agent and mistress, however, suggested that female combatants could not occupy the same space as the traditional male soldier.[14] While men could claim honor and respect for their battlefield sacrifices, women with similar aspirations to fight against evil still had to be villainized in order to maintain a gender-acceptable wartime narrative. Thus, in the "The Nordic Nymphs Who Almost Killed Hitler," the female protagonists who sleep with the local

Fig. 3.3 *Brigade*, March 1963

Gestapo and important Nazi visitors from Berlin appear more tawdry than heroic.[15]

Everywhere, it seemed, women were luring men to their doom. On the home front, wives were entrapping men in a "cage of domesticity," while on the extended battlefield, temptresses played the role of pulp villain far more than they did of victim. "Kill-crazy pirate girls" prowled the coastlines of Red China in "murderous female hyena packs." Nympho spies helped lead the Japanese to defeat in World War II. Meanwhile, outcast "brothel pigeons" roamed Shanghai's Tibet Road. Betrayal looked as if it was an integral part of the female constitution.[16]

Lest readers question such gender discourses, respected scholars seemed like they might be confirming pulp narratives of women using their supposed innocence to trap and betray. In one of the most popular works on the French-Indochina War, *Street without Joy*, famed war correspondent and Howard University professor Bernard Fall maintained that no less than one-third of all French posts fell during the war thanks to the efforts of Viet Minh saboteurs, many of whom were women. For Fall, it remained a "matter of conjecture whether the element of 'vice' which [women] added to the

Fig. 3.4 *Man's Conquest*, December 1968

war was not outweighed by the element of femininity."[17] It should not surprise that American successors to the French armed forces cast wary eyes on alluring yet equally frightening Vietnamese women.

These depictions could be unnerving not just for soldiers deploying overseas, but also for young men inexperienced in sex. Surely many must have wondered if sexual pleasures were worth the risks as they fretted over their own virginity. Comics instructed them to "never turn your back on the female of the species." World War II propaganda posters displayed "loose," impure women as the primary vessels of sexually transmitted diseases. And pulps like *For Men Only* ran articles on French prostitutes who murdered their male clients.[18] Sexual threats piled ever higher in the postwar era, to terrifying heights. Writing in the late 1940s, Simone de Beauvoir saw a natural consequence of this imagined peril, of men "suffering from an inferiority complex." To the French existentialist, "no one is more arrogant toward women, more aggressive and more disdainful, than a man anxious about his own virility."[19]

In many ways, adventure magazines took advantage of prevailing anxieties and sexist attitudes rooted in deep fears of women and their supposed power to abuse sex. One *Stag* essay demonstrated the extreme. In a case that grabbed national attention, Newark resident Monique von Cleef was arrested for running a "torture-for-thrills" house in her twenty-room mansion. *Stag* disapprovingly noted how this "domineering blonde" and "priestess of a strange cult of the 'sick'" doled out "every form of degradation to her select, offbeat clientele." Fortuitously, a New Jersey detective willingly laid his body on the line to "invade her temple" and bring the "leather-suited, booted blonde" to justice. While the courts wrestled with the issue of policing private sexual conduct, men's magazines took a different approach when it came to sadomasochism. For *Stag*, the issue was not about getting pleasure from inflicting or receiving pain. That existed, to some extent the pulp argued, in "ordinary" relationships. Rather, Mistress Monique problematically wanted to dominate men instead of submitting to them. As *Stag* hissed, "Men make themselves her victims because they are so sick they must be turned into slaves."[20]

Von Cleef's transgression, of subverting traditional gender norms, easily fed into established Cold War anxieties over morality, sexuality, and masculinity. All these fears were exacerbated when interlaced with the combined threats of international and domestic communism. When *Male* published a "true" book-length adventure story on a US agent fighting against a "super-secret Red subversion corps," the magazine ensured that "full-bodied" blondes played an integral part of the story. As in so many other plot devices, violence and sexuality went hand-in-hand.[21]

That communist subversives so effortlessly could use sex as a weapon meant few men were safe, being instead imperiled by women who were inhabiting bodies that *were* weapons, a point clearly embraced by men's adventure magazines. Spy-nymphs were dangerous because of their "cunning brains" and "luscious bodies." In one story, a French agent's beauty put her in "complete control" of an Austrian target, the corpulent businessman unable to resist and falling to his knees before her.[22] Worse, it seemed, these seducers were pursuing American soldiers using "sex, Marx and blackmail to 'persuade' GIs to turn traitor." *Stag* left little doubt who held the advantage in these exchanges. In a story on an Amsterdam "seduction ring," the stunning temptress effortlessly beguiles

American GIs who are just "kids." "Brash, arrogant on the outside; underneath scared, lonely, and oh so trusting."[23] Likely, many young men deploying to Vietnam in the 1960s fit this description, further laying the groundwork for an adversarial relationship with the Vietnamese population in a frighteningly confusing wartime environment.

At its core, however, the ideological conflict of the Cold War wasn't necessary to show the dangers women posed. Women were seductresses not because they were communists, but because they were women. In one shocking example, the March 1966 issue of *Man's Illustrated* ran a story on "lustful gals" who willingly provoked "sex attacks." The piece argued that far too many rape investigations ignored the "crime-provoca- tive function of the victim" and that evidence clearly showed an "uncon- scious desire on the part of the victim to be attacked." Since any healthy woman could successfully keep a man from forcing himself on her, the article intimated that in many cases "the female 'victim' was merely engaging in the time-honored game of putting up mock resistance to an act she truly wanted." How many young readers left such stories with a lack of empathy for survivors of sexual violence? How many may not have thought twice about the "mutually enjoyable" act of raping a South Vietnamese woman?[24]

It was no coincidence the same issue showcased the US Army's 173rd Airborne Brigade fighting heroically against the Vietcong in South Vietnam. With choppers whirring overhead and bullets slamming into the ground among a group of GIs, a veteran soldier turns to his young captain experiencing his first taste of combat. "We're no longer virgins," he grins.[25]

THE EXOTIC "ORIENTAL"

The same year that *Man's Illustrated* defended men against sexual "frame- ups," Leland Gardner's exposé *Vietnam Underside* offered a slightly differ- ent view of the female seductress by recounting the sexual history of Southeast Asia. To Gardner, it was the heritage of the exotic and erotic Asian to "wallow in the sensual." These women were not inherently immoral, though buyers of the roughly 25,000 professional prostitutes in Saigon surely beware. Rather, such a high number of sex workers apparently resulted from the presence of virile American men, a refreshing contrast to the "completely inadequate" South Vietnamese male who was unable to satisfy his sexually "insatiable" female partner. In paternalistic fashion, Gardner recounted how the "Viets laugh a lot, but they also throw tantrums and go into vicious, violent rages on an individual basis. Much of their humor is childish because, as a people, they have not yet become sufficiently aware to be concerned about politics, national economy or sociological problems."[26]

This construction of Asian as child had long historical roots. Westerners sought to demonstrate their cultural superiority by comparing themselves favorably to the inferior other, all the while attaining a rationale for imperialist expansion overseas. In the aftermath of World War II, if not before, Americans particularly welcomed such notions. After having fought a brutal race war in the Pacific against a determined and "savage" enemy, depicting Japanese as "small, childlike, and feminized" allowed American occupiers, according to historian John Dower, the opportunity to transform their erstwhile foes "into a compliant feminine body on which the white victors could impose their will." With the proper rearing, these new fathers could guide their Asian wards into a more modern community of nations overseen by a benevolently patriarchal United States.[27]

In keeping with this narrative – of devaluing women in terms of both gender and race – the submissive, feminized child conveniently blossomed into a servile beauty eager to please her Western master. Amy Sueyoshi argues that these depictions of submissive Asian women proliferated in the early 1900s, "just as increasingly independent white women appeared to be undercutting marital stability."[28] The Japanese geisha, in particular, epitomized popular images of obedient, self-sacrificing Asian servants who promised a sexual alternative to modern feminist agitators back home. Instead of war-mongering savages, Asians usefully could be reconceived as feminized, "unthreatening objects for collection and consumption."[29]

American soldiers serving overseas reveled in these portrayals, applying them to their own wartime sexual experiences. In World War II, GIs stationed on Luzon encountered young Filipinas offering sex, one medic recalling that he had "never had a girl and didn't want to die without knowing." On Hotel Street in Hawaii, William Manchester found "more massage parlors, strip joints, and pornographic shops than cafés."[30] After the war, roughly 1,100 Japanese women reported sexual attacks by American occupiers, some of these assaults conceivably a result of GIs who viewed the locals as ripe for sexual conquest, if not retribution after a long, hard-fought war. The trend continued into Korea and Vietnam. Veterans spoke of the pleasures offered in Bangkok and Hong Kong, one serviceman labeling the Thai capital a "fucking colony." To many Americans, Asia seemed the "brothel of the world," a place where prostitutes offered what men ostensibly desired most – "sex in its primitive sense, untrammeled and undiluted by feelings of guilt, fear, sentimental love, respect, and competition."[31]

The macho pulps conformed to these impressions by promulgating the exotic Oriental narrative. In 1953, *Man's Day* showcased an Asian fishing village, a "male paradise" in which female divers, all clad in bikinis, collected seaweed while the men were "content to supervise and be happy henpecked husbands." *Adventure* featured a story on New Caledonia, "The Island of Lonely Girls," where local entrepreneurs had "no trouble in recruiting exotic beauties" as "girls by the score applied for work" because they "were imbued with a patriotic desire to make the stay of the brave Americans . . . as pleasant as possible." *Stag's* confidential section even shared how bra manufacturers had rated Polynesian women "as having the world's most beautifully shaped breasts."[32]

These exotic locales, though, paled in comparison with what Japan supposedly offered virile American men. Because pleasure was "Japan's best-selling commodity," *Battle Cry* judged it the place where the US Army learned about sex. One pulp maintained there was "no topping the Japanese prostitute . . . because she was sincerely able to fall in love with every man she met."[33] *Man's Illustrated* went further, claiming that a Japanese woman was able to "sense the moods and feelings of her male guest like a mindreader." The comparison with domineering American housewives could not have been clearer. "Were Japanese women really different?," the magazine asked. "Damned right they are," the author replied. "*Her* pleasure comes from catering to the wants and whims of her man, and she does it like nobody else in the world."[34]

For those readers who truly believed they were being emasculated at home, such storylines must have struck a deep chord. Unlike "aggressive"

American women who were contesting Cold War gender roles, the purportedly subservient Japanese held tremendous appeal. So much so that one company in Newport Beach, California actually marketed itself to lonesome men on the basis of the exotic Oriental fantasy. "For centuries," its ad claimed, "Japanese girls have been trained since childhood in the art of pleasing men and catering to their every wish and desire." For only one dollar, membership in Japan International included "hundreds of Japanese girls . . . of all ages." This commodification of Asian women might be viewed as a response to the depiction of the female body as weapon. Submissive women were less threatening, perhaps less duplicitous. Of course, on the battlefields of South Vietnam, one could never be sure. At least on R&R in Japan or Bangkok, storylines boasted, American soldiers could revel in the best Asia had to offer.[35]

To be sure, the imaginary exotic Orient proved a popular entry not only in the macho pulps, but in Cold War movies as well. Films reinforced the idea that Asian women were merely sexual playthings for American adventurers overseas. The opening scene in John Frankenheimer's *The Manchurian Candidate* (1962), for example, depicts American GIs drinking and carousing in a Korean bar during the war. Pin-up girl photographs are tacked to the wall, perhaps as a reminder that the bar's inhabitants are temporary wartime substitutes for hometown gals left behind. It is clear the local women, many of whom are shirtless in their brassieres, are there only to please their clientele and earn some easy cash, one placing money in her dress as the camera pans across the smoky bar. For a brief moment, a lanky American soldier enters the scene wearing only boxer shorts and combat boots. The fighting in Korea might be grueling, but the movie implied that respites with local bar girls offered pleasures few men back home could enjoy.[36]

Looking back, the irony of the bar scene now seems palpable. GIs covered the walls with desirous white pin-up girls yet deemed the erotic Asian as offering unique sexual gratification against which American women could not compete. Women at home were difficult and smothering. Women in foreign lands were deferential and gratifying. With such sexist attitudes prevalent across Cold War popular culture, no wonder men's magazines presented storylines accentuating women of "dark" or "dusky" races.[37] The pulps clearly fetishized over the topless

Polynesian woman or the polygamous Ottoman lying about in an exotic harem. However, this "supposed sexual licentiousness" of the uncivilized foreigner did not extend to African Americans back home. While the "oversexed-black-Jezebel" loomed large in both American mindsets and discriminatory practices, especially in the antebellum era, the macho pulps excluded African American women from any discussion on sexual fantasies. Openly admitting to a relationship with a black woman likely would have been taboo, if not abhorrent, to most white, working-class readers of the pulp genre.[38]

Rather, adventure magazines took readers overseas to fulfill their racialized, exotic fantasies. In "The Nude in the Blue Lagoon," *Valor* rhapsodized over a Samoan girl representative of "the exotic Polynesians who believed in nature; and nature meant complete freedom in matters of sex; that is until they married." Luckily for the story's hero – whom Mauie calls "Mr. America" – the eighteen-year-old has not yet wed, her "tight, well-formed breasts ... tanned by daily exposure." His "savagely" pounding heart alludes to the fact that pulp champions could expend their beastly side without damaging the more wholesome white pin-up girl next door. Of course, Mauie needs rescuing by the American after she is attacked by a giant sea turtle while swimming in the lagoon, rewarding her savior with kisses after the harrowing experience. Yet the appeal of these tribal women came from more than just sexual promise. In the same issue of *Valor*, an American explorer travels to the "forbidden" heart of Africa and encounters a tribe that lives in "a man's world." The autobiographical account noted how the social hierarchy was based on both age and sexual discrimination and that "marriage means complete subjugation for the Xosa women."[39]

Regardless of the woman in question being black or white, the pulps made clear that nowhere in American suburbs or working-class neighborhoods could men enjoy the "eastern hospitality" offered in far-flung lands. And nowhere did that hospitality loom larger than in Oriental harems. Adventure magazines relished in imagining what harems might look like, their artists painting bare-breasted concubines alongside exotic accoutrements, hookah pipes, and peacock feathers. *Sensation* featured a World War II army sergeant in Oran, North Africa taking advantage of the supply system to tender "three slave girls" the proper "inducements" so he could enjoy their company. Another offering in *Stag* focused on a similar tale, the North African campaign an apparent cultural crossroads where white men gained sexual access to the local population. Societal and geographic accuracy, though, did not preclude writers from locating harems in faraway places like India, where "temple women" guaranteed "to turn the most fumbling, inept man into the world's finest lover." Apparently sexual gratification could be found almost anywhere in the imagined Orient.[40]

Fig. 3.5 *Sensation,* April 1959

It would be wrong, however, to dismiss the imaginary East as exclusively pleasurable. For every representation of the docile and reverential geisha, there were equal stereotypes of the wily and calculating "dragon lady" who lacked any empathy or emotion. Like the red seductress, Asian women, in particular, seemed just as deceitful and capable of using their bodies as weapons of war. *Stag* opined how "Asia's comfort houses" had used "nymph decoys" to bait and lure in unsuspecting men during the Chinese Civil War. *Male* featured a story on a "half-trustworthy Kowloon 'Passion Kitten'" who aided American agents in seducing a Chinese intelligence chief to defect to the West. The Hong Kong woman is an expensive call girl, her main role to have sex with the potential turncoat and hand him over to the CIA. No wonder American GIs, typically conflating all Asian races, recalled how their orientation to Vietnam included stark warnings of "gook whores and Vietnamese women in general."[41]

Whether Japanese, Samoan, or Vietnamese, none of these women had much opportunity to speak for themselves in the macho pulps. Often, they were little more than props in the storyline. A sensual vamp, luring men with sex. An unnamed girl, raped in her village. A voluptuous pin-up, strategically placed between war stories.[42] While pulp writers made the decision to silence female voices, they hardly were exceptional in their choices. Edward Said found that in western models of the Oriental woman, "she never spoke of herself, she never represented her emotions, presence, or history." Instead, it was the male author who "spoke for and represented her." In the process, these women seemed to lose a bit of their humanity. Neither ideology nor race seemed to matter all that much. Women were the "other," plain and simple.[43]

This type of objectification thrived in both pulp advertisements and storylines. One 1975 study analyzed the ways in which magazines commonly depicted women, from "dependent on man" to "overachieving housewife." Perhaps unsurprisingly, the researchers found that "woman as sexual object . . . appeared more frequently than any other category in both men's and general magazines." Pulp ads reinforced this conclusion. Men could purchase "Harem Jamas" for their significant others, a "nite time garment inspired by the fashions of the near East, where often hundreds of women compete to attract one man." Alternatively, they could peruse fashions from "Nightie Nights on the Nile" and order a sheer "Egyptian Slave Girl" lounging robe.[44]

Adventure stories must have tempted readers to consider purchasing these outfits, in hopes they might role play and realize their fantasies at home. *Man's Conquest*, for example, included a piece titled "Buy a Slave Girl!" In the story, a World War II veteran working in Cairo poses as a wealthy businessman to write a story on the Arab "flesh markets." For only $160 he purchases a nineteen-year-old Jordanian, a beautiful "nice kid," freeing her not long after getting the bill of sale and key to her chains.[45] In *All Man*, an American is forced to help run a female slave trade across the Arabian Peninsula, shuttling "livestock" of Bedouin women of ages ranging from twenty-five to fourteen. Finally, in "The Love Slave of Hadramut," an American oil engineer buys a "sweet and gentle Arab girl" for $64. Since he is superior to the local men, he considers himself an "ideal master" and appears content with his acquisition. "Mimsha was docile and delightful. She made no trouble at all. At my beck and call, she was soothing, exciting and wicked, a veritable personification of a Houri maiden." The eroticization of power relations could not be more obvious.[46]

It mattered, of course, that the oil engineer was white. In the pulps, if not broader Cold War culture, American masculinity rested on notions of racial superiority. White men were no match for the savage other in the pages of these magazines. In the imagined Orient, adventurers could revel in sexual decadence, yet still maintain their civility and thus dominance over the local population. Women in "primitive tribes" appeared forever sexually available. Pulps like *Stag* persistently represented female natives as having soft black hair, tanned skin, firm breasts, and "many lovers before mating." All of them seemed to admire Americans. The illusion undoubtedly attracted young male readers whose definitions of masculinity were being progressively shaped by notions of physical prowess, racial authority, and sexual assertiveness. And what better place to satisfy male impulses than in the arena of war?[47]

GENDERED FANTASIES

If the pulps are to be believed, air and sea travel must have been a precarious business in the middle of the twentieth century. Stories of downed pilots or sailors lost at sea inundated the adventure mags. Not surprisingly, these faulty modes of transportation functioned as convenient plot devices in which the hero washes ashore or lands on an island inhabited by sexually attractive and available local women. Beyond the frontiers of civilization, the unshaven and usually bare-chested protagonist quickly establishes his authority over the male tribal leaders, an unintentional colonialist effortlessly mastering his new domain. Exotic tales like these evoked images of John Smith and Pocahontas, with the latter cheerfully giving herself to an outside explorer representing an ordered Eurocentric society at odds with

Fig. 3.6 *Male*, August 1964

native savagery and sexuality. In these narrative constructions, the white male stands tall in a land of puerile indigenous people.[48]

The South Seas proved a popular locale for castaway stories. One merchant mariner hit a storm between the Philippines and Guam and went on to "live a native's life for six years" after washing ashore on a tiny tropical island. There he found "scantily clad women," marrying one according to local traditions that allowed him to star in his own pornographic feature – it was "custom for the populace to watch the consummation of a marriage." Another *Male* adventurer, stranded on the island of Borneo, apparently lucked into a setting with attractive locals. "Now they always tell you native women are beautiful," he declared; "they're not – I've seen plenty and most of them are dogs." In Borneo, though, he meets plenty of young women, all whom have a "nice figure and a pretty face. When they get old, they get ugly, and they get old fast – 35 or so." Once more fortunate, the hero attracts the young Lini, who fits perfectly the mold of obedient and sensual Oriental lover, her breasts like "two giant scoops of coffee ice cream."[49]

Such lustful imaginings allowed pulp writers the chance to combine fantasies that knew no geographic boundaries. Thus, shipwrecked sailors could land on Japanese islands of "castaway geishas" or touch down on the Malabar coast in southern India and indulge in "delightful beauties," any of whom "would have been enough to knock the breath out of a man."[50] *Action for Men* featured the tale of an American washed ashore on an atoll in the Melanesian archipelagos in 1934. For ten years he lived happily on a lost southwest Pacific "harem island," the tribal chief offering him a wife of his choice not long after arriving. Only in 1943, nearly a full decade later, did the American learn of World War II, ultimately fending off Japanese invaders with only spears and an "ancient first World War pistol." Even on the very outskirts of western civilization, men could fulfill their dual roles as sexual conqueror and heroic warrior.[51]

This conquest of savage lands reinforced the macho pulps' predilection for aggrandizing the hardy frontiersman at the center of heroic wartime stories. Had not World War I sharpshooter Alvin York flourished in battle because of his ability to pull from a mythic frontier past? Survival along these spaces where the "civilized" encountered the "savage" had long required martial skill, but adventure mags emphasized how military and sexual conquest seemingly went hand-in-hand. There, the sexual subjugation of local women took center stage as American (and occasionally British) heroes battled against a non-white, savage enemy.[52]

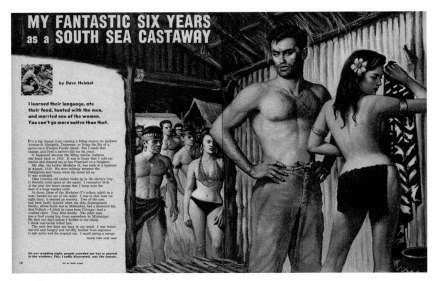

Fig. 3.7 *Battlefield*, August 1958

In the January 1961 issue of *Stag*, for instance, the protagonist, aptly named Hunter, skirmishes with Japanese patrols on Borneo, his World War II mission to "stab ice cold fear into the hearts of the Japs." During the fighting, he enlists three beautiful local girls, author Bill Wharton taking an almost obligatory pause to describe their "small, firm breasts and lithe, firm limbs." After training a "force of guerrilla head-hunters" who mercilessly defeat the Japanese, our hero decides to remain on the island and tutor additional local warriors to combat the communists in Malaya. With his three wives, he fathers eight children. There is no question Hunter is a virile warrior. By story's end, the "great man" miraculously retains his civility despite engaging in this skulking way of war and living in a hut strung with Japanese skulls.[53]

While these stories promoted a form of sexual conquest that had reinforced earlier European imperial projects, they also revealed that white men still could demonstrate their superiority over uncivilized, darker-skinned men. The supposedly hypersexual nature of African Americans certainly stood apart. Whites long had worried over blacks' "aggressive sexuality," thought to be an "anatomical peculiarity of the Negro male."[54] In pulp world, however, men in alien cultures appeared far less intimidating. Adventure mags fortified cultural stereotypes where insipid brown men from the Pacific, the Middle East, or Southeast Asia were deemed conniving, immoral, and decidedly feminine. The ease with which a downed pilot rated the finest-looking native on the island said as much about the native man as it did about the castaway hero. In many ways, the magazines' stories illustrated how depictions of colonization endured even as the actual colonies of Europe were collapsing under the weight of post-World War II nationalistic fervor.[55]

It was important that these gendered fantasies occurred overseas where there was no fear of interracial coupling or a mixing of races that might pose a menace to American social norms. During World War II, the US government viewed interracial marriages as an unwelcome and "unintended consequence" of the global conflict. While some magazines like *Ebony* and *U.S. Lady* published a few positive stories of US servicemen marrying European or Asian women, men's adventure mags generally avoided such topics.[56] Likely, storylines bringing overly sexualized foreigners back to the United States would have aggravated Cold War racial insecurities. Besides, it would have taken great narrative skill from the pulp writer, and a leap of faith from the reader, to convert a woman from Peru's "Forbidden Amazon Female Compound" into a domesticated American housewife. The two types of women were meant to be separated, in both fantasy and reality.[57]

Wartime prison camps also conveniently separated foreign women from American society. Here, pulp writers repurposed popular American captivity narratives dating back to the late 1670s with Mary Rowlandson's abduction by Native Americans during King Philip's War. The possibility of a young white woman being sexually violated by a savage Indian clearly offended Puritan sensibilities.[58] In the pulps, however, prison camps seemed more like carnal playhouses. Male captives might be sent to a Russian camp of "banished wives" or be caught in a Japanese "comfort girl" stockade, only to escape with a "glowing-eyed" beauty who sexually rewards her savior as anti-aircraft guns fire in the background. *Stag* even ran an exclusive, "Inside a Communist All-Woman Penal Camp," that focused on "sex-starved females." According to the article, "conversation and sexual intercourse" were the "two greatest pleasures of the poor and the imprisoned." When a Russian infantry unit decides to bivouac near the Siberian penal camp, the prisoners gape at the bare-chested soldiers, a few women breaking out, not to escape, but to rush across a stream and throw themselves at the waiting men who take them to "love nests in all directions."[59]

Not surprisingly, these camps were perfect locations for heroic warriors to liberate. In one *True Action* offering, undercover CIA agent Joe Coogan breaks into a wilderness stockade of "captive blondes," the "passion prisoners" being held by former Nazi henchmen. When their rescuer reaches the camp, the "dozens of young, attractive girls" become "Coogan's playmates," as they are "starved for attention and even a superficial love."[60] *Male* served up a similar tale, this one set on a Turkish penal plantation where women are forced to participate in wild parties. The only American prisoner, Jessup, is amazed to find thirty female internees. As a guard tells him, "thank Allah. It would be a very dull place without them." Not long after his capture, the American earns a spot on the household staff, the commandant's "blonde favorite" seeking him out for a quick love-making session that is filled with "explosive savagery." Yvette then hatches an escape plan with Jessup that involves poisoning the guards. Leaving the prison courtyard a "ghastly carnival grounds," the American leads the refugees to safety in Syria, though he loses Yvette along the way, rumored to have become the mistress of a British general. "She always did attract men at the top," Jessup utters.[61]

While Siberia and Turkey may have been trendy locales for pulp writers, they paled in comparison with Nazi Germany, perhaps the most common setting to mix sex with war. Looking back, the macho pulps blatantly misconstrued the ways in which American soldiers and German civilians experienced sexual violence both during and after the war. Wartime incidents of looting, destruction, and rape were common after the arrival of GIs. In the spring of 1945, instances of rape far exceeded contemporary civilian rates back home in the United States. Postwar occupation forces acted no better. According to one source, between "May 1945 and June 1947, the Army recorded nearly 1,000 rapes by American servicemen in Europe."[62] It seemed as if sexual violence had become a routine part of the allied drive toward Germany's unconditional surrender. Without doubt, American GIs' rape of German women demonstrated a power differential between victor and vanquished. This was more than just men seeking female companionship.[63]

The adventure mags, however, told a far different story, one in which German women, often with whip in hand, held sexual authority. Most pulps downplayed the more unseemly tendencies of GIs, instead placing them in the role of victim. The melodramatic presentation of female SS sadists seemed to resonate with men already anxious about their sexual status, no doubt in ways unintended by pulp writers. One former photo editor for a national men's magazine recalled how his own "early rape fantasies were to imagine raping the female Nazi camp guards, slowly and with great relish. I was doing it to righteously punish these vicious blond Brunhildas for what they had done to others." Of course, not all young readers so directly fantasized about sexual violence based on these phantasmatic renderings of Nazi prison camps. At the same time, however, the pulps openly intended for the "sadistic burlesque" to thrill and arouse.[64]

Ilse Koch ranked as the most sensational perpetrator within the "Nazi-with-whip" genre. Married to Karl Koch, commandant of the infamous Buchenwald concentration camp near Weimar, Germany, Ilse gained a notorious reputation for sexually abusing and torturing prisoners. The pulps took note. *Battlefield* described the "bitch of Buchenwald" as a "reddish-blonde beauty" who would swagger around camp "provocatively attired in halter top and shorts, a heavy riding crop under her arm." The magazine made sure readers knew that Koch, a clear "nymphomaniac," had sadistically reversed normal gender relations in the camp. "Thousands of men were her slaves, could be forced to gratify every natural or unnatural whim and caprice." As in the Jessup story, incoming prisoners who "struck her fancy were assigned to her house as servants. Their services consisted mainly of love-making." While *Battlefield* noted how Koch was "guilty of the most atrocious crimes against humanity," the article still spared readers from the worst of Buchenwald's viciousness. Sex, it appeared, was more interesting than genocide.[65]

Real Men published a similar tale in late 1960, "The Lady with the Whip." Here, an American GI is captured in North Africa after the battle at Kasserine Pass and tortured by Inga Karel, an officer in the Hitler *Jugend*. She is paradoxically the most beautiful woman the soldier has ever seen, and the only one he loathes with every fiber of his body. In the story's climactic ending, Inga engages in the "most exquisitely refined

Fig. 3.8 *Battle Cry*, August 1962

torture," sexually tempting the American even though he detests her. She undresses in tantalizing fashion and then whips her victim, demanding that he make love to her. Only after tanks from Patton's Third Army burst into the camp is he saved, our hero killing his captor by fashioning a noose out of the prison fence's barbed wire. "Inga was right," he declares as she lay bleeding. "There is a great deal of pleasure in inflicting pain – on those you hate."[66]

For younger, sexually inexperienced readers, these stories must have been discomfiting. Ilse and Inga plainly were despicable people. Yet they were beautiful and lascivious at the same time. Were all female enemies so lustful? The macho pulps certainly made German women seem so. In a story evocative of an X-rated version of *Hogan's Heroes*, "Lusty Ludwig's Love Lager," a POW camp commandant promises to throw a party if his allied prisoners do not try to escape for a whole month. The scheming POWs accept the deal, as long as "Munich broads" are invited to the festivities. Both sides fulfill the bargain, and what ensues is a "scene from a Hollywood production of a German orgy." The event seems less surprising given other pulp stories in which top German generals kept scores of mistresses, some of the "lushest, most beautiful women in Europe."[67] Maybe the ugly side of war wasn't so ugly after all.

If Hitler maintained brigades of "man-hungry" women in the German army, adventure magazines suggested men actually might enjoy the act of being sexually exploited. Sharp differences separated men's fantasies of becoming the sex slave of a warrior priestess or sadistic Nazi and a woman being raped by savage tribes, the former far more acceptable, even desirable, than the latter. Indeed, these men seemed to relish being sexually assaulted. A story on the liberation of Paris noted how a tall, muscular American sergeant "was literally raped by two girls in a café in the Rue Lauriston." A purportedly autobiographical account in *True Men* followed a Polish Canadian sold to "love-hungry" women in Madagascar, part of a modern-day male slave market.[68] *For Men Only* equally featured a 1966 story in which a Yank adventurer lands in the unexplored jungles of Guatemala, where "for 200 days he was forced to be king and – for 200 nights the 'love slave' of a female army." Naturally, the tribal priestess, a "woman of tremendous beauty," demands sex, the American complying and "leaving her utterly exhausted." Thus, even in captivity, real men could demonstrate their masculinity, strength, and endurance, bringing balance back to narratives wherein female captors had violated cultural prescriptions limiting overly aggressive, sexual behavior.[69]

In this way, gendered fantasies incorporated bondage narratives and sadomasochistic plot devices as yet another way of demonstrating that war and sex, ideally intertwined, were the most effective man-making experiences. If prisoners could endure their captivity and torture with dignity, they would prove their worth as men. If, in the process, they also could demonstrate their superiority by withstanding the worst of female sexual advances, all the better. Moreover, "a great deal of research" suggested that assertive women did not mind being assaulted in return, one psychologist in *Man's Life* claiming it was a fact "that about one in every eleven women possesses a streak of masochism to an extent that she positively requires some sensation of pain in order to achieve sexual relief."[70] The message rang clear. If GIs violated women in a wartime setting, chances were good the soldiers' victims had been hoping to be punished anyway.

For fictional war heroes, enduring pain – even if pleasurable – while at the mercy of a sexually voracious woman became yet another display of masculinity. Even wounded soldiers could perform sexually. In Vietnam veteran Larry Heinemann's *Paco's Story*, the novel's protagonist, though grievously wounded, receives oral sex from his nurse. (Only later do we find that Paco's platoon had raped a fourteen-year-old Vietnamese girl, the source of his emotional troubles.)[71] Fellow vet James Webb's *Fields of Fire* includes a marine ambulatory patient who empties "his anxieties into a half-dozen Japanese whores." Finally, in *Men*, Mario Puzo's short fiction story "The Seduction of Private Nurse Griffith" finds the hero convalescing in a VA hospital, all the while longing for a nurse who is a "dazzling, full-bodied goddess of a Florence Nightingale." Ultimately, his dreams are "made flesh" and the two share a night of passion that GI Pete "had never known and would never feel again."[72] In each of these stories, wounded soldiers somehow retained their sexual proficiency despite their wartime injuries. Was there any better way to define a man's virility?

The pulps' fantasies of "savage" women hence played upon a "dominance/submission dynamic" that ultimately sought to reinforce Cold War gender roles. Villainous Fräuleins or man-hungry slave traders might challenge conventional norms, but only until the story's climax. In the end, male heroes won the day, any assaults on captive men ultimately morphing into heterosexual intercourse in which the man dominated a subordinated woman. Sheer manliness triumphed, with sexual conquest as the reward. That these men could prevail over Nazi dominatrices or savage tribal leaders seemed to make victory all the sweeter. The same might be said of besting women strong enough to fight alongside men in battle.[73]

THE SEXUAL WARRIOR

Comic books, a parallel form of Cold War popular culture, contained few, if any, storylines explicitly blending war with sex. After facing charges from politicians, and critics like Fredric Wertham, that comics were corrupting America's youth, publishers sought less controversial topics in the hope of increasing flagging sales. Still, superhero and war-themed comic books did introduce young readers to a genre showcasing extreme battlefield heroism and, in some instances, violence against women. The two, however, usually remained separated, at least in war comics. The popular DC character Sergeant Rock never performed as a sexual conqueror, usually too busy fending off German tanks or assaulting heavily defended enemy positions. When women did enter the story, often as army nurses, they more often than not served as damsels in distress rather than love interests. In the comics, Sergeant Rock and his fellow Easy Company infantrymen exceled as near-superhuman warriors, but as asexual ones for sure.[74]

Nevertheless, women did suffer at the hands of comic villains. In *Phantom Lady* No. 21, for instance, the female victim is shown wearing nothing but lace underwear as she is strangled to death by the evil Chessman. Wertham railed against these frequent renderings of women tied up "in all kinds of poses, each more sexually suggestive than the other." Even heroines like Wonder Woman and American intelligence agent Señorita Rio often had their bodies shackled by outlaws, the disturbing "masturbation fantasy of a sadist" in Wertham's mind.[75] Equally depraved, complained critics, were the artists depicting female bodies with exaggerated features, their large breasts, known as "headlights," making "young girls genuinely worried long before puberty." Wertham, in particular, fretted that child readers would confuse "violence with strength" and "sadism with sex." While war and sexual violence may not have intermingled as vividly in the comics as they did in the macho pulps, the two themes certainly were present in Cold War era cartoons.[76]

If writers regularly placed heroines like Phantom Lady in compromising positions, it seems plausible that comics prepared young readers to become more receptive to similar storylines in men's adventure magazines. Yet it also is important to remember that Wonder Woman served alongside her male colleagues in the Justice Society. So too in the macho pulps did women fight next to men. More than just passive sexual objects, women warriors engaged in combat, albeit not in traditional roles like frontline infantry or armor units. Rather, as underground saboteurs, double agents, or "girl commandos," they could participate in war without fully challenging conventional gender constructs.[77]

While male fantasies of armed female combatants may not have involved the victimization of helpless women, they did suggest the desire to dominate strong female figures. Ian Fleming's *Casino Royale* character Vesper Lynd, for example, supposedly was based on World War II British Special Operations Executive (SOE) agent Christine Granville. Despite Granville's impressive wartime accomplishments – born Maria Krystyna Skarbek, she worked in Eastern Europe helping build the Polish resistance – Fleming's character adaption of her is both as lover and as double agent. In the Bond novel, she retains her role as seductress. Granville may have found her time in the SOE liberating, but her story ultimately promoted postwar martial masculine values rather than upsetting any hierarchical power structures in the long term. That Bond could successfully entice such a strong woman only burnished his own credentials as a man.[78]

The pulps maintained this gendered narrative, mostly by locating women in resistance units behind enemy lines. There, they could more easily use their bodies to seduce, as in one story where a Norwegian "resistance blonde" leads evil German officers to momentarily forget the war, thereby upsetting Hitler's bid to make an atomic bomb. An account in *Men* from a French resistance fighter shared how the movement relied on "brothel girls" and "chambermaids" to take advantage of their "unique opportunities" for gaining valuable information from German occupiers.[79] Pulp writer Walter Kaylin took the co-ed war to North Africa, where the American hero, Anders, meets Miss Lily Murat, a former nightclub entertainer. Though at first he rejects her plans to create a local women's auxiliary corps, he reconsiders after remembering that "Oyobe women frequently fought alongside their men in tribal wars and could probably assist a guerrilla unit in many ways." While the female fighters perform courageously in combat, Anders clearly is in charge throughout as they hold off their German and Italian adversaries.[80]

What is more, the pulps indicated that most women were not cut out for war. In *Man's World*, French milkmaid Françoise Mourant joins up to fight with the Americans after being raped by drunken German soldiers. She steals a GI uniform, transforming herself into a private from the US Army's 28th Infantry Division. For the next month, Mourant fights alongside her unsuspecting comrades, even as they make fun of her "beardless jaw" and call her "Pretty Boy." Only after being wounded in combat and evacuated to a field hospital is the masquerade uncovered.

To the magazine, the lesson was obvious. Combat had persuaded Mourant that "war was no game for a woman." Men's place remained secure.[81]

On occasion, women did take up more traditional combatant roles in pulp war stories. The adventure mags, though, did not miss an opportunity to highlight their sexuality. In one World War II account on female pilots in the Soviet Air Force, artist Samson Pollen depicts sensual aviators rushing to an airfield in nothing but their revealing underwear. Their hair is perfectly coiffed, red lipstick on each woman's face. The one pilot who is wearing a flight suit has it halfway unzipped, baring her cleavage as she wrestles with her parachute caught in an airplane's prop wash. In the story, these lascivious Russians rescue an American B-17 bomber pilot, who makes love to one of his saviors after a vodka-laden celebration. After, as they prepare to undertake a combat mission together, he is amazed at how quickly the women learn to fly a US aircraft. Readers thus could share in the American's voyeuristic fascination with these aces who were assuming a wartime role.[82]

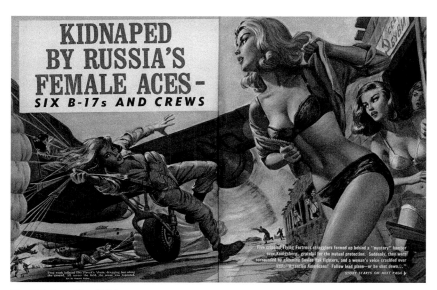

Fig. 3.9 *Stag*, May 1964

In a late 1959 issue of *Battlefield*, Russian women fulfilled more time-honored martial duties. An autobiographical account from Kyra Petrovskaya chronicled her experiences as an army nurse and entertainer of frontline troops during the war. Caught in the siege of Leningrad, she fights against the Germans and is wounded in the process, not long after leaving the army and returning to her stage career. The magazine was sure to contrast a 1942 snapshot of Kyra in Red Army breeches and tunic with a postwar photo of her barefoot and in full makeup and flowery dress. Anything less would have challenged her customarily subservient role.[83]

While Petrovskaya reverted back to postwar life as actress and spouse, other Russian women stayed in the fight to finish off the Nazis. In "Battalion of Nymphs," pulp writer William Ballinger left little doubt these female warriors were at once sexy and deadly. The "blood thirsty Amazons … carried bayonets strapped to their thighs and grenades under their blouses" as they set out to destroy the German high command. In battle, they rush forward "firing their rifles" and "screaming with rage, with exhilarating, mind-dazed anger." The female commanders competently maneuver their units against the German invaders, while their soldiers are equally at ease with a machine gun or a Molotov cocktail. According to the story's artwork, these warriors also fight with their tight-fitting tops tied in front so they can lunge bare midriff against their harried foes.[84]

Ballinger's use of the term "Amazon" is instructive, for the macho pulps regularly employed the concept throughout the 1950s and 1960s. Like the exotic harems, Amazons too could be found around the globe, ensuring that adventurers could partake in the sexualization of war no matter where they went. In the jungles of New Guinea, Yank pilots shot down during World War II are captured by nude Amazon women, "female Tarzans" who torture the Americans until they make their escape.[85] In Greece, US commandos team up with Ionian female divers who, like their Amazonian ancestors, are noted for their physical skill and "for leading a free-wheeling independent love life." *Adventure Life* took the story to Tasmania, where a captive sailor avoids being killed and then boldly shames his captors. "I see you are not really warriors, but still women who kill best when their victims are tied to a stake." Ultimately, he collects his own harem, successfully meeting both the military and the sexual challenges posed by the Amazon tribe.[86]

The global reach of Amazonian lore allowed pulp writers the chance for their heroes to best the "femme sauvage" wherever she lurked.

Westerners could command battalions of "naked, love-hungry Amazons" in East Africa or fight against pygmy warriors in the Amazon itself, their women "as beautiful in their own way as any lighter skinned girl in the Folies Bergere."[87] This code-switching even took form in Southeast Asia, where an American pilot crashes behind enemy lines during the French-Indochina War. The Amazon women who take him hostage are a "band of torture-trained females currently terrorizing the border region of Vietnam." The guerrillas are Hoa Hao, a quasi-Buddhist sect, apparently more warrior than monk. When the women strip their uniforms to cool off in a mountain lake, the American is struck by their "hard, young, athletic" bodies and the abrupt "transformation from grim young warriors to laughing young girls." Without doubt, GIs fighting their own war years later equally would question if Vietnamese women were vicious fighters, sexual objects, or a dangerous combination of both.[88]

Fig. 3.10 *For Men Only*, March 1959

Not all women, however, were simple military instruments for male combatants. Some took matters in their own hands, especially when seeking revenge against perpetrators of sexual violence. *Stag* ran a 1961 story on a group of Yugoslavian girls and young women who were brutally raped by Italian occupiers in World War II. They band together after escaping and inadvertently run into a roadblock. One of them, Mila, opens the top buttons of her shirt to distract the guards before savagely bayoneting them to death. When they next reach a concrete blockhouse guarding an important crossroads, they successfully employ the same ruse, amassing weapons as they proceed. With each raid, the partisans become more adept at killing before teaming up with an American airman. Not surprisingly, the Yank takes more of a role in planning as Mila's aggressiveness leads to casualties within the group. By story's end, though, this "killer brigade" is capable of marching through difficult mountainous terrain with heavy machine guns on their backs and cases of ammunition in their arms. Despite deprivation and losses, the women Mila leads are ready to fight "to the last."[89]

Mila's tale reveals how easily war and sex could work in tandem within men's adventure magazines. Strong warriors were sexual champions, plain and simple. Perhaps that is why *Man's Illustrated* noted how US marines in Vietnam were "hopping mad" over the tactics of their army brethren in the Special Forces. According to the men's mag, Green Berets were spreading rumors among "Saigon doxies and other Oriental dolls that Marines are impotent as a result of surgical operations designed to make them better fighting men, but ineffective in the sack."[90] The disassociation of military acumen and sexual prowess made the prank work, but also implied that US servicemen had embraced fully the heroic warrior–sexual conqueror paradigm.

If the marines indeed were miffed at being labeled impotent, it seems worth evaluating the power of heterosexual fantasies and how they are linked to aggression. The environment of war clearly legitimizes violence, an unrivaled place where men can wield massive power. Yet that power is not solely directed at enemy forces. In South Vietnam, the civilian population equally bore the brunt of hard fighting. In the process, if savage women posed a threat, a truism in the world of macho pulps, did war then offer men the chance to exorcise their fears? On an extended battlefield, where lines blurred between combatants and non-combatants, soldiers could be as aggressive as they wanted against the female population without concern of retribution. One American GI in Vietnam recalled not even desiring a prostitute because of the presumed availability of women. "You've got an M-16. What do you need to pay for a lady for? You go down to the village and you take what you want." That soldiers could come back from their tours a "double veteran" demonstrated visibly the strong connective tissues between war and sex.[91]

It seems likely that adventure magazines encouraged adolescent fantasies combining battlefield aggressiveness, misogynistic attitudes, and domineering sexual behavior. Whether nymphs or Amazons, women in war were savage others, either prizes to be attained or challenges to be overcome. The macho pulps, however, suggested that these attitudes had deep cultural roots, influencing young readers long before they went off to war. Take, for instance, an advertisement in *Brigade*. Prospective buyers could mail in a coupon for "Sassy Stories," a collection of "old-time French favorites" that included tales like "Assault and Flattery" and "Wife Beating – Evil or Good." How many readers saw few if any distinctions here between sexual pursuit and sexual violence? Did ads like this intimate that some men were more aroused by physically subduing women than by engaging in non-violent, consensual sex? Or did these "Sassy Stories" help reify in men's minds that they still commanded Cold War gender relations?[92]

Most likely, younger, working-class magazine readers did not plunge into deep theoretical thought exercises on the relationships between power and gender. The stories appealed on a more fundamental level. For many readers, they were simply entertainment. Yet these same stories must have established certain expectations about what war might be like as American men began to arrive in Vietnam. If Korea was any indication, there would be plenty of "love-and-money hungry girls" to obtain if the pulps could be trusted. In fact, as the Johnson administration debated the merits of sending US ground combat troops to South Vietnam, *Male* published an exposé on "Korea's 800,000 Give-Give Girls." The article included photographs of Asian women in heavy makeup, short dresses, and high heels, noting how they were a "major relaxation in a desolate oriental country." In the story, a nineteen-year-old infantry soldier visits a local dance hall with "swarms of Korean B-girls, dressed in oriental slit skirts, black net stockings and skin-tight white jerseys." The young Nebraskan enjoys the "most sensual night" he ever spent, conceivably making his overseas tour more than worthwhile.[93]

Eighteen months later, as US forces were fighting across the embattled South Vietnamese countryside, *For Men Only* implied that militarized sexual fantasies still might resonate among its readership. In its September 1966 issue, the magazine considered the "Ten Best Draftee Deals in the Armed Forces." After listing out benefits such as education, medical and legal aid, and travel, the article noted how overseas duty offered "a number of distinct advantages. First, there are the babes." While there were "nice American girls" working abroad, most GIs, according to the author, preferred the "not-so-nice foreign girls." The final "deal" was Vietnam. There, new recruits apparently could find a "sense of adventure and patriotism," including the chance to experience combat and share "ordeals and triumphs with their fellow Americans." Unironically, the piece ended on an uplifting note: "if you are one of those selected for duty in that far-flung area in which America is defending freedom at a heavy cost, you may be getting the best deal of all!"[94]

On the verge of US combat troops deploying to Vietnam, a precedent had been firmly established in the cultural milieu of working-class pulp readers. Men's magazines had helped create a narrative where heroic warriors were not only battlefield victors, but sexual conquerors as well. An idealized version of manhood – however warped it may have been – appeared enticingly within reach. Yet a predicament quickly emerged in the villages and rice paddies of a distant country locked in brutal civil war. Pulp readers now in uniform soon found that the reality of fighting in South Vietnam ran far afield from the fantasies that seemed so convincing in sensational magazines built upon sex and adventure.[95]

CHAPTER 4

The Vietnamese Reality

U NDER A DARKLY LIT NIGHT SKY SOMEWHERE IN VIETNAM, an American GI leans his back into the trunk of a palm tree, forest green elephant grass concealing part of his well-toned body. His torn shirt exposes a muscular yet bloodied shoulder, though his resolute face suggests he has little inclination to deal with his wounds right now. Next to him stands a slim, attractive brunette woman with Eurasian features. Her clothes also are ripped, a short red dress shredded to reveal her shoulders, chest, stomach, and thighs. Whereas she holds a pistol in her hand, the American lurches forward as he sprays bullets from his semiautomatic rifle into a thatch-roofed building. Communist soldiers fall to the ground as expended shell casings arc up from the rifle's ejection port. Our hero has taken his prey completely by surprise. The woman beside him appears calmly pleased.

So ran the cover art for the December 1966 issue of *Stag* magazine. Mort Künstler's depiction of combat action in Vietnam is alive with color – the darkened blue sky, the hot orange flash from the rifle's muzzle, the woman's crimson red dress. In bold yellow letters, the cover exclaims that this month's original full book bonus centers on a "Yank GI–Viet Doll Escape Team," a tale of survival in the face of "Cong terror." Readers are promised a "strangely wild relationship against a wartime nightmare." The accompanying story from pulp writer W.J. Saber does not disappoint, while an offering from "Stag Confidential" a few pages later reinforces the underlying message from both Künstler and Saber. "More than any war yet fought by U.S.," the short piece advises, "the Viet War is one of small units, and there is a great chance for heroism by enlisted men, right down to the greenest of draftee privates."[1]

Fig. 4.1 *Stag*, December 1966

At the same time the US Military Assistance Command in Vietnam (MACV) was arguing that 1966 might mark a "turning point in the fortunes of this strange and difficult operation," men's adventure magazines were leaving the impression that wartime events still could produce heroes worthy of praise and sexual reward. True, MACV acknowledged, the communist enemies continued their efforts in "terrorism, harassment, sabotage, propaganda, and small hit-and-run attacks aimed at controlling the population and blocking any significant gains in [South Vietnamese] nation-building."[2] But the macho pulps shared widely held convictions that young American soldiers nonetheless could find a man-making experience in the jungles, rice paddies, and villages of South Vietnam.

Many GIs, however, soon would come to realize that the depiction of combat advanced in the macho pulps left much to be desired. While senior military officers, like General William C. Westmoreland, argued that the war in Vietnam could not be won by military solutions alone, men's mags portrayed a conflict that looked eerily familiar to the conventional battlefields of World War II. In the magazines, the political aspects of irregular warfare seemed ill-suited for offering young GIs the chance to prove themselves as men. In fact, pulp writers hardly, if ever, mentioned the multilayered political war in South Vietnam. Likely, few authors had a deep understanding of Vietnamese politics. Plus, it would have been easier for them to rely on well-established tropes where real men defeated their enemies in a standup fight. Thus, adventure mags such as *Man's Illustrated* published exhilarating stories like "Riding Shotgun in Helicopter Hell," where chopper missions against the Vietcong meant having to "fly like a pilot, dig-in like a GI – and fight like a Marine."[3] Presumably only a small number of readers would have been excited to negotiate like a diplomat.

For those young men concerned about proving themselves in Vietnam, the reality of war there must have been disconcerting in the extreme. The experience of combat did not relate so easily to the triumphal rhetoric in magazine articles and illustrations. Without question, the macho pulps were not alone in offering up an unrealistic version of Vietnam, one official chronicler describing *National Geographic's* wartime coverage as "innocent."[4] Adventure magazines, though, stood apart by reinforcing narratives where traditional accounts of battlefield combat remained central to waging war, all while offering readers a supposedly tried-and-true method for attaining their manhood. There was one problem, however. Vietnam failed to deliver.

The American experience in South Vietnam exposed the lie of pulp war stories. Sons came home thinking their World War II fathers, so prevalent in the magazines, had somehow deceived them, their initiation into manhood betrayed by a gruesome, deadly, and ultimately unsuccessful war. One veteran recalled being shocked that the Vietnamese looked upon him with fear and hatred. "I still naively thought of myself as a hero, as a liberator."[5] In many ways, the war in Vietnam proved implicitly frustrating to Americans, but arguably more so for young men raised on the images and storylines perpetuated in adventure mags. For these "warrior teenagers," the conflict had failed miserably to live up to expectations spawned by their fathers' generation.[6]

Worse, Vietnam apparently had disappointed boyhood dreams wherein war's man-making experience shepherded postwar veterans into a close-knit "band of brothers" who reaped praise and admiration from the society sending them off to war. "We went to Vietnam as frightened, lonely young men," William Jayne remembered. "We came back, alone again, as immigrants to a new world." Thus, neither the Vietnamese whom Americans ostensibly came to help nor antiwar civilians back home had regarded these GIs as valiant and noble heroes. The pulps, it appeared, had been nothing more than provocative fiction all along.[7]

THE NEW FACE OF WAR

Western notions of Southeast Asia long had been colored by racialized interpretations of recalcitrant and politically immature native peoples. French colonizers, who formed Indochina in the late 1880s, viewed the ethnic Vietnamese as primitive, effeminate, and lacking initiative. Americans tended to agree. One consul reported to Washington, DC in 1924 that the inhabitants of central Vietnam "as a race are very lazy and not prone to be ambitious." Such depictions clearly spoke in racialized terms, hardly considering the political and social complexities of a multifaceted Asian community grappling with the consequences of European colonialism. Moreover, raw power undergirded the tense relationship between West and East. French imperialists held dominance over their Vietnamese subjects, extracting natural resources to benefit the metropole while the local rural population bore the brunt of foreign rule.[8]

All that changed in World War II as Japanese invaders unseated the French colonial state to impose their own brand of imperial rule. Vietnamese nationalist groups – including the powerful communist Viet Minh under Ho Chi Minh – saw in this wartime upheaval their chance to claim independence. In September 1945, after Japan's unconditional surrender to the allies, Ho proclaimed a Democratic Republic of Vietnam (DRV), free from foreign influence. The French, however, were intent on regaining their possessions. Fearing the loss of western-oriented Asian nations to communist aggression, the Truman administration offered France economic assistance and political backing in their plans to retain Indochina. While the resulting French-Indochina War (1946–1954) ravaged the Vietnamese countryside, American officials worried the conflict was auguring in a new era of communist-inspired revolutionary warfare. They were not to be disappointed. Despite massive US assistance, the French could not maintain their colonial holdings, leaving behind two competing political entities, North and South Vietnam.[9]

While Ho Chi Minh consolidated power in the communist north, Ngo Dinh Diem fought to gain supremacy in the politically fractious south. Diem's anti-communist fervor appealed to Americans anxious about the larger Cold War competition and helped ensure external backing when the government of South Vietnam (GVN) needed it most. Even with his gains, though, an internal insurgency slowly grew to challenge Diem's rule. While Ho remained hopeful of unifying an independent Vietnam, the Hanoi Politburo debated how best, if at all, to support their southern brethren. By the early 1960s, the National Liberation Front (NLF) had taken root across much of the South Vietnamese countryside, placing the military struggle on equal footing with their political efforts. The armed faction of the NLF, the People's Liberation Armed Forces of South Vietnam (PLAF), soon followed with a campaign of targeted assassinations, subversive political activity, and even armed attacks against Diem's governmental outposts and army bases. South Vietnam was inching closer and closer to full-scale war.[10]

While the PLAF – pejoratively dubbed the Vietcong, or VC, by Diem and his American allies – increased their assaults against the GVN, the Kennedy administration sent thousands of US advisors to South Vietnam in hopes of stemming the communist tide. By 1963, there were more than 16,000 American military personnel in country. The situation only deteriorated in November when a military junta overthrew Diem in a bloody coup, leaving the countryside in a state of political turmoil. Hanoi, sensing an opportunity, boosted its support to the NLF and slowly began infiltrating North Vietnamese Army (NVA) units into the embattled south. Kennedy's assassination, only three weeks after Diem's, left President Lyndon B. Johnson little choice, so he believed, other than to continue supporting America's Southeast Asian ally. By mid 1965, US ground combat troops were deploying to South Vietnam, soon to turn the country into one of the bloodiest battlefields of the Cold War era. America once more was at war.[11]

There is little in men's adventure magazines to suggest that pulp writers fully appreciated the nuances of the political and military origins of America's war in Vietnam. Rather, they focused on repurposing the soldier-hero image of World War II. If John Wayne had boosted morale back in the 1940s with tales of individual heroism, might he be able to do so again two decades later? The Duke certainly thought so, best conveyed in his 1968 film *The Green Berets*. *True* magazine called it one of the "most action-packed, realistic war movies ever." Film critics were far less enthusiastic. Renata Adler, of the *New York Times*, described the picture as "vile and insane … so full of its own caricature of patriotism that it cannot even find the right things to falsify."[12] By the time of its release, soldiers in Vietnam tended to agree with Adler. Wayne's movie seemed more surreal propaganda than an accurate rendering of a complex war. The pulps, though, stayed on message. Just one year before the film's release, *Male* shared a story on Green Beret Sergeant Harold T. Palmer, a "tough, two-fisted" commando who "rallied his battered and bleeding band of GIs" to launch a million-to-one assault against the "steel-toothed jaws" of a Vietcong death trap.[13] Men's adventure editors still believed martial heroism could sell magazines.

They were right. In Vietnam, the officials running the post exchange (PX) system chose which magazines to stock, and how many copies, by referring to stateside Audit Bureau Circulation data, sales returns, and soldiers' reading habits. Clearly, GIs were consuming plenty of reading material, an average of thirty sea-vans of periodicals being delivered to a Saigon warehouse each month for distribution to fifty-eight outlets across South Vietnam. Major categories included news periodicals like *Time* and *Stars and Stripes*, general interest offerings like sports and comic books, and adventure monthlies which included "girlie magazines." Officers debated what was considered in "good taste" and thus conflated "sex titles" with macho pulps because the latter included racy photo spreads and salacious articles.[14] As one senior staff officer disappointedly noted, "Reasonably good magazines are disappearing and there is a proliferation of trash." Readers, though, made their preferences known. In 1967, thirteen of the top twenty best-selling magazines in the PX system fell

Fig. 4.2 *Male*, July 1966

into the men's adventure category. By April 1969, the rankings had changed little. While *Playboy*, perhaps unsurprisingly, topped the list, adventure mags filled most of the remaining spots, each selling in the tens of thousands every month – *Cavalier, Climax, All Man, Stag*, and *For Men Only* to name but a few. Annual magazine sales reached $12 million, which yielded a hefty profit for the private contractor Star Far East Corporation.[15]

No doubt soldiers consumed these magazines for a variety of reasons. One US Army survey found that younger readers were "satisfied with the 'girlie-type' magazines," whereas older readers preferred *Newsweek* and *Popular Mechanics*.[16] Newly arrived recruits may have been searching for examples to follow in combat, hoping to be inspired by tales of courageous Green Berets besting their Vietcong enemies. Others may have focused on the sexy cheesecake photo spreads, or simply have perused ads for items to purchase or jobs to fill once back home. Regardless, soldiers were consuming adventure magazines in massive quantities, and not just in Vietnam. The Korean Regional Exchange (KRE) similarly ordered pulps by the thousands. In 1969, KRE's annual requisition left little doubt of the pulps' continuing appeal – 45,600 copies of *Stag*, 42,000 of *For Men Only*, and 30,000 of *Real Man*. Senior military officials may have considered them "low quality magazines," but American soldiers overseas buying the macho pulps evidently thought otherwise.[17]

If the sheer volume of men's adventure magazines in Vietnam contributed to soldiers' false expectations of combat, pulp writers at least acknowledged that this was a new kind of war. Skipping over the political origins and aims of the NLF, the magazines concentrated on what appeared to be *the* distinctive nature of combat in Vietnam – guerrilla warfare. Even before US ground troops arrived in Southeast Asia, *Stag* was calculating that one guerrilla equaled 400 soldiers. In 1963, *Brigade* described a "phantom war" where entire villages were "being massacred by the Congs when the headmen are suspected of cooperating with the Saigon government." US advisors were not even sure how many of the enemy existed in such a "sonofabitching war." One lashed out against the NLF for conducting raids "like wild animals on innocent civilians." The people, men's mags argued, were living in terror. Guerrilla war was a "pestilence of the human race," the "cruelest form of warfare on earth."[18]

Once ground combat troops arrived in force, Americans wondered if GIs were prepared to fight and win in what veteran ABC correspondent Malcolm Browne called a "different kind of conflict." Clearly, the United States' stockpiles in H-bombs and ICBMs were ill-suited to the guerrilla war inside South Vietnam. *Stag* thus ran a 1966 story on "simple, unsophisticated hardware" such as grenade launchers, walkie-talkies, and even hatchets, weapons more appropriate to the "brutal in-fighting that is the key to GI life and death."[19] That same year, *Male* introduced readers to the subterranean efforts of the "tunnel rats," who were fighting a "new kind of war, so terrifying and dangerous that it makes above-ground combat in Viet Nam look like a field exercise." If the enemy appeared inhuman, some in fact were. While soldiers and marines employed newfangled "radar personnel detectors" against the Vietcong –

"They were after our throats," said one infantryman – *Stag* published a short piece on a "new terror for GIs in Vietnam." According to the story, a marine corporal on patrol near the demilitarized zone was mauled by a tiger. Browne clearly was on to something. This *was* a different kind of war.[20]

Pulp writers were not alone in their struggle to make sense of such a disorienting experience. The war's incomprehensibility even left soldiers and marines unsure why they were in Vietnam. As veteran James Webb wrote, the conflict felt "undirected, without aim or reason."[21] Sure enough, men's mags also failed to grasp the larger strategic and cultural nuances of this new kind of war. In the late 1950s, as authors were writing in the aftermath of the French-Indochina conflict, pulp war stories focused on the genre's basic pillars. One tale related the exploits of an American pilot captured by the Viet Minh who spent six months with the "guerrilla women of Viet Nam." *For Men Only* shared the combat diary of a French paratroop commando, while *Battle Cry* criticized US politicians for not supporting French forces at the climactic battle of Dien Bien Phu. None of these articles offered insights into the Vietnamese civil war, instead focusing on how the Reds were intent on taking over Southeast Asia.[22]

On the eve of full-scale American deployments to Vietnam, when the macho pulps did venture into the strategic realm, their prognoses seemed based more on hope than evidence. In February 1965, *Male* opined that the "Viet Cong Reds [might] fear a Chinese communist invasion even more than an American invasion." While the relationship between Hanoi and Beijing could be prickly, this was pure speculation at best. True, the communists did worry about their neighbors to the north, but the DRV was far more concerned in 1965 about a US incursion than a Chinese one. That same issue, *Male* struck an optimistic chord. "As bad as things look in Viet Nam, some of our military men hope that the country can hold together just a little while longer." Citing food short-ages and low morale, the magazine suggested that the northern com-munists were in deep trouble. And never mind, *Male* told its readers, if the situation worsened – "we could win the war, just by 'gutting it out.'" No doubt more than a few senior policymakers in Washington, DC felt the same way.[23]

Besides, "gutting it out" is what real men did, at least according to the pulps. How could a young recruit prove his manhood in battle if he wasn't tested, pressed to his limits, before coming out victorious? In Vietnam, though, simply withstanding pain did not equate to military or political progress. Along the way, the very definition of heroism seemed to be changing. By the time of *The Green Berets*, John Wayne's military antics on the big screen were provoking ridicule from soldiers in the field, not admiration. Being "gung ho" was less important than having a "good head."[24] One lieutenant differentiated his men from "those phony popcorn heroes in the movies who go down fighting to the end." Another GI recalled how the "whole John Wayne thing went out the window" after his first taste of combat.[25] All this despite the continuing brisk sales of men's adventure magazines within the Vietnam PX system. Old habits die hard, and no doubt, for some, the pulps remained popular for the escapism they offered. Not until the early 1970s would they eventually fall out of favor with their prospective readers. For far too many young GIs, the allure of martial masculinity remained strong throughout the 1960s, despite the deadly, countervailing evidence provided by combat action in Vietnam.

That combat was proving far different than the set-piece battles of World War II and Korea. One Department of Defense study found that more than ninety-five percent of communist attacks occurred below the battalion level, a clear indicator of the unconventional fighting style preferred by the Vietcong. Moreover, in a war without front lines, intelligence analysts struggled to maintain a clear picture of the enemy situation. Bill Ehrhart recalled how it was like putting together a "jigsaw puzzle from the bits and piece of information that poured into" his operations center.[26] Each time Americans departed an area supposedly cleared of enemy forces, the VC drifted back again to regain influence over the population. One veteran had the feeling "the blind were leading the blind." *Male* even surmised that the lack of progress might be the fault of the US Army's infantry schools, which "emphasized conventional warfare, not dirty jungle guerrilla tactics." On frustratingly long marches, GIs scoured the countryside, more often than not returning to their bases empty-handed with no "trophies" to show for their efforts.[27]

Despite the incongruences between World War II and Vietnam, the adventure magazines' narratives remained wedded to earlier conceptions of warfare even as they occasionally offered more realistic assessments of the current conflict. *Stag*, for instance, shared the optimism of "Pentagon old-timers" who felt the war would be won "because of our greater maneuverability. It takes the Cong ten days to move three of its battalions. The U.S. can move five battalions in a day. The result is that ten American battalions can fight 50 Cong battalions." Left unstated was the obvious reality, at least in 1966 when the *Stag* issue came out, that the insurgent forces in South Vietnam never considered massing fifty battalions to fight the Americans.[28]

The following year, pulp writers trumpeted American actions that fit more easily within a World War II-style narrative. Both *Saga* and *Stag* ran articles on the 1st Infantry Division's ten-week excursion into War Zone C, northwest of Saigon, in late 1966. Dubbed Operation Attleboro, the series of battalion-size sweeps ultimately included more than 22,000 American and South Vietnamese soldiers. On one day alone, 8 November, the 1st Division's artillery expended over 14,000 rounds. Body counts tallied more than 1,000 enemy dead, while the Americans seized 2,400 tons of rice, 24,000 grenades, and 2,000 pounds of explosives. As *Saga* boasted, when the smoke and flames had cleared, the operation "had been added to the glorious history of the Fighting First Infantry Division." By the metrics of World War II, American forces were making solid progress against the southern insurgency and their NVA brothers. US operations like Attleboro, however, proved the exception in South Vietnam, and, more importantly, ultimately failed to solve any of the war's underlying political problems.[29]

True, Attleboro's conventional metrics reflected a faith in numbers and statistics so embraced by the US Department of Defense in the mid 1960s. On the ground, however, American soldiers more often encountered mines and booby traps that were left behind by a phantom menace far more difficult to quantify. Writing for *True*, Malcolm Browne shared GIs' exasperations with this "new kind of war" where the "waits are long, battles brief, and no one knows when the VC will fight or flee." Booby traps and mines incited a unique brand of fear. "Like serpents they surround you," wrote one vet poet. Mirroring soldiers' memoirs, the macho pulps highlighted the VC's hidden instruments of death – toe poppers, punji sticks, trip wires, and tiger traps all evidently covered the landscape.[30] According to *Stag*, "forty of 57 wounded in one 199th Light Infantry Company got their Purple Hearts via booby traps." All told, some twenty-five percent of allied casualties came from booby traps and mines. How could one become a hero, gain a clear sense of triumph, when the war's main threat came from deadly, inanimate objects? One young soldier from the 1st Infantry Division recalled the infuriation of losing buddies to an enemy he could not find. "It was very frustrating because how do you fight back against a booby trap?"[31]

The fact that Americans could not distinguish between friend and foe in a foreign Asian land only made matters worse. Contemporary racial attitudes did not help. Wartime racism, a tradition dating back to the colonial era, was not hard to find in men's adventure magazines. During and after the Korean War, the pulps ran autobiographical sketches from GIs who had "smacked the Gooks in the guts with everything we had" or had flown suicide combat missions in "Gook Alley." World War II vets chimed in with their experiences in the Pacific, one taking pleasure in finding two "Gook guerrillas" and cutting them "to pieces."[32] Whether Japanese, Korean, or Vietnamese, any darker-skinned adversary could be linked back to the original mythic race-enemy, the Indian. The pulps were not alone in conflating racial foes. In the Captain America comics, for example, when Cap first encounters Japanese soldiers, they are posing as Native Americans. No wonder, in an odd twist, that *Battle Cry* highlighted a Sioux GI serving in Korea who collected "commie scalps" while fighting the Chinese Reds. Racist perceptions shaped much of American thinking during the Cold War era.[33]

If the enemy-as-savage metaphor made sense to many GIs fighting in Vietnam, the vast majority discovered they had little if any prospect of actually joining in the contest. Sold by the pulps that Vietnam, like World War II, would offer them a man-making experience, readers who deployed to Southeast Asia found they rarely made it to "Indian country." At least seventy-five percent of American troops in Vietnam never saw combat. Instead, most of them served on large bases where they could enjoy ice cream shops, basketball courts, and service clubs. Could one really become a hero on the Long Binh post softball field?[34] *Bluebook* noted the support ratio in a 1967 article, yet still lavished praise on the US fighting squad, "considered by professionals as the most elite military group in the history of American warfare." For those young men in their late teens or early twenties seeking a chance for martial glory, perhaps they might beat the odds and have the chance to "zap" a VC. Besides, the magazine noted, "Older men cannot cope with the demands of jungle fighting."[35]

With so many GIs serving in support units, frontline combat infantry-men predictably cast aspersions toward the rear areas, popularizing a new term in the military lexicon – REMF. While grunts held these "rear echelon mother fuckers" in contempt, living on base camps alternatively could be filled with the threat of mortar and rocket fire or with abject boredom. One infantry officer derisively remarked of REMFs that the "most dangerous thing they've got is getting killed in a traffic accident or VD."[36] In the pulps, however, even support troops could break free from their supposedly mundane existence and demonstrate their courage under fire. *Male* printed a story in which a transportation soldier driving a semi-trailer barrels through enemy barricades to keep a vital supply line open. Leading a convoy, the "Yank marauder" proves that the enemy's "highway of death" is just as lethal to the Vietcong as it had been to the Americans. *For Men Only* ran a similarly themed article on a rugged, no-nonsense engineer officer unplugging trouble spots to feed ammunition and supplies to the battlefield. Vietnam might be a different kind of war, but in the pulps, at least, every GI had a chance to find meaning by undertaking a dangerous mission against a battle-hardened enemy.[37]

BATTLING THE CONG

Pulp readers must have wondered how the People's Liberation Armed Forces of South Vietnam came from such an ostensibly lazy, effeminate society, when the Vietcong, in contrast, seemed bred for war. One general officer ranked both VC and NVA soldiers as "the best enemy we have faced in our history. Tenacious and physically fit." A young lieutenant serving with the 25th Infantry Division in 1967 agreed, sharing with war correspondent Robert Sherrod his amazement of the Vietcong's grim resolution: "I just don't understand what motivates these people."

Americans may have conceptualized their Vietnamese foes through racist lenses, but any prejudices did not stand in the way of bestowing upon the VC a grudging respect. Here was a steadfast and capable opponent.[38]

Even before American combat troops deployed to Vietnam, men's adventure magazines portrayed the Vietcong guerrilla as "the most amazing soldier in the world. He wears his hair long, rarely shaves, wears filthy clothes, and his skin is full of jungle sores. Yet he can outwalk, and outcrawl any Western fighting man."[39] *Male* noted how the Vietcong had covered nearly all of the South with camouflaged spike pits and seemed in awe of the enemy's feats in physical endurance. "If you offered a tank or howitzer to a Red guerrilla in Vietnam he'd laugh in your face," the mag declared, "turn you down flat. He can average 45 miles a day traveling light, and speed is his game."[40] To ensure that its readers made the connection between the VC and savage frontier Indians, *Men* shared how it was "not an uncommon sight to see a U.S. helicopter in Vietnam brought down with an arrow sticking in its belly."[41] Nowhere in these portrayals did the pulp writers discuss the revolutionary struggle's political component. Perhaps such omissions help explain how young lieutenants could not fathom their enemy's motivation.

As the American war got under way, the macho pulps continued to highlight the Vietcong's competence, while never overlooking the evils of communism. *Male* revealed how the devious "Cong" targeted green American troops by hiding grenades in beer cans, spiking water with glass splinters, and even packing coconuts with TNT. *True Action* described the local VC in Pleiku province as "a murderous army of raping, kill-crazy Cong [that] was ruthlessly plundering the countryside." Their leaders were "butchers" or "sadistic, scar-faced Communist cutthroats" who brutally slaughtered anyone among the rural population foolish enough to challenge their power.[42] Moreover, to demonstrate Hanoi's role in this war, adventure mags were sure to highlight the communist aggression from North Vietnam. In one account, an inspection of dead guerrillas found they were not southern insurgents, but rather carefully selected agents from the North Vietnamese Intelligence Bureau – "the equivalent of Ho Chi Minh's own KGB." Thus, the pulps could more directly tie the external threat from Hanoi to their communist masters in Moscow. Of course, the relationship between the two capitals proved far more intricate.[43]

These competing interpretations of the Vietnamese communists – praiseworthy fighters yet brutal savages – left an ambiguous message to both pulp readers and deployed GIs. Australian correspondent Phillip Knightley believed that "racism became a patriotic virtue" in Vietnam, helping explain the common epithets of gooks, dinks, and slopes. And yet the "pint-sized VC" remained a "tough and aggressive foe even after capture."[44] If they did not fight like real men, refusing to "come out in the open and fight," they also could mount ferocious counterattacks when surrounded by American or South Vietnamese units. One typical marine captain was astonished by the "bravery of some of those little guys." What then to make of elite American units that copied the enemy's skulking way of war?[45] *True* showcased a team of US Navy Seals who had "adapted Viet Cong tactics" on their long-range patrols. Did these American warriors become less masculine in the process? Apparently not, as by story's end, the Seals had gained an edge over their enemy. As one sergeant claimed, "There's no better feeling in the world than knowing you are able to live and fight like Charlie and beat him at his own game."[46]

Fig. 4.3 *Stag*, February 1967

Unfortunately for the US military command in Saigon, their South Vietnamese allies had yet to match the proficiency of the communist foe. American condemnation for the Army of the Republic of Vietnam (ARVN) was near universal. GIs considered ARVN soldiers and their leaders corrupt and lazy, lacking morale and bravery. Regional and Popular Forces, akin to local militia, fared no better. "They aren't worth a fuck," growled an American.[47] One veteran from the US 25th Infantry Division emphasized the distrust many felt toward the ARVN: "They were losers. They didn't have any initiative whatsoever." As with so much in this war, the reality proved far more complicated. South Vietnamese soldiers were underpaid, many questioned the legitimacy of their own government in Saigon, and most lacked effective ideological training so they might more readily embrace the national cause. Still, ARVN units fought tenaciously to the bitter end, a sure sign that when properly led and motivated, the South Vietnamese were just as capable as their communist enemies.[48]

The pulps, however, sided with American critics. During the pre-1965 US advisory period, men's magazines derided the "Arvins" who "jumped like scared rabbits" – a popular refrain among GIs. *Stag* doubted the trendy idea of extending the war into North Vietnam because of the ARVN's supposed poor worth. "We can't get the South Vietnamese to fight on their own soil. What makes anyone think they'll do better in enemy territory?"[49] As the first American combat troops began their deployments to Vietnam, the story only worsened. In June 1965, *Man's Magazine* published a piece on the "Sheer Hell in Vietnam." While the US marines fared well in this battlefield account, ARVN soldiers took it on the chin. According to the mag, GIs were risking their necks for an ally who "can't or won't fight" and "who – in some cases – WANT to die!" If the US military command was going to lose this war, a convenient scapegoat already was forming in military circles and in the popular mindset.[50]

As the war dragged on, estimations of the South Vietnamese only deteriorated. American advisors working with the ARVN saw their assignment as a "thankless and unrewarding job." Increasing desertion rates did not help matters, nor did the fact that battlefield initiative seemed ever outside of the ARVN's reach. Incredibly, as *Stag* related, American officers were admitting in private that "they wish they had the North Viets on their side, instead of the South."[51] In *True*, correspondent Malcolm Browne called the ARVN a "military white elephant, increasingly content to let the U.S. pay the cost of battle in blood as well as money." Even after shaming their allies, the Americans still had to take charge of tense combat situations. In one pulp story on the Green Berets, "tall, rawboned" advisor Major Charles Beckwith finds a "scrawny" South Vietnamese soldier feigning a wound during a weeklong battle. "You damn coward!," the American roars. "Get your butt out there and fight like a man!" For the remainder of the fight, Beckwith keeps a cocked .45 pistol in hand to ensure the unscathed "smiling wounded" do not scramble aboard evac helicopters and take the place of critically wounded men.[52]

If the South Vietnamese were falling short in proving their manhood in war, the communists apparently had no such trouble. Even the Vietcong who defected seemed more adept than the Americans' true allies. Dubbed Kit Carson Scouts, former communist fighters who agreed to fight alongside US soldiers and marines made a positive impression on their new colleagues. True, some officials worried about the converts' fidelity, one officer wondering aloud how "the Vietnamese could switch sides so easily."[53] Yet, through hard fighting and sharing information on the insurgency network, the Kit Carsons normally won over skeptical Americans. *Male* even published a story on a marine staff sergeant working alongside Vietcong defector Thuong Kinh. After establishing himself in the field on a trial basis, Thuong becomes an integral part of the squad, a "human bloodhound" who leads the Americans through thick foliage, all while avoiding snipers and booby traps. Throughout several engagements, the scout proves "his worth with his uncanny knowledge of enemy tactics and trickery." By story's end, Thuong is credited with thirty-one kills, helping turn a potential defeat into tactical victory by spotting a VC ambush.[54]

If South Vietnamese soldiers appeared reluctant warriors compared even with Vietcong defectors, one ARVN unit did stand out – the Rangers. The macho pulps lavished praise on these elite detachments that ultimately earned eleven US Presidential Unit Citations. Unlike the bulk of the South Vietnamese armed forces, these rugged troops were "more than a match for Communists in hit-and-run fighting."[55] They also seemed ruthless warriors. *Male* included a full-page photograph of an ARVN ranger jamming a Ka-Bar knife against the stomach of a bare-chested Vietcong guerrilla during an interrogation session, the muddied prisoner visibly wincing in pain. *Bluebook* highlighted the "incredible valor" of the 44th Ranger Battalion, a group of "Satan-spawned killers" who never quit, even when wounded. Of course, US mentors often hovered nearby, ready to offer support and sage advice when the fighting escalated. Yet, despite the Rangers' praiseworthy actions, Americans still worried these elite units might falter once their advisors withdrew from the war.[56]

Adding insult to injury, the political situation looked more appalling than the military one. A seemingly fractious, incompetent, and corrupt Saigon government conveyed that it was doing its best to undermine American efforts in political reform. In reality, GVN leaders inevitably were struggling with the competing demands of building a stable political community in a time of war. Their American benefactors, officially there to help, only proved to NLF propagandists, and far too many rural villagers, that Saigon was nothing more than a puppet of the United States. *For Men Only* deemed the propaganda war "almost impossible to fight" because the Vietnamese population had taken so much abuse from the French and their own corrupt regime that "they find it hard to believe we're any better." Charges of unrestrained corruption and a rampant black market even incited calls for the Americans to "throw a really tight blockade around Saigon."[57]

Could it be that the problem was less political than inherently cultural? At least some pulp readers believed so, perceiving fundamental flaws in the South Vietnamese makeup. A Boston resident wrote to *Man's Illustrated* in early 1965 sharing his disgust with the "hell of a mess" in Vietnam. The solution, however, seemed evident: "if the people of that God-forsaken country wanted to do something about the Communist Viet Cong they could get off their asses and get to work." While the Americans were doing "everything humanly possible" to help win the war, their sacrifices clearly were not being matched. According to the reader, the southern Vietnamese "are probably the laziest people in the world." If the US mission in Vietnam was hoping to build domestic support for a long war of political attrition abroad, they still had plenty of work to do.[58]

These concerns over the GVN's fitness to govern had to be balanced with the prevalent view that all communists were inherently evil and impulsively cruel. If ARVN soldiers were inept "good" Asians, then the Vietcong must be deemed ruthless "bad" Asians. Thus, *Man's Action* offered a story on the "naked terror" of VC "butchers" who mutilated three US Green Berets and dismembered local civilians.[59] *Stag* ran an analogous piece in which members of the NLF abducted the daughter of a village chieftain friendly to the Americans, and cut off her arm "as a means of frightening the villagers into silence about the Cong where-abouts." The same issue noted how "Cong pilots" – the NLF had no air force – were being trained by Russian air heroes, a reminder that the Vietnam conflict still should be placed within the larger narrative of the communists' bid for world domination.[60]

While the NLF did engage in terror tactics, most infamously at the Hue massacre in early 1968, men's mags tended to mislead their readers by delineating clear lines between assailant and victim. Yet the fighting in Vietnam never proceeded so neatly. One US marine believed that both sides had made a "habit out of atrocities," while another veteran judged that his enemy "never cared whether he lived or died... We'd shoot them, and y'know, they just didn't care. They had no concept of life."[61] In the pulps, however, the war seemed far more black and white. Like the Nazis or Chinese communists before them, the Vietcong were funda-mentally wicked. By 1967, this lack of nuance even could break into fantasy. Despite the war's obvious stalemate, *Male* recorded that the Americans had turned the tables on the NLF and were winning the intelligence war. "By just feeding a card into a computer, U.S. command-ers can find out anything they need to know about any Cong unit." Nothing could have been further from the truth.[62]

In actuality, the communists too often held the basic tactical initiative. American patrols might be "in the bush incessantly," yet only make contact with the enemy when they stumbled into an ambush. The macho pulps told a different story, one in which Americans consistently were on the offensive and making sound progress across most of South Vietnam, whether in the Central Highlands or the Mekong Delta. Often noting how GIs were beating the Reds at their own game – even though many soldiers deemed ambushes an inferior, cowardly form of warfare – men's mags argued that US counterguerrilla tactics could lead to a war-winning strategy.[63] A 1967 pulp exposé on Lt. Richard Marcinko, author of the popular *Rogue Warrior* series in the 1990s, illuminated how "darkly handsome," deadly Americans were operating successfully behind enemy lines. *Male* praised this "Cong-killing" Seal team as a group of "blast 'em-and-get-out raiders'" who earned the title "super-commandos of the century." Marcinko later admitted in his memoir this was an "atrociously written piece of fiction," yet he also shared how the Vietcong had tacked up wanted posters of him throughout the Mekong Delta after the article was published. Apparently, not only Americans were reading the pulps in Vietnam.[64]

If the enemy indeed were perusing men's adventure magazines, their capacity to read did little to change prevailing American attitudes that the Vietcong were nothing more than savages. Every instance of violence only reaffirmed the view that Vietnamese communists, whether from the north or the south, came from a long line of "native cut-throats." Like the "Moslem fanatics" of West Java or the Mau who "spread terror" in their quest to "drive the white man out of Africa," the Vietnamese fit well into preconceived pulp notions of beastly others who threatened peaceful civilians overseas.[65] Since the adventure mags conflated the southern insurgents with North Vietnamese regulars, they not only obscured the enemy's point of origin, but helped promote GI opinions that "If it's dead and it's Vietnamese, it's VC." Of course, in pulpworld, killing savage enemies is what true warriors did best.[66]

AMERICAN WARRIORS

If the 1950s mass consumer society spurred fears of a new breed of lifeless "organization men" blandly following behind their tougher, more resilient forefathers, similar concerns seeped into the US armed forces. With war becoming more complex in the atomic age, critics worried that technocrats, focused more on management than on leadership, would rise to the highest levels of command and somehow forget that victory in battle came from hard fighting. Though the image of the "warrior" may have been changing for some in these Cold War years, the pulps retained the notion that physical violence remained at the core of militarized masculinity.[67]

Consequently, adventure magazines heralded strong, individual leaders who could inspire a new generation of American warriors. *Stag* called Colonel Henry "Gunfighter" Emerson, who commanded a battalion in the 101st Airborne, the "toughest paratroop commando in Vietnam." *Man's Conquest* highlighted marine general Frederick Karch, who had been "blooded in battle against the Japs" in World War II and now was beating "the Reds at their own dirty guerrilla war."[68] Meanwhile, *Stag* judged Colonel Harold G. Moore, who led American forces at the Ia Drang battle in late 1965, as the "General Patton we need in Vietnam." Even Patton's own son, a colonel commanding the 11th Armored Cavalry Regiment, received accolades, along with his "Cong-blasting tankers" who were carving out a legend for themselves in the rice paddies and jungles of Vietnam.[69]

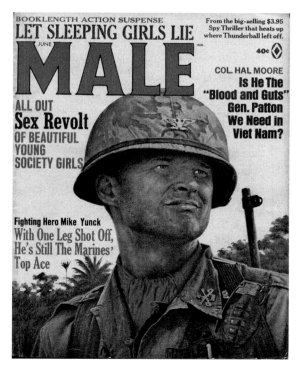

Fig. 4.4 *Male*, June 1966

No doubt this linking to the World War II generation was purposeful. Conflicts need heroes, and Vietnam proved no exception. Numerous veterans recalled being "seduced by World War II," so it was only natural for adventure mags to feed into this hero worship. They made sure to cover all the bases by trumpeting each service. In their story on the head of the US Army Special Forces, "Tough Bill" Yarborough, *Male* noted how this "combat wizard" had soaked up jungle-fighting "tricks" in the Philippines and claimed that he had faced some of Hitler's toughest SS divisions in Tunisia during World War II. Now, he was putting these "Daniel Boone" skills to good use by training "parachutist-ranger-commandos" for military service around the globe. *Man's Illustrated* ran a 1965 story on Creighton Abrams, the future MACV commander, his exploits as a tank commander in Patton's Third Army draping "the cape of a legend around his shoulders."[70]

So as not to play favorites, the pulps gave equal time to the US Navy and Marine Corps. Vice Admiral Roy L. Johnson, who "blasted the Reds at Tonkin Gulf" in 1964, had led fighter sweeps over the Philippines, Iwo Jima, and Okinawa. No "paper tiger," he was the "real thing – teeth, claws and guts." For their coverage of General Victor "Brute" Krulak, *Stag* went into detail on the marine's World War II exploits in the Pacific before noting how he had maintained "the same kind of courage, daring, and military know-how that make his Marines so rough on the Vietcong in Vietnam now. It's an unbeatable combination."[71] *Man's Magazine* ran a comparable story on Krulak's peer, Lewis W. Walt. In "The Marine the Japs Couldn't Stop," Walt steadfastly leads his unit on New Britain under barrages of enemy fire en route to earning the Navy Cross. By 1966, Walt was commanding all US Marines in Vietnam, pulp writer Glenn Infield observing that "the Viet Cong and North Vietnamese already have discovered the general is just as much at home fighting their kind of 'dirty war' as he is the more conventional battles." These heroes' shared sense of masculinity clearly was reaping dividends in Southeast Asia.[72]

The correlation between the Second World War and Vietnam meant that even older warriors, outwardly past their prime, still could offer their services to the nation. Lloyd "Scooter" Burke, who received the Medal of Honor in Korea, was forty-one years old when he was shot down in Vietnam. Two years older, Sergeant Major Bill Wooldridge deployed to

Vietnam with the famed 1st Infantry Division. *Male* recorded that this "Human Assault Wave" had fought in the bloodiest battles of World War II and Korea before heading to Vietnam, his "raw courage gut-fighting repeatedly rewarded by a string of medals" on his chest.[73] *Man's Magazine* more overtly demonstrated how Vietnam offered a chance for older men to continue fighting and validate their manhood. A story on one Korean War vet, Air Force Colonel Devol Brett, noted how he was a "generation apart, an 'old man' of 44 who still flew into combat." Though younger pilots were "skeptical of his heavy, muscular build and his advanced age," Brett knew there was a place for him in this war. He still could carry the "battle straight to the heart of the enemy."[74]

This dream of vaulting over messy, terrestrial battlefields and directly attacking one's enemy had inspired airpower advocates from the earliest days of World War I, if not before. Modern-day knights, mounted on mechanical steeds, certainly had captured young readers' attention in postwar aviation magazines, a trend that continued well into the 1960s. One American pilot flying over the rice paddies and canals of Vietnam saw his aerial missions, akin to "old African hunting trips," as his own "rite of passage into manhood." A US Air Force fighter jockey shared his deep enjoyment flying with close friends. "They loved being there."[75] Still another flier, Robin Olds, an ace who earned a special feature in *Man's Magazine*, wrote in his memoir of being enticed by the "dream of victory in aerial combat." War might be ugly and brutal, but the F-4C Phantom jet pilot knew there was more to it than just hardware. In the pulp, Olds educates a superior officer, "They're not going to win with machinery, sir. We're going to win with *men*." No wonder US Ambassador to South Vietnam Maxwell Taylor claimed that Hanoi's inability to respond to American airpower would demonstrate communist "impotence," leading to a political solution.[76] In the air, as well as on the ground, manly warriors stood ready to defeat Red aggression.

While adventure magazines showcased rugged pilots battling communist MiG jets or conducting bombing runs over Hanoi through a "blast furnace of lethal flak," they also highlighted death-defying pilots who saved fellow warriors shot down behind enemy lines. This focus allowed pulp writers to impart tales of individual heroism, with downed Americans defending against or evading an approaching enemy. The knight, knocked off his steed, struggles to rejoin the fray, aided by a steadfast companion.[77] *Stag* illustrated the plot line with a story that made national headlines in early 1966. Air Force Major Bernard Fisher was leading a strike of A-1 Skyraiders to aid a besieged US camp near the Laotian border when one of his pilots, Major Stafford Myers, was hit and forced to crash land. Fisher decided to land his own plane on a debris-littered airstrip and rescue his friend, despite his own aircraft being pummeled with small arms fire. *Stag* called the performance "one of the most heroic – certainly the most 'impossible' – rescue of the Vietnam war." Writing for the *New York Times*, journalist Neil Sheehan agreed, noting that Fisher might be recommended for the Air Force Cross. On 19 January 1967, he received the Congressional Medal of Honor.[78]

In a war without front lines, rescuing downed pilots returned drama to an ugly war against an invisible insurgency. Yet knights historically performed best when liberating a fair maiden. The pulps concurred. In one *Man's Life* tale, a young Vietnamese woman, Maria Quin Dongh, lives in a small village terrorized by the Vietcong. Her father can identify the insurgents, but remains silent for fear of communist retribution against his family. Five miles away, a group of Green Berets has set up camp and Maria makes the dangerous journey to plead for their help. Of course, the Americans agree, and Maria leads them back, all of them fighting through a VC ambush along the way. After killing some thirty-five communists – who find "there actually are such places as heaven and hell" – the Green Berets free the village from the insurgency's clutches. Maria is designated a heroine, but the pulp makes clear that the American soldiers are "doing a big, perhaps the biggest part." The rescue is made significant thanks to the male–female relationship, the Green Berets' actions reminding Maria and her family that they have rescuing knights standing ready nearby.[79]

Through similar storylines, the macho pulps could fashion the American war in Vietnam war as a heroic, man-making experience and, at least before 1968, a relatively successful one as well. Writers dusted off World War II narratives in which American GIs excelled at the tactical level. *Male* ran a 1966 story on a group of "unkillable" marines led by Staff Sergeant Jimmie E. Howard, who received the Medal of Honor for leading a reconnaissance unit behind enemy lines. The tagline was pure pulp splendor – "the V.C. streamed like maggots from the death-night jungles in human sacrifice waves to storm the vital high ground held by one iron-gutted sergeant and a handful of no-quit leathernecks."[80] Not to be outdone, *Stag* touted that the Vietcong were avoiding US marines "like the plague." As an indicator of the GIs' tactical acumen, the magazine reported that army doctors were pleased by the "low incidence of 'battle fatigue' or 'breakdown under stress'" they were encountering among those hardy Americans serving in Vietnam.[81]

Courageous exploits like these collectively intimated that the United States was making progress in a hard-fought war. In the southern Mekong Delta, sailors in the "brown water" riverine navy were clearing areas of VC influence and eliminating the threat to local villages and their valuable rice supplies.[82] Farther north, *Male* claimed in early 1967, the enemy had "fewer and fewer places to hide and that sooner or later, the only safe places for him will be outside of South Vietnam." Only occasionally would reality break through onto the magazines' pages. One account relayed how an American position had come under mortar fire before facing a "savage suicide attack" by a local Vietcong force. Hand-to-hand combat ensues. The cavalry troopers acquit themselves well in this "death embrace" with the North Vietnamese – thanks to heavy doses of firepower – before the enemy disperses, the high body count a testament to the GIs' skill and bravery. Yet the piece acknowledged that the communists had destroyed a howitzer, badly damaged five others, and inflicted "moderate to heavy casualties" on the courageous defenders. If the Americans were making progress, their enemy was exacting a high price.[83]

Even after the 1968 Tet offensive, in which communist forces attacked across the breadth of South Vietnam, the adventure mags publicized heroism at the tactical level. Critics believed the attack exposed the irrelevance of US military power in Vietnam, while MACV commander William Westmoreland accepted the fact that the enemy had "dealt the GVN a severe blow."[84] In February, *Man's Conquest* published a piece on a handful of brave Yanks in the Mekong Delta who were "turning Ho Chi Minh's Sea Trail into a corpse-clogged canal." *True Action* similarly featured the combat saga of Lieutenant Colonel David Hackworth in May, who thus far had won sixteen medals and was fast becoming America's

"'No. 1' Cong Killer." Though it had been an "uneven battle" to date, both the decorated officer and the magazine seemed optimistic for the future. "Ahead on points," author Caleb Kingston noted, "Hackworth is looking for a K.O. next time."[85]

Properly told, Hackworth's story also demonstrated that the war in Vietnam remained as meritocratic as World War II. According to *True Action*, the future combat leader had dropped out of high school at fifteen, forged his birth certificate, and enlisted in the army. Only later did he earn his GED and gain acceptance into Austin Peay State College before securing his officer commission. Thus, even into the 1960s, any young teen might be captivated by the chance to prove his courage, and his manhood, in battle.[86]

In the pulps, baby-faced warriors certainly demonstrated their grit. A young Indiana hot rodder, "still sporting peach fuzz," led his platoon in a "brilliant, slashing maneuver" that destroyed half an enemy company. A twenty-year-old former lifeguard, now a marine platoon commander, outraced VC bullets to save his men who were stuck in a burning vehicle. This "Brooklyn boy who started out saving lives in the waters of Coney Island" had gone on "to do the same in the bullet-swept muck of Vietnam."[87] Even the lowliest of privates could excel in the worst of combat situations. *Man's Magazine* highlighted the bravery of PFC William H. Wallace, who helped coordinate the actions of an entire infantry company after it was pinned down and surrounded by enemy forces near Dau Tieng. Despite being a radio operator, only Wallace "stood between the survivors of C Company and death." Two days after the ordeal, the 25th Infantry Division's assistant commander pinned a Silver Star on the Long Island native, the medal awarded for "an outstanding act of courage."[88]

On occasion, the pulps even publicized the valor of minority soldiers fighting in Vietnam. In *True Action*'s "Grenade-Duel at Cong Ravine," Sergeant Manuel J. Perez, Jr. led his men after being pinned down in a well-laid ambush. Only twenty years old, the young Latino devised "a new heroic tactic for his soldiers to ponder over: if trapped by the enemy – charge!"[89] *Stag* featured medic Lawrence Joel, an African American soldier who had enlisted in the army back in 1946. The article noted how the "husky six-footer" had grown up in extreme poverty, as "jobs were exceedingly hard to come by" for blacks living in Winston-Salem, North Carolina. Now thirty-seven, Joel found himself serving in Bien Hoa province with the 173rd Airborne Brigade. Like Perez, his unit was assaulted by a superior enemy force and, with casualties mounting among the paratroopers, the twice-wounded medic bravely assisted his comrades, despite taking heavy fire. As Lyndon Johnson later draped the Medal of Honor around Joel's neck in a March 1967 White House ceremony, the president remarked on a "very special kind of courage – the unarmed heroism of compassion and service to others."[90] Anyone, it seemed, could be a hero.

If these brave Latino or African American soldiers only periodically showed up in the macho pulps, even more rare were stories hinting that American GIs were not performing in exemplary fashion. Contemporary and postwar critics certainly exaggerated the US armed forces' woes in Vietnam. To naysayers, the signs of disintegration were evident – rampant drug use and racial tensions, high rates of desertion and battle fatigue, and a general feeling of malaise within the ranks. Adventure magazines, however, generally avoided such defamatory topics.[91] Perceptive readers may have wondered why most combat stories began with the enemy launching an effective surprise attack, but the pulps retained their faith in the "quietly professional" troops, merely acceding that "it would be misstating facts to say they are 'gung ho' about this war and really hate the enemy with a passion." Only after the 1968 Tet offensive did a few short pieces surface of marijuana use and "pot-smoking" parties among those serving in Vietnam. The heroic warrior narrative left little room for countervailing testimony.[92]

Instead, the pulps sought to highlight fearless men who held true to their nation's martial values. Prisoners of war emerged as appealing candidates. If some pundits viewed Vietnam as a "war without heroes," *Time* assessed that "many Americans were intent on making the prisoners fill that role." Pulp writers helped lead the memorialization effort, seemingly agreeing with General Westmoreland that POWs "displayed a special kind of long-term valor."[93] As early as 1965, adventure mags like *Saga* were publishing accounts of captured pilots who "survived a Red nightmare of beatings, nude temptation, and a blood break for freedom." In March, the magazine ran a story on US Navy Lieutenant

Charles F. Klusmann, whose F-8 Crusader was shot down over Laos. Pro-communist Pathet Lao captured the "ruggedly handsome" officer, but his "ill fortune was to prove no match for his determination to survive." Though surely a humbling experience, Klusmann's imprisonment offered him the chance to fulfill his own resistance and escape narrative, his courage earning him front-page coverage in the *New York Times*.[94]

Another naval lieutenant turned POW, Dieter Dengler, earned two separate stories in the men's mags, plus a 2010 biography that reinforced the pulp narrative of heroic warrior–sexual champion. "When it came to the opposite sex," his biographer gushed, "Dieter was a charmer with an unquenchable appetite." This "inveterate ladies man" ultimately heads to Vietnam where his A-1 Skyraider is downed by enemy fire on 1 February 1966. Captured by Vietcong soldiers, Dengler plans his escape from the moment he is abducted, suffering through bouts of malaria, dysentery, and maltreatment from his captors, one of whom he calls "Little Hitler." In late June, the lieutenant finally attempts his breakout. Though exhausted, bleeding, and feverish, he evades the enemy for nearly three weeks before an air force rescue helicopter lifts him to safety. Like the World War II captives before him, Dengler has retained his identity as an honorable warrior.[95]

Fig. 4.5 *Men*, December 1961

For a president seeking "peace with honor" as he withdrew the United States from its long, unsatisfying war in Vietnam, calling for the release of brave POWs offered singular political advantages. Richard Nixon skillfully exploited the prisoner issue, hoping to unite Americans at a time when the antiwar movement threatened his plans for an orderly departure from Southeast Asia. Surely, the president was not alone in seeing value – and political capital – in identifying with dauntless men held in captivity. To Air Force officer Robbie Risner, he and his fellow American prisoners endured because they considered their principles more valuable than their lives. Nixon took note. In fact, the release of POWs and a full accounting of those missing in action became a precondition for any peace agreement. No longer a tool for achieving wartime political objectives, American prisoners had morphed into a central aim of the war itself.[96]

Adventure magazines mostly overlooked this political appropriation of POWs. Their heroism was enough to move popular storylines forward. Like earlier accounts of World War II and Korea, pulps articles concentrated on warriors' battlefield exploits, leaving discussions on grand strategy or American policy in Southeast Asia to the more high-brow periodicals. When editors and writers did comment on the larger national aspects of the war in Vietnam, they remained categorically supportive, in stark contrast to Hugh Hefner's monthly. *Playboy* walked a fine line when it came to the war, sending playmates to tour South Vietnam while its editor ran articles questioning US involvement in the conflict and encouraging a diplomatic solution. The pulps, however, maintained their backing, advocating for perseverance against communist aggression. Besides, they claimed, American GIs were doing their jobs, upsetting the "Cong timetable" and reversing the enemy's momentum to a point where they might never recover.[97]

Supporting government policies, like the draft, meshed well with the pulps' conception of Cold War manhood. To be antiwar was to be decidedly feminine. Such views were not uncommon, one protestor recalling that he heard epithets of "faggots" and "queers" as often as "commies" or "cowards." One infantryman returned from Vietnam and deemed those who stayed at home as "spoiled, gutless middle class kids who cowered in college classrooms to escape the battlefield."[98] Peace activists like Joan Baez and Jane Fonda appeared in sharp relief to the warriors fighting inside the pages of the macho pulps. Indeed, the contempt many veterans still hold for Fonda is a function of their desire to punish a "dangerous" woman with the nerve to speak out against militarized masculinity. Never mind that it also took great courage not to go to war, best seen in Muhammad Ali's decision to refuse being drafted. Was Ali a coward? Were the Baltimore Colts football players with a "military problem" acting like sissies as they were quietly enlisted into the Maryland National Guard? Was singer Bruce Springsteen a "yella belly" for viewing draftees as "cannon fodder" and doing his best to gain a draft deferment?[99]

The pulps seemed to think so, spitting venom at the "bums" who sought to evade or buy their way out of the draft. *Saga* lashed out at members of the "new left" and the blatant "draft dodging underground" taking hold on college campuses. *Man's Illustrated* condemned the "card-burners" and "slackers" who had worked the system to stay out of uniform.[100] *Male* relied on more gendered language as it railed against "guitar-twanging longhairs" who "blast our courageous GI's in Vietnam, even though the most dangerous weapon they've ever held is a banjo pick." Author Ray Lunt advocated how Americans should "slap down" these unpatriotic complainers lest they influence impressionable kids, "laying the seeds for another draft-dodger generation." Finally, *Bluebook* exposed the "draftable young eggheads" who were using every gimmick to "keep far away from the firing line." Most of these critiques included a not-so-subtle class component, as feminized antiwar protestors seemed to reside mostly on college campuses.[101]

While the adventure mags rebuked draftees who were trying to duck service through fake limps or staggering into draft boards high on LSD, they conveniently avoided any discussion on the veteran antiwar movement. The Vietnam Veterans Against the War (VVAW) seemed to turn the militarized version of masculinity on its head. When protesting vets marched on Washington, DC in April 1971, for example, roughly 800 of them tossed their medals onto the steps of the US Capitol. As one marine sergeant declared, "We strip ourselves of the medals of courage and heroism ... We cast these away as symbols of shame, dishonor, and inhumanity."[102] The disparity between warrior myth and reality could not be more clear. And because more than fifty percent of the vets who joined the VVAW had seen combat in Vietnam, critics could not so easily dismiss them as spoiled, cowardly brats. Men's mags discreetly side-stepped criticism of these antiwarriors, barely mentioning the growing GI counterculture or the underground newspapers proliferating on military bases. Rather, they published letters from young enlistees who were writing their congressmen in hopes of gaining orders for Vietnam. In the macho pulps, "real" men always stood ready to serve their nation in combat.[103]

Since antiwar veterans did not reflect gendered notions of military manhood, it is not surprising they were absent from the pages of *Bluebook* or *Man's Conquest*. Yet as the war lumbered forward, year after year in bloody stalemate, it became increasingly difficult for adventure magazines to avoid criticism of US foreign policy in Southeast Asia. Like *Playboy*, they rarely passed judgment on those US soldiers fighting in the rice paddies and villages of South Vietnam. Occasionally, however, they did speak out against politicians who appeared to be mismanaging the war effort. At the end of 1967, *Stag* maintained that the fighting along the demilitarized zone between North and South Vietnam had been so murderous for US marines because "political considerations" forced them into defensive positions. If Americans were in an "all-out war," they would have been able to hit the enemy from the rear, instead of allowing the Vietcong to "simply come out and fight" before disappearing "whenever they like." Political limitations were not sitting well with pulp editors or their readers.[104]

Senior military leaders equally bristled at what they considered to be civilian interference. To them, DC policymakers were forfeiting the strategic initiative by "ignoring or overriding the counsel of experienced military professionals." Political micromanagement seemed at the heart of the generals' woes. One officer claimed that "policy restraints hindered – if not absolutely precluded – the proper utilization of available forces."[105] In his own memoirs, Westmoreland argued that the president and his civilian advisors had "ignored the maxim that when the enemy is hurting, you don't diminish the pressure, you increase it." Both senior officers and the macho pulps thus helped plant the seeds for future arguments that the US armed forces in Vietnam had been forced to fight with one hand tied behind their back. According to *Bluebook*, the Pentagon even had laser ray guns that, if put to use, would have had Ho Chi Minh screaming for any kind of peace. Warriors in the field apparently had been stabbed in the back by feckless civilians. It would be an appealing reprise for years to come.[106]

By the late 1960s, the warrior image so central to men's adventure magazines appeared far murkier than a decade earlier, perhaps even less convincing to young, working-class readers. After the 1968 Tet offensive, the macho pulps generally followed media trends of being more critical of the war, even if the vast majority of articles continued to focus on the individual exploits of brave soldiers and marines. *Stag* was comparing the rankings of America's most unpopular wars, while *Saga* uncovered the "monstrous lie" of Tet's intelligence failure.[107] Cracks in the myth were beginning to surface as more and more Americans questioned the worth of a wretched, destructive, stalemated war. Might it be possible that the pulps had been selling a version of battlefield heroism that scarcely existed in the real world?

THE UNDISCOVERED ADVENTURE

War is designed to be traumatic and disorienting. It challenges combat soldiers physically and psychologically, forcing them to confront tensions and fears unlike any other human activity. One reconnaissance specialist remembered his time in the field as an "uncomfortable, chronic, nausea-inducing condition" that came from an unshakeable, "ever-present fear." It should be of no surprise that twenty-five to thirty percent of all American casualties in World War II were psychological cases. War comes with a cost. In men's adventure magazines, however, GIs rarely suffered through these emotional ailments. As 1966 came to a close, for instance, *Stag* lauded how there were "so few mental crack-ups among our troops."[108] Pulp warriors might admit they were afraid in the heat of battle, but those fears never incapacitated them when they were needed most.

Because reality in Vietnam often ran far afield from how the war was portrayed in popular culture, soldiers were forced to reconcile this yawning gap between truth and fantasy, to make the irrational seem rational. In the January 1966 issue of *True*, not long after the Ia Drang battle, Malcolm Browne commented on the young draftees in their early twenties then serving with the 1st Cavalry Division. "For all of them, combat is a new and terrible unknown." Surely, some of them must have been excited by the chance to unleash a level of destruction forbidden in their civilian lives. *Stag* took note later in the year of the "staggering number of rounds fired for every Cong killed."[109] Yet how many of these young draftees would have agreed with Philip Caputo that combat was a far different experience than training exercises? To the marine lieutenant, "the real thing proved to be more chaotic and much less heroic than we had anticipated." When *Stag* reported in late 1967 that only half of South Vietnam had been secured despite "close to 100,000 casualties – roughly 12,000 dead – and an investment of nearly 50 billion dollars," the pulp fantasy must have lost some of its luster. Such measly results for so much blood and treasure exposed fundamental flaws in the magazines' portrayal of war.[110]

In large sense, this dichotomy arose because pulp writers and artists were making up their own version of Vietnam. Both the imagined "Orient" and the heroic battlefield were romantic creations conceived in New York City publishing offices. One of the war's more perceptive journalists, Jonathan Schell, argued that Vietnam had a "dream-like quality" because, like a dreamer, Americans faced a reality of their own making. The dream war in Southeast Asia could be at once dangerous and enticing, full of sensuality and sin, all the while offering opportunities to prove one's manhood on the field of battle. Long-standing tropes about Western adventurers taming the "exotic other world in Asia" still resonated in the 1960s. Yet the logic never quite added up. When *Male* argued, for instance, that the US Army's Special Forces were training the "deadliest and most effective guerrilla fighters in the world," the magazine also confessed that Americans were having trouble with "difficult Asian tongues." How was it possible that an unfamiliarity with local dialects did not impede the Green Berets?[111]

Pulp artists reinforced these fantasies with thrilling illustrations of men at war. The March 1966 cover for *Man's Illustrated* showed a grim-faced GI running across a field, M16 rifle in hand, as two Huey helicopter gunships trail behind him. In the background, flames and black

HAIR-RAISING ESCAPE FROM THE ROUMANIAN EXECUTION SQUAD

BLOOD TRAP FOR A CARAVAN OF FREEDOM!

SEPT. 35¢ PDC

man's Life

The Action Magazine For Men

BOOK-LENGTH NOVEL

AMBUSH BY THE BRIDGE AT NANG NAM

SPECIAL MEDICAL REPORT--

HOW AMERICAN WOMEN RATE THEIR MENFOLK!

$26,000,000

WE FOUND THE TREASURE OF THE PIRATE OF BENGAL

BUT WE COULD ONLY TAKE OUT HALF

EXPOSING: THE GIRLS WHO BEG TO BE MASTERED!

Fig. 4.6 *Man's Life*, September 1966

smoke rise into the sky, likely from a hamlet set ablaze. For *Male*'s March 1967 issue, Mort Künstler displayed a US Navy patrol boat careening through a Vietnam river's waters, an old-fashioned sampan off the starboard side. Seven gun and grenade-wielding sailors crowd atop the vessel, spraying bullets in all directions. One year later, *Man's Epic* showcased a Green Beret assaulting a Vietcong-infested tunnel. The American is armed to the nines, firing a rifle while grenades, a pistol, dynamite, and a bayonet all are strapped to his body. Dressed in their recognizable black pajamas, the insurgents clearly are taken by surprise, their faces full of terror. In all these depictions, the Americans unmistakably are on the offensive. These are brave men, each continuing the heroic traditions of their World War II predecessors.[112]

It's likely that few, if any, of these artists had any intimate knowledge of US military operations in South Vietnam, yet they were the ones helping translate a foreign war to young readers back home. Writers followed suit. In *All Man*, a CIA agent goes undercover as a communist sympathizer to learn about North Vietnamese "guerrilla operations," author Magnin Tobar clearly conflating conventional NVA forces with the southern Vietcong. The agent's cover story has him vacationing in Hanoi, where he meets two Russian women whom he quickly seduces. They turn out to be double agents themselves, and all three bring out vital microfilm that deals a heavy blow to the communist regime. The fantasy seems all the more absurd given the story's October 1966 publication date. By then, North Vietnam likely would not have topped many Americans' tourist attraction spots, even if the vacationers were sympathetic to Hanoi's plight. That the American charms two Russian "lovelies" and spends several "highly sensual – and acrobatic – hours" with them only adds to the outlandishness.[113]

As they interpreted the war in such fantastical ways, pulp artists and writers ultimately concocted a Vietnam that bore little resemblance to the real world. The pulps' depiction of Vietnamese culture, geography, politics, and combat all drifted farther away from what the GIs themselves were experiencing. In fact, these fabricated representations began to form even before American combat troops arrived. In early 1962, *Man's Illustrated* ran a piece noting how the NLF was having little trouble enlisting soldiers because each recruit rated three nights in a "local joy house" as part of his basic training. (Of course, readers were not told how South Vietnamese women felt about these transactions.)[114] The following year, *Man's World* noted that "among some Vietnamese tribes it's considered putrid manners if you sleep with a girl without slapping her mother in the mouth first." By 1966, *Male* was suggesting the United

States "go after the Viet Cong with witchcraft" and "make use of the well-known superstitions of the Viets." Thus, whether it be advocating for voodoo or for physical violence against Vietnamese mothers, the pulps were constructing a base of knowledge that left longtime readers wildly unprepared for their military tours in South Vietnam.[115]

One US foreign service officer, Gary Larsen, recalled the outcomes of this ignorance, which he believed led to arrogance. Larsen spoke fluent Vietnamese and argued that when Americans were unaware of the consequences of their presence, they proceeded "blissfully with actions based on ... [a] one-dimensional view of the country and the people."[116] In the pulps, blissful heroic warriors never dealt with any aftereffects of war. Even when seriously wounded, these champions' grit still shone through. In the same issue recommending voodoo in Vietnam, *Male* highlighted marine Colonel Mike Yunck, whose leg was amputated at a Da Nang hospital after his HU-1B helicopter had been hit with .50 caliber machine gun fire. This "courageous fighter," though, was learning how to fly again, despite "the loss of one crummy leg." To *Male*, Yunck was "still the Marines' top ace."[117]

The reality of such injuries often resulted in far less uplifting stories. Ron Kovic's searing memoir *Born on the Fourth of July* offers a prime example of how wounded veterans struggled to maintain their sense of dignity after serious injury. After being paralyzed from the chest down in Vietnam, Kovic lands in a dreadful Bronx VA hospital. It is like "being in a prison." When he complains to an aide that he is a veteran and deserves to be treated decently, the ward fires back "Vietnam don't mean nothin' to me or any of these other people. You can take your Vietnam and shove it up your ass." The event leaves a dejected Kovic wondering what he had lost his legs for and why he and others had gone to Vietnam at all. If *Born on the Fourth of July* does inspire, it is because of Kovic's colossal resiliency in the squalor of a run-down hospital, not in his glorious return to the battlefield in the manner of Colonel Yunck.[118]

When pulp heroes returned home, they did so not as broken warriors like Kovic but as men ready for sexual rewards and adventure. In *Stag's* "Hottest Tease in Town," an ex-Green Beret sergeant, "a year out of the jungles of Vietnam," is enticed by the wife of the richest man in Colby. Though "civilian wear still felt strange to him," Jim successfully meets the "challenge of passion" and has an affair with the beautiful woman. "You're quite a lover," she approvingly utters. By the end of the story, we find the husband has hired Jim to prove his wife is a cheat. The veteran has recorded the entire affair with a reel-to-reel tape recorder hidden in his briefcase but destroys it before heading back to the army recruiting station to reenlist. Thus, he demonstrates both his potent sexuality and, supposedly, his moral superiority over the unfaithful woman.[119]

In another tale from *Stag*, a marine corporal wounded at Khe Sanh returns home after promising a buddy, killed in the same action, that he would check on his wife. When Richard arrives in San Francisco, he meets Judy Prideaux, a "gleaming blond beauty." Soon after, they begin dating, and one evening Judy is accosted by two men on Hyde Street attempting to steal her purse. Despite a bum arm, Richard fends off the assailants before being hit from behind by a thug wearing brass knuckles. Not surprisingly, the marine is rewarded sexually for his knightly valor and spends the next five days in Judy's bed. They ultimately part because she is unwilling to marry, though Richard is "half relieved" to be free of any obligations. Only later does he find that Judy has wed a marine lieutenant on his way to Vietnam.[120]

That Jim and Richard so easily charm such beautiful women suggests they have lost none of their sexual appeal after serving in Vietnam. Their homecomings are an extension of the adventure they experienced on the battlefield. In reality, many veterans arrived home to receive warm welcomes only from family members or close neighbors. An American public frustrated and angry with the war itself seemed ill at ease with soldiers in their midst. As one observer noted in 1980, veterans "returned not as heroes, but as men suspected of complicity in atrocities or feared to be drug addicts."[121] Without question, the vast majority of vets pro-ductively reintegrated back into society, heading back to school, starting families, and rejoining the work force. Yet the pulps' version of the returning champion, a warrior sexually compensated for his heroism displayed in war, never quite seemed to pan out as magazine readers may have hoped.

Nor did the captivity narrative work as advertised in the macho pulps. Some American prisoners of war were accused of collaborating with the enemy while in captivity, and formal military charges were filed soon after their release. Others, like Sergeant George E. Smith, harbored anti-military feelings after returning stateside and were confined by the army for a long "debriefing" period that included threats of a court martial. A 1970 raid on the Son Ty prison camp in North Vietnam, rather than rescuing POWs, came up empty-handed. One senior general curiously deemed the mission "an intelligence failure but an operational success," implying military leaders were uncomfortable with the idea that there might be limits to what Americans could achieve in attempting to rescue their captured warriors. Not all captivity tales ended with a heroic escape from the likes of Dieter Dengler or Charles Klusmann.[122]

In reality, the war in Vietnam for those who fought it proved far more dirty, frightening, and unrewarding than ever depicted in men's adventure magazines. Pop culture fantasies had left young soldiers innocent of war's full fury. As one army sergeant shared in 1970, "If anybody had told me three years ago I'd be doing this stuff – the dead guys and all – I'd have told them they were crazy." Perhaps it was too difficult to relate the true horrors of combat. To a marine lieutenant, words could "hardly describe, if you've never been there, the smell of war, the smell of death, the constant fear of knowing that you were zeroed in."[123] Yet the pulps rarely, if ever, depicted these horrors. On occasion, a photo might appear of a medic waving a "blood-soaked bandage in an effort to get further help to [a] wounded trooper," but these were juxtaposed, on the same page, with shots of pretty Stockholm women wearing "minikinis." The "fierce fighting" after being dropped into the middle of a North Vietnamese regiment might have seemed chilling, but surely boys' eyes lingered on the Swedish models far longer than on the injured soldiers.[124]

The March 1967 issue of *True Action* perhaps best illustrated the jarring transitions between discourse and reality. An article on Vietnam acknowledged that "Cong raiders managed to elude U.S. troops who mounted an all-out search for them through the Viet Nam jungle underbrush." Two pages later, however, the magazine returned to a more appealing storyline as "seven strapping Rangers" led by a "battle-hardened U.S. captain" put "Hitler's Deathmaker Fortress" out of business. Turning the page again led the reader to a cheesecake pictorial on scantily clad Diane, a "luscious legal secretary." A bit farther along, one could find advice for winning women by following Dr. Efrem Schoenhild's "25 Keys to Female Response." The war in Vietnam might not be going well, but at least male readers still could take heart in American victories during World War II and in the pursuit of sexual women back home.[125]

Sensational artwork and dramatic storylines no doubt helped sell magazines. Yet pulp writers and artists too often closed their eyes to the darker side of war. Stories never related fully how Audie Murphy, the boy hero of World War II, actually came home a broken man who saw himself as a "fugitive from the law of averages." Nor did they share public fears that the experience of war in Vietnam might bleed back into the United States. If Murphy, the hero of *To Hell and Back*, had returned a damaged veteran from a "good war," what did that mean for soldiers coming home from a "bad" one like that in Vietnam? If young Americans had become so corrupted by Asian guerrilla fighting that they were killing their own officers in "fragging" incidents, might they also bring those notions back and pose a threat to American society?[126]

These worries manifested themselves most acutely in contemporary fears of the militarized African American. Alarmed that "Negro fighting men" had been radicalized by the Black Power movement and might spread violence once back home, many white Americans cast a wary eye on African American veterans. *Saga* even published an extraordinary letter from a sergeant in Nha Trang who shared how the Black Power movement was taking hold in Vietnam, his anger palpable in only a few short lines – "and when I return from this war that you non-Blacks are forcing me to fight, I'm going to be as militant as your military system has taught me to be. Only you won't like it because it's going to kill you."[127] Of course, few popular media outlets tackled how these vets felt betrayed by a military system that supposedly had been integrated since the Korean War. One black lieutenant shared how his fellow white soldiers hated him as much as "Charlie" did, referring to the Vietcong enemy. Another African American soldier in the 25th Infantry Division remembered feeling "insulated" and "intimidated" by the racism in his basecamp area. For the most part, adventure mags avoided discussion of any racial tensions in Vietnam (or at home), further contributing to a war story isolated from the real world.[128]

As the indecisive war in Vietnam dragged on year after bloody year, American soldiers found it ever more challenging to discover the adventure promised in men's magazines. The trumpets of heroism and victory, extolling how stalwart marines were finally controlling the night in South Vietnam, increasingly rang hollow. A "spooklike" enemy left gaping holes in soldiers' morale. GI dissidents wondered aloud why "American anti-Communist bombs" seemed more effective in killing Vietnamese children rather than the Vietcong.[129] One soldier, Bill Ehrhart, "had no idea – had not the slightest inkling – what I was fighting for or against." Even after the 1968 Tet offensive, the NLF, though damaged, retained its framework, and thus influence, in villages and hamlets across much of South Vietnam.

In the macho pulps, brave warriors had fought for honor, for their comrades, for a sense of triumph. In Vietnam, GIs simply wanted to leave the fighting behind. As one officer recalled, the emphasis became "Let's get the damn thing over. Let's close it out, with as much dignity as we can, but let's just back off and come home." The gaps between truth and fiction seemed insurmountable.[130]

The undiscovered adventure thus generated a lingering sense of anxiety that Vietnam might not be the man-making experience as publicized in the macho pulps. The modern battlefield engendered a sense of helplessness, not heroism. Working-class boys – for the most part – came home from the war without having their manhood validated, rather being judged by sympathetic commentators as "surplus" who "got caught and who died."[131] Moreover, when winning seemed a receding possibility, weary soldiers lowered their sights in the hope of simply surviving the whole ordeal. In the process, some GIs came to view heroism as a "synonym for madness." George Stover succinctly recalled of his time in the 1st Infantry Division, "All heroes do is die good." In the pulps, though, heroes did more than just die. They sacrificed for a greater good, were remembered for their battlefield courage, contributed to the martial lineage of the United States of America. Not so, it appeared, in the lived experiences of the men who actually fought and died in Vietnam.[132]

By the early 1980s, the American public seemed more willing to accept President Ronald Reagan's rebranding of Vietnam as a "noble cause." In the mid to late 1960s, however, the war bred only confusion and despair. Still, the pulps hung on to the fantasy of war as a crucible of manhood, despite the overwhelming evidence invalidating such illusions. More honest reviews spoke of soldiers "confronted by impotence and failure day after day."[133] Frightened American infantrymen felt depressed and powerless, more victim than vanquisher, at least on the shadowy fields of unconventional battle. In the process, uneasy spectators worried that GIs would lash out against the Vietnamese population. A group of "concerned Asian scholars" maintained that operations against the NLF tended to frustrate US soldiers, resulting in "acts of impulsive violence (including murder and rape) on the part of individual GIs."[134]

Debate no doubt will continue for years to come on whether or not these violent acts were "frequent occurrences." Yet, it is undeniable that more than a few discouraged American soldiers in Vietnam took advantage of wartime opportunities to behave aggressively toward the very people they were there to protect. As we have seen throughout this book, the pulps played an outsized role in contributing to a portrait of a manly warrior, conquering enemy forces in alien, savage lands, and, frequently, the women who resided there as well. For the men who were schooled by the Cold War pulps, actual experiences in Vietnam proved nothing like what they expected from stories of adventure and domination. Therefore, a climate of deep frustration against the backdrop of a bloody but vague war might have contributed to violence against Vietnamese people in general and women in particular. After all, had not the macho pulps for years been promising them the sexual rewards of an exotic Orient?[135]

CHAPTER 5

War and Sexual Violence Come to Vietnam

ABOVE DROWNED MANGROVE SWAMPS and mud-banked canals, a UH-1B Huey helicopter flies low to the ground, roughly 175 miles northeast of Saigon. An American pilot sits at the controls, the chopper circling around a lone, thatch-roofed hut. Captain Kok Quong, a liaison with the South Vietnamese Army (ARVN) Rangers is on board. "It could be a Viet Cong arms or food depot," he surmises. As the pilot lands to investigate, shadowy figures emerge from the reeds on both sides of the hut. A short, violent firefight ensues but the guerrillas flee, leaving Quong to recommend that his Rangers in an accompanying transport helicopter land, fan out, and make a sweep on foot and in rubber boats. The American aviator is skeptical – the VC never mass together to make large-scale offensives worthwhile. Still, they decide to pursue, and, over the next two days, the Rangers "bag" sixty-five Vietcong, thanks largely to this small US "Huey air force." As *Stag*'s Carl Sherman reports, the Americans are a bright spot in a "long, discouraging war with the communists" that has been "dragging along for over eight, frustrating years ... without making an appreciable dent in either the number or activities of the Viet Cong guerrillas." It is January 1964.[1]

These frustrations continued long after American ground combat troops arrived in South Vietnam the following year. Like their ARVN counterparts, US soldiers and marines also would make assumptions about whether rural farmers were National Liberation Front (NLF) sympathizers or loyal government supporters. Worse, their combat experiences rarely lived up to dreams stoked by Cold War popular culture, where brave cavalry troopers always defeated the savage Indians.

In Vietnam, the ambushes never seemed to end and, along the way, a "gook syndrome" became pervasive – to frightened Americans, all Vietnamese were "equally bad." As their fantasies of heroic combat dissolved, GIs progressively viewed the war as an absurd, morally inverted misadventure. One exasperated soldier asked, "What am I doing here? We don't take any land. We don't give it back. We just mutilate bodies. What the fuck are we doing here?" Every year the war dragged on, fundamental questions like these became harder and harder to answer.[2]

If some young American men felt terrified and disillusioned by their combat experiences, surely among them were those who still hoped to prove their masculinity while in Vietnam. Many turned to local women in hopes of filling the void. Likely, military leaders realized this, one deployed officer noting how his in-processing briefings included subjects "from the current Viet Cong infrastructure to the common venereal diseases in Vietnam." Another GI, who interviewed some 100 new arrivals in Cam Ranh Bay, found they had little to say about the war's larger issues, as "the men's personal concerns were mostly sexual." As developed in the pulps, women were ripe for the taking in war-torn Asia, especially by the heroic warriors who occupied the country.[3]

In some veteran narratives, the male protagonist clearly triumphed as both heroic warrior and sexual champion. John "Doc" Bahnsen's memoir – aptly titled *American Warrior* – fits this description well. Only fifty pages in, Bahnsen recounts how he left behind "four small kids and a faithful wife" in Georgia, swearing that he would never become involved with a "native woman." "I broke that vow shortly after arriving in Vietnam," he recalls. At a local bar, the young captain encounters Thach Thi Hung, the "Dragon Lady of Bien Hoa," whom he seduces the very first night they meet. She is an "enchanting woman" and Bahnsen finds her "wise" beyond her twenty-five years. He tells Hung that he will not give up his family for another woman, "a fact incongruous with my behavior at the time, but no less the truth." Bahnsen is quick to point out that Hung does not mind, since she thinks the American is "cute" and she has a "*thing* for pilots." To no avail, the American aviator encourages a pregnant Hung to have an abortion, returning to the United States unsure "what she was gaining by having our child without me around to help." Brave men rarely suffer war's consequences.[4]

Yet what happened when Vietnamese women did not throw themselves at American GIs like they did in Bahnsen's memoir or in men's adventure magazines? According to popular understanding, all local women were ripe for the picking. One American psychiatrist who spent a year at the University of Saigon believed Vietnamese women had "the softest skin in all the Orient," while a pulp writer supposed they were "among the most sensual in the world." If so many US servicemen felt "impotent" from indecisive fighting against an elusive enemy, might they not gain a sense of satisfaction through the sexual conquest of women apparently hard-wired to please? Shrapnel and bullets exposed the weakness of human flesh. Perhaps sexually dominating the "most beautiful flowers" of Vietnam would reinforce one's masculinity, a shield behind which to deal with war's frustrations.[5]

The problem, of course, was that relatively few Vietnamese women acted according to male fantasies. Certainly, female prostitutes contributed to Senator J. William Fulbright's assessment that Saigon had become "both figuratively and literally an American brothel." But most Vietnamese were not the erotic seductresses of pulp illusion. Many young readers must have assumed that Asian women were available to them, overlooking the inherent racism within writers' depictions of Saigon as a "slant-eyed Sodom."[6] American men were exceptional, so they imagined, and thus desirable. Likely, few GIs thought twice about their sexual aggressiveness, their hassling of women on Saigon streets, their demands for female attention, or their foul treatment of bar girls. Even fewer presumably considered how their sexual ultimatums might be an outgrowth of the anxiety and rage they felt from being locked in a stalemated war.[7]

In their unique way, men's adventure magazines contributed to a culture which found it acceptable to engage in sexual aggression toward and violence against Vietnamese women. The causal links, of course, were never so neat. Reading macho pulps did not mean GIs inevitably committed rape in Vietnam. But the mags did provide rhetorical space for readers to think along the lines of sexual conquest, to deem all "Oriental" women as opportunities – for sex, for proving one's manhood, for demonstrating power over the savage other. The pulps were a cultural, if not ideological lens through which American men viewed

Southeast Asia, long before they ever deployed there. In adventure magazines, sexual coercion was normal, consent and female subservience assumed. Moreover, wartime apparently suspended any moral questioning over acceptable male behavior. Many GIs perceived both consensual sex and forcible rape as time-honored byproducts of war, either a "just reward" or inevitable "collateral damage." For nearly two decades, the macho pulps had conveyed long-standing assumptions on these bonds between war and sex. Thus, soldiers arriving in Vietnam disembarked carrying high expectations alongside their olive drab duffle bags.[8]

When these expectations failed to materialize in an increasingly meaningless war, the resulting disappointments threatened to undermine GIs' sense of manhood and identity. An inability to exercise control over the enemy had ruptured martial fantasies. On the largely unconventional battlefields of South Vietnam, many soldiers decidedly had *not* affirmed their masculinity. Far different from adventure mags, military heroism had proven frustratingly elusive. How many working-class soldiers then looked to sexual triumphs as a way to compensate, to regain their sense of superiority? When half of the pulp vision – the noble warrior – collapsed, it is plausible that many GIs turned to the other half – the sexual conqueror of foreign women – as a way to satisfy their psychological needs for control.[9]

At least soldiers and marines could prevail over the civilian population, or so was the hope. In line with such thinking, Vietnamese women became natural targets, Americans' fears over losing control fostering sexually violent fantasies that might then be acted upon. The pulps surely encouraged such illusions. If an Asian woman was implicitly erotic, as the magazines reiterated year after year, did not the ability to overcome her sexual prowess, to satisfy her, demonstrate a "real" man's masculinity? This must have fueled the imaginations of more than a few teenage readers-turned-soldiers. Of course, sexual violence and rape in war hardly center on satisfying the victim. Far from it. More often than not, these aggressive actions were (and are) blatant displays of power over individuals, if not entire societies. Vietnam proved no different, with immensely tragic results. Women were now squarely on the front lines of war.

A POPULATION AT WAR

Even before American combat troops arrived in Southeast Asia, senior leaders in the US Military Assistance Command, Vietnam (MACV) realized that promoting a healthy relationship between the rural population and the Saigon regime would be crucial to defeating the communist insurgency. Success depended on local government being "responsive to and involving the participation of the people." To MACV, this was the heart of the allied pacification program. Gaining control over the population surely mattered, but only as a stepping-stone toward the people voluntarily contributing to the political process. The Americans could partner in this development, but ultimately the population had to trust that its government was *the* legitimate entity in South Vietnam and committed to bettering the lives of all South Vietnamese.[10]

In many Americans' eyes, however, that population seemed incapable of acting in a trustworthy manner. GIs regularly complained of locals being openly friendly yet secretly disdainful. Portable lie detector tests to evaluate "the loyalty of native troops" proved ineffective. Even women and children could not be trusted. *Male* noted how US troops would enter a village and question a young boy who insisted he spent all his time taking care of his mother and sisters. "Ten minutes later," the mag related, "all hell breaks loose, with U.S. unit almost annihilated – and when they go looking for that 'innocent' kid they never find him."[11] Army nurse Winnie Smith remembered in her memoir taking care of a wounded Vietnamese girl with a 106 degree temperature. The on-call doctor was hardly sympathetic. "Let her die! She was probably tossing a grenade at our guys when she got shot." When Smith protested, the surgeon doubled down. "She's a gook! Bust your ass to save her life, and she's likely to return the favor by blowing up another one of our guys." If MACV leaders were hoping to nurture a democratic political process, they confronted major obstacles when so many individual Americans felt they were being "cheated" by the Vietnamese.[12]

Within this atmosphere of distrust, US and ARVN troops struggled mightily to gain an advantage, not just over enemy combatants, but over the population as well. While Americans castigated rural Vietnamese as being politically unsophisticated, local grievances mattered, thus facilitating the NLF's attempts in constructing a shadow government that might contest GVN rule. Eliminating political competition, however, inescapably brought terror to villagers' doorsteps.[13] *Stag* underlined this point with an early-1967 photograph of a US marine surveying a dummy, lashed in a hangman's noose, swinging from the roof of a deserted hut near Da Nang. The effigy represented "death to South Vietnamese leaders who cooperate with the Americans." The social implications of such wartime terror were readily apparent. That same year, *True* ran a set of artist John Groth's sketches, one of them depicting young boys watching while American GIs dug foxholes. "Solemn-faced Vietnamese children are omnipresent," the caption read. "Only the very young ones ever smile. The children are old at 10." Everywhere, it seemed, war-weary civilians might turn against their protectors at any moment, blurring the battlefield lines between democratic aspirations and communist intrigue.[14]

Undeniably, American soldiers worked hard to help build a stable South Vietnamese state as they sought to destroy their ally's external and internal enemies. Nation-building and warfighting always were parallel efforts, and men's magazines made sure to highlight the benevolent, modernizing efforts of these "gentle warriors." In *True*, Malcolm Browne spotlighted one Green Beret sergeant who "could be ruthless in battle, but he could also spend a whole month's pay to help out an impoverished Vietnamese family." The following issue, Browne made note of a medic, sweat pouring "down the young soldier's face as he found himself in war trying to save a woman's life."[15] In other magazine offerings, navy technicians adopted children from Catholic orphanages, medics administered smallpox vaccines to Montagnard mothers, and "Warriors on Bulldozers" constructed vital transportation infrastructure. When US Army Captain Paul L. Miles, a "tanned and whip-thin" Rhodes Scholar from Metter, Georgia, oversaw operations at Cam Ranh Bay, the engineer officer was "working wonders with men who were mostly young, some of them just two months off the farm or away from the corner drugstore." These citizen-soldier warriors might destroy, but the pulps hoped to show that they could build just as well.[16]

Yet inherent paradoxes existed within the simultaneous process of building while destroying. The South Vietnamese refugee population spiked in the wake of devastating military operations. Capitalism proved far more exportable than democracy, wreaking havoc on the local economy. If *True Action* was correct in 1967 that "the war has gone on too long and the people are sick of it," then how could it ever be possible for Americans to win over the "hearts and minds" of the Vietnamese people?[17] Worse, any gains made in the political arena tended to be incommensurate with the damage inflicted by military operations, a destructive yet necessary component of the larger war effort. As frustrations mounted, counterinsurgency scholars of the day warned that the "pressure to meet terror with counterterror will at times seem irresistible, but to do so is to play into the guerrilla's game... Brutality, fear, and the resultant social disorganization can only work for the guerrillas." That may have been true, but as Americans increasingly adopted the motto "never trust anybody" as their best chance of survival, a supposedly ambivalent, if not hostile, population came more and more to be seen as an adversary rather than an objective.[18]

In such a wartime environment, where pulp readers were promised both power and pleasure, where the helping hand became a hand of destruction, it was not difficult for American soldiers to view sex as both an outlet and a weapon. If the people were hostile, might not GIs retaliate against women with threats and acts of sexual violence? As an instrument of war, rape long has been effective in terrorizing and humiliating the local population, an efficient tool to forcibly gain the compliance of civilians. It is hard to support assertions, however, that official US policy called for sexual violence against the Vietnamese population.[19] Without doubt, at least some boot camp drill instructors assured recruits they could rape Vietnamese women. Once deployed, many soldiers and marines failed to question orders that led to them violating innocent civilians caught in the crossfire of war. Too often, commanders only lightly punished sexual assaults or looked the other way when their subordinates acted irresponsibly. Yet none of these transgressions resulted from command policy. Rape was not a sanctioned strategy for attaining US political objectives in Vietnam.[20]

Still, Americans did engage in sexual violence throughout much of the war. Part of this could be explained by "Orientalist" attitudes which depicted Asian women as "creatures of a male power-fantasy." Surely, the

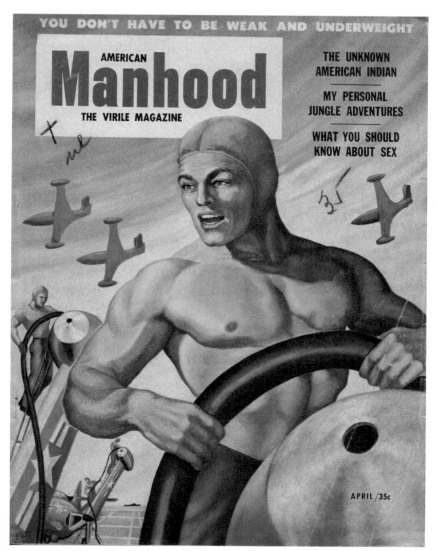

Fig. 1 *American Manhood*, March/April 1953

Fig. 2 *Battle Cry*, July 1959

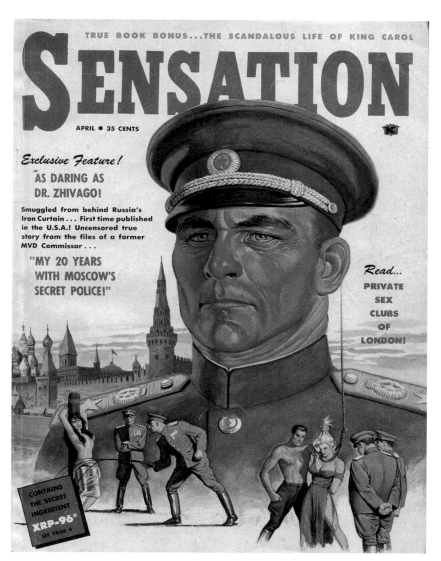

Fig. 3 *Sensation*, April 1959

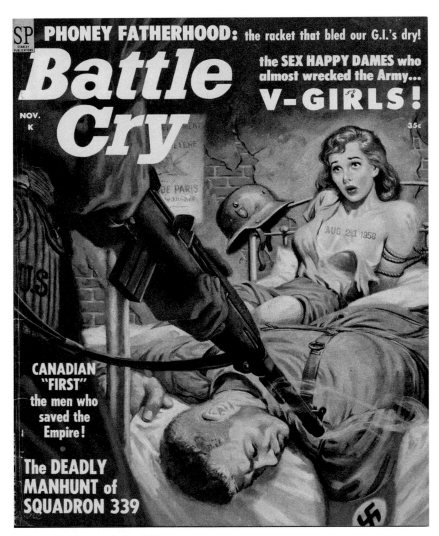

Fig. 4 *Battle Cry*, November 1958

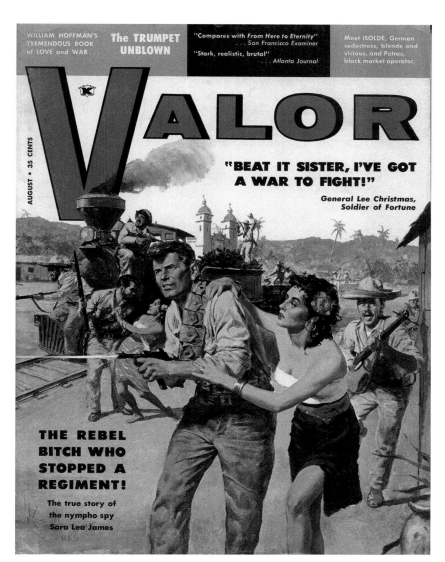

Fig. 5 *Valor*, August 1959

SEX BELOW THE 38TH PARALLEL

A naked look at the war within a war: how U.S. fighting men handled those wild and wacky Asian women

BY DIRK BRADLEY

ILLUSTRATED BY JOHN McDERMITT

■ IN mid-summer of 1950, the fortunes of the U.S. Korean Expeditionary Force were at their lowest point. Armored Communist patrols were prodding the thin defenses of the Pusan Perimeter, and alarming pips on sonar screens in the Straits of Korea made the Navy fear that marauding Russian submarines would slash our vital supply line from Japan.

Among those most concerned was the provost marshal of Pusan. Studying a chart that illustrated the staggering amount of petty gear and groceries being siphoned out

Fig. 6 *Saga*, August 1963

Fig. 7 *Big Adventure*, June 1961

Fig. 8 *Men*, May 1962

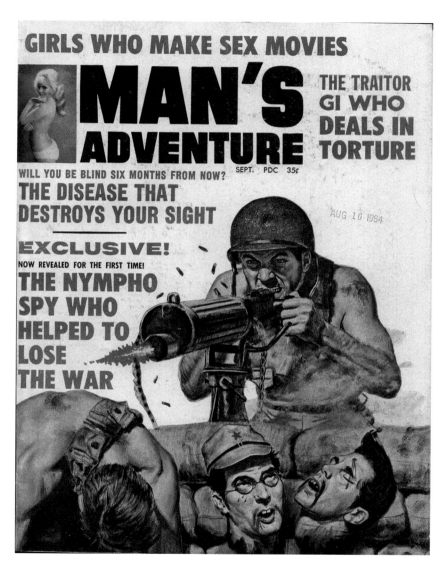

Fig. 9 *Man's Adventure*, September 1964

Fig. 10 *True Men Stories,* October 1958

Fig. 11 *Brigade*, March 1963

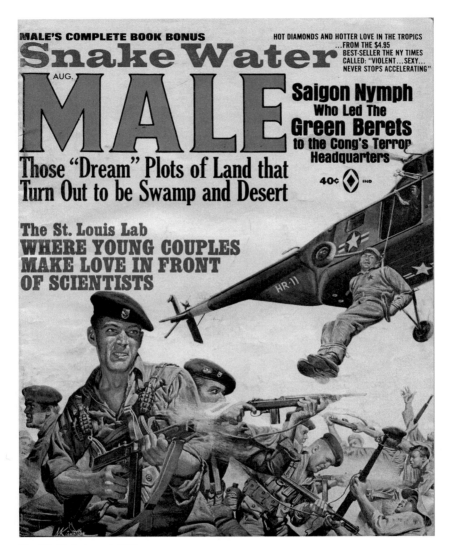

Fig. 12 *Male*, August 1966

Fig. 13 *Man's Illustrated,* March 1966

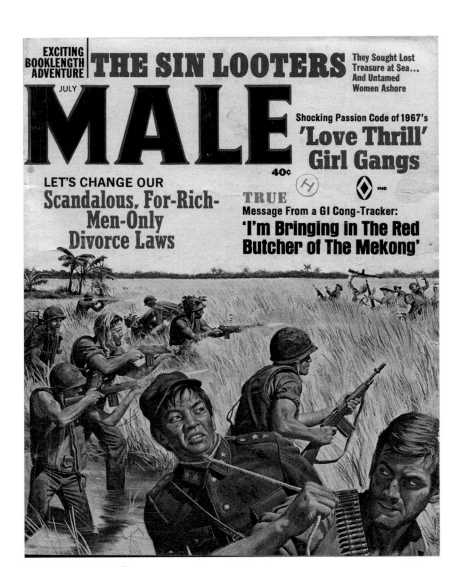

Fig. 14 *Male*, July 1967

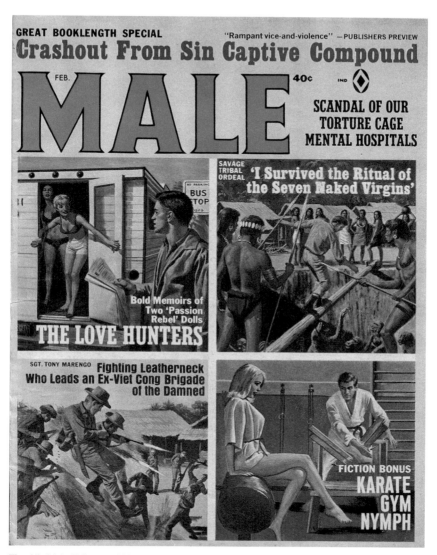

Fig. 15 *Male*, February 1968

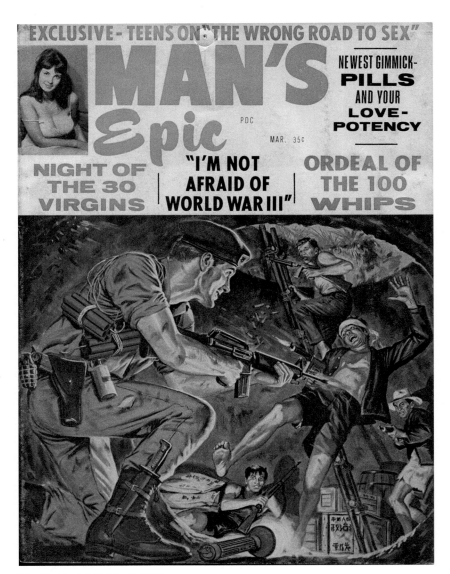

Fig. 16 *Man's Epic*, March 1968

macho pulps made clear that readers' sexual fantasies were possible. *For Men Only* ran a photo spread of Maria Minh, "Mademoiselle from Saigon," who was "one part French, one part Asian and two parts just terrific." *Male* also published a story in which the half-French, half-Vietnamese Lilli-minh serves as the female protagonist.[21] Yet Orientalism also rested on the belief that these women were not only licentious, but also culturally inferior, perhaps even subhuman. The European blood in Maria and Lilli's veins no doubt made them more acceptable to ravenous Americans. These beautiful women, however, were still part of a "primitive" society, illiterate peasants cut off from "civilization" whose minds and morals had atrophied beyond saving. For GIs pursuing sexual release in a disheartening war, the Vietnamese "nymph" must have appealed as an alluringly easy target of their desires.[22]

While countless Americans saw Asian women only as objects, an inability to differentiate the real from the imagined also contributed to wartime sexual violence. In Vietnam, GIs engaged in a variety of sexual encounters – from consensual sex and commercial prostitution to forcible rape. In the process, many often failed to discriminate between "available" and "unavailable" women, frequently misconstruing violence with sex. One marine described a horrific scene in which members of his unit gang-raped a girl, the last man making "love" to her before shooting her in the head. In a similar episode, a soldier noted how the female victim "submitted freely" to rape so she would not be killed.[23] These GIs' descriptions suggest how cultural representations of sex and gender were being reproduced in Vietnam. The September 1966 issue of *Stag*, for instance, spoke in eerily similar terms. "When a woman cries before sex – especially if she's new at it – it's no sign she wants you to stop," the magazine claimed. "Usually [it] means just the opposite and the tears only mean she's a little ashamed of her own desire." If men heard "yes" when women said "no" at home, what chance did a Vietnamese woman have who protested acts of sexual aggression in a time of war?[24]

Conflating consensual sex with rape might also be seen as the result of American arrogance and disregard leveled toward a population immersed in war. While many US advisors gained a deep admiration for their Vietnamese comrades, innumerable GIs looked down upon local women, their roles as "hooch maids," bar girls, and prostitutes only reinforcing soldiers' condescension. Dependency on Americans to make a wartime living left these women with a stark dilemma. The war had forced many of them to engage in unseemly activities to help provide for their families, yet when they did, Americans found them objectionable, if not repulsive.[25] Worse, the entire Vietnamese society appeared complicit. One US helicopter crew chief believed that children would "sell their mothers and sisters for a gang rape for enough piasters." Not all, though, placed blame on the Vietnamese. A sympathetic pulp reader shared with *Man's Magazine* how most Americans behaved overseas. "All the women here are easy game and I can buy your girl, wife or sister for a carton of cigarettes. With this GI attitude," the letter writer argued, "no wonder American soldiers aren't liked." Here was the definition of misogyny – desiring someone you despised.[26]

As in so many Orientalist narratives, women's voices remained silent. Likely, few Americans considered how Vietnamese families felt as their daughters interacted with outsiders. When Duong Van Mai fell in love with her future husband, Sergeant David Elliott, her father was "distressed by the shame," declaring that if she married an American, "everyone in Vietnam would take [her] for a whore."[27] For those women in far crueler situations, forced to use their bodies as "bargaining chips" for food or money, the sexual debasement must have been excruciating. One account of the 1968 fighting in Hue details a female refugee offering sex in exchange for a C-ration meal. "There was no shortage of takers." Similar barters took place in World War II, with both French and German women, suggesting many women in war viewed this trading of sex for food as a matter of life or death. This "entitlement rape" further blurred the lines for how some GIs thought about consensual sex and prostitution. If a woman sold her body to save herself and her family from starvation, how consensual was the sexual exchange?[28]

Arguably, not many American soldiers in Vietnam ever bothered to consider such troubling questions. For GIs growing up on the macho pulps, wartime sex was about satiating masculine needs, most certainly *not* an economic necessity for survival. Many Vietnamese women, though, approached sex from a far more dehumanizing perspective. Le Ly Hayslip's harrowing memoir, for instance, is replete with sexual trauma, detailing how young women she knew made money by selling products like cigarettes and chocolate to American soldiers at basecamps. This eventually led to prostitution because the exchange garnered more money.[29] GIs thus participated willingly in the commodification of women's bodies, viewing prostitution as little more than a time-honored tradition of the Orient. The pulps long had made that notion clear, a trend continuing throughout the war. Given the supposedly inherent eroticism of Asian women, Americans like journalist Peter Arnett almost reflexively imagined that "heads of families did not think twice before routinely selling their daughters if they needed the money." Of course, Vietnamese women, not American GIs, were suffering most from the burdens and moral injuries of this sexual capitalism.[30]

These ties between capitalism, consumerism, and sex were prevalent themes in Cold War adventure magazines. The experience of war in South Vietnam only buttressed impressions of seductive Asian women who "had something to gain" from the American presence. When a prostitute offered herself to a GI, did the proposition reinforce stereotypes from the macho pulps? *Saigon after Dark* author Philip Marnais described the GVN capital in 1967 as "a terribly lonely town for the average GI, and his loneliness is ruthlessly exploited by the city's pimps and prostitutes."[31] *Male* ran a short piece the same year, noting one Vietnamese lawyer who was calling for a relegalization of prostitution, which had been outlawed by President Ngo Dinh Diem back in 1955. While the editorial praised how this change might cut down on the "skyrocketing" venereal disease rates in South Vietnam, it also highlighted a Pleiku brothel in which the "girls, all supervised by a matron, are able to take care of 100 to 300 soldiers a day – earning from $60 to $112 per month plus room and board." Prostitution may have been relatively profitable, but these types of exchange must have been physically and emotionally devastating. Nor could they have contributed to Americans thinking very highly of Vietnamese women more generally.[32]

Of course, men's magazines tended to focus on the exploits of US servicemen, not the psychological or physical injuries borne by Vietnamese women who may have lost a piece of themselves in the degrading solicitation of wartime sex. Rather, the pulps viewed prostitution as promoting men's "rugged individualism," an opportunity for soldiers to spend a night with "pretty tramps."[33] But what happened when a

Vietnamese woman did not willingly give herself to an entitled American GI as the magazines had promised? Did her refusal lead to frustration, to resentment, and, in some cases, even to violence? In the world of men's adventure, an Asian woman had one function – to sexually gratify the heroic warrior. When she declined to fulfill that purpose, popular notions of American manhood appeared to sanction men taking their allegedly rightful prizes regardless of consent.[34]

"WAR CULTURE"

In late January 1971, the Vietnam Veterans Against the War (VVAW) held a three-day event in Detroit to publicize war crimes and atrocities in Southeast Asia. Dubbed the Winter Soldier Investigation, the forum produced more than 200 allegations of criminal behavior on the part of American GIs. Lance Corporal Thomas Heidtman, formerly of the 1st Marine Division, reported seeing frequent instances of women with their clothes ripped, "just because they were female and they were old enough for somebody to get a laugh at." One participant argued the war had devolved into an "atrocity-producing situation," another maintaining that the deliberate and indiscriminate killing of civilians had become "standard operating procedure." Sergeant Jamie Henry, who had served with the US Army's 4th Infantry Division, testified watching two men take a young, naked Vietnamese girl out of a "hootch" and assuming "she had been raped, which was pretty SOP." If men were supposed to demonstrate their heroism in war, to proudly embody American democracy abroad, these Winter Soldiers told a far less ennobling tale.[35]

Blame for these moral transgressions, to include wartime rape, reached far and wide. Some critics alleged that MACV's pressure for high body counts to measure the number of enemy dead led to GIs embracing the "mere-gook rule" which deemed Vietnamese lives as cheap. Others blamed stateside drill instructors, whose hypermasculine training methods produced soldiers who wanted to "prove themselves as men by becoming killers." Still others, like legal scholar Rhonda Copelon, have impugned war itself, which, she argues, tends to "intensify the brutality, repetitiveness, public spectacle and likelihood of rape."[36]

Finally, there are those who level charges against the corrupt socializing influences of military culture. Duke University law professor Madeline Morris illustratively maintains that military organizations can foster the "acceptance, transmission, and elaboration of rape-conducive norms" that may lead to wartime sexual violence. Of course, any nation's armed forces are an extension of the society which they serve, making it difficult to fully disassociate military norms from larger cultural ones. If Vietnam-era soldiers believed war gave them a license to rape, those expectations likely had some cultural underpinnings.[37]

Men's adventure magazines occasionally demonstrated that combat, in fact, did hold the potential to erode one's moral standards, a common refrain of GI memoirists from Vietnam. Back in 1952, with the war in Korea still raging, an article in *Men* suggested that when a combat soldier lost his senses, he became a "terrible, effective and vindictive killer." Ten years later, the magazine showcased a World War II marine sergeant, Clark Kaltenbaugh, who undertook an "incredible revenge campaign" after losing buddies during hard fighting on Guadalcanal in 1942. For three years, the leatherneck battled across the Pacific in some of the most bitter operations of the entire war. When shipped home in July 1945, he had killed forty-three enemy soldiers.[38]

If the marine sergeant had become numb to so much killing, his successors in Vietnam would have understood the moral descent. Philip Caputo recalled members of his company passing "beyond callousness into savagery." Army lieutenant James McDonough seemed to agree, describing war as "the absence of order; and the absence of order leads very easily to the absence of morality."[39] In both cases, the men under these officers' command often seethed with revenge, as did Kaltenbaugh a generation before. Fear may have blurred the ethics of combat, but so too did anger. In one 1968 issue of *True Action*, a Vietcong raiding party overwhelms a South Vietnamese garrison and executes the local mayor and his three sons. The response is obvious, at least to the magazine: "To recover face for the American forces, the Viet Cong raiders must not be allowed to go unpunished." Such storylines understandably sought to punish the VC aggressor, but they also put Americans, and their South Vietnamese allies, in a cycle of perpetual violence.[40]

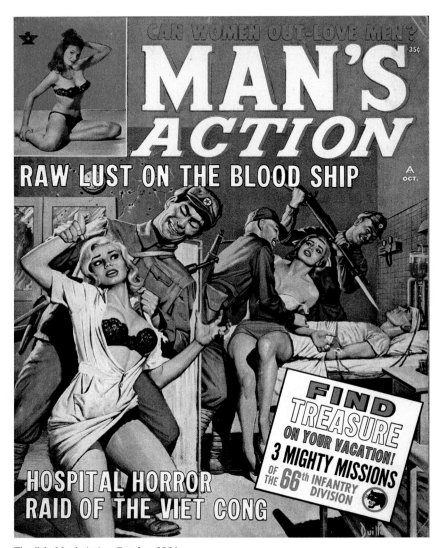

Fig. 5.1 *Man's Action*, October 1964

The language of violence used by Vietnam-era soldiers mirrored that in the macho pulps. GIs spoke of having a "sense of power" and a "sense of destruction." Many admitted they enjoyed the act of killing, one marine clearly working through the psychological wounds of war as he shared his story. "I really loved fucking killing, I couldn't get enough," the veteran recalled. "For every one that I killed I felt better. Made some of the hurt went away [*sic*]." Adventure mags seemed to reinforce the ease with which GIs slipped into a "primitive state of mind."[41] A Korean War vet wrote a personal account for *Action*, divulging that he had gone "kill-crazy" after Chinese troops had killed his half-brother. In "Blood Feast in the Hürtgen Forest," *Battle Cry* published the tale of an American sergeant who "loved to fight" and "lived to kill Krauts," the NCO's idea of fun apparently being to grab extra ammunition and go "Kraut-hunting." When *Man's World* ran a 1967 story of a "go-it-alone guerrilla demon" who fought a "no-holds-barred private war that left the occupied Philippines littered with Japanese corpses," the locale and enemy easily could have been moved to South Vietnam without altering the plotline in any significant way.[42]

Indeed, the March 1968 massacre at My Lai exemplified the murderous violence inflicted upon a war-weary population. Debate endures over whether the killing of roughly 500 noncombatants was an aberration or emblematic of US military operations in South Vietnam. Still, language similar to what readers might find in the macho pulps resonated throughout testimonies of the horrific episode. One soldier in the infantry company committing the atrocity, while not firing his own weapon, believed his peers had decided the "epitome of courage and manhood was going out and killing a bunch of people."[43] Another veteran spoke of the killings as "scratching an itch," just something that veterans in Korea and World War II had done only a few decades earlier. That soldiers viewed Quang Ngai province as hostile "Indian Country" only heightened their sense of anxiety. Lieutenant William L. Calley, Jr., the only officer convicted of wrongdoing, recalled his fear that tragic day – "nearly everyone had it. And everyone had to destroy it: My Lai, the source of it."[44]

Without question, Calley failed miserably as a leader at My Lai by not enforcing distinctions between combatants and civilians. He participated in the murders as well, compounding moral deficiencies that became apparent only after the story broke publicly in late 1969. Yet the episode may have rung familiar to pulp readers. Like Sergeant Kaltenbaugh's "revenge campaign," Calley's men were seeking payback after their unit sustained casualties in the weeks leading up to the massacre. Audie

Murphy, an adventure mag hero himself, said he was "distressed and shocked" over the guilty verdict imposed upon Calley. Evoking "kill-crazy" phraseology, the convicted lieutenant acknowledged not seeing old men, women, and children in Son My village, simply the "enemy." Once more, the pulps did not initiate this kind of violence. But they did aid in promoting a narrative framework in which the violence against foreign peoples made sense to the perpetrators.[45]

In pop culture combat stories, the enemy warranted little quarter and even less sympathy. (Such was the outcome of underlying racial and cultural conditioning.) Given the problems of differentiating between friend and foe in Vietnam, no wonder GIs held an indifferent, if not hostile, attitude toward the population. Marine Lieutenant Lewis B. Puller, Jr. remembered being "deeply offended by the notion that the hideous atrocities committed by Calley and his men were common-place." But soldier testimonials suggested that the mindsets underpin-ning the My Lai killings were not so exceptional.[46] GIs recalled kicking pregnant women, shooting children, burning "hooches," and not con-sidering rural farmers even people. *Stag* noted in early 1967 that GIs were griping when placed in defensive positions protecting the population. "They feel they should be in combat – killing Cong." Unless leaders stepped in to draw a line, army lieutenant James McDonough declared, men would gradually, but directly, move from stealing sodas to raping young women.[47]

Puller surely was correct in arguing that the men he led in combat were "like any cross section of American youth, capable of good and evil." It seems worth considering, though, how GIs who committed evil deeds may have judged them normal given the wartime setting. What made killing or raping civilians immoral at home yet acceptable in Vietnam? If a "war culture" had desensitized men into accepting violence as ordinary, preexisting sociocultural dynamics must also have eased men into thinking along such lines. For decades, the postwar pulps had linked American manhood with power – physical, social, economic, and military power. In Vietnam, when combat failed to deliver ways of realiz-ing that power against an elusive enemy, armed soldiers at least might find meaning by exercising dominance over a frightened population. As one veteran pronounced, "A gun is power. To some people carrying a gun constantly was like having a permanent hard on. It was a pure sexual trip every time you got to pull the trigger." The best of the pulp writers could not have said it better.[48]

Of course, none of these American GIs operated in a moral vacuum, and both pulp writers and veteran memoirists made sure to highlight the barbarism of the Vietcong. The October 1964 issue of *Man's Action* included a story of an American doctor who joins a Vietnamese medical mission. Two "stunning" female nurses are part of the team, one of whom already has been sexually assaulted by the VC. When the same communists raid the doctor's hospital, they forcibly strip the women and kill a man before being subdued by our hero. In another 1966 tale from *Man's Life*, a South Vietnamese militia soldier comes across the ghastly remains of a local village wife who had been raped by five Vietcong and then bayoneted to death. McDonough's memoir recounts a similar scene in which his platoon encounters a dead village elder, her breasts "half-severed from her body" because she had taken in children "whose parents had been scattered by the war." He and his men are left grieving over this "particularly grotesque" act of violence. Critics might have claimed that the VC were far more selective in their use of terror, but such arguments persuaded neither American GIs nor long-suffering South Vietnamese, who grew tired of the Vietcong's annual demands for more taxes and manpower. In this grinding war of military and political attrition, malevolence could be found in spades on either side.[49]

In such a *guerre sale*, winning over an understandably reluctant population was immensely difficult. Village and hamlet leaders often entered into tacit agreements with each side in hopes of riding out the storm. Americans, particularly those engaged in pacification efforts, surely did their best to assist local communities and persuade local residents into supporting the Saigon regime, either through rural construction projects or by medical assistance programs. On occasion, the pulps took notice. *Male* credited gentle GIs who, "very quietly, have shown themselves to be more generous and compassionate in Viet Nam than any other fighting group in history. When they get food packages from friends and relatives in the States, their first impulse is to distribute this to the Vietnamese needy." Yet Americans remained wary of civilians caught between two competing political entities, one advisor believing that the VC "shrewdly were getting the better of the bargain" because of the population's lack of confidence in the GVN. For all the effort put into winning hearts and minds, the impact appeared minimal at best.[50]

In some measure, the pacification effort simply could not overcome American attitudes that had been reproduced for years in the postwar pulps. The magazines had claimed that real men were superior, in every way. Those presumptions settled into the lexicon of the American war in Vietnam, ultimately helping inspire fear and hatred of the population itself. Colonel David H. Hackworth recalled that men in his battalion not only considered ARVN soldiers thieves and "lazy bastards," but their contacts with the people came from dealings with the "dregs of Vietnamese society – corrupt soldiers, bar girls, whores, pimps, hustlers, dope peddlers and clip-joint operators."[51] Another infantryman admitted that "the death of any Vietnamese, not just the enemy, was looked upon with no more pity than a hunter gives his prey." Neither of these commentaries suggested much sympathy with civilians who daily had to prove, sometimes to both sides, they truly were noncombatants. Adventure magazines may not have been a cause of the war culture in Vietnam, but a parallel language certainly was present as Americans interacted with a population many judged as completely inferior.[52]

If macho pulps inspired a sense of cultural, if not racial, superiority, they also encouraged the fantasy, which had been built up over more than a decade, that sex was a vital part of war. Vietnam seemingly proved no different. *Man's Illustrated* reported in early 1966 that there were "damned few complaints from GI's about bedroom cooperation from the local belles." The only "gripe," readers learned, was that "formerly sheltered Vietnamese gals haven't much imagination. That's why a couple of enterprising noncoms have imported a half-dozen doxies from Japan – to teach the Viets a few tricks." One year later, *Man's Magazine* erroneously informed their subscribers of the GVN's efforts in setting up "red light districts," specifically catering to US servicemen, in major cities like Saigon and Da Nang. These locales, however, paled in comparison to the port city of Alongapo, in the Philippines' Subic Bay. According to *True Action*, this favorite spot of the US Navy had 20,000 residents in the town, 17,500 of whom were prostitutes. Surely, pulp readers would be hard pressed to find a small town back home where nearly ninety percent of the population existed only to pleasure American men.[53]

Veterans imitated this demeanor in their own recollections of the war. One USAID officer spoke of the problems communicating and having a "real" relationship with Vietnamese women. "So you just tried to screw a lot, and you could do that in Saigon very easily." Lewis Puller wrote home to his wife of the "all-consuming horniness of lonely warriors," perhaps offering a reason why some female American nurses serving in Vietnam felt like a "commodity" simply because they were women.[54] The implications of regarding Vietnamese as little more than whores or thieves could be seen in expressions reminiscent of adventure magazines. Journalist Michael Herr recalled the same, "tired" sexual remark every time an American GI came across a dead woman. "No more boom-boom for that mama-san." What was it about American culture and its historic attitudes toward women that made men susceptible to this type of thinking?[55]

Perhaps there is no better illustration of the pulps' cultural influence than the fact that unit newspapers in Vietnam replicated, almost precisely, adventure magazine formats. These semi-official publications could be found in almost every major command – the 25th Infantry Division's *Tropic Lightning News*, the 12th Combat Aviation Group's *Blackjack Flier*, and IV Corps' *Delta Dragon*. Each week, these broadsheets would highlight the fighting prowess of American GIs and include a cheesecake girl ready for pinning up in any makeshift barracks. An August 1968 issue of *Tropic Lightning News* read like a full-blown stag magazine. The cover page highlighted a successful recon mission, "Wolfhound Fists Fix Fleeing VC," that ended up in a face-to-face fist fight with six "panic-stricken" Vietcong. A few pages in, readers could delight in "White Warriors Wipe Out Snipers in Village Cordon," before gazing upon that week's "Tropic Lightning Girl." As the caption under the bikini-clad blonde read, "Her name is unknown to us but then, is it really that important?"[56]

Far from an anomaly, *Tropic Lightning News* competed with other pulp-emulating command newspapers. The 6 March 1968 publication of the 1st Cavalry Division's *Cavalier*, comparable to other issues, contained all the adventure mags' long-standing tropes. The cover page trumpeted a recent operation in which one brigade "scored" 2,454 enemy kills, showcased Medal of Honor recipient Lewis Albanese, and ran a story on a military police unit that adopted a local orphan. Inside, the paper lavished praise on a Silver Star awardee, while displaying a photo of a pin-up girl in a short, fishnet miniskirt. Not to be outdone, the Americal Division's *Southern Cross* followed suit with stories on the "Brave and Bold" killing nearly 100 NVA troops alongside photos of cheesecake girls in scanty bikinis. A story on "tunnel rat" William Hanks noted how the young specialist had discovered a pin-up photograph of model Chris Noel in an enemy foxhole. Apparently, GIs were "not the only ones who appreciate the American way of life."[57]

Perhaps extolling the virtues of American women – similar to *The Manchurian Candidate*'s bar scene – helps explain why so few of these pin-up girls were Vietnamese. At home, the pulps exposed the secrets of passionate Asian women, apparently ready to please upon command. In Vietnam, however, GIs flipping through their unit newspapers seemingly preferred white American or Australian models. Conceivably, such inclinations implied that GIs found sexual pulp fantasies as fraudulent as combat stories. If Asian women were so desirable, why the focus on cheesecakes back home? An April 1970 edition of the *Pacific Stars and Stripes* proved a rare exception, its color cover spotlighting Miss Tuyet Huong, posed seductively in a red, white, and blue floral bikini, her eyes dark with heavy mascara. "Song Birds" like Miss Huong might still tantalize as the American war was winding down, but depictions of Vietnamese women surfaced only occasionally in the command weeklies. Like combat, it seemed, the Asian seductress was failing to deliver on the promise of Vietnam being a man-making experience.[58]

One alternative remained. For years, men's adventure magazines had reinforced the links between race, gender, and militarized masculinity. Not surprisingly, many Americans in South Vietnam saw themselves as selflessly fighting a war on behalf of a downtrodden people. They were there to help defend against the evils of communism. To some GIs, however, their wartime sacrifices allegedly sanctioned a sense of sexual prerogative, with local women a reward for martial exertion. Male privilege ran through the core of pulp offerings. So too did ideas on battlefield domination and sexual entitlement. We should not be startled, then, when American GIs conflated the two. As one veteran tellingly recalled, "I enjoyed the shooting and the killing. I was literally turned on when I saw a gook get shot."[59]

How many of those young men disappointed by the inability to prove their manhood on the field of battle, yet aroused by the incessant killing, shifted their sense of entitlement toward the Vietnamese population? In their quest to dominate someone, anyone, might not an avowedly submissive Asian woman fulfill their needs? In such a scenario, a "friendly" South Vietnamese woman could serve just as capably as a female defender of the NLF. In either case, the environment was rich with potential for sexual domination and violence based on popular notions of race, place, and gender.

RAPE AS MORE THAN A WEAPON

Philadelphia native Timon Hagelin served in a Graves Registration platoon, an army unit charged with processing Americans killed in action. He had no experience with such grim duties, arriving to Vietnam in August 1968 as a shoe repairman. Hagelin quickly made friends with his company mates, "basically nice people," he recalled. One night while walking on base, the logistics specialist heard cries of help from a Vietnamese woman. As he approached, one of his friends "punched this chick on the side of the head." Hagelin then watched in disbelief as seven GIs "ripped her off." The gang rape left him incredulous. "I know the guys," he remembered, "and I know basically they're not really bad people, you know. I couldn't figure out what was going on to make the people like this do it. It was just part of the everyday routine, you know."[60]

The notion of wartime rape as routine is a common thread running through Vietnam War memoirs and veteran narratives, suggesting that in war, good people do bad things. Hagelin's incomprehension of the motives behind the sexual assault he viewed is instructive. Why did "basically nice people" engage in sexual violence? Were they deprived of sexual intimacy on an overseas army base and simply needed physical stimulation? Did they seek to punish the young Vietnamese woman, somehow holding her responsible for their deployment far from home? Or were they seizing upon what popular culture long had promised them, the sexual gratification of an exotic Oriental woman? Perhaps some assailants among the seven men did not even consider why they were raping, merely bowing to pressure so as not be isolated from their peer group.[61]

Regardless of their individual motives that evening, the rapists had acted out a violent form of aggressive masculinity, one tied directly to power and dominance. By imposing themselves on a young woman, they had weaponized their own bodies. So too did macho adventurers in men's magazines. Pulp heroes were forceful, uncompromising, and mercilessly virile. They didn't just engage in sex. They conquered their prey. In the process, the pulps never definitively drew neat lines between consensual sex, prostitution, and outright sexual assault. It is clear, however, that such a sexual continuum in war rested on the exploitation of women's vulnerability, whether physical or economic. On one end of this spectrum, pulp readers might view wartime rape, prostitution, and sexual harassment. On the other, they could read stories of "duration wives" or ongoing relationships with local women. The thread tying together this spectrum was a view of women caught in war as available and the ideal American man as both strong and aggressive.[62]

This veneration of aggressive masculinity, central to the glorification of both war and sexual conquest, often could be found in instances of wartime rape, what Susan Griffin called "the perfect combination of sex and violence." If the war in Vietnam was a contest over power and control, then soldiers might use rape, in some instances, as a way to exhibit dominance over the local population. Simply put, the brutalization of a largely rural society could take forms beyond just napalm strikes or search-and-destroy missions. In cases where rape was not just an "opportunistic perpetration of sexual violence," to quote Sara Meger, might it instead be an instrument of policy?[63]

Some critics have suggested that gang rapes were a "horrifyingly common occurrence" during the war, in part, because American soldiers and marines carried out a systematic, deliberate command policy of violence against the Vietnamese population. No evidence exists, however, that MACV's leadership viewed rape as part of its wartime arsenal, suggesting that the motivations for committing sexual violence were far more complex than the result of overt command influence. Surely some GIs, viewing women as symbols of their local villages, considered the rape of female communists, real or perceived, as a way to prove their masculinity while suppressing communist activity in one fell swoop. But this seems far different than senior commanders calling for sexual violence as a means of targeting the population.[64]

Complicating any evaluation of incentives is the difficulty in accurately assessing how many rapes actually occurred in Vietnam. Many GIs never reported these crimes – nor did all of the female victims – one lieutenant sharing that if he brought his soldiers up on charges, it would have required unit members to testify against one another and thus "tear the platoon apart." Some servicemen were more comfortable admitting to killing rather than rape, while higher-level commanders often refused to acknowledge their subordinates' capacity for sexual violence. Goodhearted, young American boys simply did not engage in such ravenous behavior.[65]

Just as importantly, the Uniform Code of Military Justice (UCMJ) system prejudiced the rights of Americans over Vietnamese. As in the pulps, legal procedures were not attuned to protecting local women or even hearing their stories. In one graphic example, military authorities detained a twenty-year-old Vietnamese woman who later claimed she had been raped by ten US soldiers while being held in detention. Investigators questioned the "alleged victim," who could only tentatively identify two of her assailants. Later, she indicated that "she was not sure," and the case was summarily closed on account of there being "insufficient evidence to substantiate" her claims. Like the mistrusted native women in the postwar pulps who never had the chance to speak for themselves, the victims' silence undergirded male narratives of wartime sexual conduct. As a result, GI assailants might view rape as a tolerable, routine act with little fear of legal consequences.[66]

Deficiencies within the UCMJ system are equally apparent in the low numbers of allegations and convictions reported by the Department of the Army, the only service to keep count of its war crimes cases. According to one source, court-martial convictions involving Vietnamese victims between 1965 and 1973 included only twenty-five instances of rape committed by army soldiers and sixteen by marines. It is impossible to say how accurately these figures represented the true levels of sexual violence in Vietnamese. Yet insights can be gained by the case of a GI who was tried by a general court martial for raping a thirteen-year-old Vietnamese girl while interrogating her as a VC suspect. He was sentenced to a dishonorable discharge and confinement with hard labor for twenty years. Upon appeal, however, his sentence was reduced to just one year. In all, he served only seven months and sixteen days in confinement. Thus, in rape allegations, convictions, and sentencing, the US military legal system clearly privileged the American assailant over the Vietnamese victim.[67]

The potential for such outcomes to legitimize acts of sexual violence in some men's minds rose with every dismissed allegation or light punishment. From an organizational perspective, then, military legal proceedings inadvertently helped make this type of violence acceptable, or at very least understandable, to GIs who fell under UCMJ authority. Still, this ethos did not simply appear out of thin air. The legal system's treatment of violence against women must have had encouragement from some cultural inputs back home. To blame the "pressure cooker" of combat as the sole reason for incidents of rape, a way for men to satiate their sexual desires in a stressful wartime environment, arguably misses the ways in which perpetrators understood themselves and their actions. Gender norms were imparted to male servicemembers long before they joined the armed forces. It seems vital, therefore, to examine how culturally produced representations of sex and violence helped shape GI behavior among the Vietnamese population.[68]

For working-class warriors serving in South Vietnam, the pulps embodied the macho outlook of these cultural representations. The pulps were among the most widely read cultural products of the Cold War era, and the powerful ideas about American manhood which they expressed surely resonated with GIs. In terms of sexual violence, their influence actually may have increased during the war because of fewer restraints on soldiers' fantasies and behavior, the easy access to weapons, and an active participation in violence more generally.[69]

Indeed, within men's magazines, rape seemed part of the adventure. In April 1959, *Sensation* quoted novelist George Moore's 1888 *Confessions of a Young Man*, which claimed that "Nature intended woman for the warrior's relaxation." That same year, *Valor* included a story of the Wild West in which "Handsome Hank's special talents were for raping banks of their money and robbing women of their virtue. Sometimes," the pulp declared, "he combined the two sports." Of note, the outlaw preferred married women because there was an "added thrill of danger." *Big Adventure*'s first story in its June 1961 issue began with a young female being raped by a dozen sailors in a San Francisco store window. The accompanying illustration by Arne Arnesen is frightening, a grimacing woman in the clutches of two men, one of them wielding a knife, as they tear her clothes and drag her away from her mother.[70]

Fig. 5.2 *Battle Cry*, July 1959

In "The Strange Case of the Stagecoach Rapist," *Sir!* magazine noted in the story's tagline that Sam Carlisle had "terrorized half the women of the Old West – while the other half waited hopefully to be waylaid and seduced by the handsome, well-educated and debonair outlaw." If the pulps were correct, might not Vietnamese women also secretly be hoping that American soldiers would seduce them as well? Finally, in an offering from *Man's Action* on a "deadly rape gang sadist," a group of rapists who terrorize women get away with it "because the poor women were too scared or ashamed to go to the police." Here, life imitated art as victims of sexual assault in Vietnam frequently did not come forward for fear of shaming their family. If Mai Elliott's father was disappointed she had entered into a consensual relationship with an American, how would

The two sailors wrenched the girl away from her mother, and dragged her, screaming, toward the darkened lobby.

The sailors were out of control; men and women ran for safety!

THE DAY THEY RAVAGED FRISCO

by SIDNEY GEORGESON
illustrated by ARNE ARNESEN

A YOUNG GIRL RAPED by a dozen sailors in a furniture store window. . . . A pretty streetcar conductorette whose clothes are ripped off by a raving, drunken mob. . . . An old man killed by a flower pot kicked off a high building ledge. . . . Shattered store windows and looting men. . . .

These are some of my wartime memories.

Only they aren't part of the slogging, muddy, sun-scorched, rain-soaked, killing hell I remember from Europe. They are part of my home-coming. They all happened in San Francisco. They happened that summer night of August 14, 1945 when the still unofficial word of Japan's surrender kicked off celebrations all over the free world.

In San Francisco, the celebration turned into orgy, and the orgy became a terror that held the City by the Golden Gate in its grip of rape, manslaughter and pillage for more than 48 hours.

Newspapers printed little about it, then or since. It would have been bad "publicity" all around. At first they glossed over the truth, and finally they admitted in pretty small type that 11 persons were killed, over 1,000 treated at civilian hospitals, and countless women raped during the victory shindig. Nobody reported later how many of the injured had died. Nor did the military ever announce their own casualties in the riot. These statistics will probably remain secrets forever.

But now, at last, the truth finally can be told about those frantic hours when rowdy, reeling mobs of drunken, boot camp sailors, led by criminal elements within their ranks, ran wild with lust and vandalism.

I've wanted to tell about (Continued on next page)

6

Fig. 5.3 *Big Adventure,* June 1961

other family patriarchs react, daughters feared, if they had been forcibly taken by a foreign soldier?[71]

At least one pulp mag took on the matter of GI rapists directly. In October 1956, *True War* asked the question if military uniforms really did make "sex fiends out of innocent boys." Was military service a "brutalizing influence" that made men "wantonly attack women and girls"? Writer Kenneth Towne offered a laundry list of GI sexual deviancy, from assault to rape and murder, before concluding that the "American serviceman is far from being either a rapist or a sex degenerate." Towne noted that military sex crime rates were far lower than civilian ones and suggested that the media was to blame for highlighting the "GI Slayer" angle because "it sold a lot of papers." Worse, the story concluded, the problem intensified overseas as women falsely accused servicemen of rape or sexual assault so they could "obtain money or force their GI boy friends to marry them and thus obtain a U.S.-style meal ticket." Rape might be inevitable – "boys will be boys," Towne noted – but the uniform was not to blame.[72]

While the *True War* story problematically impugned media outlets and foreign women, Towne stood on firmer ground when arguing that military culture alone did not lead to men becoming rapists. Larger cultural influences were at play. Without question, military socialization processes bred a sense of hypermasculinity among some servicemen, a contempt for women that was part of a long tradition within the armed forces. Yet contemporary understandings of sexual violence, replicated in the macho pulps, suggested a much deeper misinterpretation, well outside military channels, of what rape actually meant.[73]

In line with Cold War ideas on sexual relationships, men's magazines intimated a cavalier attitude when it came to nonconsensual sex. One reader from Albany wrote to *Bluebook* arguing that "a woman can't be raped unless she's drugged, tied down or threatened with bodily harm." A pulp writer for *Men* was incredulous that a wife in California attempted to charge her husband with rape. Worse, he claimed, "statutory rape" could be a "dangerous trap" if an underage woman, though a "quivering bundle of eager acquiescence," proved to be a single day short of the legal age of consent.[74] The same magazine ran a story which reasoned that "rape is by definition impossible when a girl is more than willing." As in so many articles, men might be excused for their reactions, given that they were preyed upon by passionate female thrill seekers. One 1969 story in *Man's Life* claimed that women who openly solicited a man occasionally made "themselves available for rape!" Women like this had goaded men into attacking them.[75]

Transported to Vietnam, these sexist mindsets flourished in locales where unofficial base brothels suggested that military leaders were sanctioning, if not institutionalizing, wartime prostitution. Long-standing civilian and military attitudes melded together in Vietnamese brothels. One letter writer to *Male*, likely speaking for many men in the mid 1960s, claimed that "a certain percentage of women are born prostitutes and nothing in this world will ever change them."[76] Other popular assumptions maintained that war hypersexualized men, which might lead to rape, and thus the need for prostitutes so warriors could "let off some steam." Sex, it appeared, was the perfect distraction from combat. Even military tradition factored in, one World War II veteran remembering that some sixty percent of the men in his company had relations with "professional prostitutes or pick-up girls." Nowhere did sex advocates consider how an industry built upon gratifying American lust might affect South Vietnamese social values.[77]

Nor did such discussions contemplate the degradation to the local Vietnamese women who were performing "basic services" in support of local economies outside US military bases. One account maintained there were 400,000 prostitutes at the height of American occupation, nearly one for every GI. While dubious, the claim rested on an incontestable truth. Sex sold. As one Saigon official candidly explained, "The Americans need girls; we need dollars. Why should we refrain from the exchange?" This commodification of women's bodies had roots in earlier wars, *Male* noting in Korea the "growing practice of occupation troops 'buying' their own girls." In war zones across Asia, it appeared, US servicemen were exercising a level of control over local women unheard of back home.[78]

Given contemporary narratives of the duplicitous seductress, pulp readers likely were not surprised to find that these Asian prostitutes failed to have much loyalty to their American customers. According to *Man's Conquest*, intelligence reports were unnecessary for tracking the enemy's progress in South Vietnam. "Whenever the Viet Cong is on the offensive, the price of paid sex in Saigon temples of pleasure drops 50%. Even the free stuff is easier to get when times get tough at the front."[79] No wonder that veterans spoke of Vietnamese women in demeaning terms. One Special Forces officer wrote of judging a "pubic hair contest" to find out who among two "Eurasian girls," both "strikingly beautiful," had more French blood in them. Another vet recalled "playing around with Vietnamese girls who just wanted our money" and shaking their heads until lice fell out. As in earlier stories, the female voices were inaudible, though it is not hard to imagine these women feeling humiliated by their interactions with American GIs.[80]

While it is doubtful that many young men arrived in Vietnam premeditating acts of rape, they nonetheless were primed to envisage how their fantasies of sex with an "Oriental" woman might play out in real life. Erotic pulp stories certainly enticed. In adventure mags, Americans had sex with "wild and wacky" Korean women, met the "fabulous bare-breasted beauties of Bali," and found that in most of Polynesia, girls were "essentially willing." *Man's Magazine* printed a 1966 story of a virgin soldier lured in by "Juicy Lucy" and her "seductive slant eyes," the "pussy cat" ultimately working on the frightened lad with "loving devotion and skill."[81] From tales like these, young pulp readers heading to Vietnam had been conditioned to fantasize about the exotic Orient for years. But what happened when these dreams never materialized? Did servicemen see a lack of options for paid or consensual sex as a rationale for forcibly committing rape? Not all areas where US soldiers operated in South Vietnam offered the chance to barter with prostitutes or meet with women untouched by war's devastation, yet many of those GIs expected to be sexually gratified regardless.[82]

Of course, consensual sex and rape were far from equivalent acts. Linking them together, however, was GIs' widely held view of the Vietnamese female body as available. In this way, gender and Orientalism combined, in potentially dangerous ways, so that local women were seen as lesser, sexually loose, and thus "rapeable" by the masculine American warrior. When *Stag* mentioned that Montagnard tribesmen of Vietnam's central highlands had become "blood brothers" with US soldiers and given them "free rein with the available women of the village," what message did that send to pulp readers?[83] Not surprisingly, GIs spoke in analogous terms. They took time off to engage in "intercourse and intoxication" and "balled chicks" because they were "forcibly willing – they'd rather do that than get shot." An army investigation found that a helicopter crew in Vinh Long province had landed, shoved a Vietnamese woman onto the bird, and forcibly removed her clothes. While she denied having been sexually assaulted – raising questions about how the investigation proceeded – the fact that Americans could swoop in from the sky and seize female prey offers painful insights into the power differentials between US servicemen and Vietnamese women.[84]

A process of dehumanization coincided with such actions, perhaps helping explain them. Veteran memoirs are replete with language portraying Vietnamese as subhuman "gooks." As one vet testified, "When you shot someone, you didn't think you were shooting at a human." Another explained that "no one sees the Vietnamese as people. They're not people. Therefore it doesn't matter what you do to them."[85] What some soldiers did could be horrific. Tales abound of GIs ripping off women's clothes and stabbing them in the breasts or thrusting rifles and entrenching tools into their vaginas. One private recalled watching a fellow soldier interrogate a suspected VC woman after a comrade had been killed in an ambush. The burly American stood over his naked victim, her legs held apart, screaming at her. "Cunt! Whore! You gonna die, oh, you gonna die bad, Mama-san!" Murdered in gruesome fashion, the woman's screams offer the only hint that she actually might be a human being capable of feeling pain.[86]

Brutalizing the Vietnamese made national headlines when the My Lai story broke in 1969, but military legal documents confirm that the sexual violence committed by Calley's men was not an isolated act. Army investigators found that approximately twenty women were raped at My Lai, some girls as young as thirteen. As Calley himself recalled, "I guess lots of girls would rather be raped than be killed anytime. So why was I being saintly about it."[87] In other rape cases, though, similar attitudes emerged, not just from perpetrators but from investigators as well. When two women forcibly were taken from their village by US marines and raped, they remembered three Americans watching the assault from only ten meters away. Not unusually, the Vietnamese had difficulty positively identifying their assailants. Worse, the examining physician at the local US hospital claimed that both women had previously had sexual intercourse and he therefore discounted their stories since they were not virgins before the assault. Investigators summarily closed the case file. In such a hostile environment, women had little chance of defending themselves, physically or otherwise, from American GIs intent on doing them harm.[88]

While these acts were neither officially orchestrated nor a centerpiece of MACV strategy, they still created disorder within South Vietnamese society. In this narrow sense, some GIs likely considered rape a standard part of war. The postwar pulps certainly included stories where soldiers had incorporated sexual violence into their battle plans. An autobiographical account in *Real War* featured a US Army nurse who had been captured and raped by the Japanese during World War II. (Only five pages later, readers could delight in a photo spread of a cheesecake girl in various stages of undress.) By the midpoint of the American war in Vietnam, adventure mags often ran stories of the Vietcong raping and killing innocent South Vietnamese women, quietly avoiding reports of hometown GIs acting in similarly brutish fashion. The message, though, seemed clear – sexual violence was an inherent part of war.[89]

Moreover, since the pulps argued that US military leaders kept "our boys woman-hungry," readers likely would have expected frustrated GIs also to consider rape as an act of revenge. Could taking a Vietnamese woman by force avenge those American nurses despoiled by Asian men in World War II? Or, more tangibly, the life of a comrade recently killed in battle? When local villagers kept silent after US troops sustained casualties, for fear of retribution, how many American soldiers assumed that vengeance was theirs to take?[90] With ambushes the hallmark of this war without front lines, raping a woman might be a chance to exact payback, but also a way to regain a sense of power in an unsettling war. In the process, rape could be viewed as an attack not just on a female body, but on the Vietnamese "body politic" as a whole. When William Calley claimed that "inside of VC women, I guess there were a thousand little VC," he expressed widespread anxieties that all Vietnamese women, regardless of their support for communism, were both the enemy and vessels of a toxic ideology.[91]

Still, not all wartime rapes were linked to the larger ideological struggle. In some cases, young men, feasibly terrified by the act of rape, nonetheless performed out of peer pressure. Within a cohesive group setting, squad mates might be more willing to carry out adolescent aggressiveness toward women. Or, fearing being labeled a homosexual, they could bond with their comrades in a presumably masculine endeavor. Sexual violence, in this manner, became a rite of initiation. As one officer in Vietnam shared with a journalist, "Add a little mob pressure, and those nice kids who accompanie[d] us today would rape like champions."[92] Daniel Lang's 1969 *Casualties of War* centers on such an incident. In late 1966, a US infantry squad on a recon mission abducted a young Vietnamese woman, Phan Thi Mao, and four soldiers raped her in turn before killing her the next day. When one GI, "Eriksson," objects, he is derided as "queer" and "chicken" by his peers. Additionally, after Mao's rape and murder, a squad mate tells him to "relax about that Vietnamese girl... The kind of thing that happened to her – what else can you expect in a combat zone?" With the perpetrators ultimately being tried under court martial, the gang rape suggests they are not heroic warriors but brutal boys capable of abhorrent acts.[93]

The act of rape, however, cut both ways. A young GI could exhibit sexual power over a Vietnamese woman, but he also might betray his inability to measure up to the men depicted in adventure magazines. Power differentials clearly were at play. Rape tangibly demonstrated that a woman had been vanquished by a superior power. In Vietnam, however, fear and insecurity impelled many GIs to lash out against the Vietnamese population. Of course, they often did so with a sense of immunity, as gang rapes suggested that neither culprit nor witness had much to fear.[94] Still, men worried they might flunk their supposed test of manhood. One specialist in the 4th Infantry Division expressed his anxieties that he couldn't "get it up to do it" with a prostitute "because you're not even excited." His reasons covered a wide gamut: she was young, not "really attractive," and did not speak English. He also feared contracting venereal disease. When *Male* claimed in 1967 that GIs attracted to Vietnamese women tended to be "sexually hung-up and frightened," did soldiers either purchasing sex or raping women question their own sense of masculinity or the possibility they might be "embittered at certain aspects of American life"?[95]

The 4th Infantry Division soldier's fear of sexually transmitted diseases also alluded to the disquiet Vietnamese women provoked despite their sexual subordination. For years, the macho pulps had told readers that Asian women were both desirable and dangerous. Japanese doctors had experimented with "the use of diseased native women to incapacitate American troops." In Korea, female camp followers carried "guns and grenades for Gook guerrillas" in the hills.[96] By the 1960s, it seemed young soldiers had much to fear. *For Men Only* claimed in late 1966 that the Vietcong were "planning autumn terror attacks on beaches where GIs sunbathe, using lithe Frog Girls who'll swim in with promises of fun, but carry explosive packs in their bikini tops." The following year, *Man's World* alleged that a "top VC jungle fighter" was, in fact, "a former Saigon brothel girl who fights with two tommy guns and carries grenades in her bra." Female bodies could be toxic vehicles of STDs, but communist women's sexuality also afforded them the chance to deploy weapons into the very core of the American war effort.[97]

These pulp narratives reappeared in veterans' memoirs and even military legal documents. Vet John Ketwig recalled how the more seasoned GIs would warn "new arrivals against falling asleep after sex, for fear of castration." In imagery evoking the myth of *vagina dentata*, rumors thrived of Vietnamese women hiding razors in their "sex organs" and castrating their male victims. One official army investigation interrogated an American platoon that had captured a Vietcong nurse and decided to rape her. The lieutenant, "in deference to his rank," was afforded the first opportunity but "sustained injuries caused by a razor blade concealed in [her] vagina... Immediately thereafter, members of the platoon shot and killed the Viet Cong nurse." While investigators could not substantiate the allegations, stories like these proliferated. As one marine who found such razor blade stories plausible recalled, "Vietnamese women were made into objects of fear and dread, and it was easy to feel angry at them." To GIs like this, regardless of the "physical logistics" required by blade-carrying *femmes fatales*, evil women were out to castrate any American who let his guard down. [98]

Given women's castrating potential – did this not inspire fear at home, as well? – some GI rapists arbitrarily dismissed their victims as prostitutes who, because of their sex work, merited few, if any, protections. Deemed a "VC whore," any casualty of rape could be judged by wrongdoers as deserving of their fate. Unquestionably, Vietnamese women, often because of the disruptions of war, were available as prostitutes or entered into the GI world as bar girls or entertainers. For alienated American men, however, these distinctions mattered little. Even Lieutenant Calley reported that a man in his platoon assaulted a prostitute after she refused to have sex with every member of the unit, *twice*, for what he initially paid her. The pulps may not have inspired this type of viciousness, but both in magazine fantasies and in the reality of Vietnam, the lines between sex and violence had blurred beyond recognition.[99]

For those soldiers with ambitions of power, fueled by the larger pulp fantasy, the heroic warrior became ever more indistinguishable from the sexual conqueror. Likely, many soldiers took full advantage when presented with opportunities to be seen as either, their language clearly reflective of Cold War macho mags. One helicopter pilot shared with journalist Michael Herr the exhilaration of flying above enemy bunkers, "like wasps outside a nest." "That's sex," the captain said, "That's pure sex." For those infantrymen on the ground, though, who might not achieve such delight in heroically combatting their North Vietnamese or southern insurgent enemies, the chance to perform as sexual conquistador may have seemed within much closer reach. Such aspirations, in fact, may have been more likely than being the true action hero as depicted in the magazines. In a war fought among the population, Vietnamese women were far easier targets than battle-hardened NVA or VC troops.[100]

Yet not all sexual assaults occurred on the front lines or even just against Vietnamese women. Support troops ventured into brothels and committed rape just as did infantrymen, one "REMF" titling an entire chapter in his memoir "Fornication." American women equally could find themselves targets. Nurse Linda McClenahan recalled that her compound's high fences, lined with barbwire, and security guards were "not for protection from the VC, but to keep us separate from the gentlemen in the late hours of the evening."[101] In *Nam*, Mark Baker related the story of a GI who encounters an American Red Cross Donut Dollie on one of the massive US military bases. When she offers the soldier a cookie, he crudely replies "Fuck the cookie. I want your pussy." Frustrated – "You couldn't get them," the GI grumbles of the female volunteer – he soon after ventures into his platoon sergeant's "hooch," where he is unable to recognize his own reflection in the mirror. "I was looking at a stranger. I'd changed. I'd never seen myself before." Perhaps the war had transformed him, yet the misogynistic language of this vulgar episode had far deeper roots within pop culture renderings from the Cold War era.[102]

If both American and Vietnamese women felt defenseless against GIs' sexual aggression, so too did the Saigon government, which wrestled with its inability to protect the population. Any expansion in prostitution did little to curb the rapes of women, indicating that sexual violence was not simply about sexual gratification. Once more, though, powerful differentials came into sharp relief. While GVN leaders seemed incapable of safeguarding their people, this humiliation extended to men serving in the South Vietnamese armed forces as well. ARVN soldiers long had suffered the brunt of American contempt. The sexual exploitation of Vietnamese women only reinforced GI disdain, one veteran dismissing many of his supposed allies as "fucking queers." *Stag* also weighed in, noting how local men were complaining that US troops had "caused the prices paid to prostitutes to go into orbit. A native doesn't stand a chance when a fat-cat G.I. comes to town." Such views exposed a harsh yet contradictory reality. Americans were physically abusing Vietnamese women, but when local men could not protect them, those same men were judged deficient by the very perpetrators exploiting women in the first place.[103]

This mistreatment at the hands of American GIs left countless Vietnamese resentful. They blamed foreign troops not only for inciting sexual violence but also for distorting sexual politics inside South Vietnam. Both unwelcomed imports held the potential to tear apart the social fabric of a largely traditional, patriarchal society. Of course, hard fighting in a stalemated war did not help matters. For at least some Vietnamese men, feelings of masculine inadequacy, outside the gaze of Americans, must have been generated by these political and military upheavals. It seems few US servicemen considered the long-term consequences of these local sentiments. Rather, pulp stories on "duration wives" or the "wild rise in VD rates and a lot of 'red-headed' babies being born out of wedlock" left the impression that virile American fighting men had easy access to Asian sex whenever they desired it.[104]

If Saigon had been turned into a "large whorehouse," as some GIs believed, then the wartime American presence had done more than just threaten the moral society of South Vietnam. The US occupation also left behind deep psychological scars. As the final American troops withdrew from a still ongoing war, President Nguyen Van Thieu sullenly told his advisors that Nixon no longer wanted an "ugly" and "old mistress hanging around." This gendered language clearly demonstrated Thieu's resignation with the subordinate relationship he maintained vis-à-vis the United States. Yet it also alluded to a far deeper sentiment. A feminine, emasculated state no longer served its purpose for a dominant, more masculine nation.[105]

While the term "mistress" tellingly has no male equivalent, it suggested that Americans had simply used South Vietnam for sexual gratification, a way to help fulfill the fantasy of war as a man-making experience. Yet the reality of Vietnam indicated that sex purchased or seized did not transform boys into men. Nor did the logic of macho fantasy play out in real life. As Viet Thanh Nguyen astutely asks, "If war makes you a man, does rape make you a woman?" In Vietnam, neither proved the case. Like the war itself, rather than inspire tales of heroism and valor, prostitution and rape instead degraded and corrupted. In its final iteration, the pulp fantasy had failed to deliver.[106]

THE LONG-HAIRED WARRIORS FIGHT BACK

Bui Thi Me was born in the southern province of Vinh Long in 1921. She married at nineteen and joined the revolutionary movement in 1955, soon after the French defeat at Dien Bien Phu. While taking part in the revolution for Vietnamese unification and independence, she birthed four sons, each enlisting as "patriotic soldiers" in 1967. Three were killed during the American war, the fourth seriously wounded. In 1995, Ms. Bui received the title of "Vietnamese Heroic Mother," an honor signifying that women were not simply passive victims in war or damsels in distress as seen in so many men's adventure magazine stories. Rather, women warriors had an extensive history in Vietnam, dating back to the very beginning of the country's history. By the middle of the twentieth century, they had become an integral part of a revolution aiming for Vietnamese independence, active agents in a struggle for liberation from past injustices.[107]

In popular culture, however, these women mostly remained "invisible combatants," only periodically appearing as objects of rescue or desire. Similar to female US Army nurses in Vietnam, their stories were overlooked, not considered a legitimate part of the "true" war story. And like their American counterparts, they saw some of the worst of combat and its aftermath. As nurse Lynda Van Devanter recalled, though, no one wanted to listen because she had no "cute little love stories" to tell. "On our battlefields, there were no knights in shining armor rescuing damsels in distress. The stories, even the funny ones, were all dirty. They were rotten and they stank." Indeed, women suffered post-traumatic stress as painfully as men, struggled with terrible nightmares, and often felt alienated from others after war's end. American and Vietnamese female fighters may have existed, apparition-like, on the fringes of heroic adventure stories, but they shared the horrors of war and could be affected by its bloodletting as much as any man.[108]

For Vietnamese women, as Bui Thi Me's tale reveals, casting out foreign invaders long predated the Americans' arrival. In 40 AD, Trung Trac and Trung Nhi, two sisters mobilized into the revolution against Chinese occupation forces, commanded an army of 80,000 warriors, thirty-six of whom were female generals. A second rebellion erupted in 248 AD, this one led by Trieu Thi Trinh, the "Vietnamese Joan of Arc." Lady Trieu's leadership, like the Trung sisters before her, was evoked in an oft-repeated local proverb: "When the enemy comes, even the women must fight." In the following centuries, female warriors participated fully in this culture of resistance. By the early 1900s, women were once more at war with foreign invaders. They actively engaged French colonialists by rallying villagers against European garrisons, serving in guerrilla units, and spreading revolutionary propaganda among the population.[109]

The French-Indochina War (1946–1954) equally saw women assuming critical roles in revolutionary activity and combat. By one account, some 840,000 female guerrillas operated in the northern regions of Tonkin and Annam, another 140,000 in southern Cochinchina. They also functioned on the extended battlefield by mobilizing communities, gathering intelligence, and transporting supplies. One young girl, Vo Thi Sau, joined a guerrilla unit when she was only fourteen, spying on French soldiers and killing thirteen with a well-placed grenade.[110] Captured, she faced a firing squad and became the youngest female revolutionary to be shot without a trial. As stories like this spread, ordinary women rallied to the cause, becoming part of larger social transformations of gender roles in the post-World War II era. By the climactic 1954 battle at Dien Bien Phu, half of the more than 260,000 laborers supplying the Viet Minh army were women. Thanks to comparable sacrifices throughout the French-Indochina War, as Karen Gottschang Turner observes, "the tradition of resourceful, patriotic women was firmly imbedded in the imagination of Vietnamese citizens by the time the Americans entered in force."[111]

Popular representations aside, the social gains these women made during wartime often were fleeting. Relatively few served as full-time soldiers in the People's Army during the American conflict, and the communist state downplayed female combat participation after war's end. In western conceptions, however, old tropes resurfaced. The *Los Angeles Times* reported on the "jungle Amazon terror" of Vietnamese woman warriors who wielded swords and daggers and kept prisoners alive to "kill them slowly by mutilation." Not surprisingly, the macho pulps added a sexual component to their own storylines. In one photo essay on "Women in Uniform," *Real* claimed that "pint-sized Asian war-chicks" were the "sexiest in the world. Not even a bulky uniform and a heavy rifle can stifle their ever present sense of sex." A caption above a photograph of camouflaged female insurgents went further. "Unlike men, women in war are more passionate after combat." Apparently, to pulp writer Leon Sudarski, female combatants didn't suffer the emotional traumas of war but rather were aroused by it.[112]

While these stories may have been laden with gendered clichés, they nonetheless intimated that women were not simply victims of war. Of course, even combatants, male and female, could be victimized. Yet the pulps' version of sexualized Amazonians who took men prisoner and made them their sex slaves never quite materialized in the wars for Vietnamese independence. Rather, true women warriors regularly fought close to their villages and homes, defending against foreign intruders while fulfilling more traditional family roles. The daughter of one woman from Dinh Thuy in Ben Tre province, for example, helped her mother hide NLF insurgents in nearby tunnels and bunkers, all three of her brothers ultimately being killed in fighting far from home. When ARVN always requesting something of absolutely no importance. And please take note that I was only thirty-four at the time. During my sixteen years in the Red Army I had known many women, of many nationalities and colors, in all the Soviet Republics, in Latvia, China, and Poland. Quite frankly, I was not ready to become a monk."

The most interesting part of Colonel Sverdlov's book is the chapter in which he describes the night he was "attacked" by three husky girls, their faces disguised by boot polish. "I was drinking alone in my tent," he writes, "when suddenly an arm reached in and smashed the light. I was knocked off my cot in a flying tangle of arms and legs. It was not half as enjoyable as it sounds, but somewhere I forgot all about the directive from headquarters." Now safe from official reprisals, Colonel Sverdlov feels that he can talk freely about his experiences in a womens' army. Not only that, but he has become vitally interested in the problems of female soldiers in other armies. Last summer, traveling as a correspondent for an Austrian magazine, he discovered that the cute, pint-sized girl soldiers of Vietnam are the "sexiest in the world. Not even a bulky uniform and a heavy rifle can stifle their ever-present sense of sex," the Colonel wrote later. Asked to name the second sexiest girl soldiers in the world, Colonel Sverdlov promptly named the girls of Israel. "Perhaps it comes from drilling all day in that hot sun," the Russian expert said. "Believe me, it was all I could do to keep my mind on my work." In a recent article Colonel Sverdlov declared that he has only scratched the surface of sexual investigation into the lives and loves of girl soldiers. "There is still a great deal to be done," he says.

Two shapely machine gunners cut loose at Viet Cong guerillas.

28   REAL

Fig. 5.4 *Real*, February 1964

soldiers threatened her in an attempt to make her reveal the Vietcong locations, she refused and suffered beatings before being shot in the side of the back. Still, she did not give in. It seems highly doubtful the young woman became more "passionate" after the harrowing episode.[113]

Fig. 5.5 *Real*, February 1964

In adventure magazines, though, sex regularly intertwined with war, female combatants being part of a long line of seductresses who used their sensuality as a way to deceive men. *For Men Only* suggestively related how "Vietnamese girls knew how to 'relax' a man – and make him talk."

These female "decoys" would distract careless sentries so saboteurs could infiltrate onto US military bases and steal secrets, seducing American servicemen and "setting them up for a slow slaughter." Of course, nowhere did these depictions include the diverse roles women undertook in supporting the war effort. The national Women's Union, for instance, launched a "three responsibilities movement," which encouraged women to participate in war production, to run family affairs and encourage men to join the army, and to directly support the front and the fighting. Nor did popular representations consider that women were sacrificing their childbearing years to the revolutionary struggle, taking a further toll on their physical and emotional health. In the pulps, only beautiful Eurasian girls surfaced to "spoon sex and song" to lonely GIs before betraying them to communist subversives.[114]

Themes of Asian women's duplicity had sustained Orientalist narratives for decades, the "dragon lady" an archetypal figure in western interpretations of the east. Perhaps no one better embodied this myth than Tran Le Xuan, widely known in the United States as Madame Nhu. The sister-in-law of President Ngo Dinh Diem, Madame Nhu placed herself firmly within the lineage of women warriors dating back to the Trung sisters, often being photographed wielding a pistol while dressed in "glamorous clothes." Her 2011 Associated Press obituary described Madame Nhu as an "outspoken beauty" who wore tight silk tunics showcasing "her slender body," revealing how pulp language inspired long after the demise of men's adventure mags. Madame Nhu's "bouffant hairdo" apparently proved far more interesting than her role in establishing the southern Women's Paramilitary Corps.[115] With little imagination, readers could discern a resemblance in a 1968 *Men*'s story, "Saigon's Queen of the Assassin Angels." Al Rossi's dramatic artwork portrays a female VC terrorist leader, the "Dragon Lady," wearing tight, western-style clothes, an unzipped leather jacket noticeably exposing her cleavage. Leaning back on her motorcycle, she tosses a Molotov cocktail at a burning American building, a lone MP firing back against the attack.[116]

If Rossi wasn't directly channeling Madame Nhu, who became vociferously critical of US policy in South Vietnam, his illustration nonetheless conveyed another popular trope of the "long-haired warriors" – women's wartime deceit warranted harsh treatment once their treachery was exposed. Since the beginning of the US mission in Vietnam, Americans struggled with defining spatial lines between battle-fields and safe areas. Women only complicated this process, at least in the popular mindset. General characterizations depicted them as single combatants or snipers who refused to fight by the rules of war and who mutilated male bodies whenever the chance arose. Given these attitudes, the opportunity for violence against women surely increased as the American war dragged on.[117]

The pulps obviously contributed to male anxieties over the duplicitous Asian, *Stag* printing a full "dramatic escape" book bonus on Sky-raider pilot James "Bing" Crosby, who crashes behind enemy lines and shortly thereafter meets Frances Qui Lo, a "knockout" with "neatly curved thighs and classically-rounded buttocks." She volunteers to help him escape, but by story's end readers find that she is a communist spy, covertly sharing with the VC Crosby's plans to destroy a bridge as they make their way through hostile territory. When an ARVN officer finally shoots Frances, twice between the shoulders for good measure, he turns to the American and matter-of-factly states, "Very dangerous girl."[118]

Fig. 5.6 *Stag*, March 1966

None of these adventure stories included much context into why Vietnamese women might be fighting back against American invaders in the first place. The toll of a decades' long war had been substantial. Villagers forcibly removed from their ancestral homes. Refugees crowded into urban relocation camps. Family structures upended. Pulp writers seemed surprised that passive Asian women would retaliate against such injustices, despite them displaying phenomenal amounts of courage in combat. One female fighter recalled the difficulties of "our 30 gunners, including six or seven sisters," fighting an entire battalion of the US 25th Infantry Division with its helicopters, artillery, and support planes. Instead, the pulps railed against these "bitches in baggy pants" who roamed the battlefield scavenging off dead GIs in search of weapons and ammunition or engaged in murderous "seduce and destroy" operations.[119]

Reality ran far afield from these interpretations. While considerable work remains to be done on women's contributions to the Vietnamese wars of the twentieth century, it is clear that they played an integral role in a protracted insurgency, wielding political and military influence over much of South Vietnam's population. They took up arms, spread propaganda, harassed soldiers, and raised families in a social environment disrupted by armed conflict. Many had little choice but to defend their homes caught within a deadly struggle between two competing governments. War also created an "all-encompassing and inescapable military space," forcing changes to long-standing gender norms, if only temporarily. In one famous example, Nguyen Thi Dinh aspired to join the anti-French movement in 1945 but men in her village told her that if she wanted to carry out revolutionary activities, she could do it at home. By the end of the American war, she had served as a member of the Presidium of the National Liberation Front and headed the Women's Liberation Association, an organization with village cells in areas controlled by the Vietcong. Dinh's impressive achievements may not have been the norm, but they reflected reality far better than most adventure magazine tales.[120]

Additionally, the voices of South Vietnamese women still need uncovering. More than just bar girls or housemaids, they participated in a variety of crucial war-related activities. Thousands enlisted in the

Women's Armed Forces Corps (WAFC), the *Los Angeles Times* noting in pulp-like language how these "Vietnamese girls" were trading "frills for war drills." Others served with the National Police, participated in revolutionary development work, or joined the People's Self-Defense Forces. They were nurses, social workers, and ARVN camp supporters. Not simply victims of the war, women of South Vietnam actively engaged with their communities, whether as part of the wartime economy or as diligent members of the GVN's national security apparatus. On the whole, these sacrifices escaped the notice not just of pulp writers, but of almost all Americans covering the war. Perhaps the exotic Oriental mold was too hard to break, especially when places like Saigon appeared, on the surface, to validate long-held fantasies. Hard-working female political cadre or community development workers did not invite attention as much as the seductive "dragon lady."[121]

Nor did the postwar consequences that Vietnamese women suffered elicit much comment. For those who were raped during the war or forced into prostitution for survival, feelings of shame and guilt followed them home to their families. In many cases, the emotional trauma could not as easily be mended as the physical wounds of war. (Pulp fantasies left out these nightmares.) Some victims of sexual violence felt stigmatized by their communities and could not shake a gripping sense of insecurity.[122] Mothers with Amerasian babies faced neighbors' "half-breed dog" taunts aimed at their infants, while others suffered along with children pained by disabilities stemming from the ecocide caused by US herbicides and other chemical agents. Nor did a sense of gender equality last long after war's end. A firm sense of gender stratification reemerged upon unification, any social and political advances fleeting despite the recognition bestowed upon Vietnamese Heroic Mothers. If the war in Vietnam had largely failed to empower men, to provide them with a sense of masculinity, neither did it help women realize their own dreams of a life fulfilled.[123]

In the end, men's adventure magazines endorsed a vision of militarized masculinity that proved wildly misleading when compared with the reality of a revolutionary war in Southeast Asia. And yet, for some, male fantasies made the violence enacted upon the Vietnamese population feel somehow acceptable, even necessary. Renderings of war in the macho pulps included a cast of villainous characters that all seemed deserving of Americans' hostility – brutal communist insurgents, corrupt Saigon officials, and cheap urban prostitutes. It should not surprise us that so many young GIs, fueled by resentment and anger, and feeling insecure about their manhood in a disappointing war, lashed out so viciously against the very people they were there to protect.

Conclusion: Male Veterans Remember Their War

ON A BRISK APRIL MORNING at the University of Kansas, a group of scholars and veterans of the American war in Vietnam are meeting for a sweeping discussion on manpower and morale issues after the 1968 Tet offensive. While the conversations are engaging, the veterans, nearly all men now in their sixties and seventies, noticeably are most impressed with the luncheon speaker, Chris Noel. Host of the Armed Forces Radio show "A Date with Chris," the former actress and pin-up model was a favorite among GIs serving in Vietnam. It is clear she still is. Wearing a tiger-stripe camouflage blouse over her bright red pantsuit, Noel stands tall in cowboy boots, each emblazoned with an embroidered American flag. She is contagiously cheerful, full of energy, and her respect for the roomful of vets is undeniably genuine. They wait patiently in line to have their photographs taken with her, wide smiles on their faces.

Noel holds some papers in a black notebook, which she briefly peruses before setting them aside. She scans the room and then straightaway apologizes to the women in the audience. It seems odd, but she explains. Yes, there were women in Vietnam – Red Cross volunteers, USO entertainers like herself, and female nurses. But, she pauses for effect, "This was a man's war!" Noel shares how she traveled to Vietnam as a young woman to "go build up the morale of the troops." It was humbling to serve, she says, yet something happened along the journey. "It turned me from a young girl into a woman, just like it did for the men in Vietnam." Her comments are brief, yet Noel leaves with one simple message: "These guys were the best in our society."[1]

Some fifty years after American troops had begun their unheroic withdrawal from Vietnam, Noel's comments suggest the myth of war turning boys into men has not much suffered from the weight of history. Yet in the late 1960s and early 1970s, a new generation of draft-eligible youths were questioning the orthodoxy of war as a man-making experience. In the process, men's adventure magazines faded in popularity. The pulps could no longer attract readers from a society uneasy with, if not mobilized against, hypermasculine images and bloody war stories. Amid an avalanche of social change in the early 1970s, men's mags became a relic of the Cold War past.[2]

While the sexual liberation and counterculture movements posed stark alternatives to pulp conservatism, a new wave of "radical" feminism proved just as equipped to defy the macho narratives of men's adventure magazines. Feminists spoke out against a gendered "caste system," arguing that women were "oppressed as women, regardless of class or race" and appealing to Americans for an end to "male dominance." The very definition of masculinity seemed under assault.[3] No wonder pulp stories tendering advice on how to "keep a woman sexually subjugated" looked increasingly anachronistic by the late 1960s. Nor did stories on "grimy beatniks" who "disgrace us abroad" find much traction among those young readers willing to contest US foreign policy in Southeast Asia and the well-heeled elite in Washington, DC. As America's Vietnam war began winding down, even the term "macho" – within some circles, at least – came to be seen as a "dirty word."[4]

Out of synch with the cultural revolutions of the early 1970s, adventure mags blending war and sex offered little of value to a new generation of young male readers. True, long-standing Cold War gender anxieties remained. In February 1970, *Bluebook* warned of a new "assault on American virility," where "inverted sex practices" were making it difficult to determine who was straight and who had "given over to homosexuality and other sex aberrations." Worse, women had taken on an "aggressive role" and were demanding that men be "submissive regardless of what it may do to him." By the time of publication, though, stories like these sat uneasily alongside more modern social and cultural constructions of masculinity, suggesting that a universal model of manhood as had long been depicted by the pulps actually never quite existed.[5]

Neither did pulp writers and editors find that war stories were as easily transmitted to young men coming of age in the mid to late 1960s. Compared with World War II, Vietnam tales lacked popular appeal. A stalemated, bloody conflict, punctuated by the public awareness of atrocities like My Lai, hardly inspired military service, thus contesting the symbolic power of war itself. By the latter stages of Vietnam, veterans like Tobias Wolff were questioning their convictions of war as a man-making experience. As Wolff recalled, the whole ordeal was just "something I had to get through." When fellow vets returned home with disappointed aspirations of being lauded a hero by an appreciative nation, the warrior myth appeared even more wanting. For the pulps, there was little nostalgia in looking back upon such an unpopular conflict.[6]

Moreover, the American war in Vietnam complicated questions over who was good and evil. The one-dimensional, triumphalist narratives of earlier pulp stories and comic books no longer held up when compared with unfavorable news reports and veteran narratives. One vet who served three combat tours in Vietnam could not make sense of the evil he had seen or become. "I mean real evil. I wasn't prepared for it all." How could American GIs be "just warriors" if they were horrified at what they had turned into?[7] Pulp writers took note, Mario Puzo recalling that he could pen only a handful of tales on Vietnam because the topic was "absolute poison." According to the author of *The Godfather*, readers "hated" Vietnam because "we weren't the heroes." By the early 1970s, even *Sgt. Rock* comics were ending their stories with "Make War No More." As legendary comic book artist and editor Joe Kubert explained, "I wanted to make it clear that, despite the fact that I was editing war books, we were not glorifying war."[8]

The pulps also retreated from the glorification of war. Covers no longer displayed the lush artwork of Mort Künstler or Samson Pollen, instead featuring photographs of female models in various states of undress. With the popularity of magazines like *Penthouse*, *Oui*, and *Swank* in the 1970s, men's adventure magazines ultimately made the leap into the "skin" market. As the editorial director for *Stag* and *Men*, Noah Sarlat, rationalized in late 1976, "We try to reach the guys who want to read sophisticated magazines like *Playboy* and *Penthouse* but can't understand them. We have no pretensions." *Stag*'s covers occasionally promised a riveting World War II story, but the magazine became explicitly more sexual by the middle of the decade. The May 1976 issue, for example, leads with bare-breasted cover model Nellie Bridge staring seductively into the camera, the list of stories beside her proof that this is an "all-new Stag" with "more girls" and "more daring." Potential buyers are enticed with a review of the ten hottest porno films of 1976, a male/female masturbation handbook, and X-rated answers to readers' wildest sex letters by porn star Tina Russell. Tales of adventure, war, or heroism are conspicuously absent.[9]

If the magazines' more sexually explicit material suggested a temporary rending of war from popular definitions of masculinity, the acceleration of sexual liberalism in the late 1960s and early 1970s placed additional obstacles in front of pulp writers who hoped to reassert traditional gender hierarchies through their stories. This sexual revolution encouraged a wider acceptance of pornographic images and films in mainstream popular culture. Even Gerard Damiano's *Deep Throat*, a 1972 X-rated release, earned reviews from leading film critics Judith Crist and Vincent Canby.[10] While detractors slammed the obscenity and exploitation of women in these movies, a rising number of Americans came to approve of sexual activity between unmarried partners. The cultural landscape clearly was shifting. Though magazines like *Hustler* continued to view the female body as an object for consumption, increasingly more women than ever before were willing to contest being stripped of their public voices and demand they take part in the singles culture that the sexual revolution had inspired.[11]

No less challenging to a militarized sense of masculinity, women's participation in the All-Volunteer Force (AVF) also complicated narratives that war was just a masculine endeavor. As the draft law expired on 1 July 1973, the armed forces no longer could rely on conscription to staff their formations. Concerns over manpower shortages helped stimulate recruiting efforts aimed specifically at female recruits. Their participation in the enlisted ranks exceeded expectations, rising from 1.3 percent of the total force in 1971 to 7.6 percent in 1979.[12] Traditional male attitudes, however, proved savagely resilient. Vietnam veteran and future Democratic senator James Webb wrote a scathing piece in the November 1979 issue of *The Washingtonian* titled "Women Can't Fight." The Annapolis graduate lamented that civilian policymakers, by allowing in female midshipmen, were attempting to "sexually sterilize the Naval Academy environment in the name of equality." To Webb, the entire process of combat leadership training had been undermined, and the nation's military forces were "doomed to suffer the consequences." Lest Americans think these views were confined to bitter Vietnam vets, conservative antifeminist Phyllis Schlafly argued that the "very idea of women serving in military combat is so unnatural, so ugly, that it almost sounds like a death wish for our species." Resistance to changing gender norms thus ranged from outright disdain of women to sheltering protectiveness.[13]

Defiance to the US armed forces' supposed feminization equally could be found in the rise of a paramilitary culture in the mid and late 1970s. It is no coincidence that *Soldier of Fortune* magazine started in 1975, not long after traditional adventure magazines, combining war and sex, had fallen out of favor. If "stag" mags were going to focus more on sex, then *Soldier of Fortune: The Journal of Professional Adventurers* could retain the macho pulps' emphasis on wartime heroism and martial masculinity. By embracing a re-imagined warrior ethos, veterans of the recent war in Southeast Asia might find redemption from their disenchantment with the outcome of Vietnam. Not surprisingly, in these "new" war stories, vengeance took center stage. Beginning in 1980, *Soldier of Fortune* even started publishing classified ads to hire would-be mercenaries. Veterans could market their expertise as a "jungle warfare" or "weapons specialist," suggesting an authenticity to this new form of men's magazine. Apparently, a market existed. Major news outlets like the *New York Times* reported an increase in crimes committed by perpetrators hired from the *Soldier of Fortune* classifieds. Perhaps "real" men capable of action still roamed post-Vietnam America.[14]

Hairy-chested adventurers certainly were operating overseas. In the late 1970s, hundreds of American mercenaries, mostly Vietnam vets, traveled to Rhodesia and Angola to fight on behalf of the white minority governments there. Troubled that the United States wasn't doing enough to halt the spread of communism in Africa, these guns-for-hire saw it as their duty to respond to recruiting ads in venues like *Soldier of Fortune.* As one mercenary lamented, "The West isn't doing its job. The US especially isn't doing its duty. If they're too scared to fight the Communists, then people like me have to act independently." Even former Special Forces Sergeant Barry Sadler, who catapulted to fame with his 1966 hit "The Ballad of the Green Berets," eventually moved to Central America, running guns and authoring the popular Casca pulp novel series. Arguably, many of these mercenary soldiers traveled to global hotspots hoping to prove their masculinity after a failed American war in Southeast Asia. Sadler intimated that might be true for him. "The hardest thing to do," he recalled, had been "to live up to the illusion of those who wanted me to be a hero."[15]

In fact, stories of returning veterans hardly lived up to the ideals proffered in men's adventure mags. Popular stereotypes certainly over-emphasized the broken, maladjusted warrior image. Closer to the truth, the vast majority of Vietnam veterans returned home to pursue success-ful lives unencumbered by the aftereffects of war. Still, boys had not come back as victorious heroes who had symbolically earned their man-hood. Rather, much of an ambivalent American society viewed them as either victims or survivors of a bad war. (Most female veterans were not incorporated into this narrative for well over a decade after the 1975 fall of Saigon.)[16] The whole experience seemed terribly unfulfilling. As one veteran remembered, "If this was manhood, I would prefer to have remained a child." Vietnam had thus turned the macho pulp narrative on its head. Heroic masculinity seemed farther out of reach thanks to the war, not the principal reward for a job well done.[17]

However, discerning pulp readers might have expected that not all vets adjusted so easily to their postwar lives. An editor's note at the end of a 1961 *Man's Magazine* story on "The One-Man Army of Bataan" remarked how the World War II hero Arthur W. Wermuth had divorced and was drifting "from place to place." In civilian life, the Silver Star awardee "did not adjust too easily," toiling away in a service station, selling pharmaceut-ical supplies, and joining a flying circus. Even Bill Mauldin's famous characters Willie and Joe are found struggling in a postwar world. In a *Man's Day* feature from early 1953, we see Willie "back to fighting with his wife" and working a forty-hour week. Joe, single, "drifted languidly about, hoping for bigger and better veterans' bonuses" before re-upping in the army and heading to Korea. Nor were these strains pure fiction. In early 1962, *Stag* included a full-page photo of a Korean War veteran brandishing a rifle on a housing development rooftop and threatening to shoot anyone who came near him. Policemen persuaded the ex-GI to surrender, but the episode revealed potential long-term emotional and psychological consequences of serving in combat.[18]

Popular accounts of Vietnam veterans struggling to reintegrate into society, of being violent or drug-ridden, followed suit and proliferated in the early 1970s. The comparison with stable and heroic World War II vets appeared stark. Yet narratives of the "greatest generation" conveniently sidestepped the fact that there was an enormous amount of self-medication and of struggling to adjust within the veteran community. Somehow, alcohol use (and abuse) in 1950s VFW halls seemed far more socially acceptable than smoking marijuana on college campuses a decade later. *True*, for instance, ran a rare story in late 1968 on "pot-smoking veterans" who potentially might threaten the nation's social and moral equilibrium. "Tens of thousands of veterans are returning every month from Viet Nam," the magazine warned, "most of whom have smoked marijuana at least once." If marginalized, disenchanted veteran-addicts returned home emasculated by a futile war, anxious Americans worried about a surge in domestic violence unleashed by an untold number of "walking time bombs."[19]

By the 1980s, the veteran as victim plotline had run its course. With a patriotic commander-in-chief now labeling Vietnam a "noble cause," a paranoid insomniac from *Taxi Driver* (1976) or a flashback-plagued vet in *Heroes* (1977) surely did not encourage a national narrative of regeneration and redemption.[20] Instead, hypermasculine heroes, with excessively muscular bodies, landed on the big screen with a vengeance. Sylvester Stallone's Rambo not only returned to Vietnam to rescue American POWs and finally defeat the Vietnamese communists, but also uncovered the deceit of government bureaucrats who had helped lose the war in the first place. Rambo might struggle at home, but American society clearly had not emasculated this brutally violent warrior. The brawny Vietnam vet would have been right at home within the pages of men's adventure magazines.[21]

This Reagan-era remasculinization of the Vietnam veteran suggests that popular notions of gender and masculinity can, and do, change over time. If gender is a social construct, then it remains a malleable concept as long as society continues to reevaluate its norms and values. Moreover, definitions of "heroism" and "manhood" can be used as political tools, reinforcing or, alternatively, challenging the power relationships between men and women. While the macho pulps may have fallen out of favor in the early 1970s – in part, as a consequence of second-wave feminism – the reemergence of fearless warriors like Rambo in the mid 1980s left little doubt that America's distaste with militarized masculinity was only a temporary phenomenon.[22]

REMEMBERING WAR

War stories are more than just tales of military engagements. They tell us something about how and why societies desire to remember war and, particularly, their male veterans in certain ways. While these stories are affected by larger cultural influences, they also help to shape social attitudes as well. For example, young men's conceptions of manhood and what they deem as appropriate behavior are influenced by a variety of sources: social, cultural, political, and familial. In the 1950s and 1960s, men's adventure magazines were a unique part of this socialization process. By melding together stories of war and sex, they helped sustain, if not validate, a larger cultural narrative defining gender as a hierarchy of power relationships. In the macho pulps, heroic warriors and sexual conquerors reigned supreme. Even if Cold War-era men fretted over losing their masculinity in a consumeristic, post-World War II society, they still could look to pulp champions as proof that men mattered most.[23]

Many Vietnam veteran memoirists emulated the basic characteristics of men's adventure magazines. Most certainly, these writers were angry and contested the idea that war was an ennobling experience. Yet their focus centered upon the male warrior in combat. Among the more popular remembrances, Peter Goldman and Tony Fuller's *Charlie Company* was touted as the real-life exploits of a "gook-hunting, dirt-eating, dog-soldiering combat infantry unit." The book's subtitle, *What Vietnam*

Fig. C.1 *Valor*, June 1959

Did to Us, also alluded to the belief that these warriors were victims far more than the local Vietnamese. Yet these men remained masters of war. In John Del Vecchio's *The 13th Valley*, we meet Egan, a natural fighter with a "healthy animal paranoia." In one episode, he trumpets to his platoon mates, "War. It's wonderful. It don't make a gnat's ass difference who the enemy is. Every man, once in his life, should go to WAR." Even in the most dissatisfying of wars like Vietnam, where veterans decried their lost youth, readers might still glimpse the prospect, however small, of becoming a hero.[24]

And while warriors weren't to blame for a lost war – one returning vet making note of a cab driver railing against the "damn politicians" and "bleedin' hearts" – memoirs and novels retained the pulps' dominant narrative of sexual conqueror. A vicious rape, for instance, is at the heart of *Paco's Story* by veteran Larry Heinemann. "If the zip had been a man," the narrator shares, "we would not have bothered with the motherfucker, you understand that, don't you?" Other tales focused on the easy access to purchased sex. Bo Hathaway's novel, *A World of Hurt*, relies on popular Orientalist language as a Vietnamese prostitute entices a GI with "You fuckee now. Fifteen minute we fini."[25] When John Ketwig nervously enters a brothel for the first time, he meets Lin, who seems to emerge from most any pulp magazine. "I want very much to go with you," she says gently. "I enjoy my work, and I want very much to make you feel good." Such sexually violent and sexualized imagery suggested that the cultural stereotypes linking war and sex had retained a central place in how veterans and writers were remembering the American war in Vietnam.[26]

This cultural construct endured long after Vietnam. In the mid 1980s, *Playboy* ran an essay on US military bases in the Philippines, the "last frontier" with "beaches and bars and girls and everything cheap." As one young officer shared, "I can live here the way the British lived in India in the days of the Raj." Writing for *Esquire* during the same period, Vietnam vet William Broyles remembered going off to war with a copy of *War and Peace* and *The Charterhouse of Parma* stuffed into his pack. "They were soon replaced with *The Story of O*." As Broyles argued, "War heightens all appetites."[27]

A generation later, as Americans were immersed in another overseas war, this time in the Middle East, the story of Vietnam as a venue for sexual opportunity had changed little. National guardswoman Mickiela Montoya recalled meeting a man in Iraq who claimed the "military sends women over to give the guys eye candy to keep them sane. He said in Vietnam they had prostitutes to keep them from going crazy, but they don't have those in Iraq. So they have women soldiers instead." Philip Klay's 2014 award-winning novel *Redeployment* hits upon a similar theme, with an entire chapter titled "In Vietnam They Had Whores." In the story, a group of deployed marines are eating in a chow hall when a woman passes by. "You know," one of them says, "sometimes, girls who wouldn't give you the time of day when you were in high school change their minds once you're a war hero."[28]

And, yes, heroism still could be found in war, even in seemingly meaningless ones like Vietnam. In *We Were Soldiers Once...and Young*, Harold Moore and Joseph Galloway share the "unbelievable heroism" of 1st Cavalry troopers defending a Central Highlands landing zone (LZ) against infantry regiments from the North Vietnamese Army. When Mel Gibson's film adaption hit movie theaters in 2002, veteran Philip Beidler remembered how he "shed some silent tears for the defenders of LZ X-Ray at the end." If Americans couldn't sell themselves to Vietnam in the 1960s, it seemed they finally were having success selling Vietnam back to America in the decades that followed. The success of *We Were Soldiers Once* suggests a symbiotic relationship between heroes and how we remember war. In short, how could someone become a "hero" if their story wasn't told? Pop culture renderings like movies and adventure magazines helped maintain the possibility that the title of "hero" remained ever within reach.[29]

The macho pulps surely reinforced narratives in which triumphant battlefield exploits and heroic deaths far exceeded tales involving veterans suffering through post-traumatic stress or feelings of guilt and alienation. Rarely did adventure mags relay the rage of vets like Robert Muller, who felt like he and his fellow marines "were used like fucking cannon fodder in Vietnam." Only rarely would pulp readers get a glimpse of veterans like Sergeant Al Drabik, the first GI across the Remagen Bridge into Germany in World War II, who, in 1966, was fifty-four years old, an out-of-work butcher, and a part-time cement factory laborer. More common were tales such as "John Barrow's Sex Colony." In this 1964 offering from *Men*, a "brawling ex-GI with an unquenchable thirst for women and adventure" builds a "private paradise on a South Pacific island, stocked ... with a supply of silk-skinned, burning-eyed girls from all over the world." Clearly, Barrow's "tropical love heaven" was far better than Muller's VA hospital inhabited by "fucking drunks and derelicts and degenerates." In pulp fantasy stories, ex-GIs effortlessly retained their physical brawn and sexual appeal.[30]

Men's magazines seemed to be the solution to so much, cultural guidebooks for attaining one's manhood through valorous combat and sexual virility. They were the antidotes to men's fears and anxieties – over their masculinity, their unease with women both at home and abroad, and their concerns about not measuring up in a competitive Cold War era. Their influence could be seen not only in PX sales in Vietnam, but also in the ways in which GIs made sense of the war. The popular humor magazine *Grunt Free Press*, first published in 1968, has the distinct feel of a pulp mag. In its first issue, *Grunt*, dubbed the "Magazine for Men in Vietnam," included a story asking if Vietnamese women were the most "beautiful" in the Orient, as well as cartoons of nude Asians seducing American GIs, whether in a foxhole or in a bedroom. Chris Noel, wearing white leather boots and a mini skirt, graces the pages, though she remains anonymous to the reader – "who pays attention to faces or names?," the caption asks. And yet despite its sexist, nonconformist outlook, *Grunt Free Press* still conceded that men in uniform and the weapons they carried were "instruments" for the "preservation of a society, a way of life." Apparently, even rebellious periodicals could push the boundaries only so far.[31]

For many veterans, however, the Vietnam experience repudiated much of what the pulp magazines had been selling for so long. War wasn't heroic or manly. Asian women weren't submissive or a remedy to war's disillusionments. Mel Gibson may have been inspirational on the big screen, but moviegoers did not share in the recollections of Hal Moore's troopers, who looked in the mirror every night and thought of "all those guys killed in action, wounded in action, and their friends, their relatives and all those altered lives." The real war left behind sorrow and pain, anger and frustration, self-pity and regret.[32]

It is important, then, that we think more deeply about how we remember and how we portray war in our popular culture. Young men often find meaning in images and structures of male superiority, especially when the protagonist is a bold, heroic warrior. They take voyeuristic pleasure in viewing the destruction of war. They are enticed by the anticipation of sexual encounters with and rewards from exotic foreign women. Arguably, they also feel embittered when the reality of war betrays them, leading to a pursuit for retribution, whether militarily or sexually. Along the way, many veterans also question the promise of war as a man-making endeavor. As David Donovan noted of his time in Vietnam, "I wanted so much to be a child again, not a man beset by the dogs of war."[33]

But in popular culture, John Wayne, the movie star, never had to grow up, never had to experience for himself the nuances and hardships of modern combat, never had to deal with the aftereffects of war. Even in *The Green Berets*, there was no victory by movie's end, only more fighting. As the American war in Vietnam came to a close, disappointed veterans were left to balance the weight of culture in relation to their own experiences. Many found the war wanting. Whether in John Wayne movies or men's magazines, the reality of war never quite matched the adventure and romance depicted in popular culture. The pulps, it turns out, mostly had been a façade.[34]

In the end, socially sanctioned versions of heroic warriors and sexual conquerors carry weight. How we remember war matters, and the ways in which we look back upon the past have consequences. This is why placing men's adventure magazines within their proper historical context is worthwhile. There are social, cultural, and political ripple effects when we accept, as a "natural" imperative, images of men being overtly masculine, having free range over all others, and taking what they want without penalty. The concepts of gender and masculinity, however, need not be fixed. Thus, it seems important that we search for alternative narratives, ones in which manhood is not simply defined by military heroics or sexual conquest.[35]

REDEFINING MASCULINITY AND THE "ADVENTURE" OF WAR

If Vietnam vet William Broyles indeed had replaced a copy of *War and Peace* with *The Story of O* in his wartime rucksack, he more concretely argued that the "enduring emotion" of war was comradeship. Men, and men alone, shared in the brutal spectacle of war, the "only utopian experience most of us ever have." There were other reasons why men loved war – the power of life and death, for instance – but Broyles lavished praise on the connections between "sex and destruction" that touched the "mythic domains of our soul." While the former *Newsweek* editor acknowledged that soldiers suffered death and isolation on the battlefield, he nonetheless gave the impression of war being *the* ultimate romantic, man-making experience. As Broyles argued, it was "no accident that men love war, as love and war are at the core of man." Just one short decade after Americans had departed Vietnam, war, it seemed, was back in fashion.[36]

Broyles's language and assumptions are insightful, for they demonstrate the social power of pop culture gender constructions and their relationship to war. Veteran narratives, whether in men's adventure magazines or in memoirs, help normalize expectations about uniformed service and manhood, about military occupation and sexual abuse. In the process, these gendered tropes become embedded in larger popular culture. When a young soldier in the 25th Infantry Division, for example, noted how there were a few rapes and sexual assaults in his division's area, but "nothing, unfortunately, out of the ordinary," what did this say about his definitions of "normal" in a wartime environment?[37] Such thinking could not simply have been an outcome of military indoctrination. When *Men* ran articles on a "treacherous nymph" who sold out the US Navy at Pearl Harbor or *Saga* described Korea as "a good-looking woman with gonorrhea," this form of socialization not only reinforced the experience of military basic training, but corroborated how young readers already were inclined to think about war, power, and masculinity.[38]

Without question, the macho pulps were an escape, a way to behold brave men who had surmounted the limits of an emasculating, consumeristic society. These adventurers held no fears of not being able to measure up. They were supermen, in battle and in bed. The cover alone of the April 1966 issue of *Men in Adventure* said it all – "hard hitting stories of war adventure and sex" that promised "war and pussy galore." Yet many of these tales were fabricated by pulp writers. Fiction melded imperceptibly into a constructed form of reality. Walter Kaylin owned up to the fact that he and Mario Puzo once ran out of major battles to feature in their stories. Their solution? They made one up. As Kaylin conceded, "It was a battle so close to Anzio and just as fierce. Nobody would have ever heard of it. It was a completely mythical battle, which Mario wrote about in great detail and nobody ever questioned it." Perhaps it didn't matter. As long as readers could revel in a sense of adventure, pulp writers had achieved their goal.[39]

Fig. C.2 *Male*, January 1967

For veterans, in particular, the pulps allowed them to hold onto their battlefield experiences, a social forum articulating how their military service was noteworthy and still valid. Adventure magazines ensured their stories were not forgotten. They might even help with the transition to postwar life, granting them access to others who also had seen some of war's horrors. Yet these potentially beneficial aspects of the pulps have to be balanced with their more negative attributes. Adventure mags reinforced ideas of hypermasculinity and militarized notions of manhood, and amplified the damaging influence of aggressive sexuality. These traits could be passed down to the next generation of young warriors just as easily as tales of sacrifice and comradery. It seems likely that only reflective readers would have caught these important distinctions.

The macho pulps, however, were not known for their nuance. In general, they imagined war and sex based on unrealistic conceptions that were pervasive in Cold War popular culture, ones that were grandly heroic and lustfully violent. It would be wrong, however, to assume these visions evaporated in the late 1960s and early 1970s. The editor for John Bahnsen's memoir *American Warrior*, published in 2007, relished in the pulp narrative decades after the market gave way. "Mythical military heroes," Wess Roberts claimed, "are often made out as larger-than-life figures who are fierce fighters, brave beyond compare, invincible in battle, loyal to their soldiers, faithful to their duty, defenders of their country, yet cursed with a weakness for beautiful women." That Roberts saw in Bahnsen all these features, thus confirming his status as an "American warrior," goes far in revealing the continuing allure of militarized definitions of masculinity and the supposed adventure that war provides.[40]

It seems important, then, to consider how the American experience with war has been affected by soldiers who carried with them popular narratives of the heroic warrior and sexual conqueror that proved so elusive in reality. In a way, the pulps helped to miscommunicate to their readers, if not society at large, soldiers' experiences in the Cold War era. That led to future working-class warriors making faulty assumptions about military service, war, and the relationship of gender dynamics to both. One veteran, clearly wrestling with his guilt after killing a Vietcong insurgent, shared how inaccurate perceptions of war had left their emotional mark, long after his actions in combat. "I felt sorry. I don't know why I felt sorry. John Wayne never felt sorry."[41] Nor did any of the heroes in men's adventure magazines. Pulp warriors never suffered the consequences of war.

But real soldiers do. And because they do, we all should question versions of war that rely on a warped sense of militarized masculinity. When former Marine Corps Commandant Robert Barrow testified to congress in the early 1990s that "you have to protect the manliness of war" and thus keep women out of combat, he was touting a cultural construct that proved central to men's magazines. It's unclear if Barrow ever read the macho pulps, but his language reflected a way of thinking that would have been familiar to adventure readers. Similar assessments could be found well into 2018. One marine veteran writing for *The Federalist* outlined a host of reasons why only men should serve in infantry units: women get pregnant, they undermine unit cohesion, they have less muscle mass. Besides, the vet claimed, "Men were created to be protectors – protectors of their homes and protectors of society." A pulp aficionado in 1958 or 1968 likely would have agreed with the author's assertion that war was a "man's environment."[42]

While sexist attitudes like these clearly persist, it remains possible to rethink the associative relationship between culture and experience when it comes to war. We can, and should, develop a sense of critical thinking among our warriors, opening up the possibility of them questioning long-held tropes of war and sex. Not all pulp readers were seduced by the assumption made in offerings like *Saigon after Dark* that it was "only natural that the GI looks for solace in the silken arms of a woman after a grueling day dodging death in the rice-paddies." One soldier responding to a *Stag* article on reducing VD rates argued that "there must be a better way than encouraging prostitution." Another GI serving in Japan wrote to *Man's Magazine*, declaring that there "is a lot more over here than pure sex! There are plenty of exotic places to visit and unusual things to do without the habitual emphasis on women." If at least some Cold War readers were willing to rechannel their energies away from hypersexual notions of American manhood, then surely we too can reconsider the ways in which we tell stories of war and masculinity.[43]

The challenge, it seems, is moving beyond the various pulp conceptions of "normal" male behavior. War need not be the only, even primary, rite of passage into manhood. Pop culture heroes should not rely on sexual conquest for our approval. Arguments invoking supposed gender inequalities to claim that the very nature of women disqualifies them for combat should not be part of the dominant narrative when it comes to debates over military service and even citizenship. Moreover, we should push back against clichéd portrayals of women in war – the sexy pin-up model, the exotic "Oriental" dragon lady, the duplicitous seductress, or the beautiful but deadly female sniper. War does not require sexual action on the part of the warrior. Popular narratives of what it means to be a man need not rest on soldiers dominating their enemy *and* women in the same breath.[44]

Redefining adventure in war may, in fact, help young men and women cope better with the realities they face when immersed in wartime environments. It is possible to be an empathetic warrior. Even in the midst of combat, one can be compassionate and benevolent without necessarily demonstrating impotence. The key is opening up conversations that offer alternate models of masculinity. The working-class pulp readers who ultimately went to Vietnam were both sincere and innocent, yet the prevailing representation of manhood they consumed bred only contempt for men who showed weakness of any kind. Adventure magazines' idealized vision of militarized masculinity encouraged no other possible alternatives to aggressive behavior, either on the battlefield or in the bedroom. Male relationships were about power, pure and simple. Surely, there are other ways to conceive of interactions between men and women.[45]

Moreover, other tangible outcomes potentially surface when we consider alternate versions of pulp masculinity. Adventure magazines proved to be poor preparation for combat in South Vietnam, where the political war rivaled the military one. Power wielded by the NLF, for instance, oftentimes had little resemblance to the kind advocated in the macho pulps. Would a different version of the modern-day warrior have better equipped young GIs for their tours in Southeast Asia? And, if popular notions of aggressive masculinity helped to normalize violence against the Vietnamese, we might consider the plausible outcomes if Americans had thought differently about the civilian population. The physical and psychological toll on the Vietnamese was enormous, and US vets suffered as well. In fact, one recent study found that veterans who harmed civilians or prisoners in Vietnam were among those more likely to endure postwar trauma. Violence against noncombatants harmed victim as well as perpetrator, yet rarely in the pulps did readers confront this fundamental characteristic of war.[46]

Instead, adventure magazines fostered a version of masculinity during the 1950s and 1960s that arguably demanded conformity to a narrow definition of what it meant to be a man. To many working-class teens, contesting this popular interpretation risked social delegitimization and accusations of effeminacy. In such a way, the pulps' influence on the emotional and social education of young readers appears fairly significant. It also seems likely that the magazines' sexist, if not misogynistic, constructions of women, Asians in particular, may have encouraged GIs to view wartime sexual violence during the American war in Vietnam as somehow acceptable. In an era where far too many critics today problematically link video game violence to mass shootings, we certainly need to take care in arguing a causal relationship between wartime rape and pulp adventure. One was never a direct outcome of the other. Yet it is clear that adventure mags showcased, issue after issue, an obvious correlation between war and sex. Real men dominated their enemies, whether they be a Vietcong insurgent or an exotic "Oriental."[47]

As inhibitions declined over time in a frustrating war, it may be that what the articles expressed became more stimulating to their readers. Pulp stories found interesting at home might have been more compelling as they connected viscerally with GIs who were tired, disillusioned, and frightened. Adventure tales may not have been marching orders for soldiers to engage in sexual violence, but they inculcated in their readers a sense that male aggression was central to success in the modern world. By implication, violence became associated with victory.[48]

In early March 1965, some 3,500 US marines landed in Da Nang, the first major contingent of American ground combat troops deployed to South Vietnam. The *New York Times* heaped praise on the marines who had "a historic reputation as a fighting force on the mainland of Asia dating back to pre-World War II days." That same month, *Male* magazine featured a story by Mario Puzo on American GIs who had "turned Hitler's top tank army into scrap," before offering a piece on Korean "give-give girls" who were turning areas south of the 38th Parallel into a "wild pleasure grove."[49]

Looking back, the prospect for adventure in the early spring of 1965 seems so palpable. A new war was about to offer young men a chance to follow in their fathers' footsteps, to grasp the mantle of manhood that had been won against the forces of evil in the Second World War. The pulps would help inspire a new generation of American warriors who, in turn, would encourage their own sons to mature into courageous heroes. It all appeared so glamorous. Yet less than a decade later, men's adventure magazines had faded into obscurity, the pulp fantasyland ruptured by a war that begat few heroes and far too many villains.[50]

In the end, the reality of Vietnam helped to discredit the macho adventure narrative, if only temporarily. Perhaps, this is why examining such a "low brow" form of Cold War pop culture still matters today. How we construct popular tales of war and masculinity, how we fashion our ideas on what it means to be a man, matters, especially when the narrative is found wanting. There are consequences when young men, encouraged by fantasy, assertively seek out opportunities to prove their dominance and come up short. Shattered illusions can result in disappointment and frustration, which then can lead to hostility and violence. There are costs when we idealize war as *the* essential man-making experience. The macho pulps of the Cold War era sold an appealing version of adventure to enthusiastic readers, but not all battles so easily place young men on the road to martial glory.

Notes

INTRODUCTION

1 On Wayne as a "god" from popular culture, see Katherine Kinney, *Friendly Fire: American Images of the Vietnam War* (New York, NY: Oxford University Press, 2000), 12. See also Antony Easthope, *What a Man's Gotta Do: The Masculine Myth in Popular Culture* (Boston, MA: Unwin Hyman, 1990), 20. On Wayne's relation to the Cold War, see Bernard F. Dick, *The Screen Is Red: Hollywood, Communism, and the Cold War* (Jackson, MI: University Press of Mississippi, 2016), 210–216. On Wayne's characters as "cool-under-pressure," see Melinda L. Pash, *In the Shadow of the Greatest Generation: The Americans Who Fought the Korean War* (New York, NY: New York University Press, 2012), 11.

2 Clear-cut hero in Michael Anderegg, "Hollywood and Vietnam: John Wayne and Jane Fonda as Discourse," in *Inventing Vietnam: The War in Film and Television*, ed. Michael Anderegg (Philadelphia, PA: Temple University Press, 1991), 25. On *Sands*, see John Bodnar, *The "Good War" in American Memory* (Baltimore, MD: The Johns Hopkins University Press, 2010), 139. Wayne in relation to Vietnam in Lloyd B. Lewis, *The Tainted War: Culture and Identity in Vietnam War Narratives* (Westport, CT: Greenwood Press, 1985), 25. Self-doubt in Lewis B. Puller, Jr., *Fortunate Son* (New York, NY: Grove Weidenfeld, 1991), 63.

3 Macho pulps in Bill Osgerby, "Muscular Manhood and Salacious Sleaze: The Singular World of the 1950s Macho Pulps," in *Containing America: Cultural Production and Consumption in Fifties America*, eds. Nathan Abrams and Julie Hughes (Birmingham: The University of Birmingham Press, 2000), 125. On the production and representation of popular culture, see Katie Milestone and Anneke Meyer, *Gender and Popular Culture* (Cambridge: Polity, 2012), 5–9; and Henry Jenkins, *The Wow Climax: Tracing the Emotional Impact of Popular Culture* (New York, NY: New York University Press, 2007), 15, 57. Of note, the term "pulps" is a contested one. Hardcore fans of pre-World War II pulp magazines, for example, chafe when the term "pulp" is applied to anything else. Because men's adventure magazines share thematic and artistic DNA with the classic pulps, I use "pulp" as a shorthand, an adjective to describe a style of media that involved action and adventure and was more gritty than cerebral. My thanks to Robert Deis for helping me navigate this terrain.

4 Walter Kaylin, "The Yank Who Led a Legion of Russian Convict Women," *Male*, January 1964, 13. For a discussion on warrior hero characteristics, see Nyameka Mankayi, "Male Soldiers' Constructions of Masculinity, Sexuality and Sexual Violence," *Journal of Psychology in Africa* Vol. 20, No. 4 (2010): 592.

5 Philip Atlee, "Nude Tribe Caper," *Stag*, February 1967, 28, 92, 101. Kurt Mengel clearly was a nod to Josef Mengele, the Auschwitz Angel of Death. "Sin Captive Compound" by Erik Broske contains a similar storyline of an ex-GI seeking revenge against his fiancé's killers. *Male*, February 1968, 14–17, 94–101.

6 Lee Server has described the pulps as "publishing's poor, ill-bred stepchild." *Danger Is My Business: An Illustrated History of the Fabulous Pulp Magazines* (San Francisco, CA: Chronicle Books, 1993), 15. Low-brow in David M. Earle, *All Man! Hemingway, 1950s Men's Magazines, and the Masculine Persona* (Kent, OH: The Kent State University Press, 2009), 2; and Kathryn Weibel, *Mirror Mirror: Images of Women Reflected in Popular Culture* (Garden City, NY: Anchor Books, 1977), 28–29. Disposability and hard-boiled in Woody Haut, *Pulp Culture: Hardboiled Fiction and the Cold War* (London: Serpent's Tail, 1995), 3, 6. On kitsch, see Clement Greenberg, *Art and Culture: Critical Essays* (Boston, MA: Beacon Press, 1961), 10. James Gilbert argues that the "majority of Americans, when given the choice, seemed to prefer the commercialized culture of Hollywood, radio, comic books, and the Book-of-the-Month Club." *A Cycle of Outrage: America's Reaction to the Juvenile Delinquent in the 1950s* (New York, NY: Oxford University Press, 1986), 6. Sen. Jacob K. Javits, Letter to the Editor, *Man's Magazine*, April 1960, 6. Tom Cole, Special Asst. to Sen. John G. Tower, *Man's Magazine*, December 1963, 6. Circulation in Osgerby, 133. Net sales revenue reached $1,500,000.

7 Insecurity and paranoia in Jonathan Mitchell, *Revisions of the American Adam: Innocence, Identity and Masculinity in Twentieth-Century America* (New York, NY: Continuum, 2011), 2. Change in Myron Brenton, *The American Male* (New York, NY: Coward-McCann, 1966), 33. Joseph H. Wherry, "How Stalin Stole Our B-29," *Male*, September 1952, 12–13. Shailer Upton Lawton, "Sex Life and the Average American Male," *Male*, September 1952, 14–15. Perhaps unsurprisingly, when readers turned the page after Dr. Lawton's gloomy article, they could share in the exploits of Capt. Harry K. Copsey's "Cowboy in Korea," a heroic tale of the Third Rescue Squadron operating behind communist lines to save surrounded GIs. Lawton, who wrote on the sexual behavior of teenagers, bachelors, and married couples, also published a piece in the October 1960 issue of *Man's Magazine* on the average man needing to understand the "true nature" of the "seducer." "Study of a Sex Braggart: The Seducer," 26. Sexual anxieties were still present in the late 1960s, as evidenced by one article on men who had an "abnormal fear of women" and were dealing with the consequences of "faulty childhood conditioning toward sex." Thorp McClusky, "How 'Tranquilizers' Can Affect Your Sex-Life," *Man's Epic*, March 1968, 16–17. On the relationship between struggling and being a man, see Elisabeth Badinter, *XY: On Masculine Identity* (New York, NY: Columbia University Press, 1995), 129.

8 Savages in Richard Slotkin, *Gunfighter Nation: The Myth of the Frontier in Twentieth-Century America* (Norman, OK: University of Oklahoma Press, 1998), 11. Michael Kimmel argues

that in tales like these, men were rewarded with "large-breasted women as a kind of masculine payoff." *Manhood in America: A Cultural History* (New York, NY: The Free Press, 1996), 254. On popularity of men's magazines, see Theodore Peterson, *Magazines in the Twentieth Century* (Urbana, IL: University of Illinois Press, 1964), 310–311. Maureen Honey discusses the "power of the media to reinforce" certain portrayals of men and women and how magazines are a worthy model of analysis in *Creating Rosie the Riveter: Class, Gender, and Propaganda during World War II* (Amherst, NY: The University of Massachusetts Press, 1984), 13–15. Unlike Henry Jenkins, I use "popular culture" rather than "popular art" in describing men's adventure magazines, since these texts very much were integrated into the lives of ordinary Americans in their roles as consumers. Jenkins, 11. Erin A. Smith sees similar texts as "social processes," rather than just "linguistic artifacts." *Hard-Boiled: Working-Class Readers and Pulp Magazines* (Philadelphia, PA: Temple University Press, 2000), 5. Finally, Gary Cross claims the pulps played to a "downmarket crowd" in *Men to Boys: The Making of Modern Immaturity* (New York, NY: Columbia University Press, 2008), 97. For a short overview of this medium, see James Boylan, "Survey Sample: Men's Magazines," *Columbia Journalism Review* Vol. 3, No. 3 (Fall 1964): 30–31. Objectification in Arthur Brittan, *Masculinity and Power* (New York, NY: Basil Blackwell, 1989), 66. George L. Mosse suggests that "distinct images of masculinity" are "the way men assert what they believe to be their manhood." *The Image of Man: The Creation of Modern Masculinity* (New York, NY: Oxford University Press, 1996), 1. Susan Brownmiller moves the argument further still, discussing the myth of the "heroic rapist" in *Against Our Will: Men, Women, and Rape* (New York, NY: Fawcett Books, 1975), 289.

9 On pulp audiences, see Smith, 23–26. On the links between working-class and masculinity, see: Megan Vokey, Bruce Tefft, and Chris Tyiaczny, "An Analysis of Hypermasculinity in Magazine Advertisements," *Sex Roles* Vol. 68 (2013): 565, 572; Gina Marie Weaver, *Ideologies of Forgetting: Rape in the Vietnam War* (Albany, NY: State University of New York Press, 2010), 85; Barbara Ehrenreich, *Fear of Falling: The Inner Life of the Middle Class* (New York, NY: Pantheon, 1989), 108–110; and, more broadly, David Morgan, "Class and Masculinity," in *Handbook of Studies on Men & Masculinities*, eds. Michael S. Kimmel, Jeff Hearn, and R. W. Connell (Thousand Oaks, CA: Sage, 2005), 168–172. Draft inequalities in Gary L. Long, "A Sociology for Special Circumstances: Using the Vietnam War in the Classroom," *Teaching Sociology* Vol. 21, No. 3 (July 1993): 261–266. Christian G. Appy found that "Roughly 80 percent came from working-class and poor backgrounds." *Working-Class War: American Combat Soldiers and Vietnam* (Chapel Hill, NC: The University of North Carolina Press, 1993), 6.

10 According to Peter Haining, the "pulps were not just intended to entertain the reader – they were also meant to make him feel better about himself, his prospects, and especially his sex life." *The Classic Era of American Pulp Magazines* (Chicago, IL: Chicago Review Press, 2000), 21. Bradd Shore, "Cultural Knowledge," in *Encyclopedia of Semiotics*, ed. Paul Bouissac (New York, NY: Oxford University Press, 1998), 157–161. Rebelliousness and inadequacy in Kimmel, *Manhood in America*, 244–245. On differences with middle-class masculinity, see R. W. Connell, *Masculinities*, 2nd ed. (Berkeley, CA: University of California Press, 2005), 36.

11 Gold in Ron Milam, "Missing Home: How Popular Culture Was Used to Remind Us of What We Were Missing," in *The Vietnam War in Popular Culture, Vol. 1: During the War*, ed. Ron Milam (Santa Barbara, CA: Praeger, 2017), 61. Widely read literature in Tom Engelhardt, "An Air-Force Hospital: The War-Wounded Come Home," *Dispatch News Service International*, 21 June 1971, 6. Other veterans noted the role of magazines in their own writings, to include John M. Del Vecchio, *The 13th Valley* (New York, NY: Bantam, 1982), 145; and W. D. Ehrhart, *Vietnam–Perkasie: A Combat Marine Memoir* (Jefferson, NC: McFarland, 1983), 51.

12 PX data in "Minutes of Meeting of Joint Vietnam Regional Exchange Council," 29 April 1969, Folder 301-05, Box 3, USARV, Non-Appr. Funds Div, RG 472, NARA. See also Madeline Morris, "By Force of Arms: Rape, War, and Military Culture," *Duke Law Journal* Vol. 45, No. 4 (February 1996): 713–714 on military personnel consuming soft-core pornography. Text and phenomenon in Bethan Benwell, "Introduction," in *Masculinity and Men's Lifestyle Magazines*, ed. Bethan Benwell (Malden, MA: Blackwell, 2003), 8.

13 Letters to the Editor, *Man's Illustrated*, May 1968, 10. The three letters, from two privates and one corporal serving in Vietnam, suggest that young men were clearly engaging with these magazines. *Stag* even shared a photograph of San Francisco's "topless queen" Carol Doda, holding her official "Girl Most Desirable Plaque" awarded by the 1st Marine Air Wing in Da Nang. According to *Stag*, "Even the Vietcong would agree – she's the greatest." September 1966, 23. Moreover, soldiers stationed in Germany, Alaska, and Iceland all wrote approving letters. Letters to the Editor, *Man's Magazine*, January 1960, 6. Letters, *Saga*, February 1961, 8. Letters to the Editor, *Man's Magazine*, July 1961, 6. This Funny Life, *True*, July 1968, 64.

14 On links between violence and virility, see Mark Gerzon, *A Choice of Heroes: The Changing Faces of American Manhood* (Boston, MA: Houghton Mifflin, 1992), 38; and Martin Barron and Michael Kimmel, "Sexual Violence in Three Pornographic Media: Toward a Sociological Explanation," *The Journal of Sex Research* Vol. 37, No. 2 (May 2000): 161–168. In "Sergeant Mulligan's Private Belly Girl," for example, a supposedly autobiographical account in *Battle Cry* from July 1959, a Marine Corps veteran brags how he killed his first man on Guadalcanal in World War II, had "been in more invasions than most guys have been in classrooms," and "chased women of more races, creeds and colors than you'd believe existed." John "Deucey" Mulligan, "Sergeant Mulligan's Private Belly Girl," *Battle Cry*, July 1959, 34.

15 Dominant set and paradigm in Chris Blazina, *The Cultural Myth of Masculinity* (Westport, CT: Praeger, 2003), xiv–xv. Violence and sexuality in Lee Ellis, *Theories of Rape: Inquiries into the Causes of Sexual Aggression* (New York, NY: Hemisphere, 1989), 33. Not even the violent Mickey Spillane pulps concentrated so heavily on wartime exploits, even if the fictional hard-boiled detective Mike Hammer himself was a World War II veteran. On violence in the Mike Hammer genre, see Haut, 96–98; Server, 73; and David Glover, "The Stuff That Dreams Are Made of: Masculinity, Femininity and the Thriller," in *Gender, Genre and Narrative Pleasure*, ed. Derek Longhurst (London: Unwin Hyman, 1989), 69, 77. On contemporary criticisms of violence and sexuality in comics, see Carol L. Tilley, "Seducing the Innocent: Fredric Wertham and the Falsifications That Helped

Condemn Comics," *Information & Culture* Vol. 47, No. 4 (2012): 393. Jonathan Mitchell argues the popular representation of the cowboy is sexless, "the man who becomes the phallus but has no phallus." p. 36.

16 Cultural definitions and socialization in Lori L. Heise, "Violence against Women: An Integrated, Ecological Framework," *Violence against Women* Vol. 4, No. 3 (June 1998): 277–278. Producing, representing, and consuming in Milestone and Meyer, 1. On the evolution of stereotypes becoming normative, see Mosse, 4–5. On the links between fantasy and the legitimate, see Laura Kipnis, *Bound and Gagged: Pornography and the Politics of Fantasy in America* (Durham, NC: Duke University Press, 1999), 163. It is important to note that definitions of masculinity are not fixed, are understood differently by race, class, and culture, and can change over time. Jonathan Rutherford, "Who's That Man," in *Male Order: Unwrapping Masculinity*, eds. Rowena Chapman and Jonathan Rutherford (London: Lawrence & Wishart, 1988), 22.

17 On the sexual rewards of military conquest, see Elizabeth L. Hillman, "Rape, Reform, and Reaction: Gender and Sexual Violence in the U.S. Military," in *The Routledge History of Gender, War, and the U.S. Military*, ed. Kara Dixon Vuic (London: Routledge, 2018), 291; Beverly Allen, *Rape Warfare: The Hidden Genocide in Bosnia-Herzegovina and Croatia* (Minneapolis, MN: University of Minnesota Press, 1996), 89; and Cynthia Grguric, "War Rape: Unveiling the Complexities of Motivation and Reparation in Order to Create Lines of Peace and Empowerment," in *Terrorism, Political Violence, and Extremism: New Psychology to Understand, Face, and Defuse the Threat*, ed. Chris E. Stout (Santa Barbara, CA: Praeger, 2017), 131–132. Joanna Bourke notes the role of socially constructed definitions of masculinity, and their relation to power networks, in *Dismembering the Male: Men's Bodies, Britain and the Great War* (Chicago, IL: The University of Chicago Press, 1996), 14.

18 Susan Sontag highlights the "omnipresence of sexist stereotypes in the language, behavior, and imagery" of American society in *A Susan Sontag Reader* (New York, NY: Farrar/Straus/Giroux, 1982), 332. If discourses can indeed become "enshrined in practices," as Brittan suggests, we might think of the ways in which pulp magazines portrayed manhood – tied to combat yet embedded in sexual anxieties – and how closely those portrayals were reflected in the perceptions and actions of American soldiers serving in Vietnam. Brittan, 149. On links between cultural activity and gender, see Roger Horrocks, *Male Myths and Icons: Masculinity in Popular Culture* (New York, NY: St. Martin's Press, 1995), 16.

19 Relationships between basic training and aggressive heterosexuality in Heather Marie Stur, *Beyond Combat: Women and Gender in the Vietnam War Era* (New York, NY: Cambridge University Press, 2011), 169; and R. Wayne Eisenhart, "You Can't Hack It Little Girl: A Discussion of the Covert Psychological Agenda of Modern Combat Training," *Journal of Social Issues* Vol. 31, No. 4 (1975): 16. Preexisting sociocultural dynamics in Nancy Farwell, "War Rape: New Conceptualizations and Responses," *Affilia* Vol. 19, No. 4 (Winter 2004): 394. See also Weaver, 16; and Morris, "By Force of Arms," 703. James Gilbert has called this process "spectatorship masculinity," in which "identity was formed (or imagined at least) around observation and emulation of masculine heroes in sport

and public life, within the literary imagination, or through mass culture." *Men in the Middle: Searching for Masculinity in the 1950s* (Chicago, IL: The University of Chicago Press, 2005), 23–24.

20 Masculinity based on exaggerated beliefs in Vokey, Tefft, and Tysiaczny, 562. For a scholarly treatment of popular media's role on behavior, see Albert Bandura, "Social Cognitive Theory of Mass Communication," *Media Psychology* Vol. 3, No. 3 (2001): 265–299.

21 Male Call, *Male* September 1966, 86. Mary Louise Roberts notes that in World War II there was a "sexual double standard" at play: "male, but not female, sexual infidelity was encouraged." *What Soldiers Do: Sex and the American GI in World War II France* (Chicago, IL: The University of Chicago Press, 2013), 73. See also D'Ann Campbell, *Women at War with America: Private Lives in a Patriotic Era* (Cambridge, MA: Harvard University Press, 1984), 209. On stereotypes and masculinity, see Andrew Kimbrell, *The Masculine Mystique: The Politics of Masculinity* (New York, NY: Ballantine, 1995), 16.

22 On combat being deadly and impersonal, see Peter S. Kindsvatter, *American Soldiers: Ground Combat in the World Wars, Korea, and Vietnam* (Lawrence, KS: University Press of Kansas, 2003), 6. Tangible reality in Rachel Woodward, "Warrior Heroes and Little Green Men: Soldiers, Military Training, and the Construction of Rural Masculinities," *Rural Sociology* Vol. 65, No. 4 (December 2000): 644.

23 Sharon Marcus has argued that the "violence of rape is enabled by narratives." In Wendy S. Hesford, "Defining Moments," in *Haunting Violations: Feminist Criticism and the Crisis of the "Real,"* eds. Wendy S. Hesford and Wendy Kozol (Urbana, IL: University of Illinois Press, 2001), 19. Alternatively, Christopher W. Mullins highlights the "Routine Activities Theory," which essentially says "soldiers rape women because they can." "Sexual Violence during Armed Conflict," in *The Palgrave Handbook of Criminology and War*, eds. Ross McGarry and Sandra Walklate (New York, NY: Palgrave Macmillan, 2016), 123.

24 Micheal Clodfelter, *Mad Minutes and Vietnam Months: A Soldier's Memoir* (Jefferson, NC: McFarland, 1988), 3–4. "Man Triumphant" in Adam Parfrey, *It's a Man's World: Men's Adventure Magazines, The Postwar Pulps* (Los Angeles, CA: Feral House, 2003), 411.

25 Heroic deeds versus brutal acts in Carol Burke, *Camp All-American, Hanoi Jane, and the High-and-Tight* (Boston, MA: Beacon Press, 2004), 48. On the problems of perceived reality in popular media and the process of meaning production, see L. J. Shrum, "Assessing the Social Influence of Television: A Social Cognition Perspective on Cultural Effects," *Communication Research* Vol. 22, No. 4 (August 1995): 410–411; and Milestone and Meyer, 151–154.

26 Carnal conquest in Robin Gerster, "A Bit of the Other: Touring Vietnam," in *Gender and War: Australians at War in the Twentieth Century*, eds. Joy Damousi and Marilyn Lake (New York, NY: Cambridge University Press, 1995), 231. John V. H. Dippel argues that "Having their way with prostitutes or other Vietnamese women enabled some GIs to compensate for the powerlessness and fear they faced daily in the jungles of Vietnam." *War and Sex: A Brief History of Men's Urge for Battle* (Amherst, NY: Prometheus, 2010), 263. See also Roland Littlewood, "Military Rape," *Anthropology Today* Vol. 13, No. 2 (April 1997): 13. For an example of frustrated GIs, see Bernard Edelman, "On the Ground: The US

Experience," in *Rolling Thunder in a Gentle Land: The Vietnam War Revisited*, ed. Andrew Wiest (New York, NY: Osprey Publishing, 2006), 198. The counter, of course, is that if combat didn't match magazines' descriptions, that might have made readers more suspicious of portrayals of sex and conquest, too. Yet the popularity of magazines throughout most of the American war in Vietnam suggests otherwise.

27 Promiscuousness in Kimmel, Hearn, and Connell, 406. Redirecting hostility and dehumanization in Kyle Longley, *Grunts: The American Combat Soldier in Vietnam* (Armonk, NY: M. E. Sharpe, 2008), 150. See also Kathy J. Phillips, *Manipulating Masculinity: War and Gender in Modern British and American Literature* (New York, NY: Palgrave Macmillan, 2006), 14; and Weaver, 28. Weaver argues that "misogyny provided a starting point for other forms of domination." p. 64.

28 Veteran quoted in Arlene Eisen, *Women and Revolution in Viet Nam* (London: Zed, 1984), 44. On women in war as "spoils," see Carol Lynn Mithers, "Missing in Action: Women Warriors in Vietnam," in *The Vietnam War and American Culture*, eds. John Carlos Rowe and Rick Berg (New York, NY: Columbia University Press, 1991), 83. In such ways, the rape of Vietnamese women could be seen as a "triumph," ameliorating the frustrations of combat. Timothy Beneke, *Men on Rape* (New York, NY: St. Martin's Press, 1982), 13.

29 On links between aggression and eroticism, see Camille Paglia, *Sex, Art, and American Culture* (New York, NY: Vintage, 1992), 51. On the impacts of warrior ideals being threatened, see Suzanne Clark, *Cold Warriors: Manliness on Trial in the Rhetoric of the West* (Carbondale, IL: Southern Illinois University Press, 2000), 204.

30 Perceptual norms in Grguric, 126–127. Brenton argued in 1966 that the "notion of male aggression-independence" persisted in "men's magazines." *The American Male*, 47.

31 Since gender, and thus masculinity, are social constructions, it seems likely that sociocultural factors were significant variables in deciding to commit sexual violence in war. On the theory of social constructivism, see Janie L. Leatherman, *Sexual Violence and Armed Conflict* (Malden, MA: Polity, 2011), 17–20. Jonathan Gottschall lays out a number of competing theories, to include sociocultural ones, in "Explaining Wartime Rape," *The Journal of Sex Research* Vol. 41, No. 2 (May 2004): Variables on p. 133.

32 Affirming masculinity in Dippel, 264. On the disconnects between fantasy and reality, see James R. Ebert, *A Life in a Year: The American Infantryman in Vietnam, 1965–1972* (Novato, CA: Presidio, 1993), 88. In "War and Rape: A Preliminary Analysis," Ruth Siefert considers the connections between soldier rapes and sociocultural influences. In *Mass Rape: The War against Women in Bosnia-Herzegovina*, ed. Alexandra Stiglmayer (Lincoln, NE: University of Nebraska Press, 1994), 61. See also Jennifer Turpin, "Many Faces: Women Confronting War," in *The Women and War Reader*, eds. Lois Ann Lorentzen and Jennifer Turpin (New York, NY: New York University Press, 1998), 16.

33 Cultural fantasy in Christopher Breu, *Hard-Boiled Masculinities* (Minneapolis, MN: University of Minnesota Press, 2005), 1. One marine called it "World dreaming." In Ebert, 177. Mary A. Renda argues that "Culture, embedded in individual experience, gives rise to physical violence and other material practices." *Taking Haiti: Military Occupation and the Culture of U.S. Imperialism, 1915–1940* (Chapel Hill, NC: The University of North Carolina Press, 2001), 9.

34 Betty Friedan, *The Feminine Mystique* (New York, NY: W. W. Norton, 1963), 9, 16, 36, 50–51, 72. See also Nancy Walker, ed., *Women's Magazines, 1940–1960: Gender Roles and the Popular Press* (Boston, MA: Bedford/St. Martin's, 1998), 1–15; and Covert, 23. On magazine culture more generally, see Cross, 89. Steven Dillon argues that "many of the large-scale magazines can also be seen as men's magazines." *Wolf-Women and Phantom Ladies: Female Desire in 1940s US Culture* (Albany, NY: SUNY Press, 2015), 210. Even in the first season of *The Dick Van Dyke Show*, viewers watched sitcom writer Buddy Sorrell, who has just read a magazine article, lamenting that "we're living in the decline of the American male." The story could be trusted, Buddy quips, because "It's a high-class magazine. It cost sixty cents. There wasn't one girly picture in it." *The Dick Van Dyke Show*, "The Bad Old Days," directed by John Rich, originally aired 4 April 1962.

35 *The Saturday Evening Post* first appeared in 1821. On this and *Harper's*, see James Playsted Wood, *Magazines in the United States* (New York, NY: The Ronald Press Company, 1949), 38, 76. Prices in R. D. Mullen, "From Standard Magazines to Pulps and Big Slicks: A Note on the History of US General and Fiction Magazines," *Science Fiction Studies* Vol. 22, No. 1 (March 1995): 145; and Peterson, *Magazines in the Twentieth Century*, 13. Technological advances in David M. Earle, *Re-covering Modernism: Pulps, Paperbacks, and the Prejudice of Form* (Burlington, VT: Ashgate, 2009), 60. On the roles of mass production and distribution, see Tom Pendergast, *Creating the Modern Man: American Magazines and Consumer Culture, 1900–1950* (Columbia, MO: University of Missouri Press, 2000), 17.

36 Crudely written in Richard Bleiler, "Forgotten Giant: A Brief History of *Adventure* Magazine," *Exploration* Vol. 30, No. 4 (December 1989): 309. Erin A. Smith argues such magazines were "cheaply produced escape literature designed to be thrown away once read." "How the Other Half Read: Advertising, Working-Class Readers, and Pulp Magazines," *Book History* Vol. 3 (2000): 204. Mullen argues that magazines could be classified as "those designed to be read and discarded and those designed to be read and preserved." p. 144. Wood-fiber in Bill Blackbeard, "The Pulps," in *Handbook of American Popular Culture*, Vol. 1, ed. M. Thomas Inge (Westport, CT: Greenwood Press, 1978), 195. On pulp formatting, see Ron Goulart, *Cheap Thrills: An Informal History of the Pulp Magazines* (New Rochelle, NY: Arlington House, 1972), 14.

37 *The Argosy* circulation in Inge, 200. See also Tony Goodstone, *The Pulps: Fifty Years of American Pop Culture* (New York, NY: Chelsea House, 1970), xii. Advertising in Wood, 224. Formulaic in Don D'Ammassa, *Encyclopdia of Adventure Fiction* (New York, NY: Facts on File, 2009), 147.

38 Sensational in Inge, 203; and Frank M. Robinson and Lawrence Davidson, *Pulp Culture: The Art of Fiction Magazines* (Portland, ME: Collectors Press, 1998), 9. Of note, many of these pulps were sold off the newsstands. p. 10.

39 Tarzan in Gail Bederman, *Manliness & Civilization: A Cultural History of Gender and Race in the United States, 1880–1917* (Chicago, IL: The University of Chicago Press, 1995), 219–221. Frontier heroes and social and economic conditions in Breu, *Hard-Boiled Masculinities*, 59–60. According to Elizabeth Fraterrigo, these magazine readers were packaged as "modern, sexually virile, masculine consumer[s] who paid no heed to traditional virtues like civic duty or manly self-restraint." In *Playboy and the Making of*

the Good Life in Modern America (New York, NY: Oxford University Press, 2009), 24. See also Bill Osgerby, "A Pedigree of the Consuming Male: Masculinity, Consumption and the American 'Leisure Class,'" in Benwell, 66–75.

40 Kimberly J. Lamay Licursi argues that unlike later first-hand accounts from World War II and Korean veterans, these earlier pulps were distinct for their "lack of patriotic jingoism." *Remembering World War I in America* (Lincoln, NE: University of Nebraska Press, 2018), 136, 141. One *War Stories* contributor confessed to readers his tales were "based on all the brave things I would have done in this war if I had just thought of them at the time." In fact, the popularity of aviation pulps like *Air Adventures* and *Sky Aces* suggests that the trenches of World War I may not have been the best locales for young boys to test their mettle in battle en route to manhood. As one editor recalled, "In the aviation magazine, the machine is the hero." Contributor quoted in Licursi, *Ibid.* Aviation pulps in E. L. Adams, "Between the Devil and a Dime World," in *Pulpwood Days, Vol. 2: Lives of the Pulp Writers,* ed. John Locke (Elkhorn, CA: Off-Trail Publishers, 2013), 50–51; and Robinson and Davidson, 134, 139. Editor quoted in Douglas Ellis, Ed Hulse, and Robert Weinberg, *The Art of the Pulps: An Illustrated History* (San Diego, TX: IDW Publishing, 2017), 74.

41 Soldiers and veterans constituted a large portion of the "pulpwood population." See Harold B. Hersey, *Pulpwood Editor* (New York, NY: Frederick A. Stokes, 1937), 8. Comics following overseas in Goodstone, xv. Flying tigers and Japanese in Zou Yizheng, "Flying Tigers and Chinese Sidekicks in World War II American Comics," in *The 10 Cent War: Comic Books, Propaganda, and World War II,* eds. Trischa Goodnow and James J. Kimble (Jackson, MI: University Press of Mississippi, 2016), 55–56. On the stimulation of an expanded wartime readership, see Richard Ellis, "Disseminating Desire: Grove Press and 'The End[s] of Obscenity,'" in *Perspectives on Pornography: Sexuality in Film and Literature,* eds. Gary Day and Clive Bloom (New York, NY: St. Martin's Press, 1988), 32.

42 *Esquire* in Bill Osgerby, *Playboys in Paradise: Masculinity, Youth and Leisure-Style in Modern America* (New York, NY: Oxford University Press, 2001), 53. Of note, nearly fifty percent of the 1943 "Varga Girl Calendar" (300,000 copies total) was shipped overseas to servicemen. p. 54. On the government's wartime role in these linkages, mainly via the Magazine Bureau, see Tawnya J. Adkins Covert, *Manipulating Images: World War II Mobilization of Women through Magazine Advertising* (Lanham, MD: Lexington Books, 2011), 55–58; and Honey, *Creating Rosie the Riveter,* 36–43.

43 Paper quotas in Goodstone, xv. On the general reading market in the armed forces, see Thomas Bruscino, *A Nation Forged in War: How World War II Taught Americans to Get Along* (Knoxville, TN: The University Press of Tennessee, 2010), 101. Rugged machismo and pulp titles in Bill Osgerby, "Two-Fisted Tales of Brutality and Belligerence: Masculinity and Meaning in the American 'True Adventure' Pulps of the 1950s and 1960s," in *Masculinity and the Other: Historical Perspectives,* eds. Heather Ellis and Jessica Meyer (Newcastle upon Tyne: Cambridge Scholars Publishing, 2009), 164. Though individual titles circulated monthly at around 100,000–200,000 copies, the high volume of titles, according to one source, ensured a total circulation of 12,000,000 a month. See Osgerby, "Muscular Manhood and Salacious Sleaze," 133.

44 World War I veterans reading pulps in Earle, *All Man!*, 37. Sweats and armpit magazines in Lynn Munroe, "The Art of Charles Copeland," *Illustration* Vol. 9, No. 33 (Spring 2011): 32. Magazines in postwar society in Osgerby, *Ibid.*, 127–128.

45 Bruce Jay Friedman, *Even the Rhinos Were Nymphos: Best Nonfiction* (Chicago, IL: Chicago University Press, 2000), 18. See also Pendergast, 208; and Richard Combs, "Pleasing the Man with a Magazine," *American Libraries* Vol. 3, No. 9 (October 1972): 1001–1005. Goodman's in Osgerby, "Two-Fisted Tales of Brutality and Belligerence," 173; and Bill Devine, *Devine's Guide to Men's Adventure Magazines* (self-published, 1997), 3. For a comparison with women's magazines, see Adkins Covert, 24–28.

46 Misogyny in Kenon Breazale, "In Spite of Women: *Esquire* Magazine and the Construction of the Male Consumer, *Signs* Vol. 20, No. 1 (Autumn 1994): 20. Active imagination in Amy Sueyoshi, *Discriminating Sex: White Leisure and the Making of the "Oriental"* (Chicago, IL: University of Illinois Press, 2018), 3. It is important that these magazines came out of New York, as opposed to the west coast where Asian Americans were more part of the cultural landscape. On the "big action" there, see Henry Kuttner, "New York ... Should I Come?," in *Pulp Fictioneers: Adventures in the Storytelling Business*, ed. John Locke (Silver Spring, MD: Adventure House, 2004), 99.

47 On speaking to veterans, see Max Allan Collins and George Hagenauer, *Men's Adventure Magazines in Postwar America* (London: Taschen, 2004), 8. Usurping and effete in Osgerby, *Playboys in Paradise*, 78. On feminism and the "crisis of masculinity," see Peter G. Filene, *Him/Her/Self: Gender Identities in Modern America*, 3rd ed. (Baltimore, MD: The Johns Hopkins University Press, 1998), 74; Brittan, 183; and James Penner, *Pinks, Pansies, and Punks: The Rhetoric of Masculinity in American Literary Culture* (Bloomington, IN: Indiana University Press, 2011), 15. Astrid Fellner and Marta Fernández-Morales argue "masculinity is not *in* crisis, it *is* crisis." "Introduction" to *Rethinking Gender in Popular Culture in the 21st Century: Marlboro Men and California Girls*, eds. Astrid Fellner, Marta Fernández-Morales, and Martina Martausová (Newcastle upon Tyne: Cambridge Scholars Publishing, 2017), 5. Finally, on anti-communist "rage," see Masuda Hajimu, *Cold War Crucible: The Korean Conflict and the Postwar World* (Cambridge, MA: Harvard University Press, 2015), 24.

48 Dissatisfied man in Archer Jones, "The Pulps – A Mirror to Yearning," *The North American Review* Vol. 246, No. 1 (Autumn 1968): 36. On typical pulp readers, see Smith, *Hard-Boiled*, 28. On "nagging doubts and uncertainties" of this period, see Osgerby, "Muscular manhood and salacious sleaze," 126. A similar theme could be seen in contemporary westerns. See Andrew Ross, "Cowboys, Cadillacs, and Cosmonauts: Families, Film Genres, and Technocultures," in Boone and Cadden, 87.

49 Allan K. Echols, "The Waning Woodpile," in Locke, *Pulp Fictioneers*, 205–206.

50 This power to shape attitudes in young minds stood at the heart of Wertham's attacks on the comic book industry. Though the psychiatrist distorted, if not fabricated, his clinical evidence, such falsifications should not diminish the fact that adventure magazines could exhibit real influence over their young readers. See Tilley, 386. Tawdry in Osgerby, "Two-Fisted Tales of Brutality and Belligerence," 164. On thinking about identity, see Pendergast, 13. For a discussion on influences on attitude function, see

Daniel J. O'Keefe, *Persuasion: Theory & Research*, 2nd ed. (Thousand Oaks, CA: Sage, 2002), 35–37.

51 Scribblers in Lee Server, *Danger Is My Business*, 18. Natural parts in Allan R. Bosworth, "Take to the Hills Men," in Locke, *Pulp Fictioneers*, 176. One writer listed eleven elements of a "foolproof" plot formula, including colorful hero, trick, action, climax, and emotion. Frank Gruber, *The Pulp Jungle* (Los Angeles, CA: Sherbourne Press, 1967), 179. Another argued that the "pulp writer must portray life as the reader would like it to be and not as it is." Jones, 44. Puzo wrote under the pen name Mario Cleri.

52 Andrew A. Rooney, "D-Day – The Greatest Battle Ever Fought," *Man's World*, June 1963, 20. Raymond Chandler, "Bay City Blues," *Saga*, March 1965, 68. Mickey Spillane, "The Bastard Bannerman," *Saga*, June 1964, 27. Raymond Chandler, "Killer in the Rain, *Saga*, August 1965, 28 On Dorr, see Robert Deis and Wyatt Doyle, *A Handful of Hell: Classic War and Adventure Stories by Robert F. Dorr* (Philadelphia, PA: New Texture, 2016), 11–38.

53 Hotsie-totsies from John Bowers of Magazine Management, in Parfrey, *It's a Man's World*, 34. On *Stag Party*, see Russell Miller, *Bunny: The Real Story of Playboy* (New York, NY: Holt, Rinehart and Winston, 1984), 37–38.

54 Hairy-chested quoted in Helen Damon-Moore, "Gender as an Organizing Force in the World of Mass-Circulation Magazines," report (Madison, WI: Wisconsin Center for Education Research, April 1986), 17. Picasso in Cross, *Men to Boys*, 73. Gender hostility in Carrie Pitzulo, *Bachelors and Bunnies: The Sexual Politics of Playboy* (Chicago, IL: The University of Chicago Press, 2011), 2. Middle-class in Earle, *All Man!*, 20.

55 Girl next door in Amber Batura, "How Hugh Hefner Invented the Modern Man," *New York Times*, 28 September 2017. Security from Burt Zollo, quoted in Barbara Ehrenreich, *The Hearts of Men: American Dreams and the Flight from Commitment* (New York, NY: Anchor Books, 1983), 47. Beth Bailey has noted that Hefner saw his naked women as "a symbol of disobedience, a triumph of sexuality, an end of Puritanism." In *"Sexual Revolution(s)," the Sixties: From Memory to History*, ed. David Farber (Chapel Hill, NC: The University of North Carolina Press, 1994), 247. Fraterrigo discusses *Playboy*'s depiction of the single man versus married ones in *Playboy and the Making of the Good Life in Modern America*, 4–5, 32.

56 *Cavalcade*, November 1959, 4. A story on Burt Mossman, a "one-man army of the Arizona Rangers," told the tale of a "skinny, sleepy runt whose Colt spit six bullets as soon as a man thought about drawing on him." (Even men of average physique could become epic heroes.) Jack Pearl, "Burt Mossman: One-Man Army of the Arizona Rangers," *Male*, August 1960, 32. Magazines like *Stag* also offered up "ribald and rowdy" accounts of "bedroom-bouncing" protagonists who not only could spot a "man-hungry woman," but knew what to do with them when the time came. Christopher Frey, "How to Spot a Man-Hungry Woman," *Stag*, January 1967, 40. See also, Don Calhoun, "The Love Master," *Male*, November 1967, 24.

57 Mack Reynolds, "Are You Yellow?" *Battle Cry*, March 1960, 34. On femininity and passivity, see Badinter, *XY*, 54. Capitalism in Robert J. Corber, *Homosexuality in Cold War America: Resistance and the Crisis of Masculinity* (Durham, NC: Duke University Press, 1997), 34; and Breu, 4.

58 Russell Lynes, "High-Brow, Low-Brow, Middle-Brow," *Life*, 11 April 1949, 100–101.

59 Work clothes in *Male*, September 1952, 86; and *Man's World*, February 1967, 87. Education barrier in *Epic*, March 1957, 3. "How to Pass a Genius" in *Male*, January 1952, 7. "You don't need a college diploma" in *Sir!*, July 1962, 2.

60 Clodfelter, *Mad Minutes and Vietnam Months*, 37. Exciting in John C. Shoemaker, "My Story: Personal Reflections on the Impact of the Vietnam Era," in Milam, 44. Dippel argues that many "males from low socioeconomic backgrounds grasp that volunteering offers them a good chance to fulfill their biological destiny." *War and Sex*, 12.

61 "Stag Confidential," *Stag*, July 1966, 8. On military service as an "ideal form of masculinity," especially among working-class men, see Sarah Parry Myers, "'The Women behind the Men behind the Gun': Gendered Identities and Militarization in the Second World War," in Vuic, 94. Of note, college graduates like Orville Freeman could still act heroically by courageously leading a combat patrol while wounded. Glenn Infield, "Jap Bait at Bougainville," Guy, April 1965, 16. Freeman went on to become the governor of Minnesota and the US Secretary of Agriculture.

62 Rabid patriotism in Parfrey, 215. Ray Lunt, "Hot War in the Skies of East Germany," *Men*, July 1964, 32. Of note, an essay in *Battle Cry* from October 1957 lauded German Field Marshal Erwin Rommel as a chivalrous warrior who "paid no attention to politics and fought only for national honor." Geza Andrassy, "Knight of the Desert," 24.

63 A. W. Jackson, "Peace Corps Be Damned! It's Time for America to Get Tough!," *Real*, February 1964, 22, 47. One article in support of the CIA disparaged "college 'Peaceniks' whose closest contact with espionage has been stealing exams." Joseph Disher, "Let's Stop Rapping the CIA," *Male*, July 1966, 16. Military masculinities embedded into discourses of nationalism in Paul R. Higate, *Military Masculinities: Identity and the State* (Westport, CT: Praeger, 2003), 209. See also Mary Sheila McMahon, "The American State and the Vietnam War," in Farber, 46.

64 As Carol Cohn has argued, "gender is, at its heart, a structural power relation." See "Women in Wars: Toward a Conceptual Framework," in *Women and Wars*, ed. Carol Cohn (Malden, MA: Polity, 2013), 4. Gender as power in Maryam Khalid, *Gender, Orientalism, and the "War on Terror": Representation, Discourse, and Intervention in Global Politics* (London: Routledge, 2017), 32. Social domination in Brittan, 5; and Randal Johnson, "Introduction," in Pierre Bourdieu, *The Field of Cultural Production: Essays on Art and Literature* (New York, NY: Columbia University Press, 1993), 2. Symbolism in Sara Meger, *Rape Loot Pillage: The Political Economy of Sexual Violence in Armed Conflict* (New York, NY: Oxford University Press, 2016), 39; and Horrocks, *Male Myths and Icons*, 20.

65 Judith Butler discusses the "ritualized repetition" of masculinity in "Melancholy Gender/Refused Identification," in *Constructing Masculinity*, eds. Maurice Berger, Brian Wallis, and Simon Watson (New York, NY: Routledge, 1995), 31. Joan Wallach Scott, *Gender and the Politics of History* (New York, NY: Columbia University Press, 1988), 42. Performing and enacting masculinity in John Beynon, *Masculinities and Culture* (Philadelphia, PA: Open University Press, 2002), 11; and Bethan Benwell, "Ambiguous Masculinities: Heroism and Anti-heroism in the Men's Lifestyle Magazine," in Benwell, 152. On gender as a social practice and construct, see Connell, *Masculinities*, 71; and

Margaret R. Higgonet and Patrice L.-R. Higgonet, "The Double Helix," in *Behind the Lines: Gender and the Two World Wars*, eds. Margaret Randolph Higgonet, Sonya Michel, Jane Jenson, and Margaret Collins Weitz (New Haven, CT: Yale University Press, 1987), 41.

66 Nineteen million in Halberstam, 195. Westerns in Cross, 25–27. On diversity of masculine images, see Osgerby, "Two-Fisted Tales of Brutality and Belligerence," 179; and Steven Watts, *JFK and the Masculine Mystique: Sex and Power on the New Frontier* (New York, NY: St. Martin's Press, 2016), 15.

67 Circulation data from Peterson, 24. Bloodstream in Halberstam, *Ibid.*

68 On manhood as a cultural process, see Bederman, 7. Boys internalizing models of manhood in T. Walter Herbert, *Sexual Violence and American Manhood* (Cambridge, MA: Harvard University Press, 2002), 3. Susan Jeffords maintains that "it is the crystallized formations of masculinity in warfare that enable gender relations in society to survive." *The Remasculinization of America: Gender and the Vietnam War* (Bloomington, IN: Indiana University Press, 1989), xv.

69 Philip Caputo, *A Rumor of War* (New York, NY: Holt, Rinehart and Winston, 1977), 6. Stereotypes and socialization in R. W. Connell, *Gender and Power: Society, the Person and Sexual Politics* (Stanford, CA: Stanford University Press, 1987), 34; and Brittan, 23. Pulps influencing public opinion in Joseph T. Shaw, "Letters to the Editor," in Locke, *Pulp Fictioneers*, 33. B. Mark Schoenberg argues that adolescent males are "under great pressure to conform to societal expectations of what a male should or should not be." *Growing Up Male: The Psychology of Masculinity* (Westport, CT: Bergin & Garvey, 1993), 100.

70 Rejecting elders in Osgerby, *Playboys in Paradise*, 79. Rite of passage in Longley, *Grunts*, 28. On disdain for military service in the late 1960s, see David Cortright, *Soldiers in Revolt: The American Military Today* (Garden City, NY: Anchor Press, 1975), 4.

71 Correspondent Jim G. Lucas quoted in Phillip Knightley, "Vietnam 1954–1975," in *The American Experience in Vietnam: A Reader*, ed. Grace Sevy (Norman, OK: University of Oklahoma Press, 1989), 120. Joshua S. Goldstein has argued that "Gender roles adapt individuals for war roles, and war roles provide the context within which individuals are socialized into gender roles." *War and Gender: How Gender Shapes the War System and Vice Versa* (New York, NY: Cambridge University Press, 2001), 6.

72 Pechan quoted in Philip Jenkins, *The Cold War at Home: The Red Scare in Pennsylvania, 1945–1960* (Chapel Hill, NC: The University of North Carolina Press, 1999), 69.

73 As H. W. Brands observes, most Americans "generally subscribed to the view that a communist victory anywhere would endanger peace everywhere." *The Devil We Knew: Americans and the Cold War* (New York, NY: Oxford University Press, 1993), 86. Crises in J. Fred MacDonald, *Television and the Red Menace: The Video Road to Vietnam* (New York, NY: Praeger, 1985), 19. Empire in Sidney Lens, *Permanent War: The Militarization of America* (New York, NY: Schocken Books, 1987), 22. Clandestine forces in Jenkins, 8. I. F. Stone believed there was an "almost hysterical fear of peace" during the Korean War. *The Hidden History of the Korean War* (New York, NY: Monthly Review Press, 1952), 346. For an overview of the conflict's links to the Cold War, see David R. Segal, *Recruiting for Uncle*

Sam: Citizenship and Military Manpower Policy (Lawrence, KS: University Press of Kansas, 1989), 31–38; and Hajimu, 2.

74 Defense spending numbers in John Lamberton Harper, *The Cold War* (New York, NY: Oxford University Press, 2011), 107. Continuous war mobilization in Andrew D. Grossman, *Neither Red nor Dead: Civilian Defense and American Political Development during the Early Cold War* (New York, NY: Routledge, 2001), 30. Outbreak of Korean fighting in Richard M. Fried, *Nightmare in Red: The McCarthy Era in Perspective* (New York, NY: Oxford University Press, 1990), 113. On the idea of citizen-soldiers at this time, see R. Claire Snyder, *Citizen-Soldiers and Manly Warriors: Military Service and Gender in the Civic Republic Tradition* (Lanham, MD: Rowman & Littlefield, 1999).

75 Martin Caidin, "So . . . You're Being Drafted," *American Manhood*, February 1953, 38–39. Josh Greenfield, "SAC Never Sleeps," *Saga*, July 1957, 8. The story lauded LeMay and his "ever-ready airmen." Laura McEnaney discusses how the government "asked ordinary citizens to become partners in the nation's defense." *Civil Defense Begins at Home: Militarization Meets Everyday Life in the Fifties* (Princeton, MA: Princeton University Press, 2000), 5. As this related to identity, see Clark, *Cold Warriors*, 2.

76 Martin Caidin, "So You Want to Be a Marine!," *American Manhood*, May 1953, 46, 59. "It's Tough to Be a Marine," *Real War*, December 1957, 38. Civilian businesses in Linn, 163. Politicians using masculinity in Paul Higate and John Hopton, "War, Militarism, and Masculinities," in Kimmel, Hearn, and Connell, 434. For a counter arguing for an "ambivalence toward military service," see Amy Rutenberg, "Service by Other Means: Changing Perceptions of Military Service and Masculinity in the United States, 1040–1973," in *Gender and the Long Postwar: The United States and the Two Germanys, 1945–1989*, eds. Karen Hagemann and Sonya Michel (Baltimore, MD: The Johns Hopkins University Press, 2014), 165–169.

77 "Inside for Men," *Male*, March 1967, 8. Of note, in the aftermath of the Korean War, *Battle Cry* called for tougher training regimens. "Our GIs were murdered in Korea because of inadequate training!" The answer? More realistic training that might result in peacetime casualties. As the author implored, the "public must be made to realize that the new GIs who might 'get it' in training, will be worth sacrificing for the many who will live to tell about it if there's a war." Bob Markel, "Ya Gotta Kill 'Em to Train 'Em," *Battle Cry*, December 1955, 32, 52.

78 Amram Scheinfeld, "Are American Moms a Menace?" in Walker, 108. Devouring in Brenton, *The American Male*, 170. Homosexual children in Craig M. Loftin, *Masked Voices: Gay Men and Lesbians in Cold War America* (Albany, NY: SUNY Press, 2012), 155. "Mama's boys" in Henry Jenkins, *The Wow Climax: Tracing the Emotional Impact of Popular Culture* (New York, NY: New York University Press, 2007), 192. Overinvolved in Wini Breines, "Domineering Mothers in the 1950s: Image and Reality," *Women's Studies International Forum* Vol. 8, No. 6 (1985): 604. On Hugh Hefner's concerns of a "female-oriented society," see Fraterrigo, 33.

79 "Stag Confidential," *Stag*, March 1966, 43. On mothers not teaching sons to be men, see Heather Marie Stur, "Men's and Women's Liberation: Challenging Military Culture after the Vietnam War," in *Integrating the US Military: Race, Gender, and Sexual Orientation*

since World War II, eds. Douglas Walter Bristol, Jr. and Heather Marie Stur (Baltimore, MD: The Johns Hopkins University Press, 2017), 147. Child rearing in Cross, 58.

80 Myth-making in Thomas Myers, *Walking Point: American Narratives of Vietnam* (New York, NY: Oxford University Press, 1988), 7. Martin Caidin, "So ... You're Being Drafted," *American Manhood*, March–April 1953, 34. Sexual attraction to servicemen in Bourke, *Dismembering the Male*, 156. Dividends in Paul Kirby, "Masculinities in International Relations," in *Handbook on Gender in World Politics*, eds. Jill Steans and Daniela Tepe-Belfrage (Cheltenham: Edward Elgar, 2016), 53. Lyla Hoffman has argued that "Patriarchy, militarism and sexism are all interwoven." In "Militarism and Sexism Control in America," in *The American Military: Opposing Viewpoints*, ed. David L. Bender (St. Paul, MN: Greenhaven Press, 1983), 81.

81 Clarence Doore, cover illustration, *Battle Cry*, October 1957. Harland P. Flourie, "The Street Where Sex Is King," *Big Adventure*, June 1961, 18. For a similar story, see Harland P. Flourie, "Pig Alley: Paradise with a Capital S.E.X.," *Real War*, February 1958, 36. Roberts, *What Soldiers Do*, 59. On the militarization of masculinity, see Higate, *Military Masculinities*, 29.

82 Psychiatrist quoted in Madeline Morris, "By Force of Arms," 708. Boomers in Lawrence A. Tritle, *From Melos to My Lai: War and Survival* (New York, NY: Routledge, 2000), 48. Concept of manliness in Mosse, *The Image of Man*, 107.

83 Asserting masculinity in Mitchell, *Revisions of the American Adam*, 117.

84 On good versus evil, see Elaine Scarry, *The Body in Pain: The Making and Unmaking of the World* (New York, NY: Oxford University Press, 1985), 88; and Jean Bethke Elshtain, *Women and War* (New York, NY: Basic Books, 1987), 256. Nazis in Vernon McKenzie, "Treatment of War Themes in Magazine Fiction," *The Public Opinion Quarterly* Vol. 5, No. 2 (June 1941): 232; and Robert B. Westbrook, *Why We Fought: Forging American Obligations in World War II* (Washington, DC: Smithsonian Books, 2004), 15. Worthy of hate in Paul Hirsch, "'This Is Our Enemy': The Writers' War Board and Representations of Race in Comic Books, 1942–1945," *Pacific Historical Review* Vol. 83, No. 3 (August 2014): 460.

85 Hal DuBose, "Nazi Payoff for Mass Murder," *Cavalcade*, November 1959, 9. On contemporary views of communism, see Ellen Schrecker, *The Age of McCarthyism: A Brief History with Documents* (Boston, MA: Bedford/St. Martin's, 2002), 132; and MacDonald, 53. The comics followed suit, as Red agents administered Captain America a "virus of evil" to turn him against his country. Stevens, 64.

86 Unattainable in Lewis, *The Tainted War*, 26. Manipulative in Catherine A. Lutz and Jane L. Collins, *Reading National Geographic* (Chicago, IL: The University of Chicago Press, 1993), 6.

87 Appy, *Working-Class War*, 60. Representations of America pushing the nation to war in MacDonald, vii, 12.

88 Perseverance in Michael E. Ruane, "'Killed' in Vietnam and Buried with Comrades, One Marine Returned from the Dead," *The Washington Post*, 8 July 2017. National will and security in Guy Oakes, *The Imaginary War: Civil Defense and American Cold War Culture* (New York, NY: Oxford University Press, 1994), 30. Futile in Edelman, "On the Ground,"

205. Meaning in Annica Kronsell and Erika Svedberg "Introduction," in *Making Gender, Making War: Violence, Military and Peacekeeping Practices*, eds. Annica Kronsell and Erika Svedberg (New York, NY: Routledge, 2012), 4.

89 Richard Holmes properly noted in the mid 1980s that "the soldier's behaviour in battle is accounted for by events which occurred long before he joined the army." *Acts of War: The Behavior of Men in Battle* (New York, NY: The Free Press, 1985), 58. On the social aspects of masculinity, see David D. Gilmore, *Manhood in the Making: Cultural Concepts of Masculinity* (New Haven, CT: Yale University Press, 1990), 4. Medical Corps officer Peter G. Bourne, "Sex and war are linked ..." in David V. Forrest, "The American Soldier and Vietnamese Women," *Sexual Behavior* (May 1972): 12. Adopting gender models in Rada Iveković, "Women, Nationalism and War: 'Make Love Not War,'" *Hypatia* Vol. 8, No. 4 (Autumn 1993): 115. On the "imaginative life" of sexual violence, see Herbert, 6.

90 Manly man in Harvey C. Mansfield, *Manliness* (New Haven, CT: Yale University Press, 2006), 17–18. In *Sands of Iwo Jima*, Wayne's Sergeant Stryker retains his sense of propriety. When he hits a Hawaii bar after the fighting on Tarawa and heads back to a woman's place for a drink – it's implied Mary is a prostitute – he finds instead she is a single mother who needs money to feed her baby. Stryker doesn't even consider taking advantage of Mary and departs after tossing the child all of his money. "I can't spend it on a coral reef." "You're a very good man," says Mary, hugging the sergeant. "You can get odds on that in the marine corps," Stryker replies as he departs. Stanley W. Rogouski, "The Sands of Iwo Jima," *Writers without Money*, 14 March 2016.

91 Officer quoted in Roberts, 160. Deprivation in Samuel Stouffer *et al.*, *The American Soldier: Combat and Its Aftermath* (Princeton, MA: Princeton University Press, 1949), 80. On soldiers needing a "sexual relief," see John Ellis, *The Sharp End: The Fighting Man in World War II* (New York, NY: Charles Scribner's Sons, 1980), 270.

92 Appetite and soldier quoted in Peter Schrijvers, *The Crash of Ruin: American Combat Soldiers in Europe during World War II* (New York, NY: New York University Press, 1998), 178.

93 Stan Borack, cover illustration, *Man's World*, September 1957. Cover illustration, *Battle Cry*, July 1959. For another example of the machine gun as phallus, see Mort Künstler, cover illustration, *Male*, February 1964.

94 A. Joseph Bursteln, "A Doctor Describes How You Can Make Every Woman Your Slave" *All Man*, October 1966, 32.

95 J. Glenn Gray, *The Warriors: Reflections on Men in Battle* (Lincoln, NE: University of Nebraska Press, 1959, 1970), 69. On links between gender subordination and violence, see Laura Sjoberg, "The gender of violence in war and conflict," in Steans and Tepe-Belfrage, 198. Renda links empire and military action to affirming the nation's virility in *Taking Haiti*, 64.

96 Women as objects in Susan Griffin, *Pornography and Silence: Culture's Revenge against Nature* (New York, NY: Harper & Row, 1981), 36. Prescriptive versus descriptive in Sontag, 337. Of note, FBI director J. Edgar Hoover believed a large number of "sex

crime" cases was associated with pornography. In Joanna Bourke, *Rape: Sex, Violence, History* (Berkeley, CA: Shoemaker Hoard, 2007), 142.

97 "Inside for Men," *Male*, September 1966, 6. See also *Stag*, March 1966. Within Alan M. Young's story "Summer Shack Up," we read this on the female lead: "'Hurt me,' she moaned, 'hurt me.'" p. 52. Larry Baron and Murray A. Strauss discuss violence in terms of a "cultural spillover" in *Four Theories of Rape in American Society* (New Haven, CT: Yale University Press, 1989), 9. On the media creating as well as reflecting reality, see Carolyn Kitch, *The Girl on the Magazine Cover: The Origins of Visual Stereotypes in American Mass Media* (Chapel Hill, NC: The University of North Carolina Press, 2001), 3.

98 Widely read in Robert Jay Lifton, *Home from the War: Vietnam Veterans: Neither Victims nor Executioners* (New York, NY: Simon & Schuster, 1973), 204. Unanticipated in Lutz and Collins, 11. Militarization of masculinity in Meger, 45.

99 Aggression priming and resonating in Vincent Price and Lauren Feldman, "News and Politics" and David R. Roskos-Ewoldsen and Beverly Roskos-Ewoldsen, "Current Research in Media Priming," in *The Sage Handbook of Media Processes and Effects*, eds. Robin L. Nabi and Mary Beth Oliver (Los Angeles, CA: Sage, 2009), 116, 181–182. On causal connections between media violence and aggressive behavior, see Brad J. Bushman and Craig A. Anderson "Media Violence and the American Public: Scientific Facts versus Media Misinformation," *American Psychologist* Vol. 56, No. 6/7 (June/July 2001): 480–481. Individuals and texts in Smith, *Hard-Boiled*, 8. On confusing images with reality, see Griffin, 67.

100 Aggression level studies in Susan H. Gray, "Exposure to Pornography and Aggression toward Women: The Case of the Angry Male," *Social Problems* Vol. 29, No. 4 (April 1982): 390–391. On rape as a "sexual manifestation of aggression," see Eva Fogelman, "Rape during the Nazi Holocaust: Vulnerabilities and Motivations," in *Rape: Weapon of War and Genocide*, eds. Carol Rittner and John K. Roth (St. Paul, MN: Paragon House, 2012), 20. Deviance in Mullins, "Sexual Violence during Armed Conflict," 124. Susan Jeffords discusses the "systemic assumption that women will be violated" in "Performative Masculinities, or, 'After a Few Times You Won't Be Afraid of Rape at All,'" *Discourse* Vol. 12, No. 2 (Spring–Summer 1991): 106.

101 Wish fulfillment in Andrea Dworkin, *Woman Hating* (New York, NY: E. P. Dutton, 1974), 93. Theory and practice in Linda Williams, *Hard Core: Power, Pleasure, and the "Frenzy of the Visible"* (Berkeley, CA: University of California Press, 1999), 275. Permission in Vietnam Veterans against the War, *The Winter Soldier Investigation: An Inquiry into American War Crimes* (Boston, MA: Beacon Press, 1972), xiii. Classes of people in Philip D. Beidler, *Late Thoughts on an Old War: The Legacy of Vietnam* (Athens, GA: The University of Georgia Press, 2004), 15.

102 Rape as part of war in Jacqueline A. Lawson, "'She's a Pretty Woman ... for a Gook': The Misogyny of the Vietnam War," *The Journal of American Culture* Vol. 12, No. 3 (Fall 1989): 60. Power to reinforce in Honey, 12. On conceptual links between wartime rape and peacetime culture, see Nicola Henry, Tony Ward, and Matt Hirshberg, "A Multifactorial Model of Wartime Rape," *Aggression and Violent Behavior* Vol. 9 (2004): 535–562.

CHAPTER 1

1 Proletarianized in Mark Jancovich, "Othering Conformity in Post-war America: Intellectuals, the New Middle Classes and the Problem of Cultural Distinctions," in *Containing America: Cultural Production and Consumption in Fifties America*, eds. Nathan Abrams and Julie Hughes (Birmingham: The University of Birmingham Press, 2000), 16. Little distinction in H. W. Brands, *The Devil We Knew: Americans and the Cold War* (New York, NY: Oxford University Press, 1993), 19. Conspiracy in Ellen Schrecker, *The Age of McCarthyism: A Brief History with Documents* (Boston, MA: Bedford/St. Martin's, 2002), 21–22. Countering aggression in Michael McClintock, *Instruments of Statecraft: U.S. Guerrilla Warfare, Counterinsurgency, and Counterterrorism, 1940–1990* (New York, NY: Pantheon, 1992), 24. Conformity in Snell Putney and Gail J. Putney, *The Adjusted American: Normal Neuroses in the Individual and Society* (New York, NY: Harper Colophon, 1966), 67; and David Riesman, *The Lonely Crowd: A Study of the Changing American Character* (New Haven, CT: Yale University Press, 1961), 6.

2 Suffocating in Bill Osgerby, *Playboys in Paradise: Masculinity, Youth and Leisure-Style in Modern America* (New York, NY: Oxford University Press, 2001), 74. *Femmes fatales* in George L. Mosse, *The Image of Man: The Creation of Modern Masculinity* (New York, NY: Oxford University Press, 1996), 74; and Kenneth Paradis, *Sex, Paranoia, and Modern Masculinity* (Albany, NY: SUNY Press, 2007), 5. Beth L. Bailey compares immediate postwar views of dominating American women and "pleasant" European ones in *From Front Porch to Back Seat: Courtship in Twentieth-Century America* (Baltimore, MD: The Johns Hopkins University Press, 1988), 41.

3 Theodore Rivers, "The Enemy Within: Women Who Prey on Our Servicemen," *Real Combat Stories*, April 1964, 29, 62. On prostitution, see Donald S. Bradley, Jacqueline Boles, and Christopher Jones, "From Mistress to Hooker: 40 Years of Cartoon Humor in Men's Magazines," *Qualitative Sociology* Vol. 2, No. 2 (June 1979): 49–50.

4 Persecutory paranoia in Paradis, 6. Fears in Christina Klein, *Cold War Orientalism: Asia in the Middlebrow Imagination, 1945–1961* (Berkeley, CA: University of California Press, 2003), 36. On how these fears were intertwined with policy, see H. W. Brands, "The Age of Vulnerability: Eisenhower and the National Insecurity State," *The American Historical Review* Vol. 94, No. 4 (October 1989): 963–989.

5 Richard Hofstadter, *The Paranoid Style in American Politics and Other Essays* (New York, NY: Vintage Books, 1967), 29. On paranoias driving much of the pulp narrative, see Woody Haut, *Pulp Culture: Hardboiled Fiction and the Cold War* (London: Serpent's Tail, 1995), 14. Ellen Schrecker argues the communist threat became a "national obsession." *The Age of McCarthyism*, 25.

6 Mass society and rehabilitation to meet Cold War challenges in K. A. Cuordileone, *Manhood and American Political Culture in the Cold War* (London: Routledge, 2005), xxiii.

7 Philip Caputo, *A Rumor of War* (New York, NY: Holt, Rinehart and Winston, 1977), 5. Glorified male warrior in Charlotte Hooper, *Manly States: Masculinities, International Relations, and Gender Politics* (New York, NY: Columbia University Press, 2001), 2.

Protectors and providers in Barbara Ehrenreich, *The Hearts of Men: American Dreams and the Flight from Commitment* (New York, NY: Anchor Books, 1983), 16.

8 Postwar doubts in Warren Susman, "Did Success Spoil the United States? Dual Representations in Postwar America," in *Recasting America: Culture and Politics in the Age of the Cold War*, ed. Lary May (Chicago, IL: The University of Chicago Press, 1989), 22. Mandating new villains in Bernard F. Dick, *The Screen Is Red: Hollywood, Communism, and the Cold War* (Jackson, MS: University Press of Mississippi, 2016), 148. Suzanne Clark has noted that "World War II finished off the threat from Hitler and Japan by opening a new place for the fascist imagination within the United States." In *Cold Warriors: Manliness on Trial in the Rhetoric of the West* (Carbondale, IL: Southern Illinois University Press, 2000), 7.

9 McCarran Act in Albert Fried, ed., *McCarthyism: The Great American Red Scare, A Documentary History* (New York, NY: Oxford University Press, 1997), 85–87; and David Caute, *The Great Fear: The Anti-communist Purge under Truman and Eisenhower* (New York, NY: Simon & Schuster, 1978), 38.

10 Men feeling besieged in Peter G. Filene, *Him/Her/Self: Gender Identities in Modern America*, 3rd ed. (Baltimore, MD: The Johns Hopkins University Press, 1998), 99. Overcivilized and womanized in E. Anthony Rotundo, *American Manhood: Transformations in Masculinity from the Revolution to the Modern Era* (New York, NY: Basic Books, 1993), 251–252. On debates over "sex difference" in the late 1800s, see R. W. Connell, *Masculinities*, 2nd ed. (Berkeley, CA: University of California Press, 2005), 21.

11 On obsession and crisis, see Gail Bederman, *Manliness & Civilization: A Cultural History of Gender and Race in the United States, 1880–1917* (Chicago, IL: The University of Chicago Press, 1995), 11–12. See also Bethan Benwell, "Introduction," in *Masculinity and Men's Lifestyle Magazines*, ed. Bethan Benwell (Malden, MA: Blackwell, 2003), 15. Constricted in Stephen W. Berry III, *All That Makes a Man: Love and Ambition in the Civil War South* (New York, NY: Oxford University Press, 2003), 46.

12 Traditional gender relations and Roosevelt quoted in Bobby A. Wintermute and David J. Ulbrich, *Race and Gender in Modern Western Warfare* (Boston, MA: De Gruyter, 2019), 81–82. Harvey C. Mansfield argues that to TR, manliness was "an individual construction of one's own willpower." In *Manliness* (New Haven, CT: Yale University Press, 2006), 91.

13 *Century Magazine* in Filene, 77. Physical culture in David M. Earle, *All Man! Hemingway, 1950s Men's Magazines, and the Masculine Persona* (Kent, OH: The Kent State University Press, 2009), 30–31. On links to imperialism, see Bederman, 192–193.

14 Kennan in Frank Costigliola, "'Unceasing Pressure for Penetration': Gender, Pathology, and Emotion in George Kennan's Formulation of the Cold War," *The Journal of American History* Vol. 83, No. 4 (March 1997): 1310. On strong men and a strong nation, see Brian Robertson, "The Forgotten Man: Richard Nixon, Masculinity, and the Path to Power in Southern California," *California History* Vol. 94, No. 2 (Summer 2017): 36. On "hegemonic masculinity" going hand in hand with "the culture and ideology of hegemonic nationalism," see Emanuela Lombardo and Petra Meier, *The Symbolic Representation of Gender: A Discursive Approach* (Burlington, VT: Ashgate, 2014), 23.

15 Halberstam and Kearns quoted in Mark Gerzon, *A Choice of Heroes: The Changing Faces of American Manhood* (Boston, MA: Houghton Mifflin, 1992), 93. Johnson quoted in

Geoffrey S. Smith, "Security, Gender, and the Historical Process," *Diplomatic History* Vol. 18, No. 1 (Winter 1994): 87; and Michael Kimmel, *Manhood in America: A Cultural History* (New York, NY: The Free Press, 1996), 269–270.

16 LBJ quoted in Isabel Heinemann, "Introduction," in *Inventing the Modern American Family: Family Values and Social Change in 20th Century United States*, ed. Isabel Heinemann (New York, NY: Campus Verlag, 2012), 7. Elaine Tyler May has argued that the family became a "bastion of safety in an unsecure world," a "bulwark against the dangers of the cold war." *Homeward Bound: American Families in the Cold War Era* (New York, NY: Basic Books, 1988, 2008), 9, 33. On fears of family life not exercising the proper influence over children, see James Gilbert, *A Cycle of Outrage: America's Reaction to the Juvenile Delinquent in the 1950s* (New York, NY: Oxford University Press, 1986), 17.

17 Lester W. Dearborn, "Why More Men and Women Engage in Extramarital Relations," *Cavalcade*, November 1959, 6, 94. Shailer Upton Lawton, "Sex Secrets," *Challenge*, August 1959, 20–21. On similar conceptions of "masculine unease" in Australia, see Chelsea Barnett, "*Man's* Man: Representation of Australian Post-war Masculinity in *Man* Magazine," *Journal of Australian Studies* Vol. 39, No. 2 (2015): 153.

18 Retreat to housewifery and costs to wives in Stephanie Coontz, *The Way We Never Were: American Families and the Nostalgia Trap* (New York, NY: Basic Books, 1992), 33, 40. Idle class in Philp Wylie, *Generation of Vipers* (New York, NY: Farrar & Rinehart, 1942), 49. Controlling domestic life in Haut, 41. Traditional morals in John Bodnar, *The "Good War" in American Memory* (Baltimore, MD: The Johns Hopkins University Press, 2010), 62. Elaine Tyler May notes that experts "called upon women to embrace domesticity in service to the nation." *Homeward Bound*, 98.

19 Wylie, 205. Editors of *Look*, *The Decline of the American Male* (New York, NY: Random House, 1958), 11. Advertisement in *Men*, May 1962, 55.

20 Panic in James Gilbert, *Men in the Middle: Searching for Masculinity in the 1950s* (Chicago, IL: The University of Chicago Press, 2005), 9. Rubén Cenamor, "What Have We Learned since the 1950s? The Return to Conservative Gender Roles in Sam Mendes' Film Adaptation of *Revolutionary Road*," in *Rethinking Gender in Popular Culture in the 21st Century: Marlboro Men and California Girls*, eds. Astrid Fellner, Marta Fernández-Morales, and Martina Martausová (Newcastle upon Tyne: Cambridge Scholars Publishing, 2017), 170–178. William Heuman, "Why Do We Have to Marry Women?" *Saga*, July 1957, 32.

21 Betty Friedan, *The Feminine Mystique* (New York, NY: W. W. Norton, 1963), 274. Conformity in Peter Viereck, *The Unadjusted Man: A New Hero for Americans* (Boston, MA: The Beacon Press, 1956), 6.

22 On Miller, see Robert J. Corber, *Homosexuality in Cold War America: Resistance and the Crisis of Masculinity* (Durham, NC: Duke University Press, 1997), 36–43. C. Wright Mills equally spoke of a "deep-rooted" malaise among American working men. *White Collar: The American Middle Class* (New York, NY: Oxford University Press, 1953), xvi.

23 Arthur Schlesinger, Jr., "The Crisis of American Masculinity," *Esquire* Vol. 50, No. 5 (November 1958): 63, 64. *Gray Flannel Suit* in Christian G. Appy, "'We'll Follow the Old Man': The Strains of Sentimental Militarism in Popular Films of the Fifties," in *Rethinking Cold War Culture*, eds. Peter J. Kuznick and James Gilbert (Washington, DC:

Smithsonian Institution Press, 2001), 94. See also David Halberstam, *The Fifties* (New York, NY: Villard Books, 1993), 524.

24 GI Bill as social welfare and usage numbers in David R. Segal, *Recruiting for Uncle Sam: Citizenship and Military Manpower Policy* (Lawrence, KS: University Press of Kansas, 1989), 87–88. Housing loans in Coontz, 94–96.

25 GI Bill nonusers in Suzanne Mettler, *Soldiers to Citizens: The G.I. Bill and the Making of the Greatest Generation* (New York, NY: Oxford University Press, 2005), 48. On proving one's manhood being a "constant challenge," see Elisabeth Badinter, *XY: On Masculine Identity* (New York, NY: Columbia University Press, 1995), 2. On the benefits, more generally, of economic growth leading to a just society, see Alan Brinkley, "The Illusion of Unity in Cold War Culture," in Kuznick and Gilbert, 64.

26 Heather Marie Stur, *Beyond Combat: Women and Gender in the Vietnam War Era* (New York, NY: Cambridge University Press, 2011), 148. On the crisis of masculinity becoming a "standard literary theme," see Earle, 105. See also Clive Baldwin, "'The Orgasm of the Frigidaire': Male Sexuality and the Female Other in Post-World War II American fiction," on a "dominant discursive anxiety" in post-industrial America. In *Masculinity and the Other: Historical Perspectives*, eds. Heather Ellis and Jessica Meyer (Newcastle upon Tyne: Cambridge Scholars Publishing, 2009), 143.

27 "Stag Confidential," *Stag*, July 1961, 8. Jorge Esteban, "A Young Legal Mistress for Every Man," *Men*, July 1964, 12.

28 *Cosmopolitan* in Steven Watts, *JFK and the Masculine Mystique: Sex and Power on the New Frontier* (New York, NY: St. Martin's Press, 2016), 27. Feminizing in Gilbert, *Men in the Middle*, 63; and Hooper, *Manly States*, 70. "Dominated" in *Look*, 3. Philip Wylie, "The Womanization of America," *Playboy*, September 1958, 51. Wylie earlier claimed that a man might be "frightened out of his masculinity and suddenly start behaving in a womanish manner." *Generation of Vipers*, 120.

29 On emasculation, see Bill Osgerby, "Two-Fisted Tales of Brutality and Belligerence: Masculinity and Meaning in the American 'True Adventure' Pulps of the 1950s and 1960s," in Ellis and Meyer, 166. Joe Pearson, "The Mental Castration of Husbands," *Sir!*, July 1962, 31. Andrew Petersen, "Castration of the American Male," *Brigade*, March 1963, 35. Frederich Berquist, "Are Your Sex Guilts Making You Impotent," *Man's Action*, May 1966, 28.

30 Vigorous action in Watts, 14. Alexander P. de Seversky, "Our Boys Are <u>Not</u> Afraid to Fly," *Man's Day*, March 1953, 9. Sen. Estes Kefauver, "Are You the Ninth Man?" *Real Adventure*, March 1955, 15.

31 Paul C. Ditzel, "The Day That Cicero Died," *Stag*, April 1952, 22–23. Nor did the pulps make linkages between discrimination at home and US foreign policy. On this topic, see Mary L. Dudziak, *Cold War Civil Rights: Race and the Image of American Democracy* (Princeton, MA: Princeton University Press, 2000); and Penny M. Von Eschen, *Race against Empire: Black Americans and Anticolonialism, 1937–1957* (Ithaca, NY: Cornell University Press, 1997). On whiteness and maleness combined to mark "American authenticity," see Clark, *Cold Warriors*, 3.

32 George Mandel, "Detroit's Unholy Secret Legion," *For Men Only*, November 1958, 23. On Evers, see William Bradford Huie, "Murder Trial in Mississippi," *Saga*, June 1964, 37;

and Hal Bennet, "My Brother's Killer Can't Stop Me," *Saga*, August 1965, 20. William Bradford Huie, "The Klansman," *True*, October 1967, 37. On the Klan censoring the prewar pulps, see Linda Gordon, *The Second Coming of the KKK: The Ku Klux Klan of the 1920s and the American Political Tradition* (New York, NY: Liveright, 2017), 135. On Baldwin, see Kimmel, *Manhood in America*, 271. Armstrong in Penny M. Von Eschen, *Satchmo Blows Up the World: Jazz Ambassadors Play the Cold War* (Cambridge, MA: Harvard University Press, 2004).

33 On *Ebony* and *Duke*, see Tom Pendergast, *Creating the Modern Man: American Magazines and Consumer Culture, 1900–1950* (Columbia, MS: University of Missouri Press, 2000), 68–71, 167–169, 242; Elizabeth Fraterrigo, *Playboy and the Making of the Good Life in Modern America* (New York, NY: Oxford University Press, 2009), 138–140; and Osgerby, *Playboys in Paradise*, 172–175. For a discussion on how civil rights activists were denounced as Moscow-inspired communists, see Caute, *The Great Fear*, 166.

34 Buriel quoted in Steven Rosales, "Macho Nation? Chicano Soldiering, Sexuality, and Manhood during the Vietnam Era," *The Oral History Review* Vol. 40, No. 2 (August 2013): 304. Diversity in armed forces in Thomas Bruscino, *A Nation Forged in War: How World War II Taught Americans to Get Along* (Knoxville, TN: The University Press of Tennessee, 2010), 58.

35 It is important to note how non-white men were objectified and emasculated in popular culture in other wars, most explicitly the Japanese in World War II. On this, see Osgerby, "Two-Fisted Tales of Brutality and Belligerence," 169.

36 On George Paine, see *American Manhood*, January 1953, 45; and *American Manhood*, February 1953, 40. *Challenge*'s September 1955 exposé on fighter Jack Johnson called him the "most detested champion in all boxing history." James W. Cameron, "They Hated the Champ!," 34. On this topic, see Bederman, *Manliness & Civilization*, 1–10. Joe Weider, "Sam Langford: The Boston Tar Baby," *American Manhood*, March 1953, 31. Floyd Patterson, "I Was Hell-Bent for Trouble," *Man's Magazine*, April 1957, 28. On Satchel Paige, see Ernie Harwell, "The World's Greatest Pitcher," *Male*, July 1954, 21.

37 A. M. Libasci, "What You Should Know about Venereal Disease," *American Manhood*, February 1953, 31, 52. On sexual transgressions of the "black rapist," see Christopher Breu, *Hard-Boiled Masculinities* (Minneapolis, MN: University of Minnesota Press, 2005), 33; and Susan Griffin, *Pornography and Silence: Culture's Revenge against Nature* (New York, NY: Harper & Row, 1981), 159. Racial anxieties in Steven Dillon, *Wolf-Women and Phantom Ladies: Female Desire in 1940s US Culture* (Albany, NY: SUNY Press, 2015), 159. White sexual anxieties in Linda Williams, "Skin Flicks on the Racial Border: Pornography, Exploitation, and Interracial Lust," in *Porn Studies*, ed. Linda Williams (Durham, NC: Duke University Press, 2004), 277, 288. On issues with sexual relationships between white German women and black US soldiers, see Maria Höhn, *GIs and Fräuleins: The German–American Encounter in 1950s West Germany* (Chapel Hill, NC: The University of North Carolina Press, 2002), 86, 104; and Christine Knauer, *Let Us Fight as Free Men: Black Soldiers and Civil Rights* (Philadelphia, PA: University of Pennsylvania Press, 2014), 35–36. For a different take, in which some pulp novels explored the experiences of black GIs in

occupied Germany, see Paula Rabinowitz, *American Pulp: How Paperbacks Brought Modernism to Main Street* (Princeton, MA: Princeton University Press, 2014), 54–55.

38 On Milton Olive, see *Stag*, January 1967, 38. Mark Sufrin, "The Marine Who Won America's Most Important Race," *Male*, March 1965, 28. More representative of stories on athletes excelling in combat was Glenn Infield, "Ray Houk: The N.Y. Yankee Who Saved the 9th Armored Division," *Stag*, May 1964, 17. On sports' links to "toughness," see Donald J. Mrozek, "The Cult and Ritual of Toughness in Cold War America," in *Sport in America: From Wicked Amusement to National Obsession*, ed. David K. Wiggins (Champaign, IL: Human Kinetics, 1995).

39 On gender systems linked to racial issues, see Alice Kessler-Harris, *In Pursuit of Equity: Women, Men, and the Quest for Economic Citizenship in 20th-Century America* (New York, NY: Oxford University Press, 2001), 6. On relations to World War II, see Andrew J. Huebner, *The Warrior Image: Soldiers in American Culture from the Second World War to the Vietnam Era* (Chapel Hill, NC: The University of North Carolina Press, 2008), 52; and Knauer, 20.

40 He-Man Voice ad in *Battle Cry*, February 1956, 50. George Laycock, "Your Screwy Idea Can Make You a Million," *Real*, March 1958, 24. On fiscal concerns in the 1950s, see Coontz, *The Way We Never Were*, 31. If the American consumer-based society represented a repression of true masculinity, and a growing domination of femininity in society, then it seems ironic that men still wanted to reap the full rewards of a system they viewed as contrary to masculine beliefs.

41 Expendable ad in *Stag*, June 1959, 45. Rut ad in *Men*, December 1961, 3. On class components to gender, see Joan Wallach Scott, *Gender and the Politics of History* (New York, NY: Columbia University Press, 1988), 60. For a treatment of this in the Canadian pulps, see Michelle Denise Smith, "Soup Cans and Love Slaves: National Politics and Cultural Authority in the Editing and Authorship of Canadian Pulp Magazines," *Book History* Vol. 9 (2006): 262. On how this related to dating, see Bailey, *From Front Porch to Back Seat*, 21–22.

42 Ray Lunt, "Why Your Pension May Not Be Worth a Red Cent," *Male*, March 65, 26. Ken Kolb, "What Ever Happened to The Old-Fashioned Mistress?" *Saga*, March 1956, 24–25.

43 GNP in Walter W. Young and Nancy K. Young, *The 1950s* (Westport, CT: Greenwood Press, 2004), 3. Disposable time in Andrew Kimbrell, *The Masculine Mystique: The Politics of Masculinity* (New York, NY: Ballantine, 1995), 107. Inequalities in Lizabeth Cohen, *A Consumer's Republic: The Politics of Mass Consumption in Postwar America* (New York, NY: Alfred A. Knopf, 2003), 234. For a discussion on contemporary class hostilities, see Gilbert, *A Cycle of Outrage*, 5.

44 Mills, *White Collar*, 229. Surveys in George Lipsitz, *Class and Culture in Cold War America: "A Rainbow at Midnight"* (South Hadley, MA: J. F. Bergin, 1981), 98. Self-made man in Ava Baron, "Masculinity, the Embodied Male Worker, and the Historian's Gaze," *International Labor and Working-Class History* No. 69 (Spring 2006): 145.

45 Links to Great Depression in Christina S. Jarvis, *The Male Body at War: American Masculinity during World War II* (DeKalb, IL: Northern Illinois University Press, 2004), 16–17; and Kimmel, *Manhood in America*, 199–200. Masculinity and work in Myron Brenton, *The American Male* (New York, NY: Coward-McCann, 1966), 20.

46 Job failure ad in *Man's Magazine*, April 1957, 5. Income growth ad in *Battlefield*, August 1958, 9. Dependence in Ehrenreich, *The Hearts of Men*, 2. Lack of compassion in Robert Bly, *Iron John: A Book about Men* (New York, NY: Da Capo Press, 2004), 2.

47 Repression at bay in *American Manhood*, January 1953, 3. That same month, *Male* ran a class-centered story on a World War II NCO saving his unit from a "dangerously psychotic" officer. Jules Archer, "Lieutenant, You're Crazy, Sir!," 39.

48 James Bender, "College Men Are Sexually Inferior," *Male*, July 1954, 16–17, 54, 56. On ridiculing "high culture" in pulp writing, see Erin A. Smith, *Hard-Boiled: Working-Class Readers and Pulp Magazines* (Philadelphia, PA: Temple University Press, 2000), 131.

49 On cultural concepts differentiating hardness and softness, see James Penner, *Pinks, Pansies, and Punks: The Rhetoric of Masculinity in American Literary Culture* (Bloomington, IN: Indiana University Press, 2011), 16, 67. Collectively, magazines commanded nine percent of all US advertising dollars in 1950. Young, *The 1950s*, 147. Linking consumption to status in Tracy Penny Light, "'Healthy' Men Make Good Fathers: Masculine Health and the Family in 20th Century America," in Heinemann, 112; and Theodore Peterson, *Magazines in the Twentieth Century* (Urbana, IL: University of Illinois Press, 1964), 27.

50 Dominance in Pendergast, *Creating the Modern Man*, 235. See also Erin A. Smith, "How the Other Half Read: Advertising, Working-Class Readers, and Pulp Magazines," *Book History* Vol. 3 (2000): 206–207. Validating manhood in David D. Gilmore, *Manhood in the Making: Cultural Concepts of Masculinity* (New Haven, CT: Yale University Press, 1990), 201. For a comparison with advertising in *Playboy*, see Fraterrigo, 62, 83.

51 On Atlas, see Kimmel, 210–211; and F. Valentine Hooven III, *Beefcake: The Muscle Magazines of America 1950–1970* (Cologne: Benedikt Taschen, 1995), 22. On physical culture, see John Beynon, *Masculinities and Culture* (Philadelphia, PA: Open University Press, 2002), 43–44. Atlas ads in *Male*, November 1957, 5; *Stag*, March 1966, 75; and *For Men Only*, December 1959, 9.

52 On subculture of bodybuilding, see Suzanne E. Hatty, *Masculinities, Violence, and Culture* (Thousand Oaks, CA: Sage, 2000), 126. Atlas ads in *Stag*, July 1961, 83; *For Men Only*, July 1959, 5; *Male*, March 1967, 73. For a comparison with later movies which used the body as a "register of gender," see Brian Caldwell, "Muscling in on the Movies: Excess and the Representation of the Male Body in Films of the 1980s and 1990s," in *American Bodies: Cultural Histories of the Physique*, ed. Tim Armstrong (New York, NY: New York University Press, 1996), 136; and Christian G. Appy, *American Reckoning: The Vietnam War and Our National Identity* (New York, NY: Viking, 2015), 248.

53 Editorial policy, *American Manhood*, January 1953, 3. *American Manhood*, February 1953, 29, 49, 53. Links between the male body and masculinity in Kenneth MacKinnon, *Representing Men: Maleness and Masculinity in the Media* (New York, NY: Oxford University Press, 2003), 5; and Theodore P. Greene, *America's Heroes: The Changing Models of Success in American Magazines* (New York, NY: Oxford University Press, 1970), 127. In the case of Maurice LeBlanc, the reader is told that LeBlanc was "sick and puny" growing up, his "frail body couldn't stand even ... slight strain." Since he had enrolled with Weider, though, the thirty-year-old had "gained 15 pounds of muscle, health and energy" and

held "a tough job" while also enjoying "vigorous sports." In *American Manhood*, January 1953, 6. On bodies and manhood, see Harriet Bradley, *Gender* (Cambridge: Polity, 2007), 155; and Connell, *Masculinities*, 45, 54.

54 Harold B. Hersey, *Pulpwood Editor* (New York, NY: Frederick A. Stokes, 1937), 76. Ideal versions in Antony Easthope, *What a Man's Gotta Do: The Masculine Myth in Popular Culture* (Boston, MA: Unwin Hyman, 1990), 53. Assuaging insecurities in Kathryn Weibel, *Mirror: Images of Women Reflected in Popular Culture* (Garden City, NY: Anchor Books, 1977), 155. On imperfections and deficiencies, see Bill Osgerby, "Muscular Manhood and Salacious Sleaze: The Singular World of the 1950s Macho Pulps," in Abrams and Hughes, 139. Transforming and remaking in Smith, *Hard-Boiled*, 61.

55 Martin Haver, "Quick Pill Addict," *Challenge*, November 1958, 15. Hair ad on p. 67. *Adventure Life*, March 1959, 55. *Bluebook*, May 1965, 59.

56 Mind control in Matthew W. Dunne, *A Cold War State of Mind: Brainwashing and Postwar American Society* (Amherst, MA: University of Massachusetts Press, 2013), 17, 51. Brainwashing in *Ibid.*, 14–51. See also Kimmel, *Manhood in America*, 237.

57 John F. Kennedy, "The Soft American," *Sports Illustrated*, 26 December 1960, 15. See also Rachel Louise Moran, *Governing Bodies: American Politics and the Shaping of the Modern Physique* (Philadelphia, PA: University of Pennsylvania Press, 2018), 98–100. Watts calls JFK's plans a "crusade to regenerate masculinity." *JFK and the Masculine Mystique*, 6. Kones quoted in Robert L. Griswold, "The 'Flabby American,' the Body, and the Cold War," in *A Shared Experience: Men, Women, and the History of Gender*, ed. Laura McCall and Donald Yacovone (New York, NY: New York University Press, 1998), 335.

58 Moxie in Griswold, 335. On Korean War POWs, see William Lindsay White, *The Captives of Korea: An Unofficial White Paper on the Treatment of War Prisoners* (New York, NY: Charles Scribner's Sons, 1957); and Charles S. Young, *Name, Rank, and Serial Number: Exploiting Korean War POWs at Home and Abroad* (New York, NY: Oxford University Press, 2014). Young notes that "38 percent of 7,190 American POWs died" during the Korean War, p. 24.

59 Puller quoted in Richard Slotkin, *Gunfighter Nation: The Myth of the Frontier in Twentieth-Century America* (Norman, OK: University of Oklahoma Press, 1998), 363. On brainwashing films, see Dick, *The Screen Is Red*, 210; Matthew W. Dunne, "Homophobia, Housewives, and Hyper-masculinity: Gender and American Policymaking in the Nuclear Age," in *The Routledge History of Gender, War, and the U.S. Military*, ed. Kara Dixon Vuic (London: Routledge, 2018), 106, and Klein, *Cold War Orientalism*, 36.

60 Banish sex ignorance in *American Manhood*, January 1953, 15. Sex and exercise in *American Manhood*, March 1953, 14. A. Michaels, "Sex Knowledge for Young Men," *Ibid.*, 26. A. Michaels, "Should Teenagers Pet? *American Manhood*, May 1953, 36, 64–65. On petting as a "code of sexual conduct," see Coontz, 45. *Challenge*, November 1958, included an ad selling a book *Modern Love Letters* which came with "complete instructions on writing letters of love, courtship, and marriage," p. 47.

61 How syphilis spreads chart in Libasci, 30. In the diagram, one woman ends up infecting seventeen people. Well-hidden on p. 31. Alan Effler, "Will Your Marriage Be Fertile?," *Action*, March 1953, 14. The article noted that "Husband's love often turns to hate if

couple remains childless for years. It's usually his fault." Dr. Valentine W. Zetlin claimed that "many men stumble through the crisis of the wedding night like bulls in heat." In "What to Do on Your Wedding Night," *Challenge*, September 1955, 23. "Marriage Mischief" ad in *Stag*, April 1956, 71. J. K. Carter, "How Much Is 'Too Much Sex?,'" *Showdown*, September 1958, 13. The article highlighted one man who was married to a woman fifteen years younger and his worries over having intercourse so frequently, p. 47. "How to Taste the True Delights of Ideal Sexual Union" ad in *Cavalcade*, November 1959, 53. Henry Salton, "Virginity Can Cause Cancer!," *All Man*, April 1960, 20. R. Plimsoll Howard, "Ignorance Can Ruin Your Sex Life," *Battle Cry*, March 1964, 31. On pressures of male sexual performance, see Carolyn Herbst Lewis, *Prescribing Heterosexuality: Sexual Citizenship in the Cold War Era* (Chapel Hill, NC: The University of North Carolina Press, 2010), 65, 78.

62 On pains to prove manhood, see Timothy Beneke, *Proving Manhood: Reflections on Men and Sexism* (Berkeley, CA: University of California Press, 1997), 172. Inferiority in Kathleen Barry, *Unmaking War Remaking Men: How Empathy Can Reshape Our Politics, Our Soldiers and Ourselves* (Santa Rosa, CA: Phoenix Rising Press, 2011), 22. Sex guide ad in *Stag*, January 1964, 70. See *Man's Life*, September 1966, 51, for an ad on a "sex-manual" that offered "techniques of seduction that can open up a whole new world for you." Ogling in Ray Lunt, "Our Ridiculous Horse-and-Buggy Sex Laws," *Men*, March 1963, 68. Frigidity in ad for "Illustrated Sex Facts" in *Guy*, January 1959, 51. Anonymous, "My Wife Is a Nymphomaniac," *Battle Cry*, March 1960, 32–33. Persistence in Dr. Efrem Schoenhild, "25 Keys to Female Response," *True Action*, March 1967, 32, 62. Joseph Le Baron, "Glamour Girls Are a Pain in the Boudoir!" *Cavalcade*, November 1959, 16.

63 Cartoons in *Man's Magazine*, June 1965, 78; and *Man's Magazine*, November 1961, 30.

64 Lewis B. Puller, Jr., *Fortunate Son* (New York, NY: Grove Weidenfeld, 1991), 18. Fear and desire in Simone de Beauvoir, *The Second Sex* (New York, NY: Alfred A. Knopf, 1949, 2010), 172. Bedroom barracudas in Edgar M. Sullivan, "'All-Out' Love Kittens," *For Men Only*, April 1967, 40. For an example of how these depictions promoted violence against women, see Joanna Bourke, *Rape: Sex, Violence, History* (Berkeley, CA: Shoemaker Hoard, 2007), 74; and Griffin, *Pornography and Silence*, 146.

65 Ultimate conquest in *Battle Cry*, July 58, 42. Frank S. Caprio, "How to Boost Your Sexual Batting Average," *Men*, December 1961, 22. "Inside for Men," *Male*, June 1966, 44. On depictions of tramps, see Alan M. Young, "Executive Suite Tramp," *Stag*, August 1966, 22. "Stag Confidential," *Stag*, March 1968, 6. A comic in *Stag*, February 1967, showed a man and woman at a nightclub table: "You seem like a nice girl, but frankly I'm looking for a tramp," p. 43. *Real Men* also ran a story in which the male author, in dating a girl who responded to a want ad, noted that "She wasn't an intellectual – but who wants to date an egghead!" Brandon Malone, "Wanted: Partner for Passion," *Real Men*, December 1960, 21, 46. Temporary virgins in D. Bogen, "Sex Lives of the Love Seekers," *Stag*, March 1968, 12.

66 Advisor Virginia Gildersleeve quoted in D'Ann Campbell, *Women at War with America: Private Lives in a Patriotic Era* (Cambridge, MA: Harvard University Press, 1984), 37. Confused women in Billie Mitchell, "The Creation of Army Officers and the Gender Lie:

Betty Grable or Frankenstein?," in *It's Our Military, Too! Women and the U.S. Military*, ed. Judith Hicks Stiehm (Philadelphia, PA: Temple University Press, 1996), 40. Whores and lesbians in Cynthia Enloe, *Does Khaki Become You? The Militarisation of Women's Lives* (Boston, MA: South End Press, 1983), 140.

67 *Battlefield*, November 1959, 52. Drill Instructors in Gustav Hasford, *The Short-Timers* (New York, NY: Harper & Row, 1979), 4–5; and Carol Burke, *Camp All-American, Hanoi Jane, and the High-and-Tight* (Boston, MA: Beacon Press, 2004), 13. On this type of language, see Ray Bourgeois Zimmerman, "Gruntspeak: Masculinity, Monstrosity and Discourse in Hasford's *The Short-Timers*," *American Studies* Vol. 40, No. 1 (Spring 1999): 66. Sexual harassment and slandering in D'Ann Campbell, "The Regimented Women of World War II," in *Women, Militarism, and War: Essays in History, Politics, and Social Theory*, eds. Jean Bethke Elshtain and Shelia Tobias (Savage, MD: Rowman & Littlefield, 1990), 114–115; and John Costello, *Virtue under Fire: How World War II Changed Our Social and Sexual Attitudes* (Boston, MA: Little, Brown, and Company, 1985), 43. For a different take on military training that disassociates it from sexual violence, see Hugh McManners, *The Scars of War* (New York, NY: HarperCollins, 1993), 115.

68 On Cold War sex education, see Brian McAllister Linn, *Elvis's Army: Cold War GIs and the Atomic Battlefield* (Cambridge, MA: Harvard University Press, 2016), 280. Eroticizing women in Susan Gubar, "'This Is My Rifle, This Is My Gun': World War II and the Blitz on Women," in *Behind the Lines: Gender and the Two World Wars*, eds. Margaret Randolph Higgonet, Sonya Michel, Jane Jenson, and Margaret Collins Weitz (New Haven, CT: Yale University Press, 1987), 240. See also Bruscino, *A Nation Forged in War*, 112. For an example of *Good Housekeeping* recommending how women should wear uniforms, and choose a "feminine coiffure," see Nancy Walker, ed., *Women's Magazines, 1940–1960: Gender Roles and the Popular Press* (Boston, MA: Bedford/St. Martin's, 1998), 35–37.

69 "GI Sex Instruction Films," *Battle Cry*, December 1955, 16. Charles Farrell, "The Failure of Mickey Mouse," *Battle Cry*, July 1958, 36. On Vietnam-era films, see Sue Sun, "*Where the Girls Are*: The Management of Venereal Disease by United States Military Forces in Vietnam," *Literature and Medicine* Vol. 23, No. 1 (Spring 2004): 66–87.

70 Viewing women as objects in Nicola Dibben, "Pulp, Pornography and Spectatorship: Subject Matter and Subject Position in Pulp's *This Is Hardcore*," *Journal of the Royal Musical Association* Vol. 126, No. 1 (2001): 87. *Pleasure Primer* in *Challenge*, November 1958, 65. Photos of Brigitte Bardot in *Valor*, June 1959, 83. Stag stories for men in *Real Men*, December 1960, 63.

71 Cog in Smith, "How the Other Half Read," 214. Meat cutting in *Male*, July 1954, 79. Ads in *Battlefield*, May 1959, 3; *Male*, February 1965, 57; *Action for Men*, May 1964; *For Men Only*, March 1959, 9; and *Stag*, April 1956, 49.

72 Status striving in George Spindler and Louise Spindler, *The American Cultural Dialogue and Its Transmission* (New York, NY: The Falmer Press, 1990), 37. Artisans in Smith, *Hard-Boiled*, 63. "Investigate Accidents" in *Challenge*, November 1958, 49. "Don't Stay Just a 'Name' on the Payroll" ad in *Action*, May 1953, 5. "Be a Clerk all my life? Not Me!" ad in *Battle Cry*, February 1956, 3. IBM ad in *Saga*, June 1964, 71.

73 On ads selling English proficiency, see Smith, "How the Other Half Read," 221–224. "Everyone takes Bill for a college man" in *For Men Only*, March 1959, 10. "How to Speak and Write Like a College Graduate" ad in *For Men Only*, February 1960, 53. Mistakes in English ad in *Male*, July 1954, 63.

74 High school ads *Battle Cry*, August 1962, 5; *Action for Men*, May 1964, 48; and *Men*, February 1968, 2.

75 "Exciting Outdoor Careers of Adventure," *Action for Men*, May 1964, p. 37.

76 Delivery truck in James R. Ebert, *A Life in a Year: The American Infantryman in Vietnam, 1965–1972* (Novato, CA: Presidio, 1993), 4. Burning in John A. Wood, *Veteran Narratives and the Collective Memory of the Vietnam War* (Athens, OH: Ohio University Press, 2016), 19. Afraid in James Wright, *Enduring Vietnam: An American Generation and Its War* (New York, NY: St. Martin's Press, 2017), 133. On these "soldier-adventurers," see Peter S. Kindsvatter, *American Soldiers: Ground Combat in the World Wars, Korea, and Vietnam* (Lawrence, KS: University Press of Kansas, 2003), 189.

77 Battlefield and contest in Robert Strausz-Hupe, William R. Kintner, James E. Dougherty, and Alvin J. Cottrell, *Protracted Conflict* (New York, NY: Harper & Brothers, 1959), 29. For how some states dealt with the threat of communist subversion, see Caute, *The Great Fear*, 70–71.

78 McCarthy quoted in Fried, *McCarthyism*, 80. Maryam Khalid notes how some critics linked the USSR threat to "unpredictably aggressive negative masculinity." In *Gender, Orientalism, and the "War on Terror": Representation, Discourse, and Intervention in Global Politics* (London: Routledge, 2017), 50.

79 Fanatical communists in Istvan Hildy, "Blood Bath in Budapest," *Man's Magazine*, April 1957, 12. Emile C. Schurmacher, "Red Murder of a US Diplomat," *Stag*, January 1961, 26. Ivan Colt, "The Strange Russian City That Trains Fake Americans," *True Action*, October 1961, 26. See also "Russia: Iowa in the Ukraine," *Time*, 27 April 1959. Ed Hyde, "Russia's Spy Fleet on Our Doorstep," *Bluebook*, May 1965, 32. Mikhail Antonov, "My 20 Years with Moscow's Secret Police," *Sensation*, April 1959, 8.

80 David Mars, "Is Russia Planning a Submarine Pearl Harbor?," *Stag*, July 1961, 33, 44. Seymour Freidin, "Mr. Terror: Boss of the K.G.B.," *Stag*, March 1968, 27. See also Alex Seroff, "Stalin's Secret Book of Death," *Action*, May 1953, 11; and Kurt Koeppel, "Inside Moscow's Mafia," *Bluebook*, May 1966, 16.

81 Puppet in John Lamberton Harper, *The Cold War* (New York, NY: Oxford University Press, 2011), 105. For an alternative to this, see Irwin Carter, "The Coming War between Russia and Red China," *Men*, December 1961, 20. On assumptions about China, see John Hellmann, *American Myth and the Legacy of Vietnam* (New York, NY: Columbia University Press, 1986), 12; and James C. Thomson, Jr., "How Could Vietnam Happen?," *The Atlantic*, 1 April 1968, who spoke of "a general perception of China-on-the-march," p. 48. For a general overview, see Chen Jian, *Mao's China and the Cold War* (Chapel Hill, NC: The University of North Carolina Press, 2001). Fred Sparks, "Red China: Will She Swallow the World?," *Stag*, June 1959, 26, 28. See also Fred Sparks, "Butcher of Korea: Next Boss of Red China," *Stag*, January 1967, 28.

82 On Chinese brainwashing and torture, see Kendell Foster Crossen, "The 1,000-to-1 Mission," *Stag*, October 1959, 20. Chicom horde in Neil Turnbull, "Overkill Marauder," *True Action*, March 1967, 36. Steven Tyler, "My 3 Months inside Russia and Red China," *Stag*, August 1966, 21. Wellington Keye, "Mao's Massacre Squads," *Male*, Apr 1967, 41. For a more confident picture, see Don Warner, "Why Red China Doesn't Dare Fight Us," *Male*, August 1966, 22.

83 R. B. S. Shaw, "Let's Scrap the Geneva Convention," *Battle Cry*, October 1957, 22. The article was reprinted as "There's Only One Rule for the Reds," *Battle Cry*, February 1962, 26. On inability to trust the communists, see Marv Koeppel, "Phony Russia–Red China Split," *Bluebook*, November 1965, 25.

84 Doolittle quoted in Brands, *The Devil We Knew*, 61. On savages, see Slotkin, *Gunfighter Nation*, 47. For a similar argument of American heroes no longer needing to play by the rules, see J. Richard Stevens, *Captain America, Masculinity, and Violence: The Evolution of a National Icon* (Syracuse, NY: Syracuse University Press, 2015), 68.

85 Strausz-Hupe, 42.

86 Alf Sturgess, "'Crazy Ché': Guerrilla Czar of Cuba," *Fury*, March 1961, 37, 66. On overestimating Che, see Douglas Porch, *Counterinsurgency: Exposing the Myths of the New Way of War* (New York, NY: Cambridge University Press, 2013), 237. Crucial to national security in Appy, *American Reckoning*, 9.

87 Archer Scanlon, "The Secret Red 'Subversion Clubs' in Every U.S. Town," *Male*, November 1967, 16. Maxwell Hamilton, "36 Hours That Wrecked Russia's Greatest Spy Ring," *For Men Only*, July 1959, 36. Glenn Infield, "The Hotshot CIA Pilot Who Kicked the Reds Out of Central America," *Male*, February 1965, 28, 46. Abortionists in "Stag Confidential," *Stag*, May 1964, 43. For an outlier and more sympathetic view from a *New York Times* correspondent, see Harrison Salisbury, "Russia's Man on the Street," *Male*, August 1960, 24.

88 Flailing in Lillian Hellman, *Scoundrel Time* (Boston, MA: Little, Brown and Company, 1976), 85. Iceberg from McCarthy quoted in Fried, *McCarthyism*, 76. Imminent war in Philip Jenkins, *The Cold War at Home: The Red Scare in Pennsylvania, 1945–1960* (Chapel Hill, NC: The University of North Carolina Press, 1999), 7. On the Cold War as a "continuous emergency," see Andrew D. Grossman, *Neither Red nor Dead: Civilian Defense and American Political Development during the Early Cold War* (New York, NY: Routledge, 2001), 32.

89 McCarthy quoted in Halberstam, 54. Sexual anxieties in Osgerby, "Two-Fisted Tales," 174.

90 On Marshall, see Thomas Doherty, *Cold War, Cool Medium: Television, McCarthyism, and American Culture* (New York, NY: Columbia University Press, 2003), 189–204; and Hofstadter, *The Paranoid Style*, 26–27. Ron Kovic, *Born on the Fourth of July* (New York, NY: Akashic, 1976, 2005), 70. Communism as an infectious agent in Young, *Name, Rank, and Serial Number*, 115.

91 Mark Davis, "The Red Plan to Conquer America," *Real Men*, January 1957, 22. George Reis, "The Traitor GI Who Deals in Torture," *Man's Adventure*, September 1964, 19.

92 Psychosis in Paul Boyer, *By the Bomb's Early Light: American Thought and Culture at the Dawn of the Atomic Age* (New York, NY: Pantheon, 1985), 21. On the bomb affecting military thinking, see James M. Gavin, *War and Peace in the Space Age* (London: Hutchinson, 1959), 97. On impact in the scientific community, see Jessica Wang, *American Science in an Age of Anxiety: Science, Anticommunism, and the Cold War* (Chapel Hill, NC: The University of North Carolina Press, 1999), 11, 13, 43. Sense of strategic vulnerability in Gretchen Heefner, *The Missile Next Door: The Minutemen in the American Heartland* (Cambridge, MA: Harvard University Press, 2012), 47. On balancing fear and education in the nuclear era, see: Laura McEnaney, *Civil Defense Begins at Home: Militarization Meets Everyday Life in the Fifties* (Princeton, MA: Princeton University Press, 2000), 53; and Margot A. Henriksen, *Dr. Strangelove's America: Society and Culture in the Atomic Age* (Berkeley, CA: University of California Press, 1997), 97.

93 David A. Weiss, "Can the Hell Bomb Destroy the World?," *Real Adventure*, March 1955, 30. Allan J. Dickinger, "What Are Your Chances for Survival?," *Real War*, October 1958, 10. Iris Bristol in *Sir!*, July 1962, 25. Barracks Beauty, *True War*, September 1957, 23. Radiation sickness in "Men and Medicine," *Men*, May 1962, 44. Carrie Pitzulo notes how *Playboy* was offered as a "diversion from the anxieties of the Atomic Age." In *Bachelors and Bunnies: The Sexual Politics of Playboy* (Chicago, IL: The University of Chicago Press, 2011), 19.

94 Ray Lunt, "Should GI Commanders Control Nuclear Weapons," *Male*, February 1965, 18. See also C. K. Winston, Jr., "A Military Expert's Chilling Look at WWIII," *For Men Only*, April 1967, 26. *Man's Life* illustratively decried "'push button' warfare advocates" who pointed to the "fragility of pilots" in arguing for more guided missiles. Glenn Willard, "Supermen for Supersonics," *Man's Life*, November 1952, 21.

95 Howard L. Oleck, "The Last War on Earth," *Real War*, October 1958, 39. On fears of World War III, see Masuda Hajimu, *Cold War Crucible: The Korean Conflict and the Postwar World* (Cambridge, MA: Harvard University Press, 2015), 70.

96 Emile C. Schurmacher, "The American General Russia Fears Most," *Stag*, December 1961, 16. Stone Age in Thomas Borstelmann, *The Cold War and the Color Line: American Race Relations in the Global Arena* (Cambridge, MA: Harvard University Press, 2001), 215. On LeMay, see also Halberstam, 357.

97 Ballsiness in Cuordileone, *Manhood and American Political Culture in the Cold War*, 201.

98 Damsels and multiple constructions in Stur, *Beyond Combat*, 18. See also Susan Jeffords, "Rape and the New World Order," *Cultural Critique* No. 19 (Autumn 1991): 204–205. Passive creatures in John V. H. Dippel, *War and Sex: A Brief History of Men's Urge for Battle* (Amherst, NY: Prometheus, 2010), 143. Sex objects in James C. Foust and Katherine A. Bradshaw, "Something for the Boys: Framing Images of Women in *Broadcasting* Magazine in the 1950s," *Journalism History* Vol. 22, No. 2 (Summer 2007): 97.

99 Haut, *Pulp Culture*, 106. See also Easthope, *What a Man's Gotta Do*, 42–43; and H. R. Hays, *The Dangerous Sex: The Myth of Feminine Evil* (New York, NY: G. P. Putnam's Sons, 1964), 205. Predators in Bram Dijkstra, *Evil Sisters: The Threat of Female Sexuality in Twentieth-Century Culture* (New York, NY: Henry Holt, 1996), 216. A. I. Schutzer, "I Will

Be Your Fraulein, Hugo Bleicher," *Battlefield*, July 1959, 27, 29. *Noir* thrillers in Hatty, *Masculinities, Violence, and Culture*, 175.

100 On history of Varga girls and pin-ups, see Charles G. Martignette and Louis K. Meisel, *The Great American Pin-Up* (New York, NY: Taschen, 1996), 22–27, 32–34; and Pendergast, *Creating the Modern Man*, 220–221. On Playmates, see Richard A. Kallan and Robert D. Brooks, "The Playmate of the Month: Naked But Nice," *Journal of Popular Culture* Vol. 8, No. 2 (September 1974): 329–330; Russell Miller, *Bunny: The Real Story of Playboy* (New York, NY: Holt, Rinehart and Winston, 1984), 78; and Halberstam, *The Fifties*, 575. On these depictions promoting "casual misogyny," see Pitzulo, 36.

101 Grable and Hayworth in Robert B. Westbrook, *Why We Fought: Forging American Obligations in World War II* (Washington, DC: Smithsonian Books, 2004), 75–79; and Fraterrigo, 19. Romantic escape and erotic versus wholesome in Costello, 79, 150.

102 Hyman Goldberg, "Recipe for Cheesecake," *Man's Day*, March 1953, 36. See also *Man's Magazine*, April 1960, 28–29, on photographer Herb Flatow. On voyeurism, see Earle, *All Man!*, 11. Sexual act in Maria Elena Buszek, *Pin-up Grrrls: Feminism, Sexuality, Popular Culture* (Durham, NC: Duke University Press, 2006), 11. Invitation in Annette Kuhn, *The Power of the Image: Essays on Representation and Sexuality* (London: Routledge & Kegan Paul, 1985), 41–41. For an overview, see Joanne Meyerowitz, "Women, Cheesecake, and Borderline Material: Responses to Girlie Pictures in the Mid-Twentieth-Century U.S.," *Journal of Women's History* Vol. 8, No. 3 (Fall 1996): 9–35.

103 "Racetrack-curved" in *Male*, August 1964, 31. Karen in *Man's Magazine*, April 1957, 24. For a comparison with Australian pulps, see Ross Laurie, "Fantasy Worlds: The Depiction of Women and the Mating Game in Men's Magazines in the 1950s," *Journal of Australian Studies* Vol. 22, No. 56 (1998): 116–124.

104 Varga in *Real*, March 1958, 27. Philip Wylie argued that there "was nothing wrong in the wish of a woman to become a sexually desirable object." *Generation of Vipers*, 64. Only much later did the pulps show models' fully exposed breasts, as in *Man's Epic*, March 1968, 27; and *Stag*, September 1968, 40.

105 On innocent damsels needing protection, see Adam Parfrey, *It's a Man's World: Men's Adventure Magazines, The Postwar Pulps* (Los Angeles, CA: Feral House, 2003), 178; Laura Sjoberg, *Gender, War, and Conflict* (Malden, MA: Polity, 2014), 15; and Arthur Brittan, *Masculinity and Power* (New York, NY: Basil Blackwell, 1989), 59. Generosity in Tom Engelhardt, *The End of Victory Culture: Cold War America and the Disillusioning of a Generation* (Amherst, MA: University of Massachusetts Press, 2007), 41. Saving French girls in W. J. Saber, "Strange Combine," *Stag*, July 1961, 20, 84. On a behind-the-lines mission to save nurses, see Bill Wharton, "The 13 Army Nurses in Lt. Duffy's Cave," *For Men Only*, June 1960, 27. For a similar story, see Bill Wharton, "Ambush!," *Man's Magazine*, December 1963, 37. In *Challenge*'s September 1955 issue, the protagonist has to save a woman and girl from two other men made "frenzied by hunger, hatred and lust." Gerald Powell, "Lifeboat to Hell," 21.

106 Richard Gallagher, *Male*, "Cage of Captive Women," November 1967, 32. For similar tales, see Mario Cleri, "Trapped Girls in the Riviera's Flesh Casino," *Male*, March 1967, 31;

and Richard Gallagher, "Find the Kremlin's Blonde Nympho Hostage," *Male*, November 1966, 32.

107 J. Edgar Hoover, "Juvenile Delinquency: An Unconquered Frontier," *Educational Forum* Vol. 20 (November 1955): 46. J. Edgar Hoover, "Mothers ... Our Only Hope," in Walker, *Women's Magazines*, 46–47. For a contemporary overview, see Sheldon and Eleanor Glueck, *Unraveling Juvenile Delinquency* (New York, NY: The Commonwealth Fund, 1950). On parents' roles, see Nina Mackert, "'But Recall the Kind of Parents We Have to Deal with': Juvenile Delinquency, Independent Masculinity and the Government of Families in the Postwar U.S.," in Heinemann, 201. On war women challenging definitions of womanhood, see Sherna Berger Gluck, *Rosie the Riveter Revisited: Women, The War, and Social Change* (New York, NY: New American Library, 1987), 153.

108 Walter B. Miller, "Lower Class Culture as a Generating Milieu of Gang Delinquency," *The Journal of Social Issues* Vol. 14, No. 3 (August 1958): 5. Subcultures in Gilbert, *A Cycle of Outrage*, 18; and Albert K. Cohen, *Delinquent Boys: The Culture of the Gang* (New York, NY: The Free Press, 1955), 73. On sexuality and social class, see Jeanne Gardner, "Girls Who Sinned in Secret and Paid in Public: Romance Comics, 1949–1954," in *Comic Books and the Cold War, 1946–1962*, eds. Chris York and Rafiel York (Jefferson, NC: McFarland, 2012), 94–95; and Barbara Ehrenreich, *Fear of Falling: The Inner Life of the Middle Class* (New York, NY: Pantheon, 1989), 24.

109 Teen pregnancy in Coontz, 43–45. Permissive in Philomena Mariani, "Law-and-Order Science," in *Constructing Masculinity*, eds. Maurice Berger, Brian Wallis, and Simon Watson (New York, NY: Routledge, 1995), 148.

110 Campbell, *Women at War with America*, 83. John Bodnar argues that the "call to women to enter wartime jobs was never meant to signal a change in traditional gender roles." *The "Good War" in American Memory*, 21. See also Coontz, 210; and Margaret R. Higgonet and Patrice L.-R. Higgonet, "The Double Helix," in Higgonet, Michel, Jenson, and Collins Weitz, 31.

111 Confusing definitions in Karen Anderson, *Wartime Women: Sex Roles, Family Relations, and the Status of Women During World War II* (Westport, CT: Greenwood Press, 1981), 64. On female identities being stretched, see Filene, *Him/Her/Self*, 177. On popular depictions of working women that suggested employment would not disrupt the family, see Maureen Honey, *Creating Rosie the Riveter: Class, Gender, and Propaganda during World War II* (Amherst, MA: The University of Massachusetts Press, 1984), 117. For a different view of ads reflecting women's independence, see Page Dougherty Delano, "Making Up for War: Sexuality and Citizenship in Wartime Culture," *Feminist Studies* Vol. 26, No. 1 (Spring 2000): 45.

112 Arnold Alexander, "The Young Girl Wolfpacks Who Terrorize Our Cities," *Men*, December 1961, 16, 19. William Ard, "Death Wore a Tight Bikini," *Men*, May 1962, 17. See also Brian McKeon, "Call Girls and Their Clients," *Sir!*, July 1962, 35, 61.

113 Barry Jamieson, "Housing Development Sex Parties," *Male*, August 1964, 18, 52.

114 Alex Austin, "Cycle Girl Gangs," *Stag*, November 1967, 20. Barry Jamieson, "Strange Bedroom Rampage of 1967's 'Beatnik Girls,'" *True Action*, January 1967, 12. Barry Jamieson, "Sex Revolt of Young Society Girls," *Male*, June 1966, 34.

115 Nymphomaniac Crystal Dana, "Every Night," *Male*, March 1967, 18. Archer Scanlon, "Calldoll Bait," *Ibid.*, 40. Noel Kraft, "Illegal Sex," *Stag*, March 1966, 13, 46. Daniel Olson, "All-or-Nothing Girls," *Male*, September 1966, 36. Among the key new findings, the author found that "Today's woman likes to make the decision on when to make love – and how," p. 37.

116 On the May Act and Victory girls, see Emily Yellin, *Our Mothers' War: American Women at Home and at the Front during World War II* (New York, NY: The Free Press, 2004), 315–321; and Anderson, *Wartime Women*, 104. Frederic Lampron, "V-Girls," *Battle Cry*, November 1958, 18, 53. Parasites and vultures in Stuart N. James, "Off Limits," *Battle Cry*, February 1956, 12–13; and Don Davids, "Off Limits," *Battle Cry*, April 1956, 19. See also Matt Schultz, "The Most Vicious Town in the U.S.," *Man's Illustrated*, September 1965, 23, for a story on Biloxi outside Kessler Air Force Base, "an open sewer of a city that systematically suckers-and-saps our G.I.'s to the tune of $1 million a month."

117 Jules Archer, "Sex and the Armed Forces," *Man's Magazine*, April 1960, 11, 13, 72. On VD near military bases, see Carol Harrington, *Politicization of Sexual Violence: From Abolitionism to Peacekeeping* (Burlington, VT: Ashgate, 2010), 61. Of course, it was "promiscuous women" and not men who carried venereal diseases. See Elaine Tyler May, "Rosie the Riveter Gets Married," in *The War in American Culture: Society and Consciousness during World War II*, eds. Lewis A. Erenberg and Susan E. Hirsch (Chicago, IL: The University of Chicago Press, 1996), 134.

118 Eric Volgner, "Dear John . . .," *Battle Cry*, July 1958, 34. Defending democracy in Gluck, 11. Melissa A. McEuen takes on what qualified women as "good citizens and team players" in a time of war in *Making War, Making Women: Femininity and Duty on the American Home Front, 1941–1945* (Athens, GA: The University of Georgia Press, 2011), 2, 7–8, 57, 75, 118. On woman as betrayer in Vietnam, see Jerry Lembcke, *Hanoi Jane: War, Sex & Fantasies of History* (Amherst, MA: University of Massachusetts Press, 2010), 34, 78.

119 Bob Walters, "Army Nurses . . . Saints or Sinners?," *Battle Cry*, April 1956, 26. "GI Tip Sheet," *Battlefield*, August 1958, 11. The piece admitted, though, that "New tests show that women in uniform are moral after all, . . . The 'shack-up' stories originated in the minds of GIs who got pushed out of soft jobs by the lady soldiers."

120 Charles Towne, "U.S.O Girls: Bawds for the Brass?," *Real War*, October 1957, 38, 65. Carol Burke compares "donut dollies" to local Vietnamese women in *Camp All-American*, 111.

121 Wylie, *Generation of Vipers*, 67. Stabilities in Jonathan Rutherford, "Who's That Man," in *Male Order: Unwrapping Masculinity*, eds. Rowena Chapman and Jonathan Rutherford (London: Lawrence & Wishart, 1988), 52; and Elaine Tyler May, "Explosive Issues: Sex, Women, and the Bomb," in May, *Recasting America*, 163. Doll hunter in Arnold Paulus, "Not-So Virgin Islands," *Man's Illustrated*, November 1963, 42. Victoria Morhaim, "The 'Sexually Reckless' Female," *Men*, July 1964, 42. See also Hyman Spotnitz, "Tragedy of the Sex Addict," *Male*, March 1965, 35.

122 Socialite in Alex Austin, "What Women Look for in a Good Lover," *Stag*, February 1967, 40, 46. Dr. Grantham Powell, "That Operation," *Real Adventure*, March 1955, 39, 69. See also Carson Hill, "Surgery and Your Sex Life," *Sir!*, July 1962, 10.

123 Friedan, *The Feminine Mystique*, 43–44, 71–72, 77. On this "feminist revival," see Ehren-reich, *The Hearts of Men*, 100. Articulating in Susan Gubar, "'The Blank Page' and the Issues of Female Creativity," in *Writing and Sexual Difference*, ed. Elizabeth Abel (Chi-cago, IL: The University of Chicago Press, 1982), 76. Sexual reconceptualization in Sharon R. Ullman, *Sex Seen: The Emergence of Modern Sexuality in America* (Berkeley, CA: University of California Press, 1997), 101.

124 Social freedom in May, "Rosie the Riveter Gets Married," 133. On contraceptives, see: Elizabeth Siegel Watkins, *On the Pill: A Social History of Oral Contraceptives, 1950–1970* (Baltimore, MD: The Johns Hopkins University Press, 1998); and Lara V. Marks, *Sexual Chemistry: A History of the Contraceptive Pill* (New Haven, CT: Yale University Press, 2001). Noel Kraft, "How to Know Sexually Aggressive Women," *Stag*, July 1966, 40.

125 Dominant role in "Man's Talk," *Man's Magazine*, September 1968, 6. Andrew Comfort, "Those Bachelor Girls Who Prey on Married Men," *Male*, July 1966, 19. Andrew Comfort, "'Quickie Love Affair' Girls," *True Action*, March 1967, 12. Myron Brenton argued in 1966 that masculinity was "no longer assured solely by virtue of female dependency" thanks to the pill. *The American Male*, 24.

126 Mailer quoted in Kimmel, *Manhood in America*, 256. Kathy J. Phillips discusses the Apollo Syndrome linking sexual performance to battlefield performance in *Manipulat-ing Masculinity: War and Gender in Modern British and American Literature* (New York, NY: Palgrave Macmillan, 2006), 86–88.

127 Alison Flood, "Ian Fleming: Pussy Galore Was a Lesbian . . . and Bond Cured Her," *The Guardian*, 4 November 2015. See also Watts, 140–144. On conceptions of the dominat-ing American woman, from as early as World War II, see Pitzulo, 16.

128 Joe and Angela C., "We Almost Abandoned Wife Swapping," *Man's Life*, September 1966, 18. Catherine L., "How I Discovered Wife-Swapping," *All Man*, October 1966, 20. J. Lewis Nelson, "Outrageous Sex Demands," *Man's Magazine*, February 1967, 30, 95.

129 Dr. Efrem Schoenhild, "How to Handle Those New Free Love Girls," *Men*, December 1968, 40.

130 Liberation in Watts, 167. Glenn Infield, "Airborne Vice Girls," *Action for Men*, May 1964, 20. On how the rich profited, see also Arthur Scott, "Uncensored Memoirs of a Park Avenue Call Girl," *Male*, November 1967, 18.

131 Sexual tourism in Osgerby, "Two-Fisted Tales," 171. Jim McDonald, "The Inside Story on Orgy Cruises," *Man's Illustrated*, March 1967, 12. Mod-affluents in Jim Walters, "Sea Going Call Girls," *Bluebook*, June 1968, 41. Of note, not all servicemen benefited sexually from their travels abroad. One disillusioned sailor who served in and out of Pearl Harbor throughout World War II wrote to *Battle Attack* of his frustrations about not locating that "certain kind of female" who, according to the magazine, was "easy to find." As the Miami veteran shared, "I am a normal, red-blooded American who likes women. So, whenever I got leave in Pearl, I searched for same. But, I couldn't find any. So, how come I couldn't find any?" No doubt, the editor's response proved unsatisfy-ing. "Some guys got it. Some guys were meant to be frustrated." "Mail Call," *Battle Attack*, May 1957, 6.

132 On sexual anxieties, see: Linda Williams, *Hard Core: Power, Pleasure, and the "Frenzy of the Visible"* (Berkeley, CA: University of California Press, 1999), 41–42; Cuordileone, 121; Hays, 123. Asserting virility in Haut, 35. Gratifying partners in Brenton, 29. Cartoon in *Stag*, August 1966, 46. Inside front cover ad, *Challenge*, November 1958.

133 Robert H. K. Walter, "The Failure," *Man's Magazine*, December 1963, 14.

134 On Kinsey, see Beth Bailey, "Sexual Revolution(s)," in *The Sixties: From Memory to History*, ed. David Farber (Chapel Hill, NC: The University of North Carolina Press, 1994), 236. Elisabeth Badinter argues that homophobia is an "integral part of heterosexual masculinity." *XY*, 115.

135 Ehrenreich, *The Hearts of Men*, 26. Statistics in David Allyn, "Private Acts/Public Policy: Alfred Kinsey, the American Law Institute and the Privatization of American Sexual Morality," *Journal of American Studies* Vol. 30, No. 3 (December 1996): 411; and Miller, *Bunny*, 23. Variations in Gilbert, *Men in the Middle*, 86; and Craig M. Loftin, *Masked Voices: Gay Men and Lesbians in Cold War America* (Albany, NY: SUNY Press, 2012), 34. On repudiation of homosexual attachments, see Judith Butler, "Melancholy Gender/Refused Identification," in Berger, Wallis, and Watson, 25.

136 A. Michaels, "Sex Knowledge for Young Men," *American Manhood*, March 1953, 26. Robert Burg, "New York's Homosexual Underground," *Man's Magazine*, December 1963, 46. See also Eldon Bearden, "Don't Call Us 'Queer City,'" *Men*, April 1955, 12 on the San Francisco Sex Crimes Squad.

137 Caswell Stuart, "Could Your Wife Go Lesbian?," *Cavalcade*, May 1959, 37. Brandon Malone, "What Are Your Chances of Marrying a Lesbian?," *Battle Cry*, March 1964, 20. Sandra Block, "I Married a Homosexual," *Man's Peril*, September 1966, 14. "Inside for Men," *Male*, February 1965, 44. See also *Stag*, December 1966, 36 for a short piece on shock therapy.

138 Lester David, "The Sex Change," *Man's Day*, March 1953, 15–16. Anthony Armstrong, "Women Who Became Men," *Sir!*, July 1962, 16. On sex reassignment surgery, see Paradis, 151; and Christine Jorgensen, *Christine Jorgensen: A Personal Autobiography* (San Francisco, CA: Cleis, 1967, 2000).

139 Clyde Bunsen, "How Homosexuals Ruined Hitler's Air Force," *True War*, September 1957, 26, 57. John W. Carroll, "Lawrence of Arabia: Desert Fighter and Woman Hater," *Sir!*, July 1962, 22. Sissies in Robert D. Dean, *Imperial Brotherhood: Gender and the Making of Cold War Foreign Policy* (Amherst, MA: University of Massachusetts Press, 2001), 81. Emotional instability and panic in Jarvis, *The Male Body at War*, 74. On military comradeship attracting homosexual men, see Costello, *Virtue under Fire*, 105.

140 On induction centers, see Loftin, 108; and "Stag Confidential," *Stag*, March 1968, 43. See also *Man's World*, February 1967, on draftees who "buck for 4F by coming on with the fairy bit." Apparently, one doctor threatened to "classify them homosexuals if they'll just give him a demonstration to prove it," p. 8. On gays stigmatizing the armed forces, see Margot Canaday, *The Straight State: Sexuality and Citizenship in Twentieth-Century America* (Princeton, NJ: Princeton University Press, 2009), 68–69. Anthony Scaduto, "The Phony Cops Who Blackmail Leading Americans," *Male*, September 1966, 16.

141 *To Be Takei*, directed by Jennifer M. Kroot (Dodgeville Films, 2014). Ads in *American Manhood*, February 1953, 60; *American Manhood*, January 1953, 57; *American Manhood*, May 1953, 80. On the photographers, see Vince Aletti, *Bruce of Los Angeles* (New York, NY: Antinous Press, 2008); Reed Massengill, *The Male Ideal: Lon of New York and the Masculine Physique* (New York, NY: St. Martin's Press, 2008); and Richard Meyer, *Outlaw Representation: Censorship & Homosexuality in Twentieth-Century American Art* (New York, NY: Oxford University Press, 2002), 170–179. Maladjustment in "Strength and Health," *One*, June 1953, 5–6. *One* was one of the first national magazines in the United States aimed at a homosexual audience.

142 Andrea Friedman, *Citizenship in Cold War America: The National Security State and the Possibilities of Dissent* (Amherst, MA: University of Massachusetts Press, 2014), 34. On editors, see Hooven, *Beefcake*, 58, 60. Sexual inquisition in Dean, *Imperial Brotherhood*, 95. For an overview, see David K. Johnson, *The Lavender Scare: The Cold War Persecution of Gays and Lesbians in the Federal Government* (Chicago, IL: The University of Chicago Press, 2004).

143 Justin David Suran, "Coming Out against the War: Antimilitarism and the Politicization of Homosexuality in the Era of Vietnam," *American Quarterly* Vol. 53, No. 3 (September 2001): 453, 456–458. Alan Bérubé argues that World War II helped establish "the first signs of a continuous gay political movement and press" in the United States. *Coming Out under Fire: The History of Gay Men and Women in World War II* (Chapel Hill, NC: The University of North Carolina Press, 1990), 273.

144 Taking charge in *Look*, 8–9. On pressures related to sex, see May, *Homeward Bound*, 116. Gregory Paul, "How Women Rate Their Menfolk," *Man's Life*, September 1966, 32.

145 Scissors in Hays, *The Dangerous Sex*, 60. Fragility in Beynon, *Masculinities and Culture*, 57. David Gilmore argues that "sexual vigor is critical but insufficient to prove manhood." *Manhood in the Making*, 84. For Aaron Belkin's take on military masculinity, see *Bring Me Men: Military Masculinity and the Benign Façade of American Empire, 1898–2001* (New York, NY: Columbia University Press, 2012), 33–34.

CHAPTER 2

1 "Out of This World," *Stag*, March 1968, 8.

2 Reinforcing masculinity and encouraging behavior in Michele Adams and Scott Coltrane, "Boys and Men in Families: The Domestic Production of Gender, Power, and Privilege," in *Handbook of Studies on Men & Masculinities*, eds. Michael S. Kimmel, Jeff Hearn, and R. W. Connell (Thousand Oaks, CA: Sage, 2005), 236–237. On how comics also perpetuated the idea that failing to engage with danger was "unmanly," see Jon Judy and Brad Palmer, "Boys on the Battlefield: Kid Combatants as Propaganda in World War II-Era Comic Books," in *The 10 Cent War: Comic Books, Propaganda, and World War II*, eds. Trischa Goodnow and James J. Kimble (Jackson, MS: University Press of Mississippi, 2016), 71.

3 Vietnam vet Michael Mace quoted in Michael Takiff, *Brave Men, Gentle Heroes: American Fathers and Sons in World War II and Korea* (New York, NY: William Morrow, 2003), 149.

W. D. Ehrhart, *Vietnam–Perkasie: A Combat Marine Memoir* (Jefferson, NC: McFarland, 1983), 7.

4 Multiple versions in Sara Ruddick, "Notes toward a Feminist Peace Politics," in *Gendering War Talk*, eds. Miriam Cooke and Angela Woollacott (Princeton, NJ: Princeton University Press, 1993), 111. See also Heather Marie Stur, *Beyond Combat: Women and Gender in the Vietnam War Era* (New York, NY: Cambridge University Press, 2011), 143–145. Emulation in Arthur Brittan, *Masculinity and Power* (New York, NY: Basil Blackwell, 1989), 84. On the power of war stories, see Lloyd B. Lewis, *The Tainted War: Culture and Identity in Vietnam War Narratives* (Westport, CT: Greenwood Press, 1985), 42–44.

5 Escape in John V. H. Dippel, *War and Sex: A Brief History of Men's Urge for Battle* (Amherst, NY: Prometheus, 2010), 171. On PTS, see Sheena M. Eagan Chamberlin, "Emasculated by Trauma: A Social History of Post-Traumatic Stress Disorder, Stigma, and Masculinity," *The Journal of American Culture* Vol. 35, No. 4 (December 2012): 358; and David M. Earle, *All Man! Hemingway, 1950s Men's Magazines, and the Masculine Persona* (Kent, OH: The Kent State University Press, 2009), 79. Difference between survival and annihilation in Mark Gerzon, *A Choice of Heroes: The Changing Faces of American Manhood* (Boston, MA: Houghton Mifflin, 1992), 31.

6 Protect and serve in Laura Sjoberg, *Gender, War, and Conflict* (Malden, MA: Polity, 2014), 70. On the need for a positive view of the American past, see Richard Slotkin, *Gunfighter Nation: The Myth of the Frontier in Twentieth-Century America* (Norman, OK: University of Oklahoma Press, 1998), 279. On more militaristic views of World War II appearing in 1960s popular culture, see Lisa M. Mundey, *American Militarism and Anti-militarism in Popular Media, 1945–1970* (Jefferson, NC: McFarland, 2012), 127, 136–137. Links between militarism and masculinity in Paul R. Higate, *Military Masculinities: Identity and the State* (Westport, CT: Praeger, 2003), 113.

7 Leon Lazarus, "Let's Stop Kicking Around America's GIs," *Stag*, July 1966, 36, 66. Embodiment in Roland Littlewood, "Military Rape," *Anthropology Today* Vol. 13, No. 2 (April 1997): 10. TV series in J. Fred MacDonald, *Television and the Red Menace: The Video Road to Vietnam* (New York, NY: Praeger, 1985), 111–115.

8 Bruce Springsteen, *Born to Run* (New York, NY: Simon & Schuster, 2016), 3. Would-be soldiers in Jean Bethke Elshtain, *Women and War* (New York, NY: Basic Books, 1987), 10. Models and planes in Bo Hathaway, *A World of Hurt* (New York, NY: Taplinger, 1981), 30. Imaginary wars in Tom Engelhardt, *The End of Victory Culture: Cold War America and the Disillusioning of a Generation* (Amherst, MA: University of Massachusetts Press, 2007), 82. On manhood as something "to be seized by long and arduous testing," see David D. Gilmore, *Manhood in the Making: Cultural Concepts of Masculinity* (New Haven, CT: Yale University Press, 1990), 19.

9 Bob Schwalberg, "Baptism of Fire," *Climax*, March 1953, 45. Letter from Virginia Military Institute graduate Charles Dayhuff in *Saga*, May 1960, 92.

10 Sylvester Fourre, "Crash Out at St. Lo," *Man's Epic*, November 1967, 36. This compared with earlier article by Kurt Vaughn, "Vietnam Bloodbath – The Glory and the Despair," 17. Puzo quoted in Adam Parfrey, *It's a Man's World: Men's Adventure Magazines, The Postwar Pulps* (Los Angeles, CA: Feral House, 2003), 141. Myths in Slotkin, 88. Framing

in Ron Eyerman, Todd Madigan, and Magnus Ring, "Cultural Trauma, Collective Memory and the Vietnam War," *Croatian Political Science Review* Vol. 54, No. 1–2 (2017): 20.

11 Scrimmage in Ralph LaRossa, *Of War and Men: World War II in the Lives of Fathers and Their Families* (Chicago, IL: The University of Chicago Press, 2011), 83. Gallup and *Harper's* in Mundey, 109, 118. Sanitized in Hugh McManners, *The Scars of War* (New York, NY: HarperCollins, 1993), 8.

12 On the many obstacles to communicating the veteran war experience, see the final chapter, "The Real War Will Never Get in the Books," of Paul Fussell, *Wartime: Understanding and Behavior in the Second World War* (New York, NY: Oxford University Press, 1989), 267–297.

13 Editorial director Noah Sarlat in *Stag*, April 1968, 4. On Kaylin, see Robert Deis and Wyatt Doyle, eds., *He-Men, Bag Men & Nympho: Classic Men's Adventure Stories by Walter Kaylin* (Philadelphia, PA: New Texture, 2013). On Burma, see Walter Kaylin, "Mud, Maggots, and Massacre," *Male*, August 1964, 21. On achieving masculinity through "vicarious experience and emulation," see James Gilbert, *Men in the Middle: Searching for Masculinity in the 1950s* (Chicago, IL: The University of Chicago Press, 2005), 3.

14 Kaylin quoted in Randall Beach, "'The Great Walter Kaylin' Has Been Rediscovered," *New Haven Register*, 20 October 2013. David Saunders quoted in Parfrey, 43. On majority of soldiers not seeing combat, see Thomas Bruscino, *A Nation Forged in War: How World War II Taught Americans to Get Along* (Knoxville, TN: The University Press of Tennessee, 2010), 14.

15 Survey data in Samuel A. Stouffer *et al.*, *The American Soldier: Combat and Its Aftermath, Volume II* (Princeton, MA: Princeton University Press, 1949), 631–632. Vietnam vet quoted in Peter Marin, "What the Vietnam Vets Can Teach Us," *The Nation*, 27 November 1982, 560. World War II vet quoted in Gerald F. Linderman, *The World within War: America's Combat Experience in World War II* (New York, NY: The Free Press, 1997), 362. On Korea, see Melinda L. Pash, *In the Shadow of the Greatest Generation: The Americans Who Fought the Korean War* (New York, NY: New York University Press, 2012), 1.

16 Democratization in Philip Dwyer, "Making Sense of the Muddle: War Memoirs and the Culture of Remembering," in *War Stories: The War Memoir in History and Literature*, ed. Philip Dwyer (New York, NY: Berghahn, 2017), 2. On what war did to those who fought in it, see John Bodnar, *The "Good War" in American Memory* (Baltimore, MD: The Johns Hopkins University Press, 2010), 2.

17 Rone Lowe, "Night Jump!" *Man's World*, September 1957, 38, 56. Walter Kaylin, "Guadalcanal," *Men*, July 1964, 18, 65. Howard L. Oleck, "Invasion!," *Battle Cry*, February 1956, 8, 63. Oleck was part of the Historical Section of the US General Staff in Europe.

18 Lemuel C. Sheperd, Jr., "The Terrible Assault of Sugar Loaf Hill," *Battlefield*, January 1959, 16, 71. For an equally heroic tale, in which marines "fought their way through hell to raise the Stars and Stripes," see L. E. Owen, "Mt. Suribachi – Iwo's Bloody Acre," *Bluebook*, October 1965, 30.

19 Letter from veteran Burton Binder in "Message Center," *Battlefield*, January 1959, 8. Sentimental military, quoting Christian Appy, in Amy Rutenberg, "Service by Other

Means: Changing Perceptions of Military Service and Masculinity in the United States, 1940–1973," in *Gender and the Long Postwar: The United States and the Two Germanys, 1945–1989*, eds. Karen Hagemann and Sonya Michel (Baltimore, MD: The Johns Hopkins University Press, 2014), 166. Lillian Hellman argued that this happened much earlier, as "America in the early 1940's fell in love with total war; and no wonder. The war was the best thing that had happened to this country in a long time." In *Scoundrel Time* (Boston, MA: Little, Brown and Company, 1976), 13.

20 Survey data in Stouffer *et al.*, 631. Vets quoted in Myron Brenton, *The American Male* (New York, NY: Coward-McCann, 1966), 15. Myths in Eric J. Leed, *No Man's Land: Combat and Identity in World War I* (New York, NY: Cambridge University Press, 1979), 117.

21 W. J. Saber, "Blow the Bridge to the D-Day Bridgehead!" *Stag*, January 1964, 24. Inconsequential in Pash, 199. See also Dippel, *War and Sex*, 245.

22 Paratrooper in "Male Call," *Male*, January 1952, 96. Medals in "It's in the Bag," *Real*, March 1958, 8.

23 Puzo quoted in Parfrey, 17. Ambush letter in "Out of the Stag Bag," *Stag*, July 1961, 82. For similar personal stories, see "Letters," *Saga*, March 1956, 6; *Man's Illustrated*, November 1963, 10; "Male Call," *Male*, August 1960, 83; and "Out of the Stag Bag," *Stag*, January 1961, 84.

24 David M. Earle, *Re-covering Modernism: Pulps, Paperbacks, and the Prejudice of Form* (Burlington, VT: Ashgate, 2009), 106. Dexter in "Bluebook Bouquets and Brickbats," *Bluebook*, August 1968, 10. For a similar request, see "Letters to the Editor," *Man's Magazine*, December 1963, 6. Decent chick in "Sound Off," *Saga*, April 1967, 4. James Bond in "Real Letters," *Real*, February 1967, 5. Another letter writer in the same unit wrote in to say that the last issue had been "read by half the guys in the squadron."

25 Censors in "Truely Yours," *True*, November 1967, 2. Comics in "Sound Off," *Saga*, February 1967, 4. Young men in "Bluebook Bouquets and Brickbats," *Bluebook*, June 1968, 10.

26 On pressuring Congress, see "Veteran's Newsletter," *True War*, September 1957, 4. "Ask Adventure," *Adventure*, October 1957, 81.

27 "The Service Bureau," *Real War*, February 1958, 10; and *Real War*, October 1957, 8. "Whatever Happened to —?" *Battle Cry*, April 1956, 39. Robert LaGuardia, "'Easy Pay' Auto Gyps Who Rob Our GIs," *Stag*, March 1968, 23. See also "Avoid GI Sucker Traps," *Battle Cry*, July 1958, 10.

28 On D-Day coming to symbolize American values, see Michael R. Dolski, *D-Day Remembered: The Normandy Landings in American Collective Memory* (Knoxville, TN: The University of Tennessee Press, 2016), 3. Robert Leckie, "Coral Inferno Called Saipan," *Man's Illustrated*, November 1963, 33. One Vietnam veteran recalled reading Tregaskis's *Guadalcanal Diary* seven times as a child. In Richard Stacewicz, *Winter Soldiers: An Oral History of the Vietnam Veterans against the War* (New York, NY: Twayne, 1997), 51. Norman Mailer, "The Gook's Last Stand," *True Adventures*, October 1958, 24.

29 Ernie Pyle, "D-Day Bloodbath," *Bluebook*, May 1965, 42. Excerpt from James Clavell, "King Rat," in *Male*, January 1964, 21. S. L. A. Marshall, "The Forgotten GIs Who Saved

D-Day," *Saga*, June 1964, 9, 80. See also S. L. A. Marshall, "First G.I. Wave on Omaha Beach," *War*, Vol. 1, No. 1 (1964): 84.

30 Stephen E. Ambrose, *Band of Brothers: E Company, 506th Regiment, 101st Airborne, from Normandy to Hitler's Eagle's Nest* (New York, NY: Simon & Schuster, 1992), 224. Dolski, 68. It seems worth asking how much "moral superiority" truly is a determinant of combat motivation. On this, see Peter G. Bourne, *Men, Stress, and Vietnam* (Boston, MA: Little, Brown and Company, 1970), 40.

31 James Neal Harvey, "Who Says We Won't Come Back?" *Fury*, April 1959, 28, 67.

32 Robert C. Doyle, *Voices from Captivity: Interpreting the American POW Narrative* (Lawrence, KS: University Press of Kansas, 1994), 3–5, 9, 26–28. Brenda M. Boyle, "Rescuing Masculinity: Captivity, Rescue and Gender in American War Narratives," *The Journal of American Culture* Vol. 34, No. 2 (June 2011): 158.

33 J. M. Jones, "The Three Who Fled Mooseburg's Escape-Proof Stalag," *Male*, August 1960, 17. David Mars, "Our Top WWII Breakout King," *War*, Vol. 1, No. 1 (1964): 26. Capt. "Bustout" in Alex Austin, "The Yank Who Led WWII's Biggest POW Escape," *Stag*, January 1964, 16. See also Robert F. Dorr, "P.O.W. Escape," *Man's Magazine*, October 1966, 24.

34 Mario Cleri, "We Go at Dawn," *Male*, February 1965, 15–17, 95–101.

35 Mark Sufrin, "The Ranger Raid to Save 512 Dying Yanks," *True Action*, October 1961, 16. Collective glory in Robert Jay Lifton, *Home from the War: Vietnam Veterans: Neither Victims nor Executioners* (New York, NY: Simon & Schuster, 1973), 25. Control in Linderman, *The World within War*, 9. On superhuman strength as part of a "revenge fantasy," see John Hellmann, "Rambo's Vietnam and Kennedy's New Frontier," in *Inventing Vietnam: The War in Film and Television*, ed. Michael Anderegg (Philadelphia, PA: Temple University Press, 1991), 140; and Jacqueline A. Lawson, "'She's a Pretty Woman ... for a Gook': The Misogyny of the Vietnam War," *The Journal of American Culture* Vol. 12, No. 3 (Fall 1989): 57.

36 Mark Sufrin, "Deadliest Yank Rifleman of All Time," *Male*, February 1965, 22, 75, 77.

37 On the 101st in the Bulge, see Laird Travis, "Slaughter in the Snow!," *True War*, September 1957, 12, 51. *Male* also shared an autobiographical account on the heroic stand of twenty-seven men who protected the entire right flank of the US First Army during the critical battle. Lt. William Forrest Dawson, "Give Each Man Four Grenades," *Male*, July 1954, 28. Howard Cohn, "The General Who Parachuted into Hell," *Guy*, January 1959, 19.

38 On links to the frontier, see John Hellmann, *American Myth and the Legacy of Vietnam* (New York, NY: Columbia University Press, 1986), 44; and Philip D. Beidler, *Late Thoughts on an Old War: The Legacy of Vietnam* (Athens, GA: The University of Georgia Press, 2004), 133. On Kennedy, see Michael McClintock, *Instruments of Statecraft: U.S. Guerrilla Warfare, Counterinsurgency, and Counterterrorism, 1940–1990* (New York, NY: Pantheon, 1992), 180.

39 Survey data from D. M. Mantell's 1974 *True Americanism: Green Berets and War Resisters* as quoted in Richard Holmes, *Acts of War: The Behavior of Men in Battle* (New York, NY: The Free Press, 1985), 93–94. On Green Berets reaffirming their faith "in their own

omnipotence and invulnerability," see Bourne, 113–114. For an article on the military's elite US Army Strike Command, see Walter Wager, "The Army's Fast, Tough, Elite Specialists in 'Instant Hell,'" *Men*, May 1962, 13.

40 Richard Charles, "I Was a Filing Tiger," *Battle Cry*, December 1955, 20. Jules Archer, "The Bloody Butchers of Milne," *Ibid.*, 22. On working deals, see Cincinnatus, 148. On the narrative of "soft clerks," see Higate, *Military Masculinities*, 31. *Coward* magazine in David Cort, "Down With the Other Sex," *The Nation*, 15 February 1958, 137.

41 William V. Horn, "I Was a Commando Raider!" *Adventure*, October 1957, 13–14, 76. Jake Dalton, "Lt. Karl Timmerman's Crash-through to Remagen Bridge," *Valor*, June 1959, 18. For a similar tale about a "rampaging U.S. Ranger," see John Drozen, "Destroy That Bloody Bridge at Coblentz," *Male*, August 1964, 36. On masculine qualities, see Donald Spoto, *Camerado: Hollywood and the American Man* (New York, NY: New American Library, 1978), 28; and Rachel Woodward, "Warrior Heroes and Little Green Men: Soldiers, Military Training, and the Construction of Rural Masculinities," *Rural Sociology*, Vol. 65, No. 4 (December 2000): 643. Steven Cohan argues that heroism in battle often was viewed as a "masquerade" by soldiers themselves. *Masked Men: Masculinity and the Movies in the Fifties* (Bloomington, IN: Indiana University Press, 1997), 104.

42 *Battle Cry*, for instance, ran a "None But the Bravest" series that showcased soldiers like paratrooper James Towle, who demonstrated "extreme heroism" by single-handedly attacking five German tanks during Operation Market Garden in World War II. In their story on recipient Carl V. Sheridan, *Stag* described the fatally wounded private first class from Maryland as "a hell of a lot tougher than those old-time knights you read about." Richard T. Wallinghurst, "The Epic of Jim Towle," *Battle Cry*, July 1958, 24. Glenn Infield, "Gaspipe-and-Guts Medal of Honor GI," *Stag*, September 1966, 16, 84. See also *Man's Action*, May 1966, which ran a story on the Third Infantry Division winning the most medals of honor in World War II. Lee O. Miller, "Combat History: Third Division," 22.

43 Glenn Infield, "Awarded for Singular Bravery," *Stag*, July 1966, 16. On Harmon, see Thomas R. Brooks, *The War North of Rome: June 1944–May 1945* (Cambridge, MA: Da Capo Press, 1996), 83–84. For similar stories, see J. P. Fried, "One-Man Suicide Squad," *Man's Magazine*, February 1967, 36; and Bruce Jacobs, "I'll Kill Japs Until I Die," *Man's Illustrated*, July 1965, 42.

44 David Fax, "Captain Bayonet: America's Greatest Cold Steel Fighter" *War*, Vol. 1 No. 1 (1964): 71, 73–75.

45 Transcending motivations in Robert McDowell, "A Rare Moment for All of Us," *The Hudson Review* Vol. 52, No. 2 (Summer 1999): 347. Citizen heroes from *The Washington Times* praise for Tom Brokaw, *The Greatest Generation* (New York, NY: Random House, 1998), inside front cover of trade paperback edition. On the strength of stereotypes, see Carolyn Kitch, *The Girl on the Magazine Cover: The Origins of Visual Stereotypes in American Mass Media* (Chapel Hill, NC: The University of North Carolina Press, 2001), 5.

46 "Stag Confidential," *Stag*, September 1968, 6. Colonel Theodore Bank quoted in Jarvis, 69. On toughness and masculinity, see LaRossa, 108. Control in Earle, *All Man!*, 13.

47 Glenn Infield, "Hell-and-Back Air Hero of Midway Island," *Stag*, July 1961, 16, 54. Newton Axelrod, "One-Man Army Who Drove a German Regiment Off Mt. Rotundo,"

Men, March 1963, 18, 73. On Britt, who lost his right arm below the elbow, see Jack C. Mason, "My Favorite Lion, Maurice Britt," *Army*, May 2008, 71–76.

48 Mark Sufrin, "Like Hell I'll Surrender," *Men*, December 1961, 24, 87. On Miller, see Stephen Harding, *The Castaway's War: One Man's Battle against Imperial Japan* (Boston, MA: Da Capo Press, 2016).

49 Yellow in John Dower, *War without Mercy: Race and Power in the Pacific War* (New York, NY: Pantheon, 1986), 162. E. B. Sledge, *With the Old Breed: At Peleliu and Okinawa* (Novato, CA: Presidio Press, 1981), 148. For a similar treatment on "insensate hatred," see William Manchester, *Goodbye, Darkness: A Memoir of the Pacific War* (Boston, MA: Little, Brown and Company, 1979), 64.

50 McFadden quoted in John C. McManus, *The Deadly Brotherhood: The American Combat Soldier in World War II* (Novato, CA: Presidio Press, 1998), 175.

51 Animals from Okinawa veteran John Moore, quoted in McManus, 175. C. L. Morehead, "It Took More Than Guts . . . Iwo Jima!," *Battle Cry*, April 1956, 34, 36.

52 Staff Sergeant Lawrence M. Ashman, "ROK Leathernecks," *Action*, May 1953, 18–19. On American views of their South Korean counterparts, see: T. R. Fehrenbach, *This Kind of War: The Classic Korean War Story* (Washington, DC: Brassey's, 1994), 149, 164; and Stanley Sandler, *The Korean War: No Victors, No Vanquished* (Lexington, KY: The University Press of Kentucky, 1999), 78–79. Kenneth E. Hamburger holds a more sympathetic view in *Leadership in the Crucible: The Korean War Battles of Twin Tunnels and Chipyong-Ni* (College Station, TX: Texas A&M University Press, 2003), 39.

53 Glenn Infield, "Battling Lepers of Vietnam," *Male*, January 1967, 28. Americans views on the AVRN in Christian G. Appy, *American Reckoning: The Vietnam War and Our National Identity* (New York, NY: Viking, 2015), 127; and Robert K. Brigham, *ARVN: Life and Death in the South Vietnamese Army* (Lawrence, KS: University Press of Kansas, 2006), 83.

54 Rasmus quoted in Studs Terkel, *The Good War: An Oral History of World War Two* (New York, NY: Pantheon, 1984), 38–39. See also Rachel Louise Moran, *Governing Bodies: American Politics and the Shaping of the Modern Physique* (Philadelphia, PA: University of Pennsylvania Press, 2018), 67. Personal interests in Bodnar, 65. On military conceptions of manhood, see James Penner, *Pinks, Pansies, and Punks: The Rhetoric of Masculinity in American Literary Culture* (Bloomington, IN: Indiana University Press, 2011), 72. Masculinity as an achievement in Candace West and Don H. Zimmerman, "Doing Gender," in *The Gendered Society Reader*, 2nd ed., ed. Michael S. Kimmel (New York, NY: Oxford University Press, 2004), 151.

55 Edward Linn, "The Ballad of Rodger Young," *Saga*, March 1956, 13. "The Ballard of 'Rodger Young': An Infantry Private Who Became a Hero Inspires a Stirring New Song," *Life*, 5 March 1945, 111–114.

56 Audie Murphy, "The Day I Cried," *Battle Cry*, August 1956, 16–17, 46–47. Murphy in Earle, *All Man!*, 79–82. Strength versus weapons in Joshua S. Goldstein, *War and Gender: How Gender Shapes the War System and Vice Versa* (New York, NY: Cambridge University Press, 2001), 165–166.

57 William J. Lederer, "O'Toole and the Missing Jap Fleets," *Real*, March 1958, 39. On boys suffering anxiety, see Peter G. Filene, *Him/Her/Self: Gender Identities in Modern America*, 3rd ed.

(Baltimore, MD: The Johns Hopkins University Press, 1998), 104. Vulnerable to charges in James Gilligan, "Culture, Gender, and Violence: 'We Are Not Women,'" in Kimmel, *Ibid.*, 431. Governed by shame in E. Anthony Rotundo, *American Manhood: Transformations in Masculinity from the Revolution to the Modern Era* (New York, NY: Basic Books, 1993), 52.

58 Farrell Cross, "The Yankee Misfit Who Conquered China," *Guy*, January 1959, 37, 70. "Freckle-faced" hero in Martin Sol, "Great Raid on Japan's '30 Ship Harbor,'" *Men*, July 1964, 34.

59 Military doctors in "Last Minute Memo for Men," *For Men Only*, July 1959, 30. Mark Sufrin, "The Zany Pole Who Became Our Deadliest Commando," *Male*, February 1962, 16. Monro MacCloskey, "The World War II Mission That Made Heroes out of 'Gutless GIs,'" *Saga*, August 1965, 12, 14–15.

60 Mundey, 111. On women in Korea, see Brian McAllister Linn, *Elvis's Army: Cold War GIs and the Atomic Battlefield* (Cambridge, MA: Harvard University Press, 2016), 62–63. Service numbers in Jeanne Holm, *Women in the Military: An Unfinished* Revolution, rev. ed. (Novato, CA: Presidio Press, 1992), 149. For an excellent overview of women serving in Korea and during the Cold War, see chapter 12. On the often unexamined role of African Americans serving in Korea, see Daniel Widener, "Seoul City Sue and the Bugout Blues: Black American Narratives of the Forgotten War," in *Afro Asia: Revolutionary Political Connections between African Americans and Asian Americans*, eds. Fred Ho and Bill V. Mullen (Durham, NC: Duke University Press, 2008), 55–87.

61 Clay Blair, Jr., "We Walk Back or Die," *Man's Magazine*, November 1960, 34, 85. On sacrifice, see Michael Rowlands, "The Role of Memory in the Transmission of Culture," *World Archaeology* Vol. 25, No. 2 (October 1993): 146.

62 Arnold M. Lanceford, "Greater Love Hath No Man," *Battle Cry*, November 1958, 23, 43. Separate from society in Jonathan Mitchell, *Revisions of the American Adam: Innocence, Identity and Masculinity in Twentieth-Century America* (New York, NY: Continuum, 2011), 7. On "sisters," see Rada Iveković, "Women, Nationalism and War: 'Make Love Not War,'" *Hypatia* Vol. 8, No. 4 (Autumn 1993): 121; and Joanna Bourke, *Dismembering the Male: Men's Bodies, Britain and the Great War* (Chicago, IL: The University of Chicago Press, 1996), 133. Of course, some women also found a special form of comradeship in the armed forces. See Jane Waller and Michael Vaughan-Rees, *Women in Wartime: The Role of Women's Magazines, 1939–1945* (London: MacDonald, 1987), 123.

63 John Ketwig, . . . *and a Hard Rain Fell: A GI's True Story of War in Vietnam* (Naperville, IL: Sourcebooks, 2002), 47. Philip Caputo, *A Rumor of War* (New York, NY: Holt, Rinehart and Winston, 1977), xvii. For a similar take on kinship, see Micheal Clodfelter, *Mad Minutes and Vietnam Months: A Soldier's Memoir* (Jefferson, NC: McFarland, 1988), 38. Impeachment in Linderman, 263.

64 Pyle quoted in Elshtain, *Women and War*, 21. Murphy quoted in Linderman, 297. Sharing fears in Stouffer *et al.*, 202. Sanitized in McManners, 8. Depersonalization in John Ellis, *The Sharp End: The Fighting Man in World War II* (New York, NY: Charles Scribners' Sons, 1980), 290.

65 Jack Lasco, "'Commando' Kessler – the Sergeant York of W.W. II," *Bluebook*, November 1965, 37, 39.

66 Docile domesticity in Rotundo, 224. Sociology professor Willard Waller quoted in Andrew J. Huebner, *The Warrior Image: Soldiers in American Culture from the Second World War to the Vietnam Era* (Chapel Hill, NC: The University of North Carolina Press, 2008), 34.

67 Lieut. Fremont Piercefield, "Toughest Korea Duty," *Man's Life*, November 1952, 24, 54.

68 Stouffer *et al.*, 87. Replacements in Fussell, 66; and Ellis, 305. Killing and dying in Samuel Hynes, *The Soldiers' Tale: Bearing Witness to Modern War* (New York, NY: Penguin, 1997), 126. Dehumanization in Kathleen Barry, *Unmaking War, Remaking Men: How Empathy Can Reshape Our Politics, Our Soldiers and Ourselves* (Santa Rosa, CA: Phoenix Rising Press, 2011), 6.

69 On clean and whole bodies, see Michael C. C. Adams, *The Best War Ever: America and World War II* (Baltimore, MD: The Johns Hopkins University Press, 1994), 13. See also Jonathan Shay, *Achilles in Vietnam: Combat Trauma and the Undoing of Character* (New York, NY: Atheneum, 1994), 10.

70 Expectations in Chamberlin, "Emasculated by Trauma," 359. On combat trauma and its relationship to gender, see Goldstein, 264.

71 R. C. Channon, "A Psychologist Looks at G.I. Marriage Problems," *Action*, May 1953, 22, 25.

72 M. L. Greene, "The Enemy Within – The Scourge of the Silent Killer," *Real Combat Stories*, June 1964, 28. Mike Lombardo, "Are Heroes Psycho?," *Battle Attack*, May 1957, 9.

73 Sense of vulnerability in Bodnar, 29. Loss of dignity in Peter S. Kindsvatter, *American Soldiers: Ground Combat in the World Wars, Korea, and Vietnam* (Lawrence, KS: University Press of Kansas, 2003), 47. For a similar treatment from Civil War veterans, see Stephen W. Berry III, *All That Makes a Man: Love and Ambition in the Civil War South* (New York, NY: Oxford University Press, 2003), 174–175.

74 Robert Benney, "Shrapnel Wound: Left Eye," *Male*, January 1952, 32–33. Thomas Gallagher, "What Makes a Hero?" *Saga*, August 1965, 39, 43, 86. Sledge, 157.

75 Chandler Price, "The Fighting Slobs of Peleliu," *Fury*, April 1959, 38. Len Simmons, "We Got Killed at Kasserine," *Battle Cry*, April 1956, 14.

76 Howard L. Oleck, "Anzio: The War's Biggest Stalemate," *Battle Cry*, July 1958, 12. Wynford Vaughan-Thomas, "Who Threw 40,000 GI's Down the Drain?," *Men*, December 1961, 12. For a similar storyline, see Emile C. Schurmacher, "Desperate Stand at Huertgen Forest," *Stag*, January 1964, 38.

77 Puzo quoted in Parfrey, *It's a Man's World*, 10. On GIs not seeing Korea as a "limited war," see Fehrenbach, 425. On suffering of Koreans, including American rape, see John Tirman, *The Deaths of Others: The Fate of Civilians in America's Wars* (New York, NY: Oxford University Press, 2011), 105. Questioning "victory" in Pash, *In the Shadow of the Greatest Generation*, 222.

78 Charles and Eugene Jones, "This Is Combat," *Battlefield*, August 1958, 26, 30. Frank D. Selvin, "We Fought with Our Fists," *Real Men*, January 1957, 26, 51.

79 Jim Yeager, "The Day They Massacred POW's," *Battlefield*, July 1959, 18. "The Look," *Battle Cry*, February 1956, 40. In "Hell Was Never Like This!" author Ted Marks wrote on the fear and pain of American GIs fighting on Triangle Hill. One medic recalled not having enough stretchers to carry the badly wounded off the battlefield, his comrades "perfect targets" for the Chinese. "When I say that blood flowed down that hill, I mean it

literally; blood of men being slaughtered contrary to all rules of warfare." *Battle Attack*, May 1957, 32.

80 Wally's tale in Shailer Upton Lawton, "The Male Body," *Challenge*, November 1958, 22. See also Louis Berg, "Castration: The Story of a Wounded G.I.," *Man's Magazine*, April 1957, 14; and H. B. Couth, "Hush Hush Purple Heart," *Real Adventure*, March 1955, 6. On the role of women in dealing with men's wartime disabilities, see David A. Gerber, "Heroes and Misfits: The Troubled Social Reintegration of Disabled Veterans in 'The Best Years of Our Lives,'" *American Quarterly* Vol. 46, No. 4 (December 1994): 550.

81 Hyperrealism in John Strausbaugh, "Oh, Those Pulpy Days of 'Weasels Ripped My Flesh,'" *New York Times*, 9 December 2004. On modernism, see Earle, *Re-covering Modernism*, 3–6. Mort Künstler art accompanying Richard Gallagher, "The Island of Sea Nymphs Who Lived with PT-Boat 629," *Male*, December 1962, 12–13. Mort Künstler, cover art, *Male*, January 1964.

82 On Minney, see Thomas Ziegler, "The Sensational Art of Bruce Minney," *Illustration* Vol. 10, No. 4 (Winter 2013): 34–76. Bruce Minney art accompanying Glenn Infield, "'Panhandle's' Ride-'Em-Cowboy Charge to Save Co. C," *Stag*, February 1967, 18–19. Bruce Minney art accompanying Mario Cleri, "2,000-Mile Jungle Breakout from the Amazon's Captive Girl Pen," *Male*, April 1967, 12–13.

83 Obituary, Colonel Charles Waterhouse, *The Star-Ledger*, 18 November 2013. Rudy Nappi art accompanying Ted Stoil, "Two-Month Island Women Furlough of AWOL Sgt. O'Neil," *For Men Only*, February 1960, 12–13. Robert Deis and Wyatt Doyle, eds., *Pollen's Women: The Art of Samson Pollen* (Philadelphia, PA: New Texture, 2018). Samson Pollen art accompanying Martin Fass, "The GI Vanishing Artist of Pyongyang," *Male*, February 1962, 12–13. "Norman Saunders in Parfrey, 43–51. For a list of artists, see Max Allan Collins and George Hagenauer, *Men's Adventure Magazines in Postwar America* (London: Taschen, 2004), 491–505.

84 Senator Millard Tydings (Democrat, Maryland) quoted in Masuda Hajimu, *Cold War Crucible: The Korean Conflict and the Postwar World* (Cambridge, MA: Harvard University Press, 2015), 149. Translating power in Engelhardt, 62. See also Richard K. Betts, *Soldiers, Statesmen, and Cold War Crises* (Cambridge, MA: Harvard University Press, 1977), 96–97. On World War II as a more satisfying conflict than Korea, see J. Richard Stevens, *Captain America, Masculinity, and Violence: The Evolution of a National Icon* (Syracuse, NY: Syracuse University Press, 2015), 59.

85 Norman Kingsley, "Hell on No-Name Hill," *Male*, May 1952, 18. See also M/Sgt. Thoams F. Sheldon, "I Won Two Silver Stars and Lived!," *Action*, March 1953, 26.

86 Mark Sufrin, "Hold Toktong Pass to the Last Man," *Male*, November 1962, 16, 56. On Barber, see also Bob Drury and Tom Clavin, *The Last Stand of Fox Company: A True Story of U.S. Marines in Combat* (New York, NY: Atlantic Monthly Press, 2009).

87 James V. Parnell, "Bloody Bastards of Chipyong-Ni," *True War*, September 1957, 8, 68. For a similar story, see T/Sgt. Carl S. McPherson, "George Company's Pinned-Down Patrol," *Battlefield*, November 1959, 16.

88 On Korean War films, see William L. O'Neill, "The 'Good' War: National Security and American Culture," in *The Long War: A New History of U.S. National Security Policy since*

World War II, ed. Andrew J. Bacevich (New York, NY: Columbia University Press, 2007), 524–525; Rutenberg, "Service by Other Means," 167; and Bernard F. Dick, *The Screen Is Red: Hollywood, Communism, and the Cold War* (Jackson, MS: University Press of Mississippi, 2016), 5, 162, 184, 247. S. L. A. Marshall, *The River and the Gauntlet: Defeat of the Eighth Army by the Chinese Communist Forces, November, 1950, in the Battle of the Chongchon River, Korea* (New York, NY: Time Incorporated, 1953), xi, 11.

89 Andrew Geer, *The New Breed: The Story of the U.S. Marines in Korea* (New York, NY: Harper & Brothers, 1952), 55–56, 222, 280. I. F. Stone, *The Hidden History of the Korean War* (New York, NY: Monthly Review Press, 1952), 253.

90 "A Boy Needs a Dad He Can Brag About!," advertisement for International Correspondence Schools, *Man's Magazine*, January 1960, 5. On fathers' military glories, see Tracy Karner, "Fathers, Sons, and Vietnam: Masculinity and Betrayal in the Life Narratives of Vietnam Veterans with Post Traumatic Stress Disorder," *American Studies* Vol. 37, No. 1 (Spring 1996): 68. Mark Bowden has argued that "War was stitched deep in the idea of manhood." *Hué 1968: A Turning Point of the American War in Vietnam* (New York, NY: Atlantic Monthly Press, 2017), 12.

91 Gendered codes in Carol Cohn, "War, Wimps, and Women: Talking Gender and Thinking War," in Cooke and Woollacott, 239. On the "narrative of patriotic armed civic virtue," see Elshtain, 92. Expectations in Kindsvatter, 286–287. See *Guy*, April 1965, 63 for an ad on rocket ships and p. 69 on monsters. See *Man's Magazine*, January 1960, 58 on ads for a flying helicopter and p. 73 for plastic toy cars. See *Man's Magazine*, June 1965, 67 for an ad on "giant toys," directly under an advert for a divorce lawyer.

92 John C. Bahnsen, Jr., *American Warrior: A Combat Memoir of Vietnam* (New York, NY: Citadel Press, 2007), xiv. Compulsive worries in Brenton, *The American Male*, 69. On products of and contributors to social reality, see Deborah Cheney, "Visual Rape," *Law and Critique* Vol. IV, No. 2 (1993): 192. Cynthia Cockburn argues that from "a young age, boys learn that their bodies are weapons" and military systems exploit their propensity for violence. "Militarism, Masculinity, and Men," in *Together for Transformation: Men, Masculinities, and Peacebuilding*, ed. José de Vries and Isabelle Geuskens (Alkmaar: Women Peacemakers Program, 2010), 18.

93 Steven Dillon, *Wolf-Women and Phantom Ladies: Female Desire in 1940s US Culture* (Albany, NY: SUNY Press, 2015), 22. Clean death in Bourke, 221. Bourke also argues that "combatants interpreted their battleground experiences through the lens of an imaginary camera." *An Intimate History of Killing: Face-to-Face Killing in Twentieth-Century Warfare* (New York, NY: Basic Books, 1999), 14. Civilian depictions in Dwyer, 7. As an example of articles that spoke of the sexualized "Oriental" "shorn of guilt feelings or shame," see Shailer Upton Lawton, "Oriental Love Customs," *Man's Magazine*, November 1960, 38.

CHAPTER 3

1 Judith Butler, *Bodies That Matter: On the Discursive Limits of "Sex"* (New York, NY: Routledge, 193), 187. On the relationship between knowledge and daily practices which enforce a society's power relations, see Gail Bederman, *Manliness & Civilization:*

A Cultural History of Gender and Race in the United States, 1880–1917 (Chicago, IL: The University of Chicago Press, 1995), 24. Dualisms on p. 91.

2 On fearing oppressed groups, see Arthur Brittan, *Masculinity and Power* (New York, NY: Basil Blackwell, 1989), 163–164. Exotic locales in Max Allan Collins and George Hagenauer, *Men's Adventure Magazines in Postwar America* (London: Taschen, 2004), 167. French philosopher Michel Foucault stands at the center of discussions on discourse and power. For a pithy review, see Katie Milestone and Anneke Meyer, *Gender and Popular Culture* (Cambridge: Polity, 2012), 22–28. For a more detailed consideration, see Michel Foucault, "Truth and Power," in *The Foucault Reader*, ed. Paul Rabinow (New York, NY: Pantheon Books, 1984), 51–75.

3 Honor House Products Corp. advertisement, *Battle Cry*, July 1959, 62.

4 Kent Addison, "Women – Which Nationality Is Best?" *Man's Illustrated*, March 1962, 27, 29. Russians in "Stag Confidential," *Stag*, March 1966, 42. Topless dancer in "Men in Action," *Male*, November 1967, 36. On links between discourse and power, see Stuart Hall, "Foucault: Power, Knowledge, and Discourse," in *Discourse Theory and Practice: A Reader*, eds. Margaret Wetherell, Stephanie Taylor, and Simeon J. Yates (London: Sage, 2001), 75–78. On representations being productive, see Annette Kuhn, *The Power of the Image: Essays on Representation and Sexuality* (London: Routledge & Kegan Paul, 1985), 19. Conflict in Simone de Beauvoir, *The Second Sex* (New York, NY: Alfred A. Knopf, 1949, 2010), 10.

5 On Rome, see Roberto Orsi, "City of 10,000 Wild Playdolls," *Men*, March 1963, 14; and Cyrus W. Bell, "Rome's Wild Nudie 'Games,'" *Man's Illustrated*, July 1965, 28. L. E. Owen, "Sweden – Swinging Land of the Midnight Sun," *Bluebook*, May 1965, 17, 21. Leon Ridgefield, "Rio – City of 1,000 Delights," *Man's Illustrated*, September 1965, 30.

6 Edward W. Said, *Orientalism* (New York, NY: Vintage Books, 1979, 1994), 187–188. Racialized sexuality in Linda Williams, "Skin Flicks on the Racial Border: Pornography, Exploitation, and Interracial Lust," in *Porn Studies*, ed. Linda Williams (Durham, NC: Duke University Press, 2004), 272; and Steven Dillon, *Wolf-Women and Phantom Ladies: Female Desire in 1940s US Culture* (Albany, NY: SUNY Press, 2015), 139. Racial temptation and conquest in John Cawelti, "Pornography, Catastrophe, and Vengeance: Shifting Narrative Structures in a Changing American Culture," in *The American Self: Myth, Ideology, and Popular Culture*, ed. Sam B. Girgus (Albuquerque, NM: University of New Mexico Press, 1981), 186. On white women's appeal to GIs, see Robert B. Westbrook, *Why We Fought: Forging American Obligations in World War II* (Washington, DC: Smithsonian Books, 2004), 78.

7 Sexual subservience in Mari Yoshihara, *Embracing the East: White Women and American Orientalism* (New York, NY: Oxford University Press, 2003), 91. On soldiers seeking sex devoid of emotion, see Peter Schrijvers, *The Crash of Ruin: American Combat Soldiers in Europe during World War II* (New York, NY: New York University Press, 1998), 183.

8 Farrell W. Hoaglund, "Sex Is Their Secret Weapon," *Battle Cry*, February 1962, 20, 52. Jones Milward, "Inside a Sex-School for Spies," *Man's Illustrated*, November 1963, 26–28, 29. We might ask if the fear of weaponized sexuality was so acute because of man's

fallibility in sexual scenarios where he was helpless against the female sexual deviant, suggesting limits to his abilities as a sexual conqueror.

9 Igor Osipov, "Russia's Spy Fleet of Female Bed Partners," *Men*, May 1964, 36. On selling out to the Reds in the CIA West Berlin office, see W. J. Saber, "The Fraulein Trap," *Stag*, November 1966, 33. See also Emile C. Schurmacher, "East Berlin Spy House of the Communists' Blackmail Blonde," *For Men Only*, June 1960, 20. On bordello of neo-Nazis, see Alex Austin, "House of Call-Doll Frauleins," *Action for Men*, May 1964, 14.

10 Judas joy girl in Mario Cleri, "Track Down the Nude Double Agent on Passion Boulevard," *Male*, January 1967, 12. Cleri (Puzo) noted how women used "their silken-fleshed bodies" to work as undercover spy-girls, p. 15. There seemed a timeless aspect to this construction. *Fury* featured a story on a woman in the American Civil War who was the Union's best secret weapon "because the gallant Confederate officers simply couldn't resist her charms." Mike Doyle, "The Incredible Exploits of Major Pauline Cushman," *Fury*, April 1959, 15.

11 Walter Baker, "Prostitute-Spy Invasion of the U.S." *Stag*, September 1966, 12–14. Philip Marnais, *Saigon after Dark* (New York, NY: McFadden, 1967), 56. Heather Marie Stur notes the "pervasiveness of the untrustworthy Vietnamese women in the wartime culture" in *Beyond Combat: Women and Gender in the Vietnam War Era* (New York, NY: Cambridge University Press, 2011), 44. On prostitution, see Donald S. Bradley, Jacqueline Boles, and Christopher Jones, "From Mistress to Hooker: 40 Years of Cartoon Humor in Men's Magazines," *Qualitative Sociology* Vol. 2, No. 2 (June 1979): 44. Women as symbols in Vesna Kesic, "From Reverence to Rape: An Anthropology of Ethnic and Gendered Violence," in *Frontline Feminisms: Women, War, and Resistance*, eds. Marguerite R. Waller and Jennifer Rycenga (New York, NY: Garland Publishing, 2000), 25.

12 Rejecting femininity in Andrea Friedman, *Citizenship in Cold War America: The National Security State and the Possibilities of Dissent* (Amherst, MA: University of Massachusetts Press, 2014), 33. Prevailing images and conditions in Tawnya J. Adkins Covert, *Manipulating Images: World War II Mobilization of Women through Magazine Advertising* (Lanham, MD: Lexington Books, 2011), xiii. Shifts in sexual attitudes in Sharon R. Ullman, *Sex Seen: The Emergence of Modern Sexuality in America* (Berkeley, CA: University of California Press, 1997), 14. On aggressive female sexuality, see p. 19.

13 T. V. Neville, "The Passionate Widow Who Seduced a B-17 Pilot," *Brigade*, March 1963, 12–15, 60, 70. The article's tagline read "Outside there was the London Blitz, but she was more dangerous." On Tokyo Rose, see Emily Yellin, *Our Mothers' War: American Women at Home and at the Front during World War II* (New York, NY: The Free Press, 2004), 256–261.

14 Bedroom espionage in "The Red Scene," *Men*, July 1964, 46. On a "beautiful Hungarian" trying to steal allied invasion plans, see Bill Wharton, "They Sent a B-Girl to Booby Trap D-Day," *For Men Only*, March 1959, 21. John Robles, "The Joy Girl Who Fingered Hitler's Master Killer," *Fury*, March 1961, 22.

15 David J. Hager, "The Nordic Nymphs Who Almost Killed Hitler," *Man's Conquest*, December 1968, 12. Gender-acceptable narrative from Cameron Carlomagno, feedback to author, 10 June 2019.

16 Cage of domesticity and women as lures in E. Anthony Rotundo, *American Manhood: Transformations in Masculinity from the Revolution to the Modern Era* (New York, NY: Basic Books, 1993), 105. Clarke Grant, "Kill-Crazy Pirate Girls of Red China," *Valor*, June 1959, 28–30. Shanghai Road in Clifford Coxe, "The Passionate Lady Spies Who Held Down a Japanese Regiment," *Men*, January 1962, 28. Wendell O'Dell, "The Nympho Spy Who Helped to Lose the War," *Man's Adventure*, September 1964, 28.

17 Bernard B. Fall, *Street without Joy* (Mechanicsburg, PA: Stackpole Books, 1961, 1994), 135, 141. Trap and betray in Kelly Oliver, *Women as Weapons of War: Iraq, Sex, and the Media* (New York, NY: Columbia University Press, 2007), 20.

18 Propaganda posters in Christina S. Jarvis, *The Male Body at War: American Masculinity during World War II* (DeKalb, IL: Northern Illinois University Press, 2004), 79–81. While the loose women displayed in VD propaganda posters illustrated the "wrong" type of femininity, the "correct" one was seen in posters of women in uniform, as nurses, or as supportive wives and mothers. Comics in Peter Lee, "Decrypting Espionage Comics in 1950s America," in *Comic Books and the Cold War, 1946–1962*, eds. Chris York and Rafiel York (Jefferson, NC: McFarland, 2012), 38. Arthur Kaplan, "The Vanishing Lovers of Streetwalker Madeline Libertaud," *For Men Only*, July 1959, 20. Impure in Oliver, 30.

19 de Beauvoir, 13.

20 Archer Scanlon, "Monique: Queen of Newark's Sex Torture Palace," *Stag*, November 1967, 12, 74. "Jury Convicts Pair in 'Torture' Trial," *New York Times*, 24 June 1967. Fred P. Graham, "Law: No Censorship in the Home," *New York Times*, 13 April 1969.

21 Neil Turnbull, "Am Now Red Cuba's Most Wanted Man … Will Fight On …" *Male*, August 1964, 12. Anxieties in K. A. Cuordileone, *Manhood and American Political Culture in the Cold War* (London: Routledge, 2005), 40.

22 Bodies as weapons in Oliver, xi. Albert Hendricks, "Europe's Most Dangerous Spy Nymph," *Man's Conquest*, February 1968, 41–42.

23 Stuart Charles, "How We Broke the U.S. Deserters Seduction Ring," *Stag*, September 1968, 33, 80. On the implications of a communist seductress targeting an American officer in *The Ugly American*, see Robert D. Dean, *Imperial Brotherhood: Gender and the Making of Cold War Foreign Policy* (Amherst, MA: University of Massachusetts Press, 2001), 177.

24 Kenneth W. Vinson, "Women Who Provoke Sex Attacks," *Man's Illustrated*, March 1966, 22, 55. The tagline read "Men call it 'frame-up,' women call it 'rape,' and psychiatrists call it 'wish fulfillment.'"

25 Kurt Vaughn, "Kill the Viet Cong in Zone D!" *Man's Illustrated*, March 1966, 44.

26 Leland Gardner, *Vietnam Underside* (San Diego, CA: Publishers Export, 1966), 18, 25, 32, 93–94, 96, 114, 137.

27 Inferior other in Tarak Barkawi and Keith Stanski, "Introduction," in *Orientalism and War*, eds. Tarak Barkawi and Keith Stanski (New York, NY: Columbia University Press, 2012), 4. Paternalistic discourse in Mary A. Renda, *Taking Haiti: Military Occupation and the Culture of U.S. Imperialism, 1915–1940* (Chapel Hill, NC: The University of North Carolina Press, 2001), 13. Feminized in Naoko Shibusawa, *America's Geisha Ally: Reimagining the Japanese Enemy* (Cambridge, MA: Harvard University Press, 2006), 21. Compliant body from John Dower quoted in Sheridan Prasso, *The Asian Mystique: Dragon Ladies,*

Geisha Girls, and Our Fantasies of the Exotic Orient (New York, NY: Public Affairs, 2005), 53. On Asians as children, see Donna Alvah, *Unofficial Ambassadors: American Military Families Overseas and the Cold War, 1946–1965* (New York, NY: New York University Press, 2007), 168.

28 Amy Sueyoshi, *Discriminating Sex: White Leisure and the Making of the American "Oriental"* (Urbana, IL: University of Illinois Press, 2018), 135. Servile in Shibusawa, 39.

29 Consumption in Yoshihara, *Embracing the East*, 18. Geishas in Sueyoshi, 59. On how this discourse has led to Asian Americans being seen as the "model minority," see Audrea Lim, "The Alt-Right's Asian Fetish," *New York Times*, 6 January 2018.

30 Luzon in Thomas Bruscino, *A Nation Forged in War: How World War II Taught Americans to Get Along* (Knoxville, TN: The University Press of Tennessee, 2010), 114. William Manchester, *Goodbye, Darkness: A Memoir of the Pacific War* (Boston, MA: Little, Brown and Company, 1979), 49. On World War II bringing "unprecedented opportunities" for premarital sex, see Steven Cohan, *Masked Men: Masculinity and the Movies in the Fifties* (Bloomington, IN: Indiana University Press, 1997), 85.

31 Brian Walsh, "Sexual Violence during the Occupation of Japan," *The Journal of Military History* Vol. 82, No. 4 (October 2018): 1225. Walsh argues that "heinous crimes such as rape and murder, though not unheard of, were decidedly uncommon," p. 1203. Bangkok in Peter Goldman and Tony Fuller, *Charlie Company: What Vietnam Did to Us* (New York, NY: Ballantine Books, 1983), 114; and Robert Jay Lifton, *Home from the War: Vietnam Veterans: Neither Victims nor Executioners* (New York, NY: Simon & Schuster, 1973), 207–208. Brothel of the world in Chung Hyun-Kyung, "'Your Comfort versus My Death': Korean Comfort Women," in *War's Dirty Secret: Rape, Prostitution, and Other Crimes against Women*, ed. Anne Llewellyn Barstow (Cleveland, OH: The Pilgrim Press, 2000), 21. Lure of prostitutes in Myron Brenton, *The American Male* (New York, NY: Coward-McCann, 1966), 189. Of note, Brenton was not just referring to Asian prostitutes, but speaking more generally.

32 "Male Paradise," *Man's Day*, March 1953, 60. Thorp McClusky, "The Island of Lonely Girls," *Adventure*, October 1957, 18–19. "Stag Confidential," *Stag*, February 1967, 44. See also Bryan Peters, "The Girl from Hong Kong's 'Hot Street,'" *Male*, August 1964, on an "Oriental Venus with a wild sweet tooth for men," p. 25.

33 Don Davis, "Where the American Army Learned about Sex," *Battle Cry*, October 1957, 20. See also Alex Austin, "The Day They Outlawed Geishas," *Man's World*, June 1959, 26. No topping in "Inside for Men," *Male*, November 1957, 6.

34 Robert F. Dorr, "Inside the Oriental Sin Town Where Passion's the Name of the Game," *Man's Illustrated*, August 1971, 14, 50.

35 Japan International advertisement, *Sir!*, July 1962, 62. This idea of the "submissive" may have been aided by the lack of interaction between Japanese women and American soldiers during World War II. Most contact occurred during the years of US occupation, thus Japanese women did not have the opportunity to challenge this perception in a wartime setting.

36 *The Manchurian Candidate*, directed by John Frankenheimer, United Artists, 1962. On Hollywood World War II films "filled with strange landscapes and exotic women," see

John Bodnar, *The "Good War" in American Memory* (Baltimore, MD: The Johns Hopkins University Press, 2010), 27. James Webb mentions "groin-grinding bar girls" in his Vietnam novel *Fields of Fire* (Englewood Cliffs, NJ: Prentice-Hall, 1978), 38.

37 Difficult and smothering in Shibusawa, 43. On the deep roots of the allure of darker, "dusky" skinned women, see Amy S. Greenberg, *Manifest Manhood and the Antebellum American Empire* (New York, NY: Cambridge University Press, 2005), 116–118.

38 Polynesian women in Catherine A. Lutz and Jane L. Collins, *Reading National Geographic* (Chicago, IL: The University of Chicago Press, 1993), 136–139. Polygamous harems in Reina Lewis, *Rethinking Orientalism: Women, Travel and the Ottoman Harem* (New Brunswick, NJ: Rutgers University Press, 2004), 96. On the relationship between fetishization and sexual violence, see Sara Meger, *Rape Loot Pillage: The Political Economy of Sexual Violence in Armed Conflict* (New York, NY: Oxford University Press, 2016), 17. Licentiousness and Jezebel in Candice M. Jenkins, *Private Lives, Proper Relations: Regulating Black Intimacy* (Minneapolis, MN: University of Minnesota Press, 2007), 8–11. For a discussion on African American soldiers' perceptions of Korean and Japanese women, see Christine Knauer, *Let Us Fight as Free Men: Black Soldiers and Civil Rights* (Philadelphia, PA: University of Pennsylvania Press, 2014), 153–157, 170–171. Taboo from Charissa Threat, conversation with author, 4 July 2019. One rare exception was an ad for "Gentlemen Prefer Bronze," a photo collection of women with "dusky loveliness," offered by Matt Books in Los Angeles. *Man's Epic*, March 1968, 12.

39 Harry Roskolenko, "The Nude in the Blue Lagoon," *Valor*, June 1959, 34. Xosa tribe in Jack Sholimir, "Beachcombers of the African Jungle," *Valor*, June 1959, 8, 10.

40 Martin Henderson, "Sgt. Hogan's Heavenly Harem," *Sensation*, April 1959, 32. Glenn Infield, "The Harem HQ of WWII's Missing-in-Action Major," *Stag*, July 1961, 26. Harland P. Flourie, "Holy Harlots of India," *Cavalcade*, May 1959, 17–18. On the "representational effect" of stories like these, see Julia Kuehn, "Exotic Harem Paintings: Gender, Documentation, and Imagination," *Frontiers: A Journal of Women's Studies* Vol. 32, No. 2 (2011): 32.

41 Stereotypes in Prasso, 87. James Collier, "The Nymph Decoys of Asia's Comfort Houses," *Stag*, July 1961, 12–13. Eugene Anthony, "Sleep Around Girl Who Lured Red China's Top Defector," *Male*, July 1966, 12. Vietnam vet quoted in Susan Zeiger, *Entangling Alliances: Foreign War Brides and American Soldiers in the Twentieth Century* (New York, NY: New York University Press, 2010), 215.

42 Ray Bourgeois Zimmerman notes how these women were "discursively obliterated." In "Gruntspeak: Masculinity, Monstrosity and Discourse in Hasford's *The Short-Timers*," *American Studies* Vol. 40, No. 1 (Spring 1999): 71. Unnamed girl being raped in Joanna Bourke, *Rape: Sex, Violence, History* (Berkeley, CA: Shoemaker Hoard, 2007), 5. On Vietnamese women lacking a presence in many war narratives, see Martha Raye in Keith Walker, *A Piece of My Heart: The Stories of 26 American Women Who Served in Vietnam* (Novato, CA: Presidio, 1985), 2. Barkawi and Stanski argue that orientalism is about "who is empowered to represent with authority, who is seen to speak knowledgably." *Orientalism and War*, 5.

43 Said, *Orientalism*, 6. Silencing as a decision in Susan Sontag, *A Susan Sontag Reader* (New York, NY: Farrar/Straus/Giroux, 1982), 185. On questioning whether women were even human, see Carol Rittner, "Are Women Human?," in *Rape: Weapon of War and Genocide*,

eds. Carol Rittner and John K. Roth (St. Paul, MN: Paragon House, 2012), 1–2. Otherness in Mary V. Dearborn, *Pocahontas's Daughters: Gender and Ethnicity in American Culture* (New York, NY: Oxford University Press, 1986), 5.

44 Study results in M. Venkatesan and Jean Losco, "Women in Magazine Ads: 1959–71," *Journal of Advertising Research* Vol. 15, No. 5 (October 1975): 52. Slave girl outfit in Originals, Inc. advertisement, *Male*, August 1964, 47. Harem Jamas in Smoothee Co. advertisement, *Valor*, June 1959, 92. On Egyptian-inspired pin-ups, see Maria Elena Buszek, *Pin-Up Grrrls: Feminism, Sexuality, Popular Culture* (Durham, NC: Duke University Press, 2006), 69–72.

45 Felix Muntsaarts, "Buy a Slave Girl!" *Man's Conquest*, February 1968, 12. Such storylines also reasserted ideals of American men being the benevolent "rescuer" of women.

46 Andrew McCoy, "You Can Take Your Pay in Women," *All Man*, April 1960, 19, 71. Arnold Chesterton, "The Love Slave of Hadramut," *Battle Cry*, March 1964, 18, 52. Eroticization in Alison Assiter, "Romance Fiction: Porn for Women?," in *Perspectives on Pornography: Sexuality in Film and Literature*, eds. Gary Day and Clive Bloom (New York, NY: St. Martin's Press, 1988), 103.

47 White masculinity in Jarvis, *The Male Body at War*, 141–143. Carl Sherman, "Stone-Age Island Headhunters," *Stag*, September 1966, 31, 33. On the sexually decadent other, see Patricia Owens, "The Pleasures of Imperialism and the Pink Elephant: Torture, Sex, Orientalism," in Barkawi and Stanski, 255. On how these notions relate to wartime sexual violence, see Pascale R. Bos, "Feminists Interpreting the Politics of Wartime Rape: Berlin, 1945; Yugoslavia, 1992–1993," *Signs*, Vol. 31, No. 4 (Summer 2006): 997–998.

48 On these storylines, see Lee Server, *Danger Is My Business: An Illustrated History of the Fabulous Pulp Magazines* (San Francisco, CA: Chronicle Books, 1993), 49–50. On the frontier as "geomythical space," see Jonathan Mitchell, *Revisions of the American Adam: Innocence, Identity and Masculinity in Twentieth-Century America* (New York, NY: Continuum, 2011), 19. On sexual availability, see Chris Finley, "Decolonizing the Queer Native Body (and Recovering the Native Bull Dyke): Bringing 'Sexy Back' and Out of Native Studies' Closet," in *Queer Indigenous Studies: Critical Interventions in Theory, Politics, and Literature*, eds. Qwo-Li Driskill, Chris Finley, Brian Joseph Gilley, and Scott Lauria Morgensen (Tucson, AZ: The University of Arizona Press, 2011), 34. Colonialism in Charlotte Hooper, *Manly States: Masculinities, International Relations, and Gender Politics* (New York, NY: Columbia University Press, 2001), 84.

49 Dave Heinkel, "My Six-Year South Sea Adventure," *Stag*, April 1956, 40–41, 50. In August 1958, *Battlefield* reprinted the article as "My Fantastic Six Years as a South Sea Castaway," with far more appealing artwork by Rudy Nappi, p. 18. Ansel Cooker, "Seaman Cooker and the After-Dark Girls of Borneo Bay," *Male*, August 1960, 12, 82, 86. These castaway stories represented a spatial separation from the constraints of "modernization" and consumerism, recalling days of "pure" masculinity, when men were providers and, supposedly, unchallenged by femininity.

50 Sgt. James W. Coffin, "I Crashed on an Island of Castaway Geishas," *Battlefield*, May 1959, 12. Louis B. Hutton, "To Kidnap the Joy Girls of the Malabar Coast," *Real Men*, December 1960, 19.

51 Alec Rantzen, "10 Castaway Years on Lost Harem Island," *Action for Men*, May 1964, 32, 64. Bruscino notes how American soldiers overseas confronted a much less pleasing reality. *A Nation Forged in War*, 120. These ideas highlighted how "traditional" societies often were deemed inferior, whereas "modern" (white) ones inherently were judged as superior.

52 On expansionism and martial manhood, see Greenberg, 92. Survival in Richard Slotkin, *Regeneration through Violence: The Mythology of the American Frontier, 1600–1860* (Norman, OK: University of Oklahoma Press, 1973), 55. On frontier stories in the Cold War, see Suzanne Clark, *Cold Warriors: Manliness on Trial in the Rhetoric of the West* (Carbondale, IL: Southern Illinois University Press, 2000), 40.

53 Bill Wharton, "The Amazing GI Who Took Three Head-Hunting Brides," *Stag*, January 1961, 12, 52, 54. Of note in this story, female sexuality is the primary identity of the local women – women first, warriors second. Shari M. Huhndorf notes the conquering culture's need to "reimagine the objects of its conquest" in *Going Native: Indians in the American Cultural Imagination* (Ithaca, NY: Cornell University Press, 2001), 20.

54 Winthrop D. Jordan, *The White Man's Burden: Historical Origins of Racism in the United States* (New York, NY: Oxford University Press, 1974), 81–82. On African Americans' sexual character being stigmatized as "uncivilized" in the United States, see Jenkins, 4. On the paradoxes between civilization and manhood in *Tarzan of the Apes*, see Bederman, *Manliness & Civilization*, 222.

55 Cultural stereotypes of inferior cultures, see Joe Snader, *Caught between Worlds: British Captivity Narratives in Fact and Fiction* (Lexington, KY: The University Press of Kentucky, 2000), 79. Kimloan Hill discusses earlier sexual relationships between French and Vietnamese in "Sacrifices, Sex, Race: Vietnamese Experiences in the First World War," in *Race, Empire, and First World War Writing*, ed. Santanu Das (New York, NY: Cambridge University Press, 2011), 58–61.

56 Unintended consequence in Zeiger, 163. On antebellum anxieties over "hybridism," see Dearborn, 150. *Ebony* and *U.S. Lady* in Alvah, 59. *U.S. Lady* was a magazine aimed at military wives.

57 A. V. Loring, "Forbidden Amazon Female Compound," *Stag*, April 1968, 32. June Namias discusses earlier fears that "Indian men could indeed serve as attractive and compassionate sexual partners" in *White Captives: Gender and Ethnicity on the American Frontier* (Chapel Hill, NC: The University of North Carolina Press, 1993), 99. For an alternative view, where the "beats" of the 1950s were seeking out interracial sex, see Todd Gitlin, *The Sixties: Years of Hope, Days of Rage* (New York, NY: Bantam Books, 1993), 47.

58 On Puritan captivity narratives, see: Tara Fitzpatrick, "The Figure of Captivity: The Cultural Work of the Puritan Captivity Narrative," *American Literary History* Vol. 3, No. 1 (Spring 1991): 1–26; and Robert C. Doyle, *Voices from Captivity: Interpreting the American POW Narrative* (Lawrence, KS: University Press of Kansas, 1994). On the sexuality of white–Indian contact, see Louise K. Barnett, *The Ignoble Savage: American Literary Racism, 1790–1890* (Westport, CT: Greenwood Press, 1975), 113–119.

59 Eric Pleasants, "Russia's Camps of Banished Wives," *True Action*, June 1961, 12. Alex Austin, "The Yank P.O.W. in 'Comfort Girl' Stockade," *Stag*, May 1960, 21, 89. Richard Gallagher, "Inside a Communist All-Woman Penal Camp," *Stag*, January 1964, 32, 62–63.

60 Martin Fass, "Stockade of Captive Blondes," *True Action*, March 1967, 28. For a similar story on a Geisha compound in Burma, see George Mandel, "The P.O.W.'s Who Took Over a Geisha Compound," *For Men Only*, July 1959, 12.

61 Neil Turnbull, "The Lost Blondes of Penal Plantation 9," *Male*, July 1966, p. 28, 87, 90. *Male* included one story, ostensibly from the female perspective, in Janet Lyons, "My Two Years in the 'Barracks of the Caged Young Girls,'" *Male*, September 1966, 20, 23. The author noted how "'straight' girls fought to get work assignment on [the] prison farm where they could party with male guards."

62 1,000 rapes in Alvah, 27. Susan Brownmiller has a slightly different, though no less disturbing, set of figures in *Against Our Will: Men, Women, and Rape* (New York, NY: Fawcett Books, 1975), 76–77. Comparison with civilian rates in Madeline Morris, "In War and Peace: Rape, War, and Military Culture," in *War's Dirty Secret: Rape, Prostitution, and Other Crimes against Women*, ed. Anne Llewellyn Barstow (Cleveland, OH: The Pilgrim Press, 2000), 170. Destruction and looting in Miriam Gebhardt, *Crimes Unspoken: The Rape of German Women at the End of the Second World War* (Malden, MA: Polity, 2017), 84. On occupation, see Atina Grossman, "A Question of Silence: The Rape of German Women by Occupation Soldiers," *October Magazine* Vol. 72 (Spring 1995): 42–63; and Atina Grossman, "The 'Big Rape': Sex and Sexual Violence, War, and Occupation in Post-World War II Memory and Imagination," in *Sexual Violence in Conflict Zones: From the Ancient World to the Era of Human Rights*, ed. Elizabeth D. Heineman (Philadelphia, PA: University of Pennsylvania Press, 2011), 137–151.

63 On desire for female companionship, see, Petra Goedde, *GIs and Germans: Culture, Gender, and Foreign Relations, 1945–1949* (New Haven, CT: Yale University Press, 2003), 83. On rape being seen as routine, see Grossman, "The 'Big Rape,'" 138. Peter Conolly-Smith argues that World War II films rarely showed white victims of rape, suggesting an element of Orientalism at play. "Race-ing Rape: Representations of Sexual Violence in American Combat Films," *War and Society* Vol. 32, No. 3 (October 2013): 246.

64 Rape fantasy from "Mark," quoted in Timothy Beneke, *Men on Rape* (New York, NY: St. Martin's Press, 1982), 64. Burlesque in Adam Parfrey, *It's a Man's World: Men's Adventure Magazines, the Postwar Pulps* (Los Angeles, CA: Feral House, 2003), 177. On links to postwar sexual anxieties, see Amit Pinchevski and Roy Brand, "Holocaust Perversions: The Stalags Pulp Fiction and the Eichmann Trial," *Critical Studies in Media Communications* Vol. 24, No. 5 (December 2007): 391. Downplaying GI violence in Bourke, *Rape*, 360. See also Collins and Hagenauer, 267–268.

65 Charles V. Nemo, "The Blonde 30,000 POWs Called 'BITCH,'" *Battlefield*, May 1959, 26, 42, 44. On Koch and the Nazi camps, see Laura Sjoberg, *Women as Wartime Rapists: Beyond Sensation and Stereotyping* (New York, NY: New York University Press, 2016), 2–3, 102–108.

66 Tony Sorrentino, "The Lady with the Whip," *Real Men*, December 1960, 6, 56, 58. For similar stories, see: James Collier, "Mistress of the Mediterranean's Infamous Penal Hole," *Male*, July 1961, 21; and Drake Hansen, "The Sex-Mad Harlots Who Fought for Hitler," *Battle Cry*, August 1962, 30. The tagline read "An army of women, crazed with lust, screamed for our blood." This theme also could be seen in 1970s "sexploitation" films like *Ilsa: She Wolf of the SS*, directed by Don Edmonds, Cambist Films, 1975.

67 Sgt. Rusty Miller, "Lusty Ludwig's Love Lager," *Battle Cry*, July 1959, 6, 53. The story was reprinted as "The Best Damn POW Camp in History," *Battle Cry*, August 1962, 18. Mistresses in Grant Freeling, "U.S. Agent Who Invaded Hitler's House of Hostage Frauleins," *Male*, June 1966, 28. Other nationalities could suffice in wartime fantasies. In Tereska Torrès's "French Girls' Barracks," members of a French WAC company are "willing to do anything for the war effort," the story's tagline promising "violent love and strange desires." *Male*, February 1965, 34. Of note, Torrès's *Women Barracks* (1950) was the first lesbian pulp novel in the United States.

68 Martin Fass, "Hitler's Man-Hungry 'Lost Women' Brigade," *Male*, December 1962, 21. Henri Mortain, "The Day That Paris Fell," *Battle Cry*, October 1957, 40. Peter Gusdanovich, "I Was Sold to the Love-Hungry Women of Madagascar," *True Men*, October 1958, 14. See also Geoffrey Randall, "One Man in a Woman's Army," *Battle Cry*, July 1959, 18, 45, on members of a Bolshevik Women's Battalion who, in essence, rape their captive Englishman. Margalit Fox, "Tereska Torrès, 92, Writer of Lesbian Fiction, Dies," *New York Times*, 24 September 2012.

69 Donald Honig, "Yank Explorer Who Ruled Guatemala's 'Taboo Tribe,'" *For Men Only*, August 1966, 36, 78. Violating cultural prescriptions in Snader, 82. On gendered differences in captivity narratives, see Namias, 79–81.

70 Norton McVickers, "The Girls Who Beg to Be Mastered," *Man's Life*, September 1966, 28, 68. On prisoners seeing torture as a test of will rather than something to be avoided, see Jerry Lembcke, *Hanoi Jane: War, Sex & Fantasies of History* (Amherst, MA: University of Massachusetts Press, 2010), 52–54. Apparently, the pulps' depiction of sexual violence far exceeded what was shown in *Playboy*. On this, see Joseph E. Scott and Steven J. Cuvelier, "Sexual Violence in *Playboy* Magazine: A Longitudinal Content Analysis," *The Journal of Sex Research* Vol. 23, No. 4 (November 1987): 536.

71 Larry Heinemann, *Paco's Story* (New York, NY: Vintage Books, 1986, 2005), 55–56. On the sexual aspects of *Paco's Story*, see Susan Jeffords, "Tattoos, Scars, Diaries, and Writing Masculinity," in *The Vietnam War and American Culture*, eds. John Carlos Rowe and Rick Berg (New York, NY: Columbia University Press, 1991), 210; and Keith Beattie, *The Scar That Binds: American Culture and the Vietnam War* (New York, NY: New York University Press, 1998), 55–56.

72 Webb, *Fields of Fire*, 246. Mario Cleri, "The Seduction of Private Nurse Griffith," *Men*, July 1964, 16, 88.

73 Dynamic in Stan Goff, *Borderline: Reflections on War, Sex, and Church* (Eugene, OR: Cascade Books, 2015), 21–22. On sexually available Fräuleins, see Grossman, "The 'Big Rape,'" 150. Morphing and sheer manliness from Eugenia C. Kiesling, email to author, 8 July 2019. Not surprisingly, the pulps avoided the obvious possibility of male rape, anal penetration of the male victim.

74 Avoiding controversy in Robert Genter, "'With Great Power Comes Great Responsibility': Cold War Culture and the Birth of Marvel Comics," *The Journal of Popular Culture* Vol. 40, No. 6 (2007): 953. On Sergeant Rock, see Cord A. Scott, *Comics and Conflict: Patriotism and Propaganda from WWII through Operation Iraqi Freedom* (Annapolis, MD: Naval Institute Press, 2014), 53; and Christopher J. Hayton and Sheila Hayton, "The

Girls in White: Nurse Images in Early Cold War Era Romance and War Comics," in *Comic Books and the Cold War, 1946–1962*, eds. Chris York and Rafiel York (Jefferson, NC: McFarland, 2012), 135.

75 *Phantom Lady*, No. 21, December 1948, 14–15. Fredric Wertham, *Seduction of the Innocent* (New York, NY: Rinehart, 1953), 185.

76 Headlights in Friedman, 167. Wertham, 201, 361.

77 Girl commandos in Christina M. Knopf, "'Hey Soldier! – Your Slip Is Showing!': Militarism vs. Femininity in World War II Comics and Books," in *The 10 Cent War: Comic Books, Propaganda, and World War II*, eds. Trischa Goodnow and James J. Kimble (Jackson, MS: University Press of Mississippi, 2016), 39–40. On Justice League, see Jill Lepore, *The Secret History of Wonder Woman* (New York, NY: Alfred A. Knopf, 2014), 209–211. On not being passive objects, see Carol L. Tilley, "A Regressive Formula of Perversity: Wertham and the Women of Comics," *Journal of Lesbian Studies* Vol. 22, No. 4 (2018): 5. Roles of "female fighters" in Jean Bethke Elshtain, *Women and War* (New York, NY: Basic Books, 1987), 176–180.

78 Granville in Ben Macintyre, "Through Enemy Lines," *New York Times*, 19 July 2013; and Clare Mulley, *The Spy Who Loved: The Secrets and Lives of Christine Granville* (New York, NY: St. Martin's Press, 2012), 342. Hierarchical power structures in Francine D'Amico, "Feminist Perspectives on Women Warriors," in *The Women and War Reader*, eds. Lois Ann Lorentzen and Jennifer Turpin (New York, NY: New York University Press, 1998), 120.

79 Glenn Infield, "The Amazing U.S. Flyer Who Wrecked Hitler's Bid for Atomic Weapons," *Men*, May 1962, 37. Philippe de Vomecourt, "Major 'Mayhem' and His Magnificent Dirty Fighters," *Men*, December 1961, 32. On Americans' construction of the French male, in which only World War II resistance fighters merited admiration, see Mary Louise Roberts, *What Soldiers Do: Sex and the American GI in World War II France* (Chicago, IL: The University of Chicago Press, 2013), 95.

80 Walter Kaylin, "Yank C.O. of WWII's Strangest Co-ed Commando Battalion," *Stag*, March 1966, 32, 72. See also Cyrus W. Bell, "Hell-Raising Guerrilla Queen Who Saved Marshall Tito," *Man's Epic*, November 1967, 32.

81 Ormond MacArthur, "The Girl in Pvt. Devereux' Combat Boots," *Man's World*, June 1959, 20, 23, 54. On how women were similarly viewed as unsuited for war, see Jeanne Holm, *Women in the Military: An Unfinished* Revolution, rev. ed. (Novato, CA: Presidio Press, 1992), 179. Those who did serve in uniform were expected to maintain their femininity and be attractive to men. Maureen Honey, *Creating Rosie the Riveter: Class, Gender, and Propaganda during World War II* (Amherst, MA: The University of Massachusetts Press, 1984), 114.

82 Edwin Johnson, "Kidnapped by Russia's Female Aces," *Stag*, May 1964, 24. Art by Samson Pollen. Voyeuristic fascination in Juliette Pattinson, *Behind Enemy Lines: Gender, Passing and the Special Operations Executive in the Second World War* (Manchester: Manchester University Press, 2007), 9. On women taking up arms being perceived as "sexually unconventional," see David E. Jones, *Women Warriors: A History* (Washington, DC: Brassey's, 1997), xii.

83 Kyra Petrovskaya, "Combat Diary of a Russian Woman Soldier," *Battlefield*, November 1959, 18, 21. See also Norman Dash, "Glamorous Santa Monican Looks Like Anything but Russian Hero," *Los Angeles Times*, 6 November 1960. Lyn Webster Wilde argues that "occasional masculinity, along with its privileges, is awarded to women to keep them quiet in their customarily subservient role." *On the Trail of the Women Warriors: The Amazons in Myth and Memory* (New York, NY: St. Martin's Press, 1999), 183.

84 William Ballinger, "Battalion of Nymphs," *Action for Men*, November 1968, 33, 76. Ballinger's excerpted story came from his 1967 *Women's Battalion* (New York, NY: Lancer Books, 1967), according to the cover a "raw, savage novel of WWII's amazing all-female fighting unit . . . who used guns, knives – and sex – to destroy the Third Reich."

85 Sexualization of war in Kesic, "From Reverence to Rape," 24. Gregory Johnson, "We Were Captured by New Guinea's Nude Amazons," *Battlefield*, January 1959, 13, 46.

86 Ivan Cameron, "Timothy Briggs: Captive Sailor of Tasmania's Amazon Women," *Adventure Life*, March 1959, 12, 66. Neil Turnbull, "U.S. Commando Force and the Greek Nude Girl Divers Who Broke Up Germany's 'Underwater Arsenal,'" *Male*, January 1964, 36, 45. On challenges, see Cynthia Enloe, *Does Khaki Become You? The Militarisation of Women's Lives* (Boston, MA: South End Press, 1983), 117. Amazonian sexual practices in Wilde, 27.

87 Femme sauvage in Miriam Cooke, *Women and the War Story* (Berkeley, CA: University of California Press, 1996), 132. Mike Doyle, "The Invincible Colonel and His 1,000 Congo Queens," *Fury*, March 1961, 15. Leicester Harrison, "I Fought the Amazon's 'Blood Feast' Headhunters," *True Action*, July 1967, 22, 42. For a similar tale, see Robert Martel, "I Lived with the Axe Women of the Amazon," *True Action*, November 1968, which includes a "mock battle of the sexes followed by a shocking orgy," p. 29.

88 Emile C. Schurmacher, "The Yank Pilot Who Lived with Indochina's Amazon Women," *For Men Only*, March 1959, 12, 44.

89 W. J. Saber, "Vengeance Platoon from the Village of Violated Women," *Stag*, January 1961, 29–31, 64–78.

90 "Flashes for Men," *Man's Illustrated*, September 1965, 6.

91 Soldier quoted in Enloe, 33–34. Legitimizing violence and exorcising fears in Jacqueline A. Lawson, "'She's a Pretty Woman . . . for a Gook': The Misogyny of the Vietnam War," *The Journal of American Culture* Vol. 12, No. 3 (Fall 1989): 56.

92 The Queen of Caper advertisement, *Brigade*, March 1963, 64. Domineering sexual behavior in Susan Griffin, "Rape: The All-American Crime," *Ramparts*, September 1971, 30. Consensual sex in Bourke, *Rape*, 53.

93 Bill Harrell, "Korea's 800,000 Give-Give Girls," *Male*, March 1965, 18, 80. On how other cultural venues portrayed the Korean War, see Hye Seung Chung, "From Saviors to Rapists: G.I.s, Women, and Children in Korean War Films," in *Heroism and Gender in War Films*, eds. Karen A. Ritzenhoff and Jakub Kazecki (New York, NY: Palgrave Macmillan, 2014), 115–130; Yuming Piao, "The Construction of Korean Female Images in the Korean War Novels from an Orientalist Perspective," *Comparative Literature Studies* Vol. 54, No. 1 (2017): 201–204; and Prasso, 88–92.

94 Charlton W. Killgore, Jr., "Ten Best Draftee Deals in the Armed Forces," *For Men Only*, September 1966, 20, 44, 48.

95 On the problems of young soldiers achieving their sexual fantasies, see Lynne Segal, "Look Back in Anger: Men in the 50s," in *Male Order: Unwrapping Masculinity*, eds. Rowena Chapman and Jonathan Rutherford (London: Lawrence & Wishart, 1988), 86.

CHAPTER 4

1 Mort Künstler, cover art, *Stag*, December 1966. W. J. Saber, "Yank GI–Viet Doll Escape Team," *Ibid.*, 26. "Stag Confidential," *Ibid.*, 42.

2 HQ, USMACV, Command History, 1966, Volume I, Entry MACJ03, RG 472, National Archives and Records Administration, College Park, MD, pp. 1, 3. (Hereafter cited as NARA.)

3 Kurt Vaughn, "Riding Shotgun in Helicopter Hell," *Man's Illustrated*, September 1965, 40. Westmoreland in Blair Clark, "Westmoreland Appraised: Questions and Answers," *Harper's*, November 1970, 96. One colonel, Lewis Goad, noted how Vietnam was "not a military war: it's a political war." In Robert Sherrod, "Notes on a Monstrous War," *Life*, 27 January 1967, 22B. For a less complimentary version of US military leaders' outlook, see Jeffrey Race, *War Comes to Long An: Revolutionary Conflict in a Vietnamese Province* (Berkeley, CA: University of California Press, 1972), 226, 263. Proving oneself in Kathy J. Phillips, *Manipulating Masculinity: War and Gender in Modern British and American Literature* (New York, NY: Palgrave Macmillan, 2006), 131.

4 On *National Geographic* war photography also avoiding the more brutal aspects of the fighting, see Catherine A. Lutz and Jane L. Collins, *Reading National Geographic* (Chicago, IL: The University of Chicago Press, 1993), 99–100.

5 Veteran Bobby Muller quoted in Kim Willenson, *The Bad War: An Oral History of the Vietnam War* (New York, NY: New American Library, 1987), 112. On lies from the World War II generation, see Tracy Karner, "Fathers, Sons, and Vietnam: Masculinity and Betrayal in the Life Narratives of Vietnam Veterans with Post Traumatic Stress Disorder," *American Studies* Vol. 37, No. 1 (Spring 1996): 63.

6 Warrior teenagers in Thomas Myers, *Walking Point: American Narratives of Vietnam* (New York, NY: Oxford University Press, 1988), 30. Unmet expectations in Miriam Cooke, *Women and the War Story* (Berkeley, CA: University of California Press, 1996), 81.

7 William Jayne, "Immigrants from a Combat Zone," in *The Wounded Generation: America after Vietnam*, ed. A. D. Horne (Englewood Cliffs, NJ: Prentice-Hall, 1981), 161. Fiction in Don Ringnalda, *Fighting and Writing the Vietnam War* (Jackson, MS: University Press of Mississippi, 1994), 95.

8 Consul Leland L. Smith quoted in Mark Bradley, "Slouching toward Bethlehem: Culture, Diplomacy, and the Origins of the Cold War in Vietnam," in *Cold War Constructions: The Political Culture of United States Imperialism, 1945–1966*, ed. Christian G. Appy (Amherst, MA: The University of Massachusetts Press, 2000), 14. On Western notions, see pp. 13–14, 22. Occidental versus Orient in Arjun Chowdhury, "Shocked by War: The Non-politics of Orientalism," in *Orientalism and War*, eds. Tarak Barkawi and Keith Stanski (New York, NY: Columbia University Press, 2012), 20–22.

9 For a pithy overview of the post-1945 period, see Fredrik Logevall, "The Indochina Wars and the Cold War, 1945–1975," in *The Cambridge History of the Cold War, Volume II, Crises and Détente*, eds. Melvyn P. Leffler and Odd Arne Westad (New York, NY: Cambridge University Press, 2014), 281–304. For a more complete telling, see Fredrik Logevall, *Embers of War: The Fall of an Empire and the Making of America's Vietnam* (New York, NY: Random House, 2012). For an alternate perspective, see Pierre Asselin, *Hanoi's Road to the Vietnam War, 1954–1965* (Berkeley, NY: University of California Press, 2013).

10 On Diem's relationship with the United States, see Edward Miller, *Misalliance: Ngo Dinh Diem, the United States, and the Fate of South Vietnam* (Cambridge, MA: Harvard University Press, 2013). For insights on the rise of the NLF, see David W. P. Elliott, *The Vietnamese War: Revolution and Social Change in the Mekong Delta, 1930–1975*, concise ed. (Armonk, NY: M. E. Sharpe, 2007).

11 David Kaiser takes on US escalation in *American Tragedy: Kennedy, Johnson, and the Origins of the Vietnam War* (Cambridge, MA: The Belknap Press of Harvard University Press, 2000); as does Gary R. Hess in "South Vietnam under Siege, 1961–1965: Kennedy, Johnson, and the Question of Escalation or Disengagement," in *The Columbia History of the Vietnam War*, ed. David L. Anderson (New York, NY: Columbia University Press, 2011), 143–167. For a short review of how the American Joint Chiefs of Staff saw the problem, see Richard K. Betts, *Soldiers, Statesmen, and Cold War Crises* (Cambridge, MA: Harvard University Press, 1977), 23–26.

12 Brian St. Pierre, "Viet Nam Comes to the Bijou," *True*, July 1968, 59. Renata Adler, *A Year in the Dark: Journal of a Film Critic, 1968–69* (New York, NY: Random House, 1969), 177–178. Michael Anderegg, "Hollywood and Vietnam: John Wayne and Jane Fonda as Discourse," in *Inventing Vietnam: The War in Film and Television*, ed. Michael Anderegg (Philadelphia, PA: Temple University Press, 1991), 24–26.

13 Erik Broske, "Green Beret Commando Who Blasted '1,000-Cong Forest,'" *Male*, April 1967, 16. For insights into GIs' reactions to the film, see Gustav Hasford, *The Short-Timers* (New York, NY: Harper & Row, 1979), 31–32, 135. Propaganda in Bernard F. Dick, *The Screen Is Red: Hollywood, Communism, and the Cold War* (Jackson, MS: University Press of Mississippi, 2016), 221. Gary Cross recalls mocking the "cardboard cowboy John Wayne" and the film in *Men to Boys: The Making of Modern Immaturity* (New York, NY: Columbia University Press, 2008), 121.

14 Stocking priorities and categories in Minutes of Meeting of Joint Vietnam Regional Exchange Council, 29 April 1969, Entry P1691, Box 3, RG472, NARA. Sea-vans and distribution points in Joint Vietnam Regional Exchange Council Agenda, 18 May 1970, Entry 1691, Box 9, RG472, NARA. Good taste in Enclosure, Minutes of Meeting of Joint Vietnam Regional Exchange Council, 23 November 1970, *Ibid.*

15 Copies in Minutes of Meeting of Joint Vietnam Regional Exchange Council, 29 April 1969, NARA. In April 1969, the monthly copies sold included *Cavalier*, 17,970; *Climax*, 13,782; *All Man*, 13,489; *Stag*, 12,219; and *For Men Only*, 12,035. The Star Far East Corporation ordered 1,250,000 copies of periodicals monthly. VRE Council Minutes, 20 February 1970, Entry 1691, Box 9, RG472, NARA. Star Far East ultimately lost its contract for abusing its privileges. See Report of Investigation Concerning Star Far East

Corporation, MACV IG Investigating Division, Reports of Investigation, Box 48, RG472, NARA; and Meredith H. Lair, *Armed with Abundance: Consumerism & Soldiering in the Vietnam War* (Chapel Hill, NC: The University of North Carolina Press, 2011), 171–172. On *Playboy* being coveted by soldiers, see Amber Batura, "The Cult of Playboy: Exploring *Playboy* Magazine's Popularity in the Vietnam War," in *The Vietnam War in Popular Culture, Volume 1, During the War*, ed. Ron Milam (Santa Barbara, CA: Praeger, 2017), 246.

16 Trash in memo cover note, USARV DCG, Collection of Magazines in Post Exchanges file, Entry P1691, Box 32, RG472, NARA. Survey in Minutes of Meeting of Joint Vietnam Regional Exchange Council, 15 June 1972, Entry P1691, Box 33, RG472, NARA. Of note, memoirists themselves used the term "girlie magazine" as well. See James R. McDonough, *Platoon Leader* (Novato, CA: Presidio, 1985), 69.

17 Low quality in Report of Investigation Concerning Allegations against the Star Far East Corporation, 3 April 1970, MACVJ14 Administrative Branch General Records, NND 957718, Box 3, RG472, NARA; and Computation of Percentage of Girlie and Low Quality Magazines, 24 March 1970, *Ibid.* KRE data in 1LT A. M. Shiffert, Request for Assistance, 5 December 1969, *Ibid.* Clearly, the magazines were ubiquitous. Arlene Eisen's *Women and Revolution in Viet Nam* (London: Zed Books, 1984) includes a photograph of Vietnamese children, en route to a "strategic hamlet," poring over American magazines showcasing liquor ads and blonde models, p. 48.

18 "Out of This World," *Stag*, December 1961, 48. Steven Hughes, "'Copter War on the Phantom Vietcong Guerrillas," *Brigade*, March 1963, 19, 21, 49.

19 Browne quoted in Andrew J. Huebner, *The Warrior Image: Soldiers in American Culture from the Second World War to the Vietnam Era* (Chapel Hill, NC: The University of North Carolina Press, 2008), 179. Dave R. Palmer seemed to agree, suggesting the "very nature of the war" in Vietnam was different than the past. *Summons of the Trumpet: U.S.–Vietnam in Perspective* (San Rafael, CA: Presidio Press, 1978), xxi. Richard Gallagher, "Our Secret Win-the-War Weapons for Vietnam," *Stag*, August 1966, 38.

20 Erik Broske, "King of Our Heroic Cong-Busting 'Tunnel Rats,'" *Male*, July 1966, 36. Richard Gallagher, "Newest Miracle Weapons," *Stag*, March 1968, 39, 41. On tigers, see "Out of This World," *Stag*, April 1968, 50.

21 Disorienting in Julian Smith, *Looking Away: Hollywood and Vietnam* (New York, NY: Charles Scribner's Sons, 1975), 22; and Loren Baritz, *Backfire: A History of How American Culture Led Us into Vietnam and Made Us Fight the Way We Did* (New York, NY: William Morrow and Company, 1985), 19. James Webb, *Fields of Fire* (Englewood Cliffs, NJ: Prentice-Hall, 1978), 167. On soldiers not understanding why they were fighting, see Christian G. Appy, *Working-Class War: American Combat Soldiers and Vietnam* (Chapel Hill, NC: The University of North Carolina Press, 1993), 209.

22 Colin Brady, "My Six Months with the Guerrilla Women of Viet Nam," *Complete Man's Magazine*, August 1957, 26. Philippe de Pirey, "Combat Diary of a Paratroop Commando," *For Men Only*, November 1958, 16. Bud Riley, "We Sold Them Out," *Battle Cry*, October 1957, 14.

23 "Inside for Men," *Male*, February 1965, 8, 44. On the inner workings of the Hanoi Politburo during this time period, see Lien-Hang T. Nguyen, *Hanoi's War: An*

International History of the War for Peace in Vietnam (Chapel Hill, NC: The University of North Carolina Press, 2012). Daniel Ellsberg believed the United States persisted in Vietnam not because victory seemed possible but because the situation was so bleak that all US leaders could do was hang on in the hope that the war might be ended on favorable terms. See "The Quagmire Myth and the Stalemate Machine," *Public Policy* (Spring 1971): 217–274.

24 Gung ho in Mark Bowden, *Hué 1968: A Turning Point of the American War in Vietnam* (New York, NY: Atlantic Monthly Press, 2017), 72. Ridicule in Ray Bourgeois Zimmerman, "Gruntspeak: Masculinity, Monstrosity and Discourse in Hasford's *The Short-Timers*," *American Studies* Vol. 40, No. 1 (Spring 1999): 77; and Christian G. Appy, *American Reckoning: The Vietnam War and Our National Identity* (New York, NY: Viking, 2015), 144. On earlier accounts, where Wayne was a hero, see Ron Kovic, *Born on the Fourth of July* (New York, NY: Akashic, 1976, 2005), 65.

25 Popcorn in Micheal Clodfelter, *Mad Minutes and Vietnam Months: A Soldier's Memoir* (Jefferson, NC: McFarland, 1988), 78. Out the window from Josh Cruze, quoted in Willenson, 61.

26 W. D. Ehrhart, *Vietnam–Perkasie: A Combat Marine Memoir* (Jefferson, NC: McFarland, 1983), 27. Department of Defense study in Thomas C. Thayer, *War without Fronts: The American Experience in Vietnam* (Annapolis, MD: Naval Institute Press, 1985, 2016), 45.

27 Veteran Gerry Schooler quoted in Eric M. Bergerud, *Red Thunder, Tropic Lightning: The World of a Combat Division in Vietnam* (Boulder, CO: Westview Press, 1993), 104. Infantry schools in "Inside for Men," *Male*, February 1965, 44. On some policymakers, like Roger Hilsman, advocating for Americans to "adopt the tactics of the guerrilla," see Robert D. Dean, *Imperial Brotherhood: Gender and the Making of Cold War Foreign Policy* (Amherst, MA: University of Massachusetts Press, 2001), 58–59. VC regaining influence in Kevin M. Boylan, *Losing Binh Dinh: The Failure of Pacification and Vietnamization, 1969–1971* (Lawrence, KS: University Press of Kansas, 2016), 232; and John Prados, *The Hidden History of the Vietnam War* (Chicago, IL: Ivan R. Dee, 1995), 120.

28 "Stag Confidential," *Stag*, December 1966, 42.

29 H. R. Adams, "Banzai at Tay Ninh," *Saga*, April 1967, 14. Emile C. Schurmacher, "Vietnam's Hero from Hell," *Stag*, June 1967, 30. Operation results from George L. MacGarrigle, *Taking the Offensive: October 1966 to October 1967* (Washington, DC: Center of Military History, 1998), 55–59. See also Larry Cable, *Unholy Grail: The US and the Wars in Vietnam, 1965–8* (New York, NY: Routledge, 1991), 67–68; and Shelby L. Stanton, *The Rise and Fall of an American Army: U.S. Ground Forces in Vietnam, 1965–1973* (Novato, CA: Presidio, 1985), 107–109. Even when the war in Vietnam was locked in stalemate, magazines highlighted World War II, sharing the "truth" about the Battle of the Bulge and how 1,100 green American paratroopers "smashed Hitler's last bid for victory." Sylvester Fourre, "The Truth about the Battle of the Bulge," *Man's Conquest*, December 1968, 20.

30 Malcolm W. Browne, "Hell in the Highlands," *True*, January 1966, 54. Serpents from Charles M. Purcell in *Winning Hearts and Minds: War Poems by Vietnam Veterans*, eds. Larry Rottman, Jan Barry, and Basil T. Paquet (New York, NY: McGraw-Hill, 1972), 17. Types

of traps in Ed Hymoff, "Vietnam: The Booby Trap War," *Stag*, November 1966, 39. See also "Stag Confidential," *Stag*, January 1968, 43; and Lou Prato, "They Live One Second from Hell," *Saga*, February 1967, 28.

31 "For Your Information," *Stag*, November 1967, 38. On twenty-five percent, see Lawrence A. Tritle, *From Melos to My Lai: War and Survival* (New York, NY: Routledge, 2000), 140. 1st Infantry Division soldier David Ross quoted in Al Santoli, *Everything We Had: An Oral History of the Vietnam War by Thirty-Three American Soldiers Who Fought It* (New York, NY: Random House, 1981), 49. Of note, William Calley's company sustained twenty-eight casualties, all from mines and booby traps, in the three months before the My Lai massacre. Michael Bilton and Kevin Sim, *Four Hours in My Lai* (New York, NY: Viking, 1992), 93. No sense of triumph in Appy, *Working-Class War*, 189.

32 On "gooks" in Korea, see Bill Coscarelli, "Bloody Hill 676!," *True War Stories*, January–February 1953, 10; and Alonzo Norrbom, "We Kissed the Gooks Good-By!," *Ibid.*, 16. Cut to pieces in Bryce Walton, "You Don't Count for a Damn!," *Battle Cry*, December 1955, 31, 46. Lt. Wade C. Young, "I Flew the Suicide Run in Gook Alley," *Real Combat Stories*, April 1964, 14. On racism during the Korean War, see Bobby A. Wintermute and David J. Ulbrich, *Race and Gender in Modern Western Warfare* (Boston, MA: De Gruyter, 2019), 279; and Melinda L. Pash, *In the Shadow of the Greatest Generation: The Americans Who Fought the Korean War* (New York, NY: New York University Press, 2012), 112. In S. L. A. Marshall's tale of the Korean War, Chinese attackers yell "Banzai!" as they attack American positions. *The River and the Gauntlet: Defeat of the Eighth Army by the Chinese Communist Forces, November, 1950, in the Battle of the Chongchon River, Korea* (New York, NY: Time Incorporated, 1953), 71, 153.

33 Bill Donovan, "A Commie Scalp for Injun Joe," *Battle Cry*, August 1962, 32. See also Mickey Fredericks, "Scalps for Uncle Sam," *Battle Attack*, May 1957, 12. The tagline read when "Injuns went on the warpath, the Axis bit the dust!" Stevens, 37. Mythic race-enemies in Richard Slotkin, *Gunfighter Nation: The Myth of the Frontier in Twentieth-Century America* (Norman, OK: University of Oklahoma Press, 1998), 319. See also Richard Drinnon, *Facing West: The Metaphysics of Indian-Hating and Empire-Building* (Minneapolis, MN: University of Minnesota Press, 1980), 75. On racist perceptions of Japanese, see John W. Dower, "Race, Language, and War in Two Cultures: World War II in Asia," in *The War in American Culture: Society and Consciousness during World War II*, eds. Lewis A. Erenberg and Susan E. Hirsch (Chicago, IL: The University of Chicago Press, 1996), 173–184.

34 On combat-to-support ratios and post amenities, see Lair, *Armed with Abundance*, 6, 33, 90. In World War II, twenty-five percent of the sixteen million called to serve never left the United States, and less than fifty percent overseas were ever in a battle zone. Michael C. C. Adams, *The Best War Ever: America and World War II* (Baltimore, MD: The Johns Hopkins University Press, 1994), 70. "Indian country" in Michael Stephenson, *The Last Full Measure: How Soldiers Die in Battle* (New York, NY: Crown Publishers, 2012), 360.

35 Chuck McCarthy, "What Are Your Chances of Fighting in Vietnam?," *Bluebook*, August 1967, 17–19.

36 On REMFs, see George C. Herring, "Vietnam Remembered," *The Journal of American History* Vol. 73, No. 1 (June 1986): 157. Officer Tom Lynch quoted in Yvonne Honeycutt

Baldwin and John Ernst, "In the Valley: The Combat Infantryman and the Vietnam War," in *The War That Never Ends: New Perspectives on the Vietnam War*, eds. David L. Anderson and John Ernst (Lexington, KY: The University Press of Kentucky, 2007), 319.

37 Leon Lazarus, "Our Rugged Vietnam Combat Construction Boss," *For Men Only*, September 1966, 17. George Powers, "Fourth Cong Ambush Ahead. Am Crashing Through," *Male*, March 1967, 22. On problems finding meaning, see Lair, 44.

38 General quoted in Cincinnatus, *Self-Destruction: The Disintegration and Decay of the United States Army during the Vietnam Era* (New York, NY: W. W. Norton & Company, 1981), 110. Sherrod, "Notes on a Monstrous War," 23. One marine sergeant recalled being "at the mercy of the VC." Otto J. Lehrack, *No Shining Armor: The Marines at War in Vietnam, an Oral History* (Lawrence, KS: University Press of Kansas, 1992), 29. Mark Bradley argues that poor assessments of the Vietnamese were the norm among Americans in the 1940s and 1950s, even after the French defeat in 1954. "Slouching toward Bethlehem," 28–29.

39 Amazing soldier in "Men's Newsletter," *Men*, May 1962, 40.

40 Spike pits in "Inside for Men," *Male*, November 1962, 6. The article made sure to mention that these steel spikes were "always covered with human excrement." Offering a tank in "Inside for Men," *Male*, December 1962, 6.

41 "Men's Newsletter," *Men*, March 1963, 8.

42 Decoys in "Inside for Men," *Male*, March 1967, 8. Gary Alberts, "Hero of Viet Nam's 'Corpse Valley' Commandos," *True Action*, March 1967, 16. Tom Christopher, "Destroy the Red Butcher of the Mekong," *Male*, July 1967, 25.

43 Ho's KGB in Marv Vaugh, "Outpost in Hell for the Fighting Skypilot," *Bluebook*, May 1966, 32, 34. On the Vietcong engaging in terror within a once-peaceful Vietnamese village, see Robert F. Dorr, "9 Assaults on Ira Dinh," *Man's Magazine*, September 1966, 16.

44 Phillip Knightley, "Vietnam 1954–1975," in *The American Experience in Vietnam: A Reader*, ed. Grace Sevy (Norman, OK: University of Oklahoma Press, 1989), 121. See also Ringnalda, *Fighting and Writing the Vietnam War*, 20. On racism being just below the surface at the policy level, see Thomas Borstelmann, *The Cold War and the Color Line: American Race Relations in the Global Arena* (Cambridge, MA: Harvard University Press, 2001), 191. Pint-sized in Doug Kennedy, "John Groth's Viet Nam," *True*, November 1967, 38.

45 Not fighting in the open in "Stag Confidential," *Stag*, January 1967, 8. Captain Dave Ramsey quoted in Lehrack, 67. VC units surrounded in Donald Duncan, "The Whole Thing Was a Lie!," *Ramparts*, February 1966, 22.

46 William Tuohy, "He Waits to Kill," *True*, May 1968, 32, 35, 72. On the need to both dehumanize and feminize the enemy, see Jacqueline A. Lawson, "'She's a Pretty Woman ... for a Gook': The Misogyny of the Vietnam War," *The Journal of American Culture* Vol. 12, No. 3 (Fall 1989): 58.

47 Epithets in Robert Jay Lifton, *Home from the War: Vietnam Veterans: Neither Victims nor Executioners* (New York, NY: Simon & Schuster, 1973), 310; Lewis B. Puller, Jr., *Fortunate Son* (New York, NY: Grove Weidenfeld, 1991), 129; and Guillermo Alvidrez in *Soldados: Chicanos in Viet Nam*, ed. Charley Trujillo (San José, CA: Chusma House, 1990), 65. Worth a fuck in Ehrhart, 62.

48 Michael Willis quoted in Eric M. Bergerud, *The Dynamics of Defeat: The Vietnam War in Hau Nghia Province* (Boulder, CO: Westview Press, 1991), 227. National cause in Robert K. Brigham, *ARVN: Life and Death in the South Vietnamese Army* (Lawrence, KS: University Press of Kansas, 2006), 121. For a similarly nuanced view, see Nathalie Huynh Chau Nguyen, *South Vietnamese Soldiers: Memories of the Vietnam War and After* (Santa Barbara, CA: Praeger, 2016).

49 Scared rabbits in Steven Hughes, "'Copter War on the Phantom Vietcong Guerrillas," *Brigade*, March 1963, 18, 48. See also Hasford, *The Short-Timers*, 69. On extending the war into North Vietnam, see "Stag Confidential," *Stag*, August 1964, 45.

50 Bill Francois, "Sheer Hell in Vietnam," *Man's Magazine*, June 1965, 16. The ARVN also seemingly lacked aggressiveness in battle. "U.S. advisors say that the trouble with the average Viet Nam troop is that he'd rather use artillery than go in and fight." "Inside for Men," *Male*, February 1965, 44. For a version of scapegoating, see George McTurnan Kahin and John Wilson Lewis, *The United States in Vietnam*, rev. ed. (New York, NY: The Dial Press, 1967, 1969), 363.

51 Thankless in "Stag Confidential," *Stag*, November 1967, 6. Desertions in "Inside for Men," *Male*, July 1966, 40. No initiative in "Stag Confidential," *Stag*, April 1968, 6. "Stag Confidential," *Stag*, June 1967, 6. The piece noted how the "French always claimed that the Northerners had more energy, intelligence."

52 Malcolm W. Browne, "Why South Viet Nam's Army Won't Fight," *True*, October 1967, 31. This compared with the "hand-to-hand action" undertaken by Korean troops, who apparently fared better than the ARVN. John Groth, "The ROKs Take a Hill," *Climax*, March 1953, 34. Marv Koeppel, "The Thousand to One Break-out of the Green Berets," *Man's Conquest*, December 1968, 72–73. Beckwith actually would say, "I'd give anything to have two hundred VC under my command." In Tom Engelhardt, *The End of Victory Culture: Cold War America and the Disillusioning of a Generation* (Amherst, MA: University of Massachusetts Press, 2007), 222.

53 General Bruce Palmer quoted in Willenson, *The Bad War*, 109. On Kit Carson Scouts, see Lewis W. Walt, *Strange War, Strange Strategy: A General's Report on Vietnam* (New York, NY: Funk & Wagnalls, 1970), 43–47.

54 Henry I. Kurtz, "Brigade of the Damned," *Male*, February 1968, 26, 64–67.

55 Reluctant warriors in Lieutenant General William Fulton, quoted in Harry Maurer, ed., *Strange Ground: Americans in Vietnam, 1945–1975, an Oral History* (New York, NY: Henry Holt and Company, 1989), 465. Presidential Unit Citations in Robert L. Tonsetic, *Forsaken Warriors: The Story of an American Advisor with the South Vietnamese Rangers and Airborne, 1970–71* (Philadelphia, PA: Casemate, 2009), 27. Hit-and-run in Sgt. Jim Briggs, "Combat Diary of a Yank with Viet Nam's 7th Rangers," *Man's World*, June 1963, 16.

56 Photo in "Men in Action," *Male*, March 1965, 40. For a comparable story on a soldier who seemed to be little more than a cold-hearted killer, see Charles Keeler, Jr., "Our One-Man Army Who Has Killed 1,054 Viet Cong," *For Men Only*, August 1966, 20. 44th Battalion in Ed Hyde, "The Bloody Devils Who Fight Saigon's War," *Bluebook*, May 1966, 46. Doubts in Tonsetic, 163.

57 On criticisms of the GVN, see Frances FitzGerald, *Fire in the Lake: The Vietnamese and the Americans in Vietnam* (Boston, MA: Little, Brown and Company, 1972), 314, 322; and Bergerud, *The Dynamics of Defeat*, 221. Propaganda war in "Last Minute Memo for Men," *For Men Only*, August 1966, 11. On the impact of this, see James Walker Trullinger, Jr., *Village at War: An Account of Revolution in Vietnam* (New York, NY: Longman, 1980), 163. Blockade in "Stag Confidential," *Stag*, August 1966, 8. According to "Stag Confidential," Marines who "distributed nearly a million pounds of soap to the Viet population, saw almost all of it reappear on the black market." *Stag*, June 1967, 6.

58 "Letters to the Editor," *Man's Illustrated*, January 1965, 8. On problems selling the war back home, see Karl H. Purnell, "He's Gen. Ky's Own Executioner," *True*, July 1968, 92.

59 Charles Forbes, "Naked Terror of the Viet Cong Butchers," *Man's Action*, May 1966, 40–43. Good and bad Asians in Susan A. Brewer, *Why America Fights: Patriotism and War Propaganda from the Philippines to Iraq* (New York, NY: Oxford University Press, 2009), 179. On impulsive cruelty being the essence of "Indianness," see Engelhardt, 17.

60 "Stag Confidential," *Stag*, January 1967, 42.

61 Marine Philip Caputo, *A Rumor of War* (New York, NY: Holt, Rinehart and Winston, 1977), 228. Veteran quotes in Jonathan Shay, *Achilles in Vietnam: Combat Trauma and the Undoing of Character* (New York, NY: Atheneum, 1994), 105. Massacre in Nhã Ca, *Mourning Headband for Hue* (Bloomington, IN: Indiana University Press, 2014), xxxv, 111. On the Vietcong waging war in direct violation of the Geneva Conventions, see Telford Taylor, *Nuremberg and Vietnam: An American Tragedy* (Chicago, IL: Quadrangle Books, 1970), 136.

62 "Inside for Men," *Male*, January 1967, 42. On inability to gain a clear sense of the enemy picture, see: Mark Baker, *Nam: The Vietnam War in the Words of the Men and Women Who Fought There* (New York, NY: William Morrow and Company, 1981), 171; and Ringnalda, 38.

63 Incessantly from infantryman Michael Patrick Kelley in Bernard Edelman, "On the Ground: The US Experience," in *Rolling Thunder in a Gentle Land: The Vietnam War Revisited*, ed. Andrew Wiest (New York, NY: Osprey Publishing, 2006), 194. Enemy initiative in Thayer, *War without Fronts*, 91; and Bergerud, *The Dynamics of Defeat*, 229. Ambushes as inferior in Malcolm W. Browne, *The New Face of War*, rev. ed. (New York, NY: The Bobbs-Merrill Company, 1968), 164. Counterguerrilla tactics in Kurt Vaughn, "The GI Guerrilla Raid That Rocked the Viet Cong!," *Man's Illustrated*, July 1965, 16, 62. See also Marv Koeppel, "Green Hell Raiders," *Man's Illustrated*, January 1965, 43.

64 Gregory Patrick, "The Navy's Deadliest Viet Nam Shark-Man," *Male*, November 1967, 39. Richard Marcinko with John Weisman, *Rogue Warrior* (New York, NY: Pocket Books, 1992), 125, 167–168.

65 Fanatics and cut-throats in Allen Bernard, "Westerling: 'Butcher' of Indonesia," *Climax*, March 1953, 18. Nicholas J. Leslie, "Mau," *Ibid.*, 53.

66 If it's dead in Christian G. Appy, *Patriots: The Vietnam War Remembered from All Sides* (New York, NY: Viking, 2003), 356. Obscuring origins in Marilyn B. Young, *The Vietnam Wars, 1945–1990* (New York, NY: HarperCollins, 1991), 187. See also Trujillo, 17. For a more nuanced view of the enemy, see Konrad Kellen, *Conversations with Enemy Soldiers in Late*

1968/Early 1969: A Study of Motivation and Morale (Santa Monica, CA: Rand Corporation, 1970). For an example of warriors achieving honor because they had "killed more than 5,000 Nips" in Manila during World War II, see Richard Dennis, "Angels of the 11th Airborne," *True War*, September 1957, 30, 32.

67 Thomas E. Ricks, *The Generals: American Military Command from World War II to Today* (New York, NY: The Penguin Press, 2012), chapter 14, "The Organization Man's Army." For a supporting contemporary view, see H. R. Hays, *The Dangerous Sex: The Myth of Feminine Evil* (New York, NY: G. P. Putnam's Sons, 1964), 278. Physical violence in Rachel Woodward, "Warrior Heroes and Little Green Men: Soldiers, Military Training, and the Construction of Rural Masculinities," *Rural Sociology*, Vol. 65, No. 4 (December 2000): 643.

68 Glenn Infield, "'Gunfighter' Emerson: Toughest Paratroop Commando in Vietnam," *Stag*, January 1967, 16. For more, see Henry E. Emerson, interview by Jonathan Jackson, 2004, Senior Officer Oral History, US Army Military History Institute, Carlisle Barracks, PA. On Karch, see Marv Koeppel, "Bloodbath at Danang," *Man's Conquest*, December 1965, 42. Karch later voiced his respect for the Vietcong: "I thought that once they ran up against our first team they wouldn't stand and fight, but they did. I made a miscalculation." Joe Holley, "Gen. Frederick J. Karch, Who Led First Ground Troops into Vietnam, Dies at 91," *The Washington Post*, 25 May 2009.

69 On Moore, see G. G. Burke, "Is He the 'General Patton' We Need in Viet Nam?," *Male*, June 1966, 42. On Patton, see Jeff St. John, "Fighting C.O. of Viet Nam's Cong-Blasting 'Tankers,'" *Men*, December 1968, 20. For a similar tale, see Glenn Infield, "'Danger 79': Toughest General the Cong Ever Faced," *Stag*, April 1968, 16.

70 David Mars, "If There's a Dirty War Get Me Yarborough," *Male*, February 1964, 38, 82. On Abrams, see "Thunderbolt on Wheels," *Man's Illustrated*, January 1965, 35, 56. Seduced in Baker, *Nam*, 14. On need for heroes, see Laura Sjoberg, *Gender, War, and Conflict* (Malden, MA: Polity, 2014), 65. On worshipping World War II veterans, see Smith, *Looking Away*, 4. On the tactical consequences of this worship, see Guenter Lewy, *America in Vietnam* (New York, NY: Oxford University Press, 1978), 119.

71 Glenn Infield, "The Admiral Who Blasted the Reds at Tonkin Gulf," *Stag*, February 1965, 14, 80, 83. Glenn Infield, "'Brute' Krulak's 7-Day Suicide Decoy for Bougainville," *Stag*, March 1966, 22, 63.

72 Glenn Infield, "The Marine the Japs Couldn't Stop," *Man's Magazine*, September 1966, 33, 49.

73 Emile C. Schurmacher, "Showdown for Medal of Honor Hero 'Scooter' Burke," *Stag*, August 1966, 16. On Burke, see also David Hackworth and Julie Sherman, *About Face: The Odyssey of an American Warrior* (New York, NY: Touchstone, 1989), 125. Ed Hyde, "Three War Bullet-and-Bayonet Rampage," *Male*, January 1967, 17.

74 William D. Porter, "The Pilot Who Rode the Wind," *Man's Magazine*, September 1968, 18, 21.

75 Mechanical steeds in Harold B. Hersey, *Pulpwood Editor* (New York, NY: Frederick A. Stokes, 1937), 184. Rite of passage from Richard Olsen in Appy, *Patriots*, 63. Close friends in Stanley D. Rosenberg, "The Threshold of Thrill: Life Stories in the Skies over

Southeast Asia," in *Gendering War Talk*, eds. Miriam Cooke and Angela Woollacott (Princeton, NJ: Princeton University Press, 1993), 59.

76 Robert F. Dorr, "Trap in the Sky," *Man's Magazine*, July 1967, 16, 19. Robin Olds with Christina Olds and Ed Rasimus, *Fighter Pilot: The Memoirs of Legendary Ace Robin Olds* (New York, NY: St. Martin's Press, 2010), 78. Taylor quoted in James William Gibson, *The Perfect War: The War We Couldn't Lose and How We Did* (New York, NY: Vintage Books, 1986), 330. Loren Baritz argued that "Air power supposedly made Americans potent, especially against the primitives who dared to confront us." *Backfire*, 110.

77 Blast furnace in Robert F. Dorr, "Bomb Raid on Hanoi," *Man's Magazine*, September 1967, 38. See also Jacob Konrath, "The Air War ... Goes On!" *Real*, February 1967, 24. On Air Rescue pilots "defying concentrated Viet Cong fire near [a] landing zone," see Ed Hyde, "'Angels' in Choppers," *Bluebook*, October 1965, 16, 19.

78 Emile C. Schurmacher, "The 'Crazy Guy' Rescue of Major 'Jump' Myers," *Stag*, September 1966, 26. Neil Sheehan, "Flier, Safe, Thanks 'Crazy Guy,'" *New York Times*, 12 March 1966. Sheehan called Fisher's "a particularly daring act of heroism." For similar tales, see Robert L. LaPointe, *PJs in Vietnam: The Story of Air Rescue in Vietnam as Seen through the Eyes of Pararescuemen* (Anchorage, AK: Northern PJ Press, 2001); and John T. Correll, "A Habit of Heroism," *Air Force Magazine*, January 2010, 63–67.

79 Epton Ellington, "The Curvy Cutie Who Broke Up the Viet Cong Ambush of Death," *Man's Life*, January 1969, 15. On posing as rescuing knights, see Kristin L. Hoganson, *Fighting for American Manhood: How Gender Politics Provoked the Spanish–American and Philippine–American Wars* (New Haven, CT: Yale University Press, 1998), 56. On the significance of masculine men rescuing women, see Brenda M. Boyle, "Rescuing Masculinity: Captivity, Rescue and Gender in American War Narratives," *The Journal of American Culture* Vol. 34, No. 2 (June 2011): 154.

80 Ed Hyde, "Sgt. Jimmy Howard and His Unkillable Marines of Hill 488," *Male*, November 1966, 22–23. Dusting off in Huebner, *The Warrior Image*, 175. Despite such stories, at least a few US policymakers saw Vietnam as "an escalating military stalemate." In Palmer, *Summons of the Trumpet*, 108.

81 "Stag Confidential," *Stag*, February 1967, 10. Robert Sherrod reported in early 1967 that military psychologists were "underemployed." "Notes on a Monstrous War," 22.

82 Glenn Infield, "River War in Vietnam," *Man's Magazine*, October 1966, 38–41, 46. Infield called the hero, Lt. Harold Meyerkord, the "Hornblower" of the Delta. For similar stories, see George D. Robinson, "Black Beret Raid on the Viet Cong Nitro-Navy," *For Men Only*, April 1967, 14; and Tom Christopher, "Top Gun of Viet Nam's 'Napalm River' Death Raiders," *Male*, March 1967, 16. Details on this aspect of the conflict are in John Darrell Sherwood, *War in the Shallows: U.S. Navy Coastal and Riverine Warfare in Vietnam, 1965–1968* (Washington, DC: Naval History and Heritage Command, 2016). The wife of one riverboat patrolman said her husband suffered from seeing "so much violence and death and horrible things." In Julie Davidson, "Proud but haunted, ex-Vietnam riverboat gunner is remembered," *Seattle Post-Intelligencer*, 16 July 2006.

83 "Inside for Men," *Male*, January 1967, 42. Henry I. Kurtz, "Hand to Hand Combat in Vietnam," *Man's Magazine*, October 1967, 42, 90.

84 Westmoreland quoted in William Thomas Allison, *The Tet Offensive: A Brief History with Documents* (New York, NY: Routledge, 2008), 158. Irrelevance in Appy, *American Reckoning*, 177. See also Todd Gitlin, *The Sixties: Years of Hope, Days of Rage* (New York, NY: Bantam Books, 1993), 299.

85 Ed Hyde, "Mekong Marauders: Specialists in Creating Viet Cong Corpses," *Man's Conquest*, February 1968, 17. Emile C. Schurmacher, "Sgt. Jimmie Howard's 'Lost Platoon' Heroes," *Stag*, March 1968, 16. Caleb Kingston, "16-Medal 'No. 1' Cong Killer," *True Action*, May 1968, 20, 54.

86 Samuel Hynes argues that courage, and even heroism, were possible in Vietnam. *The Soldiers' Tale: Bearing Witness to Modern War* (New York, NY: Penguin, 1997), 214. On this allure for young teens, see Kovic, 81–82; and Jan Barry Crumb in Richard Stacewicz, *Winter Soldiers: An Oral History of the Vietnam Veterans Against the War* (New York, NY: Twayne, 1997), 29.

87 C. K. Winston, Jr., "Indiana Hot Rodder Who Became Our Youngest, Toughest Cong Killer," *Male*, June 1967, 16. See also "Honored for Service: Crafton Enshrined in Military Hall of Fame," *Madison Courier*, 4 November 2017. Henry I. Kurtz, "The Brooklyn Lifeguard Who Saved His Men in Vietnam," *Man's Magazine*, September 1968, 37, 74.

88 Glenn Infield, "Ambushed by the Vietcong," *Man's Magazine*, July 1967, 36. For a similar tale, see Glenn Infield, "'Panhandle's' Ride-'Em Cowboy Charge to Save Co. C," *Stag*, February 1967, 19. As the story recounted, "U.S. Marines have always been known for their courage, especially when the chips are down," p. 86.

89 Tom Christopher, "Grenade-Duel at Cong Ravine," *True Action*, July 1967, 16, 81. See also Kurt Koeppel, "The Fantastic Danang Escape of the Marines Who Wouldn't Die," *Bluebook*, August 1967, 42, for one of the few articles with an African American protagonist, Sergeant James S. Dodson.

90 Emile C. Schurmacher, "Medal of Honor Medic the Cong Couldn't Stop," *Stag*, January 1968, 24, 71, 74. We might ask if Joel's story was less of a threat to the pulps' constructed narrative on martial manhood because he was a medic and not a combat soldier. For an overview, see James E. Westheider, *The African American Experience in Vietnam: Brothers in Arms* (Boulder, CO: Rowman & Littlefield, 2008).

91 On the "troubled army" narrative, see: Huebner, 231–232; David Cortright, *Soldiers in Revolt: The American Military Today* (Garden City, NY: Anchor Press, 1975), 10; and Gabriel Kolko, *Anatomy of a War: Vietnam, the United States, and the Modern Historical Experience* (New York, NY: Pantheon Books, 1985), 363–367.

92 Professional troops in "Stag Confidential," *Stag*, December 1966, 6. Marijuana in "Stag Confidential," *Stag*, March 1968, 43. For a more nuanced view of drug use, see Jeremy Kuzmarov, *The Myth of the Addicted Army: Vietnam and the Modern War on Drugs* (Amherst, MA: University of Massachusetts Press, 2009), 38–43. On post-Tet skepticism, see Peter S. Kindsvatter, *American Soldiers: Ground Combat in the World Wars, Korea, and Vietnam* (Lawrence, KS: University Press of Kansas, 2003), 146.

93 *Time* quoted in Michael J. Allen, *Until the Last Man Comes Home: POWs, MIAs, and the Unending Vietnam War* (Chapel Hill, NC: The University of North Carolina Press, 2009),

66. William C. Westmoreland, *A Soldier Reports* (Garden City, NY: Doubleday & Company, 1976), 373.

94 Edward Payson Brown, Jr., "My Escape from a Viet Cong Torture Camp," *Saga*, August 1965, 52. Joseph E. Brown, "Lieutenant Klusmann's Amazing Escape," *Saga*, March 1965, 29, 31. Fendall W. Yerxa, "Captured U.S. Airman Escapes from Pro-Communists in Laos," *New York Times*, 2 September 1964. Resistance and escape narratives in Robert C. Doyle, *Voices from Captivity: Interpreting the American POW Narrative* (Lawrence, KS: University Press of Kansas, 1994), 33.

95 Hal D. Steward, "Navy Ace Who Blasted His Way Out of The Cong's 'Body Rot' Jungle," *Man's World*, February 1967, 16, 68. See also William Harris, "Escape from a Viet Cong Prison Camp," *Man's Magazine*, February 1967, 18. Bruce Henderson, *Hero Found: The Greatest POW Escape of the Vietnam War* (New York, NY: HarperCollins, 2010), 26, 73. For a similar story, see S/Sgt. George Lockey, "My 72 Days of Hell in the Cong's Fortress of Daggers . . . .," *True Action*, January 1967, 17.

96 On the politicization of the POW issue, see: Allen, 15–16, 29; H. Bruce Franklin, *Vietnam and Other American Fantasies* (Amherst, MA: University of Massachusetts Press, 2000), 178; and Brewer, *Why America Fights*, 219. Central war aim in Slotkin, *Gunfighter Nation*, 621. Robinson Risner, *The Passing of the Night: My Seven Years as a Prisoner of the North Vietnamese* (New York, NY: Random House, 1973), 76. Of the POWs, *Stag* noted that there was "no evidence that one of them has ever denounced war and country. Nor is it likely one ever will." "For Your Information," April 1968, 38. For a different rendering, see George E. Smith, *P.O.W.: Two Years with the Vietcong* (Berkeley, CA: Ramparts Press, 1971).

97 On *Playboy* and the pulps' prowar stance, see Max Allan Collins and George Hagenauer, *Men's Adventure Magazines in Postwar America* (London: Taschen, 2004), 370. Timetable in "Stag Confidential," *Stag*, June 1967, 6. When criticisms did arise, they usually focused on the Saigon government. As an example, see Clement Haney, "That Dirty Mess in Vietnam!," *Real*, February 1964, 14.

98 Faggots in Mark Gerzon, *A Choice of Heroes: The Changing Faces of American Manhood* (Boston, MA: Houghton Mifflin, 1992), 46. See also Michael S. Foley, *Confronting the War Machine: Draft Resistance during the Vietnam War* (Chapel Hill, NC: The University of North Carolina Press, 2003), 183. Vet Micheal Clodfelter quoted in Jeff Loeb, "Childhood's End: Self Recovery in the Autobiography of the Vietnam War," *American Studies* Vol. 37, No. 1 (Spring 1996): 111.

99 On Ali, see Benjamin T. Harrison, "The Muhammad Ali Draft Case and Public Debate on the Vietnam War," *Peace Research* Vol. 33, No. 2 (November 2001): 69–86. Colts in Mitchell K. Hall, *Crossroads: American Popular Culture and the Vietnam Generation* (Lanham, MD: Rowman & Littlefield, 2005), 107. Bruce Springsteen, *Born to Run* (New York, NY: Simon & Schuster, 2016), 99–103. On Baez and Fonda, see Avital H. Bloch, "Joan Baez: A Singer and Activist," and Barbara L. Tischler, "'Hanoi Jane' Lives: The 1960s Legacy of Jane Fonda," in *Impossible to Hold: Women and Culture in the 1960s* (New York, NY: New York University Press, 2005), 126–151, 241–258. Fonda as a "dangerous

female" in Carol Burke, *Camp All-American, Hanoi Jane, and the High-and-Tight* (Boston, MA: Beacon Press, 2004), 186. For a story on the courage not to go to war, see Jack Todd, *Desertion: In the Time of Vietnam* (Boston, MA: Houghton Mifflin, 2001).

100 Ray Lunt, "The Bums Who Buy Their Way Out of the Draft – and the Creeps Who Help Them Do It," *Male*, August 1966, 31. Bill Surface, "Draft Dodging Underground," *Saga*, February 1967, 21. Edward Hymoff, "The 1967 Draft Scandal and You," *Man's Illustrated*, March 1967, 24.

101 Ray Lunt, "Let's Slap Down 'Snotty Brat' Entertainers Who Smear America," *Male*, January 1967, 24. Don King, "Draft Deferments: The Inside Story of Who Gets Them," *Bluebook*, August 1968, 16.

102 Ducking service in "Stag Confidential," *Stag*, April 1968, 6. Sergeant Jack Smith quoted in Andrew E. Hunt, *The Turning: A History of Vietnam Veterans Against the War* (New York, NY: New York University Press, 1999), 113.

103 GI counterculture in Cortright, *Soldiers in Revolt*, 25 On the warrior myth and its relation to the "gendered ideology that defined it," see Heather Marie Stur, "Men's and Women's Liberation: Challenging Military Culture after the Vietnam War," in *Integrating the US Military: Race, Gender, and Sexual Orientation since World War II*, eds. Douglas Walter Bristol, Jr. and Heather Marie Stur (Baltimore, MD: The Johns Hopkins University Press, 2017), 148. Percentage in Stacewicz, *Winter Soldiers*, 3. On the underground newspaper *Overseas Weekly* being "loaded with sex, crime and corruption," see Al Stump, "A GI Newspaper the Brass Can't Kill," *True*, July 1967, 52–54. The story alleged that a "vast epidemic of corruption, waste and theft was sweeping Viet Nam," p. 88. PFC hoping to get to Vietnam in "Truely Yours," *True*, June 1967, 2.

104 "Stag Confidential," *Stag*, November 1967, 6. For a similar critique on political considerations, see Malcolm W. Browne, "The New Face of Censorship," *True*, April 1967, 38. Amber Batura, "The *Playboy* Way: *Playboy* Magazine, Soldiers, and the Military in Vietnam," *Journal of American–East Asian Relations* Vol. 22, No. 3 (October 2015): 233.

105 Overriding in US, Grant Sharp, *Strategy for Defeat: Vietnam in Retrospect* (San Rafael, CA: Presidio Press, 1978), 270. Restraints and forfeiting the initiative in Palmer, *Summons of the Trumpet*, 116, 133. Micromanagement in Douglas Porch, *Counterinsurgency: Exposing the Myths of the New Way of War* (New York, NY: Cambridge University Press, 2013), 290.

106 Westmoreland, *A Soldier Reports*, 406. Hands tied in Susan Jeffords, "Telling the War Story," in *It's Our Military, Too! Women and the U.S. Military*, ed. Judith Hicks Stiehm (Philadelphia, PA: Temple University Press, 1996), 231. Edward Hymoff, "The Ultimate Infantry Weapon the Pentagon Won't Use to Win in Vietnam," *Bluebook*, May 1966, 24. For a similar theme, see Kurt Vaughn, "Vietnam Bloodbath – The Glory and the Despair," *Man's Epic*, November 1967, 17. The article noted how the ARVN soldiers were fighting with "second hand weapons."

107 Murky warrior image in Huebner, 237. Unpopular wars in "Stag Confidential," *Stag*, April 1968, 6. Intelligence failure in Frank Winters, "Vietnam Pearl Harbor," *Saga*, December 1968, 14. For a similar story on the inability to capture COSVN, see Mike Scott, "The Pentagon Foul-Up That Threatens Our Intelligence Network," *Man's Illustrated*, August 1971, 26, 62.

108 Specialist James Martin Davis quoted in Kindsvatter, *American Soldiers*, 50. Percentages in Adams, *The Best War Ever*, 95. "Stag Confidential," *Stag*, September 1966, 6.

109 Irrational in Susan Jeffords, *The Remasculinization of America: Gender and the Vietnam War* (Bloomington, IN: Indiana University Press, 1989), 111. Malcolm W. Browne, "Hell in the Highlands, *True*, January 1966, 54–56. "Stag Confidential," *Stag*, November 1966, 6. The piece noted, however, that such an outlay of ammunition was "far from a waste and acts as a good protective shield for our own troops." On satisfaction of being in combat, see Kindsvatter, 184.

110 Caputo, *A Rumor of War*, 128. "Stag Confidential," *Stag*, November 1967, 6.

111 "Inside for Men," *Male*, July 1961, 36. Schell quoted in *From Nuremberg to My Lai*, ed. Jay W. Baird (Lexington, MA: D. C. Heath, 1972), 237. On visions of the Orient, see Sheridan Prasso, *The Asian Mystique: Dragon Ladies, Geisha Girls, and Our Fantasies of the Exotic Orient* (New York, NY: Public Affairs, 2005), xi, 29, 49. Other world from Oliver Stone, quoted in Appy, *Patriots*, 253.

112 Cover illustration, *Man's Illustrated*, March 1966. Mort Künstler, cover illustration, *Male*, March 1967. Cover illustration, *Man's Epic*, March 1968.

113 Magnin Tobar, "Follow the Curves to the Viet Cong House of Spies," *All Man*, October 1966, 28, 30–31, 44. On translating foreign aspects of the Cold War, see Christina Klein, *Cold War Orientalism: Asia in the Middlebrow Imagination, 1945–1961* (Berkeley, CA: University of California Press, 2003), 63.

114 "Flashes for Men," *Man's Illustrated*, March 1962, 8. On fabricated representations and the construction of knowledge, see Maryam Khalid, *Gender, Orientalism, and the "War on Terror": Representation, Discourse, and Intervention in Global Politics* (London: Routledge, 2017), 4–5.

115 "Deadline: Man's World," *Man's World*, June 1963, 24. On "Voodoo in Vietnam," see "It's a Strange World," *Male*, June 1966, 48. On American GIs not being prepared for actual combat conditions, see Appy, *Working-Class War*, 113; and Hugh McManners, *The Scars of War* (New York, NY: HarperCollins, 1993), 113.

116 Larsen quoted in Willenson, *The Bad War*, 115. For a similar assessment, see Fitzgerald, *Fire in the Lake*, 142, 370.

117 Greg Moffett, "With One Leg Shot Off – He's Still the Marines' Top Ace," *Male*, June 1966, 16. See also Chester J. Pach, Jr., "The War on Television: TV News, the Johnson Administration, and Vietnam," in *A Companion to the Vietnam War*, eds. Marilyn B. Young and Robert Buzzanco (Malden, MA: Blackwell, 2006), 455. For a similar story of pilot heroism, see Bob Strange, "The Desperate Chopper War of 'Iron Man' Barrett," *Man's Illustrated*, August 1971, 30. Even at this late stage of the war, there were opportunities for heroism. Of note, the article included no discussion of the larger stalemated war.

118 Kovic, *Born on the Fourth of July*, 132–133, 136.

119 Larry Powell, "Hottest Tease in Town," *Stag*, December 1966, 22, 84–85.

120 Richard Gallagher, "Who's the Guy in Judy's Bed?" *Stag*, September 1968, 22. For loose parallels on a wounded (paralyzed) veteran still able to provide sexual satisfaction, see Michael Selig, "Boys Will Be Men: Oedipal Drama in *Coming Home*," in *From Hanoi to Hollywood: The Vietnam War in American Film*, eds. Linda Dittmar and Gene Michaud

(New Brunswick, NJ: Rutgers University Press, 2000), 197. Ron Kovic's experiences differed greatly. See pp. 124–129.

121 Complicity from historian Frank Freidel, quoted in James Wright, *Enduring Vietnam: An American Generation and Its War* (New York, NY: St. Martin's Press, 2017), 317. For an example of vets being disappointed with their homecoming, see Kyle Longley, *Grunts: The American Combat Soldier in Vietnam* (Armonk, NY: M. E. Sharpe, 2008), 160.

122 Michael E. Ruane, "Traitors or Patriots? Eight Vietnam POWs Were Charged with Collaborating with the Enemy," *The Washington Post*, 22 September 2017. On Smith, see Donald Duncan, "The Prisoner," *Ramparts*, September 1969, 51–56. Son Ty in Doyle, *Voices from Captivity*, 226–227. Operational success in Bruce Palmer, Jr., *The 25-Year War: America's Military Role in Vietnam* (Lexington, KY: The University Press of Kentucky, 1984), 161.

123 Sergeant Nicholas Francic quoted in James P. Sterba, "Close-up of the Grunt: The Hours of Boredom, the Seconds of Terror," *New York Times*, 8 February 1970. Lieutenant Lee Ashburn quoted in Lehrack, *No Shining Armor*, 147. See also Longley, 82.

124 "Men in Action," *Male*, September 1966, 24.

125 Gary Alberts, "Hero of Viet Nam's 'Corpse Valley' Commandos," *True Action*, March 1967, 16–17. Grant Freeling, "Find and Destroy Hitler's Deathmaker Fortress," *Ibid.*, 20. "How Diane Keeps Men Out of Trouble," *Ibid.*, 22. Dr. Efrem Schoenhild, "25 Keys to Female Response," *Ibid.*, 32.

126 Fugitive in Smith, *Looking Away*, 70. On fratricides, see George Lepre, *Fragging: Why U.S. Soldiers Assaulted Their Officers in Vietnam* (Lubbock, TX: Texas Tech University Press, 2011).

127 "Sound Off," *Saga*, December 1968, 4. Negro fighting men in Appy, *American Reckoning*, 138. Racial tensions in Borstelmann, *The Cold War and the Color Line*, 213–219. On the Panthers and "military radicals," see James E. Westheider, *Fighting on Two Fronts: African Americans and the Vietnam War* (New York, NY: New York University Press, 1997), 143.

128 Lieutenant Ezell Ware, Jr. quoted in John Prados, ed., *In Country: Remembering the Vietnam War* (London: Ivan R. Dee, 2011), 129. Specialist Haywood T. Kirkland quoted in Wallace Terry, *Bloods: An Oral History of the Vietnam War by Black Veterans* (New York, NY: Random House, 1984), 103. On the press often using controversial terms when it came to black masculinity, see Huebner, 192. For an alternative view, see William M. King, "'Our Men in Vietnam': Black Media as a Source of the Afro-American Experience in Southeast Asia," *Vietnam Generation* Vol. 1, No. 2 (1989): 94–117.

129 Controlling the night in "Inside for Men," *Male*, June 1967, 6. Bombs in Duncan, "The Whole Thing Was a Lie!," 24. Spooklike from Private Richard Ogden in Kindsvatter, *American Soldiers*, 211.

130 Ehrhart, *Vietnam–Perkasie*, 247. NLF in David Hunt, *Vietnam's Southern Revolution: From Peasant Insurrection to Total War* (Amherst, MA: University of Massachusetts Press, 2008), 217. Lieutenant Colonel Garry Riggs quoted in Santoli, *Everything We Had*, 168.

131 Helplessness in Dean, *Imperial Brotherhood*, 55. Validated from John Hellmann, *American Myth and the Legacy of Vietnam* (New York, NY: Columbia University Press, 1986), 135. Surplus from Gloria Emerson, quoted in Myers, *Walking Point*, 31.

132 Lowering sights in Peter Goldman and Tony Fuller, *Charlie Company: What Vietnam Did to Us* (New York, NY: Ballantine Books, 1983), 8. Stover quoted in *Ibid.*, 105. One

marine argued that the military experience turned boys not into men, but into beasts. In Lifton, *Home from the War*, 140.

133 Noble cause in Appy, *American Reckoning*, 286. Impotence from Daniel Ellsberg, quoted in Baird, *From Nuremberg to My Lai*, 237.

134 The Committee of Concerned Asian Scholars, *The Indochina Story: A Fully Documented Account* (New York, NY: Pantheon Books, 1970), 105. Victim and vanquisher in Appy, *Working-Class War*, 191. Depressed in James R. Ebert, *A Life in a Year: The American Infantryman in Vietnam, 1965–1972* (Novato, CA: Presidio, 1993), 178.

135 Frequent occurrences in Committee of Concerned Asian Scholars, 105. Shapeless and disjointed in Lloyd B. Lewis, *The Tainted War: Culture and Identity in Vietnam War Narratives* (Westport, CT: Greenwood Press, 1985), 72. Andrew Wiest argues that many soldiers embraced an "impotent rage" due to their frustrations. See *The Boys of '67: Charlie Company's War in Vietnam* (New York, NY: Osprey, 2012), 142, 233.

CHAPTER 5

1 Carl Sherman, "Major Slavich's Top-Ace Frontline Air Force," *Stag*, January 1964, 30, 54.

2 What are we doing here in Robert Jay Lifton, *Home from the War: Vietnam Veterans: Neither Victims nor Executioners* (New York, NY: Simon & Schuster, 1973), 37. Gook syndrome in Cincinnatus, *Self-Destruction: The Disintegration and Decay of the United States Army during the Vietnam Era* (New York, NY: W. W. Norton & Company, 1981), 94. On the western genre and ambushes, see Tom Engelhardt, *The End of Victory Culture: Cold War America and the Disillusioning of a Generation* (Amherst, MA: University of Massachusetts Press, 2007), 194, 237. Tobias Wolff recalled that "We were all living on fantasies." In *Pharaoh's Army: Memories of the Lost War* (New York, NY: Alfred A. Knopf, 1994), 5.

3 VD in Robert L. Tonsetic, *Forsaken Warriors: The Story of an American Advisor with the South Vietnamese Rangers and Airborne, 1970–71* (Philadelphia, PA: Casemate, 2009), 23. Interviews by Carl D. Rogers in James R. Ebert, *A Life in a Year: The American Infantryman in Vietnam, 1965–1972* (Novato, CA: Presidio, 1993), 91. Presumably, many GIs assigned to support roles actually liked their relatively safe and comfortable assignments.

4 John C. Bahnsen, Jr., *American Warrior: A Combat Memoir of Vietnam* (New York, NY: Citadel Press, 2007), 51–52, 122. No doubt many officers believed that "any man who won't fuck, won't fight." In Christina S. Jarvis, *The Male Body at War: American Masculinity during World War II* (DeKalb, IL: Northern Illinois University Press, 2004), 82.

5 Softest skin in David V. Forrest, "The American Soldier and Vietnamese Women," *Sexual Behavior* (May 1972): 9. Sensual and flowers in Philip Marnais, *Saigon after Dark* (New York, NY: McFadden, 1967), 12–13. Weakness of flesh from Private Jack Smith, quoted in John Prados, ed., *In Country: Remembering the Vietnam War* (London: Ivan R. Dee, 2011), 29.

6 Fulbright quoted in Amanda Boczar, "Uneasy Allies: The Americanization of Sexual Policies in South Vietnam," *Journal of American–East Asian Relations* Vol. 22, No. 3 (2015): 188. Sodom in Marnais, 22. On expectations coming from cultural depictions, see Sheridan Prasso, *The Asian Mystique: Dragon Ladies, Geisha Girls, and Our Fantasies of the Exotic Orient* (New York, NY: Public Affairs, 2005), 8.

7 Meghana V. Nayak and Christopher Malone, "American Orientalism and American Exceptionalism: A Critical Rethinking of US Hegemony," *International Studies Review* Vol. 11, No. 2 (June 2009): 254–257. Anxiety and rage in Arthur Brittan, *Masculinity and Power* (New York, NY: Basil Blackwell, 1989), 44. For how these expectations differed from those of American women serving in Vietnam, see Jeanne Holm, *Women in the Military: An Unfinished Revolution*, rev. ed. (Novato, CA: Presidio Press, 1992), 213, 227.

8 On the concept of the "violence of rhetoric," see Wendy S. Hesford, "Rape Stories: Material Rhetoric and the Trauma of Representation," in *Haunting Violations: Feminist Criticism and the Crisis of the "Real,"* eds. Wendy S. Hesford and Wendy Kozol (Urbana, IL: University of Illinois Press, 2001), 20. Subservience in Roger Saint Martin O'Toole, "Sensuous Orient and Its Scrutable Dolls," *True,* July 1968, 42, 45. Reward and collateral damage in Nancy Farwell, "War Rape: New Conceptualizations and Responses," *Affilia,* Vol. 19, No. 4 (Winter 2004): 389. Farwell notes that accepting rape as an "inevitable aspects of armed conflict can lead to condoning it." Sexual coercion as normal in T. Walter Herbert, *Sexual Violence and American Manhood* (Cambridge, MA: Harvard University Press, 2002), 32. On the links between exposure to pornography and male propensities to commit rape, see Lee Ellis, *Theories of Rape: Inquiries into the Causes of Sexual Aggression* (New York, NY: Hemisphere, 1989), 39–40.

9 Meaningless war from Lieutenant Joseph W. Callaway in Prados, 122. Affirming masculinity in R. Wayne Eisenhart, "You Can't Hack It Little Girl: A Discussion of the Covert Psychological Agenda of Modern Combat Training," *Journal of Social Issues,* Vol. 31, No. 4 (1975): 17. Michael Herr spoke of the problems when "you pursue a fantasy until it becomes experience, and then afterward you can't handle the experience." *Dispatches* (New York, NY: Alfred A. Knopf, 1968, 1978), 68.

10 Definition of pacification in Gregory A. Daddis, *Westmoreland's War: Reassessing American Strategy in Vietnam* (New York, NY: Oxford University Press, 2014), 120–121. On control, see Martin G. Clemis, *The Control War: The Struggle for South Vietnam, 1968–1975* (Norman, OK: University of Oklahoma Press, 2018), 16–19. On advocating the use of "soft power" in military guidebooks, see Donna Alvah, *Unofficial Ambassadors: American Military Families Overseas and the Cold War, 1946–1965* (New York, NY: New York University Press, 2007), 50–53.

11 Lie detectors in "Inside for Men," *Male,* August 1964, 42. Boy in "Inside for Men," *Male,* March 1967, 8. Secretly despising in Ebert, *A Life in a Year,* 297.

12 Winnie Smith, *American Daughter Gone to War: On the Front Lines with an Army Nurse in Vietnam* (New York, NY: William Morrow and Company, 1992), 54, 114–115.

13 Politically unsophisticated from CIA officer Bruce Lawlor in Al Santoli, *Everything We Had: An Oral History of the Vietnam War by Thirty-Three American Soldiers Who Fought It* (New York, NY: Random House, 1981), 195. Grievances in Ethan B. Kapstein, "Success and Failure in Counterinsurgency Campaigns," *Journal of Cold War Studies* Vol. 19, No. 1 (Winter 2017): 133–135. Eliminating political competition in William R. Andrews, *The Village War: Vietnamese Communist Revolutionary Activities in Dinh Tuong Province, 1960–1964* (Columbia, MO: University of Missouri Press, 1973), 65. See also Donald Duncan, "The Whole Thing Was a Lie!," *Ramparts,* February 1966, 21.

14 "Stag's Big Picture," *Stag*, February 1967, 27. Doug Kennedy, "John Goth's Vietnam," *True*, November 1967, 41. Aspirations and communist intrigue in John Tirman, *The Deaths of Others: The Fate of Civilians in America's Wars* (New York, NY: Oxford University Press, 2011), 128. On terror, see Eric Norden, "American Atrocities in Vietnam," in *Crimes of War: A Legal, Political-Documentary and Psychological Inquiry into the Responsibility of Leaders, Citizens, and Soldiers for Criminal Acts of War*, eds. Richard A. Falk, Gabriel Kolko, and Robert Jay Lifton (New York, NY: Random House, 1971), 282. Fears of the people turning against the Americans in "Man's Bulletin," *True Action*, November 1968, 6.

15 Gentle warrior image in Heather Marie Stur, *Beyond Combat: Women and Gender in the Vietnam War Era* (New York, NY: Cambridge University Press, 2011), 143, 153. Stur notes how this image "relied in part on notions of Vietnamese primitivism," p. 158. Malcolm W. Browne, "Ghosts of Christmas Past," *True*, December 1965, 39. Medic Malcolm W. Browne, "Hell in the Highlands," *True*, January 1966, 54, 73. On modernization efforts, see Jonathan Nashel, "The Road to Vietnam: Modernization Theory in Fact and Fiction," in *Cold War Constructions: The Political Culture of United States Imperialism, 1945–1966*, ed. Christian G. Appy (Amherst, MA: The University of Massachusetts Press, 2000), 132–145.

16 "Battlefield Baby" in "What a World," *For Men Only*, September 1966, 46. Vaccines in "Stag's Big Picture," *Stag*, January 1968, 31. Joseph E. Brown, "Warriors on Bulldozers," *Argosy*, June 1967, 31. Captain Miles in Peter Arnett, "How We Built a Super Base on a Shifty Sandpile," *True*, June 1967, 42, 95. Building and destroying in James M. Carter, *Inventing Vietnam: The United States and State Building, 1964–1968* (New York, NY: Cambridge University Press, 2008), 183.

17 "Man's Bulletin," *True Action*, July 1967, 8. On paradoxes, see Richard Slotkin, *Gunfighter Nation: The Myth of the Frontier in Twentieth-Century America* (Norman, OK: University of Oklahoma Press, 1998), 460. Refugees in Michael McClintock, *Instruments of Statecraft: U.S. Guerrilla Warfare, Counterinsurgency, and Counterterrorism, 1940–1990* (New York, NY: Pantheon, 1992), 260; and Marilyn B. Young, *The Vietnam Wars, 1945–1990* (New York, NY: HarperCollins, 1991), 177. Exportable in H. W. Brands, *The Devil We Knew: Americans and the Cold War* (New York, NY: Oxford University Press, 1993), 94. Hearts and minds in Peter G. Bourne, *Men, Stress, and Vietnam* (Boston, MA: Little, Brown and Company, 1970), 3.

18 Peter Paret and John Shy, *Guerrillas in the 1960's* (New York, NY: Frederick A. Praeger, 1962), 48. Incommensurate in Eric Bergerud, "The Village War in Vietnam, 1965–1973," in *The Columbia History of the Vietnam War*, ed. David L. Anderson (New York, NY: Columbia University Press, 2011), 283. Never trust anybody in Kennedy, "John Goth's Vietnam," 42.

19 Power and pleasure in Forrest, "The American Soldier and Vietnamese Women," 13. Hands in Carol Burke, *Camp All-American, Hanoi Jane, and the High-and-Tight* (Boston, MA: Beacon Press, 2004), 38. Rape as a weapon in Farwell, "War Rape," 393. Efficient tools in Janie L. Leatherman, *Sexual Violence and Armed Conflict* (Malden, MA: Polity, 2011), 8. Hostile population from PFC Bill Brocksieker in Otto J. Lehrack, *No Shining Armor: The Marines at War in Vietnam, An Oral History* (Lawrence, KS: University Press of Kansas, 1992), 35.

20 Drill instructors in Sara Meger, *Rape Loot Pillage: The Political Economy of Sexual Violence in Armed Conflict* (New York, NY: Oxford University Press, 2016), 61. Not questioning orders in Norden, 278. On violence as a command policy, see Nick Turse, *Kill Anything That Moves: The Real American War in Vietnam* (New York, NY: Metropolitan Books, 2013), 22, 230. For an alternative view, where soldiers would have gotten into trouble for excessive violence, see Richard Stacewicz, *Winter Soldiers: An Oral History of the Vietnam Veterans Against the War* (New York, NY: Twayne, 1997), 155.

21 Male-power fantasy in Edward W. Said, *Orientalism* (New York, NY: Vintage Books, 1979, 1994), 207. "Mademoiselle from Saigon," *For Men Only*, August 1966, 30. Mario Cleri, "Saigon Nymph Who Led the Green Berets to the Cong's Terror HQ," *Male*, August 1966, 12.

22 Licentious in Said, 190. Subhuman in Peter G. Bourne, "From Boot Camp to My Lai," in Falk, Kolko, and Lifton, 466. Atrophied in Richard Drinnon, *Facing West: The Metaphysics of Indian-Hating and Empire-Building* (Minneapolis, MN: University of Minnesota Press, 1980), 449. Sexual release in Forrest, 13.

23 Marine Michael McCusker quoted in Joanna Bourke, *Rape: Sex, Violence, History* (Berkeley, CA: Shoemaker Hoard, 2007), 366. For a similar story of a soldier attempting rape by stating that he "wanted to make love," see Serious Incident Report S-8-59-71, 24 August 1971, Entry P845, Box 2, Serious Incident Reports, Office of the Provost Marshal, RG472, National Archives and Records Administration, College Park, MD. (Hereafter cited as NARA) Soldier Arthur E. Woodley, Jr. quoted in Wallace Terry, *Bloods: An Oral History of the Vietnam War by Black Veterans* (New York, NY: Random House, 1984), 255. On Americans believing most female "hooch maids" also offered "*personal* services," see Bahnsen, 39–40. On GIs feeling entitled with servants, see Santoli, 7.

24 "Stag Confidential," *Stag*, September 1966, 6. Men hearing yes in Bourke, 67.

25 Dependency in Duncan, 16. On GI attitudes, see Prados, *In Country*, 135; and Lawrence A. Tritle, *From Melos to My Lai: War and Survival* (New York, NY: Routledge, 2000), 117. For a perspective from Vietnamese women, see Bourne, 52–56; and Mai Lan Gustafsson, "'Freedom. Money. Love.': The Warlore of Vietnamese Bargirls," *The Oral History Review* Vol. 38, No. 2 (Summer/Fall 2011): 322.

26 Letter from Harlan A. Bender, Jr., *Man's Magazine*, October 1960, 6. On the reaction spawned by these attitudes, see Alvin Shuster, "Vietnam Riot: Anti-G.I. Feelings Boil Over," *New York Times*, 14 December 1970. Crew chief John Durant quoted in Fred Turner, *Echoes of Combat: Trauma, Memory, and the Vietnam War* (Minneapolis, MN: University of Minnesota Press, 1996), 24.

27 Duong Van Mai Elliott, *The Sacred Willow: Four Generations in the Life of a Vietnamese Family* (New York, NY: Oxford University Press, 1999), 307. For another Vietnamese reaction, see Nguyen Ngoc Ngan with E. E. Richey, *The Will of Heaven: A Story of One Vietnamese and the End of His World* (New York, NY: E. P. Dutton, 1982), 47.

28 Mark Bowden, *Hué 1968: A Turning Point of the American War in Vietnam* (New York, NY: Atlantic Monthly Press, 2017), 327–328. Sexual debasement in Gina Marie Weaver, *Ideologies of Forgetting: Rape in the Vietnam War* (Albany, NY: State University of New York Press, 2010), 41. Entitlement rape in Eva Fogelman, "Rape during the Nazi Holocaust:

Vulnerabilities and Motivations," in *Rape: Weapon of War and Genocide*, eds. Carol Rittner and John K. Roth (St. Paul, MN: Paragon House, 2012), 22. Bargaining chips in Goedde, 91. See also Maria Höhn, *GIs and Fräuleins: The German–American Encounter in 1950s West Germany* (Chapel Hill, NC: The University of North Carolina Press, 2002), 129; and John Costello, *Virtue under Fire: How World War II Changed Our Social and Sexual Attitudes* (Boston, MA: Little, Brown, and Company, 1985), 248. On sexual "collusion" as a condition of survival, see Lorraine Helms, "'Still Wars and Lechery': Shakespeare and the Last Trojan Horse," in *Arms and the Woman: War, Gender, and Literary Representation*, eds. Helen M. Cooper, Adrienne Auslander Munich, Susan Merrill Squier (Chapel Hill, NC: The University of North Carolina Press, 1989), 38.

29 On Hayslip, see Leslie Bow, "Third-World Testimony in the Era of Globalization: Vietnam, Sexual Trauma, and Le Ly Hayslip's Art of Neutrality," in Hesford and Kozol, 171–176; and Weaver, 43. On the story changing in movie form, told now as an American success story, see Rebecca L. Stephens, "Distorted Reflections: Oliver Stone's *Heaven and Earth* and Le Ly Hayslip's *When Heaven and Earth Changed Places*," *The Centennial Review* Vol. 41, No. 3 (Fall 1997): 661–669. On rape as a result of sexual needs, see Maria Eriksson Baaz and Maria Stern, "Why Do Soldiers Rape? Masculinity, Violence, and Sexuality in the Armed Forces in the Congo," *International Studies Quarterly* Vol. 53, No. 2 (June 2009): 508. Dehumanizing in "Acknowledging Violations, Struggling against Impunity: Women's Rights, Human Rights," in *Common Grounds: Violence against Women in War and Armed Conflict Situations*, ed. Indai Lourdes Sajor (Quezon City, Philippines: Asian Center for Women's Human Rights, 1998), 37.

30 Selling daughters and time-honored tradition from Peter Arnett in Susan Brownmiller, *Against Our Will: Men, Women, and Rape* (New York, NY: Fawcett Books, 1975), 93. Women as commodities in Timothy Beneke, *Men on Rape* (New York, NY: St. Martin's Press, 1982), 31. One sketch artist in *True* showed children congregating around GIs, with the caption reading "They try to sell anything, including their older sisters." Kennedy, "John Goth's Vietnam," 42.

31 Marnais, *Saigon after Dark*, 23. Something to gain in Stacewicz, 133.

32 "Bring Back the Brothels!" in "It's a Strange World," *Male*, April 1967, 44. Prostitution as profitable in Jean Bertolino, "Report on American Conduct of the War in the South," in Falk, Kolko, and Lifton, 335. Behavior contributing to images in Klaus Theweleit, *Male Fantasies, Volume 1: Women, Floods, Bodies, History* (Minneapolis, MN: University of Minnesota Press, 1987), 152.

33 Individualism in Bob Wanderer, "Sin State," *Guy*, April 1965, 28. Tramp from Veteran of the Korean War, "I Married a Pon Girl," *Action*, March 1953, 22, 24. We might ask why the author, who ultimately married the Japanese woman because she treated him like a "king," preferred to stay anonymous.

34 One function and sexual gratification in Weaver, 73. On Vietnamese women being "doubly demeaned" as both women and "Orientals," see Robin Gerster, "A Bit of the Other: Touring Vietnam," in *Gender and War: Australians at War in the Twentieth Century*, eds. Joy Damousi and Marilyn Lake (New York, NY: Cambridge University Press, 1995), 230.

35 Goals of the forum in Vietnam Veterans Against the War, *The Winter Soldier Investigation: An Inquiry into American War Crimes* (Boston, MA: Beacon Press, 1972), 2. Heidtman and Henry quoted in Brownmiller, 109, 110. Atrocity-producing in Patrick Hagopian, *The Vietnam War in American Memory: Veterans, Memorials, and the Politics of Healing* (Amherst, MA: University of Massachusetts Press, 2009), 53. Allegations in Deborah Nelson, *The War behind Me: Vietnam Veterans Confront the Truth about U.S. War Crimes* (New York, NY: Basic Books, 2008), 146. Neil Sheehan claimed not long after the event that Americans' "vision was so narrowly focused on the unfolding details of the war" that they paid no heed to war crimes allegations. "Should We Have War Crimes Trials?," *New York Times*, 28 March 1971.

36 Gook rule in Resume of Hearing, Ad Hoc Committee to Investigate War Crimes, 27 April 1971, Summaries of Congressional Hearings on War Crimes, Box 5, War Crimes Working Group Files, RG319, NARA. See also Guenter Lewy, *America in Vietnam* (New York, NY: Oxford University Press, 1978), 241. Drill instructors in Arlene Eisen Bergman, *Women of Vietnam* (San Francisco, CA: Peoples Press, 1974), 67. Copelon quoted in Waitman Wade Beorn, "Bodily Conquest: Sexual Violence in the Nazi East," in *Mass Violence in Nazi-Occupied Europe*, eds. Alex J. Kay and David Stahel (Bloomington, IN: Indiana University Press, 2018), 198. For an alternative view, see Michael Bilton and Kevin Sim, *Four Hours in My Lai* (New York, NY: Viking, 1992), 18. The mother of one of the killers at My Lai told the *New York Times*, "I sent them a good boy, and they made him into a murderer." Mrs. Anthony Meadlo quoted in Richard A. Falk, "The Circle of Responsibility" in Falk, Kolko, and Lifton, 222.

37 Madeline Morris, "By Force of Arms: Rape, War, and Military Culture," *Duke Law Journal*, Vol. 45, No. 4 (February 1996): 724. On American mass media, which sent the message that to be a man, "you had to kill bad guys," see Norman Cousins in Ebert, *A Life in a Year*, 50.

38 Sgt. Lyle I. Johnson, "They Don't Like Grenades," *Men*, October 1952, 14, 52. Stefan Wolfe, "The Quiet Dutchman Who Became Ambush King of the Marines," *Men*, January 1962, 20, 83. The article was part of the "Heroes of the Great War" series.

39 Philip Caputo, *A Rumor of War* (New York, NY: Holt, Rinehart and Winston, 1977), 124. David Donovan, *Once A Warrior King: Memoirs of an Officer in Vietnam* (New York, NY: McGraw-Hill, 1985), 59. Numb to killing in Eisen Bergman, *Women of Vietnam*, 70.

40 Eric Broske, "Smash the Cong's Terror Tunnels," *True Action*, November 1968, 16, 66. Ethics of combat in Tirman, *The Deaths of Others*, 153.

41 Power and destruction in Bak Mark Baker, *Nam: The Vietnam War in the Words of the Men and Women Who Fought There* (New York, NY: William Morrow and Company, 1981), 152. Enjoying killing in Turner, *Echoes of Combat*, 29; and James P. Sterba, "Close-up of the Grunt: The Hours of Boredom, the Seconds of Terror," *New York Times*, 8 February 1970. Feeling better in Shay, 78. Primitive from Douglas Anderson in Santoli, 69.

42 Cpl. Lester Carter, "Payoff on Horror Hill," *Action*, March 1953, 18. See also Jonathan Ira Freeman, "Kill Crazy," *True War*, September 1957, 16. Don Croxley, "Blood Feast in the Hürtgen Forest," *Battle Cry*, March 1964, 32. Rick Gavin, "When I've Killed Enough Japs, I'm Taking on MacArthur," *Man's World*, February 1967, 40.

43 On the problems of accurately accounting for the number of those murdered, see Howard Jones, *My Lai: Vietnam, 1968, and the Descent into Darkness* (New York, NY: Oxford University Press, 2017), 1–2. Aberration debate in Bruce Palmer, Jr., *The 25-Year War: America's Military Role in Vietnam* (Lexington, KY: The University Press of Kentucky, 1984), 85; Lifton, *Home from the War*, 42; and Peter Goldman and Tony Fuller, *Charlie Company: What Vietnam Did to Us* (New York, NY: Ballantine Books, 1983), x. Epitome from Michael Bernhardt in Christian G. Appy, *Patriots: The Vietnam War Remembered from All Sides* (New York, NY: Viking, 2003), 350.

44 Itch in Lifton, 53. Indian Country in Drinnon, *Facing West*, 451. Calley quoted in *From Nuremberg to My Lai*, ed. Jay W. Baird (Lexington, MA: D. C. Heath, 1972), 222. He also noted that "the only lesson every GI learned was not to trust anybody." In Bilton and Sim, 54.

45 Murphy quoted in Tom Tiede, *Calley: Soldier or Killer?* (New York, NY: Pinnacle Books, 1971), 132. Only seeing the enemy in Baird, *Ibid.*

46 Lewis B. Puller, Jr., *Fortunate Son* (New York, NY: Grove Weidenfeld, 1991), 258. Kicking pregnant women in Stacewicz, 118. Dehumanization in James Wright, *Enduring Vietnam: An American Generation and Its War* (New York, NY: St. Martin's Press, 2017), 164; and Sheehan. Shooting children and burning in Baker, *Nam*, 158–159. On soldier testimonials in the aftermath of My Lai, see Nelson, *The War Behind Me*, 74, 77–78, 87, 145.

47 "Stag Confidential," *Stag*, January 1967, 8. McDonough, 59. On indifference to noncombatants in Korea, see I. F. Stone, *The Hidden History of the Korean War* (New York, NY: Monthly Review Press, 1952), 257–258.

48 Puller, *Ibid.* Sexual trip in Baker, 166. On the links between atrocities and a "perverse quest for meaning," see Robert Jay Lifton, "Beyond Atrocity," in Falk, Kolko, and Lifton, 23. Kathleen Barry argues that when the "violence of male domination that we see in wife abuse and rape engages with the sociopathy of war, we are no longer dealing with [a] 'good men in a bad situation' scenario." *Unmaking War, Remaking Men: How Empathy Can Reshape Our Politics, Our Soldiers and Ourselves* (Santa Rosa, CA: Phoenix Rising Press, 2011), 76.

49 McDonough, 73. Jackson Bowling, "Ambush by the Bridge at Nam Nang," *Man's Life*, September 1966, 38, 42. Dr. Reginald Keen, "Hospital Horror Raid of the Viet Cong," *Man's Action*, October 1964, 40, 42, 64–65. Taxes and manpower in Elliott, *The Sacred Willow*, 322. VC selective terror in Falk, Kolko, and Lifton, 266.

50 Tacit agreements and shrewd VC in Edward P. Metzner, *More Than a Soldier's War: Pacification in Vietnam* (College Station, TX: Texas A&M University Press, 1995), 33–34. On medical assistance and its "minimal" impact, see Robert J. Wilensky, *Military Medicine to Win Hearts and Minds: Aid to Civilians in the Vietnam War* (Lubbock, TX: Texas Tech University Press, 2004), 117, 130. "Inside for Men," *Male*, September 1966, 6.

51 Superiority in Kim Willenson, *The Bad War: An Oral History of the Vietnam War* (New York, NY: New American Library, 1987), 11. Fear and hatred in Tritle, *From Melos to My Lai*, 123. David H. Hackworth and Eilhys England, *Steel My Soldiers' Hearts: The Hopeless to Hardcore Transformation of 4th Battalion, 39th Infantry, United States Army, Vietnam* (New York, NY: Simon & Schuster, 2002), 131. For an alternate view in which a specialist

argued he and his unit "got to know some of the Vietnamese people as human beings," see Vietnam Veterans Against the War, *The Winter Soldier Investigation*, 82.

52 Micheal Clodfelter, *Mad Minutes and Vietnam Months: A Soldier's Memoir* (Jefferson, NC: McFarland, 1988), 149. Onus on civilians in Turse, 55.

53 "Flashes for Men," *Man's Illustrated*, March 1966, 8. John E. Sparkman, "Man's Talk," *Man's Magazine*, February 1967, 8. "Man's Bulletin," *True Action*, July 1967, 8.

54 USAID officer Robin Pell quoted in Harry Maurer, ed., *Strange Ground: Americans in Vietnam, 1945–1975, An Oral History* (New York, NY: Henry Holt and Company, 1989), 474. Puller, *Fortunate Son*, 137. Commodity from Rose Sandecki in Keith Walker, *A Piece of My Heart: The Stories of 26 American Women Who Served in Vietnam* (Novato, CA: Presidio, 1985), 10.

55 Herr, *Dispatches*, 199. Whores and thieves in Lifton, *Home from the War*, 194. On pre-Vietnam examples of Asian women being the victims of sexual violence in popular culture, see Peter Conolly-Smith, "Race-ing Rape: Representations of Sexual Violence in American Combat Films," *War and Society* Vol. 32, No. 3 (October 2013): 241–242.

56 *Tropic Lightning News*, 26 August 1968, Box 30, Entry P1660, Unit Publication Files, RG472, NARA. The 12th Combat Aviation Group's *Blackjack Flier* can be found in Box 31, *Ibid.* IV Corps' *Delta Dragon* from Box 2, Entry P1705, Publications 1971–1972, RG472, NARA.

57 *Cavalier*, 6 March 1968, Box 34, Entry P1660, Unit Publication Files, RG472, NARA. *Southern Cross*, 25 October 1968, Box 37, *Ibid.*

58 Sunday Magazine, *Pacific Stars and Stripes*, 19 April 1970. On service publications in World War II including pin-up girls, see Costello, 153; and Robert B. Westbrook, *Why We Fought: Forging American Obligations in World War II* (Washington, DC: Smithsonian Books, 2004), 73.

59 Vet quoted in Baker, *Nam*, 59. On male privilege, see Miriam Gebhardt, *Crimes Unspoken: The Rape of German Women at the End of the Second World War* (Malden, MA: Polity, 2017), 99.

60 Hagelin quoted in Vietnam Veterans Against the War, 67.

61 Sexual intimacy in Ellis, *Theories of Rape*, 1. On problems with the simplistic notion that "men must have sex" and will rape if "deprived," see Morris, "By Force of Arms," 676. On military rape rates in combat theaters climbing to several times civilian rates, see Madeline Morris, "In War and Peace: Rape, War, and Military Culture," in *War's Dirty Secret: Rape, Prostitution, and Other Crimes against Women*, ed. Anne Llewellyn Barstow (Cleveland, OH: The Pilgrim Press, 2000), 167.

62 Rape as a weapon in Jill Benderly, "Rape, Feminism, and Nationalism in the War in Yugoslav Successor States," in *Feminist Nationalism*, ed. Lois A. West (New York, NY: Routledge, 1997), 65. Dominance and aggression in Larry Baron and Murray A. Strauss, *Four Theories of Rape in American Society* (New Haven, CT: Yale University Press, 1989), 61. On women's economic vulnerabilities in war, see Carol Harrington, *Politicization of Sexual Violence: From Abolitionism to Peacekeeping* (Burlington, VT: Ashgate, 2010), 80. On romantic liaisons between GIs and Asian women in a wartime environment, see Naoko Shibusawa, *America's Geisha Ally: Reimagining the Japanese Enemy* (Cambridge, MA: Harvard University Press, 2006), 40, 261.

63 Susan Griffin, "Rape: The All-American Crime," *Ramparts*, September 1971, 29. On rape as a weapon of war and a deliberate policy, see Doris E. Buss, "Rethinking 'Rape as a Weapon of War,'" *Feminist Legal Studies* Vol. 17, No. 2 (2009): 146, 149; and Meger, *Rape Loot Pillage*, 54, 57. Opportunistic in Meger, 93.

64 Gang rapes as common occurrence in Turse, 168. MACV published a directive on 20 April 1965 outlining procedures for investigations of war crimes and "similar prohibited acts," following contemporary standards of what constituted a "grave breach" of the Geneva Conventions. While "inhuman treatment" was deemed a prohibited act, the directive did not specifically address rape or sexual violence. MACV Directive 20-4, 20 April 1965, Box 4, Reporting and Investigating War Crimes Allegations, War Crimes Working Group Files, RG319, NARA. Nor did the 10 July 1970 version of the directive mention sexual violence. On this topic, see Gary D. Solis, *The Law of Armed Conflict: International Humanitarian Law in War*, 2nd ed. (New York, NY: Cambridge University Press, 2016), 339–341.

65 Lieutenant Joseph W. Callaway, Jr. quoted in Prados, *In Country*, 245. Capacity for rape in Weaver, *Ideologies of Forgetting*, xiv Majority of rapes going unreported on p. xv. Admitting killing over rape in Viet Thanh Nguyen, *Nothing Ever Dies: Vietnam and the Memory of War* (Cambridge, MA: Harvard University Press, 2016), 80. See also "Introduction" in Barstow, 5.

66 Herbert Allegation, 3 August 1972, Box 2, War Crimes Allegations Talking Points, War Crimes Working Group Files, RG319, NARA. On another rape case being dropped for "insufficient evidence," see Brummett Allegation, 29 November 1972, Box 1, War Crimes Allegations Case Studies, War Crimes Working Group Files, RG319, NARA. On women "suffering without words," see Gebhardt, 171. Victim silence in Agnes Callamard, "Breaking the Collusion of Silence," in Sajor, *Common Grounds*, 63. Distrusted rape victims in Bourke, *Rape*, 23. For a more skeptical view of "war crime stories," see Gary Kulik, *"War Stories": False Atrocity Tales, Swift Boaters, and Winter Soldiers – What Really Happened in Vietnam* (Washington, DC: Potomac Books, 2009), 19.

67 Szolsowski Incident, 14 July 1971, Box 14, Brummett Allegation, 29 November 1972, Box 1, War Crimes Allegations Case Files, War Crimes Working Group Files, RG319, NARA. In a similar case, an infantry company captured two suspected VC nurses who were gang-raped during overnight detention. Case 43, Americal Div. Allegation, 2 June 1968, Box 1, War Crimes Allegations Talking Points, War Crimes Working Group Files, RG319, NARA. War crime statistics in Gary D. Solis, "Military Justice, Civilian Clemency: The Sentences of Marine Corps War Crimes in South Vietnam," *Transnational Law & Contemporary Problems* Vol. 59 (2000): 67–79; W. Hays Parks, "Crimes in Hostilities," *Marine Corps Gazette*, August 1976, 18; Lewy, *America in Vietnam*, 348–356; and Nelson, *The War Behind Me*, 140–143. A full listing of cases classified as "founded" by army investigators can be found in Appendix A. See also Karen Stuhldreher, "State Rape: Representations of Rape in Viet Nam," *The Vietnam Generation Big Book* Vol. 5, Nos 1–4 (March 1994): 155. Fred Turner quotes one study which claimed that "nearly one in every ten combat soldiers committed an act of abusive violence, such as torturing prisoners, raping civilians, or mutilating a corpse." *Echoes of Combat*, 29.

68 Pressure cooker in Ruth Siefert, War and Rape: A Preliminary Analysis," in *Mass Rape: The War against Women in Bosnia-Herzegovina*, ed. Alexandra Stiglmayer (Lincoln, NE: University of Nebraska Press, 1994), 54. On sexual and gender norms, see Morris, "In War and Peace," 182. Perpetrators understanding themselves in Baaz and Stern, "Why Do Soldiers Rape?," 496. For a similar discussion on "rape signs," see Beneke, *Men on Rape*, 7. Culturally produced representations in Stuhldreher, 157. On MACV making rape "socially acceptable," see Eisen Bergman, *Women of Vietnam*, 63.

69 Increased influence from Robert Slayton, email to author, 7 August 2019.

70 "What They Said about Women," *Sensation*, April 1959, 6. Wesley Hall, "Cowboy Hank Plummer and the Bed-Hopping Brides," *Valor*, June 1959, 26. Sidney Gorgeson, "The Day They Ravaged Frisco," *Big Adventure*, June 1961, 6.

71 Dean W. Ballenger, "The Strange Case of the Stagecoach Rapist," *Sir!*, July 1962, 21. H. B. Allen, "Decoy for the Deadly Rape Gang Sadist," *Man's Action*, May 1966, 12, 14. For insights into family reactions, see Nguyen Thu Huong, "Rape in Vietnam from Socio-cultural and Historical Perspectives," *Journal of Asian History* Vol. 40, No. 2 (2006): 185–206.

72 Kenneth Towne, "The Truth about GI Rapists," *True War*, October 1956, 25, 50–51. On problems with the inevitability of rape argument, see Brownmiller, 31; and Bourke, 359. On the "military mindset" as a contributing factor to rape, see Andrew F. Simon, Susan A. Nolan, and Chi Thao Ngo, "Sexual Violence as a Weapon of War," in *Violence against Girls and Women: International Perspectives, Volume 2, In Adult, Midlife, and Older Age*, eds. Janet A. Sigal and Florence L. Denmark (Santa Barbara, CA: Praeger, 2013), 83.

73 On contemporary romanticizing of violence, see Steven Watts, *JFK and the Masculine Mystique: Sex and Power on the New Frontier* (New York, NY: St. Martin's Press, 2016), 114. On social traditions reflecting male dominance, see Ellis, *Theories of Rape*, 10. On military contempt for women, see Miranda Alison, "Wartime Sexual Violence: Women's Human Rights and Questions of Masculinity," *Review of International Studies* Vol. 33, No. 1 (January 2007): 78.

74 "Bluebook Bouquets and Brickbats," *Bluebook*, May 1966, 10. On husbands not being able to rape their wives, see also "Hot Line on Women," *Men*, December 1968, 8; and Bourke, 27–28. Ray Lunt, "Our Ridiculous Horse-and-Buggy Sex Laws," *Men*, March 1963, 40, 69. In its January 1979 issue, *Family Circle* ran an article titled "Legal Rape" which began with the admission that it was not a "crime for a man to brutally force his wife to have sexual relations," p. 24.

75 Jack Gordon, "I Joined a Go-Naked Swap Cult," *Men*, December 1968, 15, 16. Norton McVickers, "Women Who Prowl the Streets Looking for Sex Thrills," *Man's Life*, January 1969, 19, 56. For a similar story, see Lilburn Hamber, "Crescendo," *Climax*, June 1953, 18, about a man who murders his "faithless wife" because she "tantalizes him beyond all human endurance." Such narratives suggested men ultimately were not responsible for rape. See Beneke, 8.

76 "Male Call," *Male*, July 1966, 86. Institutionalizing prostitution in Brownmiller, 92. Sanctioned in Appy, *Patriots*, 159. On prostitution in Vietnam as a reflection and consequence of gender ideas more broadly, see Heather Marie Stur, "Gentle Warriors,

Gunslingers, and Girls Next Door: Gender and the Vietnam War," in *The Routledge History of Gender, War, and the U.S. Military*, ed. Kara Dixon Vuic (London: Routledge, 2018), 121.

77 World War II vet in Costello, *Virtue under Fire*, 245. Steam in John A. Wood, *Veteran Narratives and the Collective Memory of the Vietnam War* (Athens, OH: Ohio University Press, 2016), 63. See also Elisabeth Jean Wood, "Armed Groups and Sexual Violence: When Is Wartime Rape Rare?," *Politics & Society* Vol. 37, No. 1 (March 2009): 135. Distraction in Baaz and Stern, 506. On brothels, see Boczar, "Uneasy Allies," 190, 195–197, 201, 210. On calls for legalized prostitution from the pulps, see "Stag Confidential," *Stag*, July 1961, 43.

78 "It's a Strange World," *Male*, February 1965, 10. Basic services in Baird, *From Nuremberg to My Lai*, 240. On 400,000 prostitutes, see Eisen Bergman, *Women of Vietnam*, 82. The number jumps to nearly half a million in her later book, *Women and Revolution in Viet Nam* (London: Zed Books, 1984), 45. Assuming a total South Vietnamese population in 1965 of 16,124,000, that would mean over three percent of the population was engaged in prostitution, a questionable claim. "Final Report, A Population Survey in Viet Nam," 31 March 1967, Folder 06, Box 43, Douglas Pike Collection: Unit 03 – Statistical Data, The Vietnam Center and Archive, Texas Tech University, Lubbock, TX. Still, *True Action* noted how the US Army in Vietnam was fighting back against an "army of prostitutes." "Man's Bulletin," January 1967, 6. Saigon official quoted in Eisen, *Women and Revolution in Viet Nam, Ibid.* On control of women's bodies in Korea, see Katharine H. S. Moon, *Sex among Allies: Military Prostitution in U.S.–Korea Relations* (New York, NY: Columbia University Press, 1997), 94.

79 "Conquest Confidentials," *Man's Conquest*, December 1965, 8. Neil L. Jamieson discusses prostitution in *Understanding Vietnam* (Berkeley, CA: University of California Press, 1993), 332–333. James William Gibson referred to brothels as "virtual sex factories." *The Perfect War: The War We Couldn't Lose and How We Did* (New York, NY: Vintage Books, 1986), 263.

80 Contest in Donovan, *Once a Warrior King*, 191–192. Lice in *Soldados: Chicanos in Viet Nam*, ed. Charley Trujillo (San José, CA: Chusma House, 1990), 5.

81 On Korea, see Dirk Bradley, "Sex Below the 38th Parallel," *Saga*, August 1963, 31. Bali in "It's a Strange World," *Male*, February 1965, 10. Polynesia in James Peterson, "Four Greatest Bargains for the Boat-Hopping Adventurer," *For Men Only*, May 1965, 41, 54, 55. Leslie Thomas, "The Virgin Soldier and Juicy Lucy," *Man's Magazine*, September 1966, 14, 84.

82 On fantasies, see Timothy Beneke, *Proving Manhood: Reflections on Men and Sexism* (Berkeley, CA: University of California Press, 1997), 28; and Laura Kipnis, *Bound and Gagged: Pornography and the Politics of Fantasy in America* (Durham, NC: Duke University Press, 1999), 8. Miriam Gebhardt found that in World War II Germany, Americans used "fraternization" as a "euphemism for rape." *Crimes Unspoken*, 107.

83 Montagnards in "Stag Confidential," *Stag*, September 1968, 6. Joanna Bourke argues that racist discourse means that women are "not really seen as human." *Rape*, 378. See also Eisen Bergman, *Women of Vietnam*, 69. On rape as a tool of "othering," see James E. Waller, "Rape as a Tool of 'Othering' in Genocide," in Rittner and Roth, 87–88.

84 Intercourse and intoxication in Kathy J. Phillips, *Manipulating Masculinity: War and Gender in Modern British and American Literature* (New York, NY: Palgrave Macmillan, 2006), 133. Forcibly willing in Brownmiller, 107. Baron and Strauss argue that rape myths rest on a belief that "women expect or enjoy being forced to have sex," p. 146. Brooks Allegation, 9 April 1970, Box 1, War Crimes Allegations Case Studies, War Crimes Working Group Files, RG319, NARA. The helicopter incident supports the "routine activity theory," which states that "soldiers rape women because they can." Christopher W. Mullins, "Sexual Violence during Armed Conflict," in *The Palgrave Handbook of Criminology and War*, eds. Ross McGarry and Sandra Walklate (New York, NY: Palgrave Macmillan, 2016), 123.

85 Gooks as less worthy humans in Elisabeth Vikman, "Modern Combat: Sexual Violence in Warfare, Part II," *Anthropology & Medicine* Vol. 12, No. 1 (April 2005): 36. Not shooting at humans in Terry H. Anderson, "Vietnam Is Here: The Antiwar Movement," in *The War That Never Ends: New Perspectives on the Vietnam War*, eds. David L. Anderson and John Ernst (Lexington, KY: The University Press of Kentucky, 2007), 260. Not people in Bilton and Sim, *Four Hours in My Lai*, 60. See also Vietnam Veterans Against the War, *The Winter Soldier Investigation*, 14, 112.

86 Tales in Eisen Bergman, *Women of Vietnam*, 71; and Jacqueline A. Lawson, "'She's a Pretty Woman ... for a Gook': The Misogyny of the Vietnam War," *The Journal of American Culture* Vol. 12, No. 3 (Fall 1989): 61–62. VC incident in John Ketwig, *... and a Hard Rain Fell: A GI's True Story of War in Vietnam* (Naperville, IL: Sourcebooks, 2002), 87–88. Poet Adrienne Rich argued in 1973 that "when you strike the chord of sexuality in the ... [male] psyche, the chord of violence is likely to vibrate in response." In Jonathan Shay, *Achilles in Vietnam: Combat Trauma and the Undoing of Character* (New York, NY: Atheneum, 1994), 133.

87 Calley quoted in Baird, 227. For a summary of the approximately twenty rapes, see James S. Olson and Randy Roberts, *My Lai: A Brief History with Documents* (Boston, MA: Bedford, 1998), 99–102. See also Bilton and Sim, 136–137; and William Thomas Allison, *My Lai: An American Atrocity in the Vietnam War* (Baltimore, MD: The Johns Hopkins University Press, 2012), 47, 69.

88 Alleged Rape of Two Vietnamese Nationals by U.S. Military Personnel, 11 December 1969, Box 69, MACIG Investigations Division Reports of Investigations, RG472, NARA. In another rape investigation, allegations prompted command concerns over "widespread publicity" and "widespread embarrassment" due to the age of the victims. Potter Allegation, 6 July 1971, Box 15, War Crimes Allegations Case Files, War Crimes Working Group Files, RG319, NARA.

89 Lt. "Ruth West," "Girl Prisoner of the Japanese," *Real War*, December 1957, 24. Mai Elliott mentions a similar tale of Japanese rape in *The Sacred Willow*, 110. For a story on a French plantation owner's daughter being raped and killed by the Vietcong, see Martin Howard, "Revenge of the Green Berets," *Man's Peril*, September 1966, 34, 38. On rape creating disorder, see Megan H. MacKenzie, *Female Soldiers in Sierra Leone: Sex, Security, and Post-conflict Development* (New York, NY: New York University Press, 2012), 100. As a systematic centerpiece of strategy, see Kerry F. Crawford, *Wartime Sexual Violence: From Silence to Condemnation of a Weapon of War* (Washington, DC: Georgetown University

Press, 2017), 5, 33. As a means to produce or maintain dominance, see Claudia Card, "Rape as a Weapon of War," *Hypatia*, Vol. 11, No. 4 (Autumn 1996): 7.

90 Woman-hungry in Corporal Jake Ogilvie, "Death Charge at Tongawe Village!," *Men in Adventure*, February 1960, 31. On the "taking" of women as a form of revenge in earlier wars, see Petra Goedde, *GIs and Germans: Culture, Gender, and Foreign Relations, 1945–1949* (New Haven, CT: Yale University Press, 2003), 84.

91 Calley quoted in Baird, 215. Body politic in Carolyn Nordstrom, "Rape: Politics and Theory in War and Peace," *Australian Feminist Studies* Vol. 11, No. 23 (1996): 152. Demonstrating power in Gibson, *The Perfect War*, 202. On women "belonging to the enemy," see Yuki Tanaka, "Rape and War: The Japanese Experience," in Sajor, 178.

92 Officer quoted in Richard Holmes, *Acts of War: The Behavior of Men in Battle* (New York, NY: The Free Press, 1985), 392. On group psychology, see Bourke, *Rape*, 377. Gang-rape as bonding in Alison, "Wartime Sexual Violence," 77; and Barry, *Unmaking War, Remaking Men*, 38. Homophobia in John Beynon, *Masculinities and Culture* (Philadelphia, PA: Open University Press, 2002), 67. Adolescent aggressiveness toward women in Beneke, *Proving Manhood*, 19.

93 Daniel Lang, *Casualties of War* (New York, NY: Pocket Books, 1969), 35, 58. Brutal boys in Robert Bly, *Iron John: A Book about Men* (New York, NY: Da Capo Press, 2004), 90. Deborah Cheney argues that in Brian DePalma's film version, the story is less about the Vietnamese victim than about the young Americans "brutalized" by war. "Visual Rape," *Law and Critique* Vol. IV, No. 2 (1993): 195.

94 Immunity in Benderly, 66; and Beverly Allen, *Rape Warfare: The Hidden Genocide in Bosnia-Herzegovina and Croatia* (Minneapolis, MN: University of Minnesota Press, 1996), 39. Vanquished in Brownmiller, 49. Compensating for powerlessness and fear in John V. H. Dippel, *War and Sex: A Brief History of Men's Urge for Battle* (Amherst, NY: Prometheus, 2010), 263.

95 Specialist Robert E. Holcomb quoted in Terry, *Bloods*, 216. "Inside for Men," *Male*, July 1967, 8. For a similar view, see Marnais, *Saigon after Dark*, 24.

96 Ray Robbins, "Korean Camp-Followers," *True War Stories*, January–February 1953, 36–37. Dean W. Ballenger, "Japan's Fantastic Plot to Wipe Out 20,000 U.S. Marines," *Man's World*, April 1959, 20, 56. On the enemy using prostitutes to infect Allied soldiers in World War II, see Costello, 84.

97 Last Minute Memo For Men," *For Men Only*, September 1966, 11. "Deadline Bulletin," *Man's World*, February 1967, 51. For a similar story of a woman having hand grenades under her dress, see Ebert, 49. In one issue from *True Men Stories*, the Vietcong are said to "booby-trap" Saigon "B-girls" by drugging them so they appear to be "merely drunk" and then affixing fragmentation grenades to their bras. The "fumbling GI customer" ends up blowing her to pieces and losing his hands in the process. "Briefing Session," *True Men Stories*, 11 November 1965, 10.

98 Ketwig, 77. Hotchkiss Allegation, 25 May 1972, Box 2, War Crimes Allegations Talking Points, War Crimes Working Group Files, RG319, NARA. *Vagina dentata* in Jerry Lembcke, *Hanoi Jane: War, Sex & Fantasies of History* (Amherst, MA: University of Massachusetts Press, 2010), 100. Razor blade stories in Stacewicz, 136. Marine quoted in Beneke, *Men on Rape*, 59. Castration in Theweleit, *Male Fantasies*, 171, 201.

99 VC whore in Bilton and Sim, 132. See also Eisen Bergman, *Women of Vietnam*, 74. Calley incident in Gibson, 263. On American views of prostitutes and access to sex, see Weaver, *Ideologies of Forgetting*, 34. One veteran recalled that "Sex for most of the men meant prostitutes." In Maurer, *Strange Ground*, 223.

100 Captain quoted in Loren Baritz, *Backfire: A History of How American Culture Led Us into Vietnam and Made Us Fight the Way We Did* (New York, NY: William Morrow and Company, 1985), 53. For a response to arguments on the "pervasiveness" of rape in wartime, see John B. Corr, "Rape, Sex, and the U.S. Military: Questioning the Conclusions and Methodology of Madeline Morris' *By Force of Arms*," *Transnational Law & Contemporary Problems* Vol. 10 (2000): 200–210. Targeting women in Alison, 89.

101 Richard Gilkey, *Vietnam REMF?* (Ashland, OR: Hellgate Press, 2016), 113–115. McClenahan in Walker, *A Piece of My Heart*, 19. On service troops committing rape in World War II, see J. Robert Lilly, *Taken by Force: Rape and American GIs in Europe during World War II* (New York, NY: Palgrave Macmillan, 2007), 58.

102 Baker, *Nam*, 92. Journalist Peter Arnett suggested that rear-area troops were driven to brothels by "discontent and boredom." In Brownmiller, *Against Our Will*, 94.

103 "Stag Confidential," *Stag*, March 1968, 43. Vet David Delgado in Trujillo, *Soldados*, 110. Not curbing rape in Cynthia Enloe, *Does Khaki Become You? The Militarisation of Women's Lives* (Boston, MA: South End Press, 1983), 36. On inability to protect women, see: Brownmiller, 37–38; Baaz and Stern, 498; and Elvan Isikozlu and Ananda S. Millard, "Wartime Rape: Identifying Knowledge Gaps and Their Implications," *Security and Peace* Vol. 28, No. 1 (2010): 37. Sara Meger notes the demoralizing aspect of this failure. *Rape Loot Pillage*, 186. Of note, male victims of sexual violence were not part of this discussion. On this, see Simon, Nolan, and Ngo, 84.

104 VD rates and wedlock in "Stag Confidential," *Stag*, September 1968, 6. Duration wives in "Men's Newsletter," *Men*, December 1968, 13. Distortion of sexual politics in Cynthia Enloe, "Bananas, Bases, and Patriarchy," in *Women, Militarism, and War: Essays in History, Politics, and Social Theory*, eds. Jean Bethke Elshtain and Shelia Tobias (Savage, MD: Rowman & Littlefield, 1990), 200. Resentfulness in Lifton, *Home from the War*, 196. On the political response to rape, see Huong, 196. For a contemporary American view of the Vietnamese man, see Bourne, *Men, Stress, and Vietnam*, 217–222.

105 Whorehouse from soldier Peter Martinsen in Weaver, 50. Moral society in Boczar, 193. Thieu quoted in Lien-Hang Nguyen, "Cold War Contradictions: Toward an International History of the Second Indochina War, 1969–1973," in *Making Sense of the Vietnam Wars: Local, National, and Transnational Perspectives*, eds. Mark Philp Bradley and Marilyn Young (New York, NY: Oxford University Press, 2008), 232. Feminine versus masculine states in Rada Iveković, "Women, Nationalism and War: 'Make Love Not War,'" *Hypatia* Vol. 8, No. 4 (Autumn 1993): 122.

106 Nguyen, *Nothing Ever Dies*, 227. No male equivalent in Jessica Bennett, "Why Do People Still Use the Word 'Mistress'? A Reporter Reflects," *New York Times*, 7 June 2016.

107 Bui Thi Me in Mahoko Kyouraku, "Gender in War: The Case of the Vietnam War and 'Vietnamese Heroic Mother,'" *Social Alternatives* Vol. 29, No. 10 (2010): 11–14. On Heroic Mothers, see also Dana Healy, "Laments of Warriors' Wives: Re-gendering the

War in Vietnamese Cinema," *South East Asia Research* Vol. 14, No. 2 (July 2006): 241. Passive victims in Margaret R. Higgonet and Patrice L.-R. Higgonet, "The Double Helix," in *Behind the Lines: Gender and the Two World Wars*, eds. Margaret Randolph Higgonet, Sonya Michel, Jane Jenson, and Margaret Collins Weitz (New Haven, CT: Yale University Press, 1987), 46. Women warriors in Sandra C. Taylor, *Vietnamese Women at War: Fighting for Ho Chi Minh and the Revolution* (Lawrence, KS: University Press of Kansas, 1999), 2, 6. Damsels "in need of rescue" in Stur, *Beyond Combat*, 6. Women as key players in Helen E. Anderson, "Fighting for Family: Vietnamese Women and the American War," in Anderson, *The Columbia History of the Vietnam War*, 298.

108 Invisible combatants in D'Ann Campbell, "Women in Combat: The World War II Experience in the United States, Great Britain, Germany, and the Soviet Union," *The Journal of Military History* Vol. 57, No. 2 (April 1993): 301. See also Susan K. Alexander, "The Invisible Veterans: Nurses in the Vietnam War," *Women's Studies Quarterly* Vol. 12, No. 2 (Summer 1984): 16–17. Lynda Van Devanter with Christopher Morgan, *Home before Morning: The Story of an Army Nurse in Vietnam* (New York, NY: Beaufort Books, 1983), 13. The best work on nursing in Vietnam is Kara Dixon Vuic, *Officer, Nurse, Woman: The Army Nurse Corps in the Vietnam War* (Baltimore, MD: The Johns Hopkins University Press, 2010). Nightmares in *Visions of War, Dreams of Peace: Writings of Women in the Vietnam War*, eds. Lynda Van Devanter and Joan A. Furey (New York, NY: Warner Books, 1991), 117. PTS in Joan A. Furey, "Women Vietnam Veterans: A Comparison of Studies," *Journal of Psychosocial Nursing* Vol. 29, No. 3 (1991): 12. Not considered legitimate in Carol Lynn Mithers, "Missing in Action: Women Warriors in Vietnam," *Cultural Critique* No. 3 (Spring 1986): 84. Cynthia Enloe discusses these "forgotten veterans" in *Does Khaki Become You?*, 109, 116.

109 For a history of Vietnamese women warriors, see: David E. Jones, *Women Warriors: A History* (Washington, DC: Brassey's, 1997), 32–33; Eisen Bergman, *Women of Vietnam*, 30–33; and Anderson, "Fighting for Family," 297–300. When the enemy comes in Helle Rydstrøm, "Gendered Corporeality and Bare Lives: Local Sacrifices and Sufferings during the Vietnam War," *Signs* Vol. 37, No. 2 (January 2012): 284.

110 Vo Thi Sau in Eisen Bergman, 169. For similar stories, see Taylor, *Vietnamese Women at War*, 10; and Jones, 33. Number of female guerrillas in Mary Ann Tétreault, "Women and Revolution in Vietnam," in *Vietnam's Women in Transition*, ed. Kathleen Barry (New York, NY: St. Martin's Press, 1996), 41.

111 Karen Gottschang Turner with Phan Thanh Hao, *Even the Women Must Fight: Memories of War from North Vietnam* (New York, NY: John Wiley & Sons, 1998), 32. Women in the Viet Minh in Eisen, *Women and Revolution in Viet Nam*, 29–32. Social transformation in "Introduction" in *Gender Practices in Contemporary Vietnam*, eds. Lisa Drummond and Helle Rydstrøm (Singapore: NIAS Press, 2004), 3.

112 "Jungle Amazon Terror Told by Viet-Nam Troops," *Los Angeles Times*, 30 June 1955. Leon Sudarski, "Women in Uniform," *Real*, February 1964, 26, 29. At least one World War II male veteran agreed, stating that the "proximity of danger finds a man obsessed with a wild exhilaration, almost sensual." In Costello, 94. On the limits of social transformations, see Rydstrøm, "Gendered Corporeality and Bare Lives," 277.

Downplaying in Joshua S. Goldstein, *War and Gender: How Gender Shapes the War System and Vice Versa* (New York, NY: Cambridge University Press, 2001), 80–81. See also Eisen, *Ibid.*, 106–107.

113 Dinh Thuy episode in Taylor, 50. On the lines between female combatants and victims not being clearly drawn, see Laura Sjoberg, *Gender, War, and Conflict* (Malden, MA: Polity, 2014), 39. On victimization as a common theme, see Peggy Reeves Sanday, "The Socio-cultural Context of Rape: A Cross-Cultural Study," *Journal of Social Issues* Vol. 37, No. 4 (1981): 5–6. Defending homes in Jones, *Women Warriors*, 34.

114 Spooning sex and song in Edwin Johnson, "GI Who Raided 'Saigon Sally's' Sin Barracks," *For Men Only*, May 1965, 26–29, 58. Slow slaughter in Erik Broske, "Ambush in the 'Alley of Perfumed Virgins,'" *Male*, November 1966, 13. Women's Union in Rydstrøm, 289; and Eisen, *Women and Revolution in Viet Nam*, 96. Childbearing years and toll on women in Heather Marie Stur, "Gender and Sexuality," in *The Routledge History of Global War and Society*, eds. Matthew S. Muehlbauer and David J. Ulbrich (New York, NY: Routledge, 2018), 289.

115 "Madame Nhu dies at 86; former first lady of South Vietnam," *Los Angeles Times*, 27 April 2011. On Madame Nhu and the Women's Paramilitary Corps, see Stur, *Beyond Combat*, 26–27; and Anna Snipes, "Race and Gender in Early Vietnam War Popular Fiction," in *The Vietnam War in Popular Culture, Volume 1, During the War*, ed. Ron Milam (Santa Barbara, CA: Praeger, 2017), 277. On the "dragon lady" trope, see Susan Zeiger, *Entangling Alliances: Foreign War Brides and American Soldiers in the Twentieth Century* (New York, NY: New York University Press, 2010), 216; and Jones, 35.

116 Jeff St. John, "Get Saigon's Queen of the Assassin Angels," *Men*, February 1968, 18–19.

117 Susan Jeffords, "Point Blank: Shooting Vietnamese Women," *Vietnam Generation* Vol. 1 (Summer–Fall 1989): 153. On women serving American GIs while working for the PLAF, see Eisen, *Ibid.*, 105.

118 W. J. Saber, "I'm Missing – Like Hell!" *Stag*, March 1966, 16, 99. Stories like these had precedence in tales of World War II, where undercover female spies infiltrated the United States' west coast. See Alan Hynd, "The Great Stakeout of L.A.'s Geisha Spy House," *Stag*, December 1961, 32.

119 "Bitches in Baggy Pants" in "For Your Information," *Stag*, September 1966, 40. Seduce and destroy in "Action for Men Final," *Action for Men*, November 1968, 36. The piece ran under the tagline "Marines Mauled By Murderous Maids." Tolls in Powell 100–101. One female fighter noted that her "strength came from anger and the need to avenge my dead comrades." In Turner, *Even the Women Must Fight*, 59. 25th ID in Hai T. Nguyen, "As the Earth Shook, They Stood Firm," *New York Times*, 17 January 2017.

120 Military space from Healy, "Laments of Warriors' Wives," 237. On the multiple roles played by "long-haired warriors," see Taylor, *Vietnamese Women at War*, 71. See also Eisen, *Ibid.*, 105–108; and William S. Turley, "Women in the Communist Revolution in Vietnam," *Asian Survey* Vol. 12, No. 9 (September 1972): 793–805. On women increasing their autonomy during wartime, see Tétreault, 43. Nguyen Thi Dinh, *No Other Road to Take*, trans. Mai Elliott (Ithaca, NY: Cornell Southeast Asia Program, 1976). Wolfgang

Saxon, "Nguyen Thi Dinh, the Senior Woman in Vietcong Ranks," *New York Times*, 30 August 1992.

121 Women's support of the ARVN in Robert K. Brigham, *ARVN: Life and Death in the South Vietnamese Army* (Lawrence, KS: University Press of Kansas, 2006), 112–118; and Anderson, 300–302. "First Women's Corps," *Los Angeles Times*, 8 April 1965. Phung Thi Hanh, "South Vietnam's Women in Uniform," Folder 21, Box 5, Douglas Pike Collection: Unit 11 – Monographs, The Vietnam Center and Archive, Texas Tech University. On the WFAC, see also Stur, *Beyond Combat*, 109–100. War economy on p. 50. Heather Marie Stur also is helping to uncover this largely underreported story. See *Saigon at War: South Vietnam and the Global Sixties* (New York, NY: Cambridge University Press, 2020).

122 Feelings of guilt and insecurity in Weaver, 20–23; MacKenzie, 109–110; and Kevin Gerard Neill, "Duty, Honor, Rape: Sexual Assault against Women during War," *Journal of International Women's Studies* Vol. 2, No. 1 (November 2000): 47. Emotional trauma in Leatherman, *Sexual Violence and Armed Conflict*, 107; and Nguyen, *Nothing Ever Dies*, 32. On male fantasies leaving out the nightmares of rape victims, see Herbert, *Sexual Violence and American Manhood*, 34.

123 Half-breeds in David Lamb, "Children of the Vietnam War," *Smithsonian Magazine*, June 2009. Gender stratification in Daniel Goodkind, "Rising Gender Inequality in Vietnam since Reunification," *Pacific Affairs* Vol. 68, No. 3 (Autumn 1995): 344. See also MacKenzie, 123–124, 130–131. On postwar gender representation, see Jayne S. Werner, "Between Memory and Desire: Gender and the Remembrance of War in *doi moi* Vietnam," *Gender, Place, and Culture* Vol. 13, No. 3 (June 2006): 306–307, 310–311.

CONCLUSION

1 Author notes, "Manpower and Morale after Tet Symposium," 27 April 2019, Center for Military, War, and Society Studies, University of Kansas.

2 On cultural changes and the pulps increasingly becoming an "anachronism," see Bill Osgerby, *Playboys in Paradise: Masculinity, Youth and Leisure-Style in Modern America* (New York, NY: Oxford University Press, 2001), 152–153; and Steven Watts, *JFK and the Masculine Mystique: Sex and Power on the New Frontier* (New York, NY: St. Martin's Press, 2016), 361, 364. On the war in Vietnam discrediting the "style of aggressive masculinity," see Barbara Ehrenreich, *The Hearts of Men: American Dreams and the Flight from Commitment* (New York, NY: Anchor Books, 1983), 105, 107.

3 Caste system in Shulamith Firestone, *The Dialectic of Sex: The Case for Feminist Revolution* (New York, NY: Quill, 1970), 23. Oppressed and male dominance in Andrea Dworkin, *Woman Hating* (New York, NY: E. P. Dutton, 1974), 17, 23. On discarding masculinity as a "useful category of expression," see Ehrenreich, 107. On counterculture, see Tim Hodgdon, *Manhood in the Age of Aquarius: Masculinity in Two Countercultural Communities, 1965–83* (New York, NY: Columbia University Press, 2008); and Todd Gitlin, *The Sixties: Years of Hope, Days of Rage* (New York, NY: Bantam Books, 1993), 215, 286–287. On a more progressive pulp author dealing with "free-love philosophy," see George R. Meadows, "The Wrong Road to Sex," *Man's Epic*, March 1968, 36.

4 Sexually subjugated in Joseph Le Baron, "How to Hold Your Own, Although Married!" *Men in Adventure*, February 1960, 22–23. Beatniks in Richard Gallgher, "Let's Crack Down on Grimy Beatnik 'Kicks-Tourists' Who Disgrace Us Abroad," *Male*, June 1967, 29. One can note a separation between generations even earlier. *Men* ran a letter from a reader who lauded a previous issue's "real story of courage under fire. Not like these spineless kids nowadays who spend all their time trying to get out of being drafted." In "Calling All Men," *Men*, January 1962, 84. Macho as a dirty word, quoting *Newsweek*, in David Savran, "The Sadomasochist in the Closest: White Masculinity and the Culture of Victimization," *Differences* Vol. 8, No. 2 (Summer 1996): 139.

5 Bill Ryder, "Unisex – The Assault on American Virility," *Bluebook*, February 1970, 38–40. On universal masculine models, see Elisabeth Badinter, *XY: On Masculine Identity* (New York, NY: Columbia University Press, 1995), 25. See also "Introduction" and Carole S. Vance, "Social Construction Theory and Sexuality," in *Constructing Masculinity*, eds. Maurice Berger, Brian Wallis, and Simon Watson (New York, NY: Routledge, 1995), 4, 42–44. On links to the second wave of feminism, see Charlotte Hooper, *Manly States: Masculinities, International Relations, and Gender Politics* (New York, NY: Columbia University Press, 2001), 22–25.

6 Tobias Wolff, *In Pharaoh's Army: Memories of the Lost War* (New York, NY: Alfred A. Knopf, 1994), 68. Symbolic power in Thomas Myers, *Walking Point: American Narratives of Vietnam* (New York, NY: Oxford University Press, 1988), 3. Returning home as a war hero in Mark Baker, *Nam: The Vietnam War in the Words of the Men and Women Who Fought There* (New York, NY: William Morrow and Company, 1981), 220. On Vietnam's relation to masculine citizenship and the warrior myth, see Heather Marie Stur, "Men's and Women's Liberation: Challenging Military Culture after the Vietnam War," in *Integrating the US Military: Race, Gender, and Sexual Orientation since World War II*, eds. Douglas Walter Bristol, Jr. and Heather Marie Stur (Baltimore, MD: The Johns Hopkins University Press, 2017), 143, 145; and Chris Blazina, *The Cultural Myth of Masculinity* (Westport, CT: Praeger, 2003), xvi. On its relation to the culture of dissent, see Margot A. Henriksen, *Dr. Strangelove's America: Society and Culture in the Atomic Age* (Berkeley, CA: University of California Press, 1997), 350.

7 Veteran quoted in Jonathan Shay, *Achilles in Vietnam: Combat Trauma and the Undoing of Character* (New York, NY: Atheneum, 1994), 33. Just warriors in Jean Bethke Elshtain, *Women and War* (New York, NY: Basic Books, 1987), 9. On triumphalist narratives in the comics, see "Introduction" in *The 10 Cent War: Comic Books, Propaganda, and World War II*, eds. Trischa Goodnow and James J. Kimble (Jackson, MS: University Press of Mississippi, 2016), 13.

8 Puzo quoted in Adam Parfrey, *It's a Man's World: Men's Adventure Magazines, the Postwar Pulps* (Los Angeles, CA: Feral House, 2003), 31. Harry Brod, "Joe Kubert's 'War No More' War Comics – Losing a Living Legend," *Huffington Post*, 17 August 2019.

9 Sarlat quoted in "Them!," *Esquire*, November 1976, 94. In the same piece, Carl Sifakis, editorial director for *Male* and *Action*, said he "aimed at the blue-collar readers with high-school educations and annual incomes of twelve thousand dollars. A majority of our readers own a home – but a home in some place like Arkansas." *Stag*, May 1976. On

the transition to "skin" mags, see Parfrey, 19. On this market, see Russell Miller, *Bunny: The Real Story of Playboy* (New York, NY: Holt, Rinehart and Winston, 1984), 170, 187–189; and Michael Kimmel, *Manhood in America: A Cultural History* (New York, NY: The Free Press, 1996), 275.

10 Sexual liberalism in Stephanie Coontz, *The Way We Never Were: American Families and the Nostalgia Trap* (New York, NY: Basic Books, 1992), 260. On the rising popularity of X-rated films, see Jody W. Pennington, *The History of Sex in American Film* (Westport, CT: Praeger, 2007), 56–58; and Linda Williams, *Hard Core: Power, Pleasure, and the "Frenzy of the Visible"* (Berkeley, CA: University of California Press, 1999), 96–99. On the rise of "sexploitation" magazines, see David Church, "Between Fantasy and Reality: Sexploitation, Fan Magazines, and William Rotsler's 'Adults-Only' Career," *Film History* Vol. 26, No. 3 (2014): 106–143.

11 *Hustler* in Laura Kipnis, *Bound and Gagged: Pornography and the Politics of Fantasy in America* (Durham, NC: Duke University Press, 1999), 128–131. On a crisis of masculinity being re-envisioned in the 1990s, where men were scapegoats for unhappy, angry women, see Stephen Wicks, *Warriors and Wildmen: Men, Masculinity, and Gender* (Westport, CT: Praeger, 1996), 3, 42.

12 Percentages in Melissa T. Brown, "Transitioning to an All-Volunteer Force," in *The Routledge History of Gender, War, and the U.S. Military*, ed. Kara Dixon Vuic (London: Routledge, 2018), 134. On concerns over manpower shortages, see Stephen J. Dienstfrey, "Women Veterans' Exposure to Combat," *Armed Forces and Society* Vol. 14, No. 4 (Summer 1988): 550. On military recruiting ads during this timeframe, which still promoted a "warrior masculinity," see Melissa T. Brown, *Enlisting Masculinity: The Construction of Gender in U.S. Military Recruiting Advertising during the All-Volunteer Force* (New York, NY: Oxford University Press, 2012), 48–49.

13 James Webb, "Women Can't Fight," *The Washingtonian*, November 1979, 146. A West Point cadet mirrored Webb's sentiment, saying he "would never openly harass women, [but] I hope they understand they are not welcome here." In Joshua S. Goldstein, *War and Gender: How Gender Shapes the War System and Vice Versa* (New York, NY: Cambridge University Press, 2001), 97. Schlafly quoted in Beth Bailey, *America's Army: Making the All-Volunteer Force* (Cambridge, MA: The Belknap Press of Harvard University Press, 2009), 169. On disdain for female soldiers dating back to World War II, see Emily Yellin, *Our Mothers' War: American Women at Home and at the Front during World War II* (New York, NY: The Free Press, 2004), 111.

14 James William Gibson, *Warrior Dreams: Paramilitary Culture in Post-Vietnam America* (New York, NY: Hill and Wang, 1994), 7–13, 28–29, 39, 48, 196–197. See also James William Gibson, "Redeeming Vietnam: Techno-thriller Novels of the 1980s," *Cultural Critique* No. 19 (Autumn 1991): 179–202.

15 Mercenary quoted in Kyle Burke, "Soldiers of Fortune," *Jacobin Magazine*, 2 June 2018. See also H. Bruce Franklin, *Vietnam and Other American Fantasies* (Amherst, MA: University of Massachusetts Press, 2000), 155. Sadler quoted in Marc Leepson, *Ballad of the Green Beret: The Life and Wars of Staff Sergeant Barry Sadler* (Guilford, CT: Stackpole Books, 2017), 179. On the ideology of masculinity needing healing after war, see Katherine

Kinney, *Friendly Fire: American Images of the Vietnam War* (New York, NY: Oxford University Press, 2000), 106. Robert Bly has argued, somewhat problematically, that if a culture does not "deal with the warrior energy ... it will turn up outside in the form of street gangs, wife beating, drug violence, brutality to children, and aimless murder." *Iron John: A Book about Men* (New York, NY: Da Capo Press, 2004), 190.

16 Victims in Christian G. Appy, *American Reckoning: The Vietnam War and Our National Identity* (New York, NY: Viking, 2015), 241; and Robert Jay Lifton, "Victims and Execu-tioners," in *Crimes of War: A Legal, Political-Documentary and Psychological Inquiry into the Responsibility of Leaders, Citizens, and Soldiers for Criminal Acts of War*, eds. Richard A. Falk, Gabriel Kolko, and Robert Jay Lifton (New York, NY: Random House, 1971), 419. For women dealing with similar postwar issues, see Winnie Smith, *American Daughter Gone to War: On the Front Lines with an Army Nurse in Vietnam* (New York, NY: William Morrow and Company, 1992), 37; and Barbara Hesselman Kautz, *When I Die I'm Going to Heaven 'Cause I Spent My Time in Hell: A Memoir of My Year as an Army Nurse in Vietnam* (Portsmouth, NH: Piscataqua Press, 2013). 65. Of course, Vietnamese women were absent from these postwar conversations. On symbolically earning manhood, see Myers, *Walking Point*, 137.

17 Remaining a child in John Ketwig, *... and a Hard Rain Fell: A GI's True Story of War in Vietnam* (Naperville, IL: Sourcebooks, 2002), 75. On unfulfilled manhood, see Tracy Karner, "Fathers, Sons, and Vietnam: Masculinity and Betrayal in the Life Narratives of Vietnam Veterans with Post Traumatic Stress Disorder," *American Studies* Vol. 37, No. 1 (Spring 1996): 65.

18 Walter R. Hecox, "The One-Man Army of Bataan," *Man's Magazine*, July 1961, 42, 80. "Bill Mauldin in Korea," *Man's Day*, March 1953, 87–88. "Stag's Big Picture," *Stag*, March 1962, 23. For a similar tale of Medal of Honor recipient Dwight Johnson's post-Vietnam struggles, see James E. Westheider, *The African American Experience in Vietnam: Brothers in Arms* (Boulder, CO: Rowman & Littlefield, 2008), 128; and Fred Turner, *Echoes of Combat: Trauma, Memory, and the Vietnam War* (Minneapolis, MN: University of Minne-sota Press, 1996), 50–51.

19 Karl H. Purnell, "How Many GI's Get Hooked on Drugs?," *True*, August 1968, 52, 82. Equilibrium and time bombs in Myers, 190. On World War II, see David A. Gerber, "Heroes and Misfits: The Troubled Social Reintegration of Disabled Veterans in 'The Best Years of Our Lives,'" *American Quarterly* Vol. 46, No. 4 (December 1994): 545–574. Fears of increasing domestic violence in Janie L. Leatherman, *Sexual Violence and Armed Conflict* (Malden, MA: Polity, 2011), 82.

20 On *Taxi Driver* and *Heroes*, see Mitchell K. Hall, *Crossroads: American Popular Culture and the Vietnam Generation* (Lanham, MD: Rowman & Littlefield, 2005), 181. On regenerative violence, see Richard Slotkin, *Gunfighter Nation: The Myth of the Frontier in Twentieth-Century America* (Norman, OK: University of Oklahoma Press, 1998), 228. For a discus-sion on Vietnam films like *The Deer Hunter* (1978), which exposed the traumas of a humiliating lost war, see Suzanne E. Hatty, *Masculinities, Violence, and Culture* (Thousand Oaks, CA: Sage, 2000), 171; Peter Marin, "Coming to Terms with Vietnam," *Harper's*, December 1980, 45; and Leonard Quart, "*The Deer Hunter*: The Superman in Vietnam,"

in *From Hanoi to Hollywood: The Vietnam War in American Film*, eds. Linda Dittmar and Gene Michaud (New Brunswick, NJ: Rutgers University Press, 2000), 159–168.

21 Hypermasculine heroes in R. W. Connell, *Gender and Power: Society, the Person and Sexual Politics* (Stanford, CA: Stanford University Press, 1987), 80. On Rambo, see: Susan Jeffords, "Debriding Vietnam: The Resurrection of the White American Male," *Feminist Studies* Vol. 14, No. 3 (Autumn 1988): 525–526; Savran, 130; and Eben J. Muse, "From Lt. Calley to John Rambo: Repatriating the Vietnam War," *Journal of American Studies* Vol. 27, No. 1 (April 1993): 88–92. Excessively muscled bodies in Antony Easthope, *What a Man's Gotta Do: The Masculine Myth in Popular Culture* (Boston, MA: Unwin Hyman, 1990), 134.

22 On gender being politically deployed, see Harriet Bradley, *Gender* (Cambridge: Polity, 2007), 4. Gender not being fixed in R. W. Connell, *Masculinities*, 2nd ed. (Berkeley, CA: University of California Press, 2005), 35.

23 On the effect of war stories, see Susan Jeffords, "Telling the War Story," in *It's Our Military, Too! Women and the U.S. Military*, ed. Judith Hicks Stiehm (Philadelphia, PA: Temple University Press, 1996), 227–230.

24 Peter Goldman and Tony Fuller, *Charlie Company: What Vietnam Did to Us* (New York, NY: Ballantine Books, 1983), ix. John M. Del Vecchio, *The 13th Valley* (New York, NY: Bantam, 1982), 19, 160–161. See also Myers, *Walking Point*, 67. On portraying war as neither noble nor uplifting, see Philip Dwyer, "Making Sense of the Muddle: War Memoirs and the Culture of Remembering," in *War Stories: The War Memoir in History and Literature*, ed. Philip Dwyer (New York, NY: Berghahn, 2017), 10. On how idiosyncratic views become accepted as universal, see Judy Lee Kinney, "Gardens of Stone, Platoon, and Hamburger Hill," in *Inventing Vietnam: The War in Film and Television*, ed. Michael Anderegg (Philadelphia, PA: Temple University Press, 1991), 160. Lost youth in Jeff Loeb, "Childhood's End: Self Recovery in the Autobiography of the Vietnam War," *American Studies* Vol. 37, No. 1 (Spring 1996): 100. The vision of every man being a "hero in immediate prospect" could be seen in the Civil War as well. Stephen W. Berry III, *All That Makes a Man: Love and Ambition in the Civil War South* (New York, NY: Oxford University Press, 2003), 167.

25 Taxi cab driver quoted in W. D. Ehrhart, *Vietnam–Perkasie: A Combat Marine Memoir* (Jefferson, NC: McFarland, 1983), 273. Larry Heinemann, *Paco's Story* (New York, NY: Vintage Books, 1986, 2005), 176. Joanna Bourke notes how threatening rape was seen as an acceptable way to gain information from prisoners of war and civilians. *Rape: Sex, Violence, History* (Berkeley, CA: Shoemaker Hoard, 2007), 368. Bo Hathaway, *A World of Hurt* (New York, NY: Taplinger, 1981), 110. See also Susan Jeffords, "'Things Worth Dying For': Gender and the Ideology of Collectivity in Vietnam Representation," *Cultural Critique* No. 8 (Winter 1987–1988): 86–87.

26 Ketwig, 129. See also Micheal Clodfelter, *Mad Minutes and Vietnam Months: A Soldier's Memoir* (Jefferson, NC: McFarland, 1988), 144. On GI sexual behavior rooted in mainstream culture, see John A. Wood, *Veteran Narratives and the Collective Memory of the Vietnam War* (Athens, OH: Ohio University Press, 2016), 61.

27 P. F. Kluge, "Why They Love Us in the Philippines," *Playboy*, September 1986, 90, 92. William Broyles, Jr., "Why Men Love War," *Esquire*, November 1984, 62.

28 Montoya quoted in Gina Marie Weaver, *Ideologies of Forgetting: Rape in the Vietnam War* (Albany, NY: SUNY Press, 2010), 161. Phil Klay, *Redeployment* (New York, NY: Penguin Books, 2014), 125.

29 Harold G. Moore and Joseph L. Galloway, *We Were Soldiers Once . . . and Young* (New York, NY: HarperPerennial, 1993), 231. Philip D. Beidler, *Late Thoughts on an Old War: The Legacy of Vietnam* (Athens, GA: The University of Georgia Press, 2004), 195. Selling Vietnam in Rick Berg and John Carlos Rowe, "The Vietnam War and American Memory," in *The Vietnam War and American Culture*, eds. John Carlos Rowe and Rick Berg (New York, NY: Columbia University Press, 1991), 3.

30 Muller quoted in *The Wounded Generation: America after Vietnam*, ed. A. D. Horne (Englewood Cliffs, NJ: Prentice-Hall, 1981), 122, 123. For similar sentiments, see Goldman and Fuller, 125, 251. Of course, women were not part of these homecoming stories. On this, see Jeanne Holm, *Women in the Military: An Unfinished* Revolution, rev. ed. (Novato, CA: Presidio Press, 1992), 240–242. On the tolls suffered by the "greatest generation," see Thomas Childers, *Soldier from the War Returning: The Greatest Generation's Troubled Homecoming from World War II* (Boston, MA: Mariner Books, 2009), 13. "Where Are They Now?," *Stag*, March 1966, 39. Martin Fass, "John Barrow's Sex Colony," *Men*, May 1964, 21.

31 *The Grunt*, Vol. 1, No. 1 (1968): 5, 22. The magazine was published in Honolulu, Hawaii.

32 Trooper Clinton Poley quoted in Moore and Galloway, 424. On the emotional cycle of war, see David Donovan, *Once a Warrior King: Memoirs of an Officer in Vietnam* (New York, NY: McGraw-Hill, 1985), 156.

33 Donovan, *Ibid.* Voyeurism in Don Ringnalda, *Fighting and Writing the Vietnam War* (Jackson, MS: University Press of Mississippi, 1994), 175. Structures and images of male superiority in Jonathan Rutherford, "Who's That Man," in *Male Order: Unwrapping Masculinity*, eds. Rowena Chapman and Jonathan Rutherford (London: Lawrence & Wishart, 1988), 54.

34 On Wayne, see Mark Gerzon, *A Choice of Heroes: The Changing Faces of American Manhood* (Boston, MA: Houghton Mifflin, 1992), 3; Samuel Hynes, *The Soldiers' Tale: Bearing Witness to Modern War* (New York, NY: Penguin, 1997), 215; and Robert Jay Lifton, *Home from the War: Vietnam Veterans: Neither Victims nor Executioners* (New York, NY: Simon & Schuster, 1973), 245. No victory in Susan A. Brewer, *Why America Fights: Patriotism and War Propaganda from the Philippines to Iraq* (New York, NY: Oxford University Press, 2009), 209. Patrick Hagopian argues that the "residue of unallocated guilt" had a "pernicious effect on the lives of Vietnam veterans." *The Vietnam War in American Memory: Veterans, Memorials, and the Politics of Healing* (Amherst, MA: University of Massachusetts Press, 2009), 75.

35 On gender and identities not being fixed, see Hooper, *Manly States*, 35, 53–54, 75. On the warrior code as a natural imperative, see T. Walter Herbert, *Sexual Violence and American Manhood* (Cambridge, MA: Harvard University Press, 2002), 60.

36 Broyles, 58, 61, 65. For a similar argument, see J. Glenn Gray, *The Warriors: Reflections on Men in Battle* (Lincoln, NE: University of Nebraska Press, 1959, 1970), 66. On war as the "ultimate romantic experience," see Goldman and Fuller, 56. For an example of

Vietnam being reframed in the 1980s in terms of gallantry and heroism, see Meredith Lair, "The Education Center at The Wall and the Rewriting of History," *The Public Historian* Vol. 34, No. 1 (Winter 2012): 54.

37 Soldier Anthony Cavender quoted in Eric M. Bergerud, *Red Thunder, Tropic Lightning: The World of a Combat Division in Vietnam* (Boulder, CO: Westview Press, 1993), 229. Journalist Dan Rather admitted that stories of soldiers perpetrating rape in Vietnam was "not something he thought of as news" because such incidents were "relatively common." In Carol Harrington, *Politicization of Sexual Violence: From Abolitionism to Peacekeeping* (Burlington, VT: Ashgate, 2010), 93. On narratives having social power, see Beverly Allen, *Rape Warfare: The Hidden Genocide in Bosnia-Herzegovina and Croatia* (Minneapolis, MN: University of Minnesota Press, 1996), 30.

38 William Harrell, "The Treacherous Nymph Who Sold Out the Navy at Pearl Harbor," *Men*, March 1963, 34. Jimmy Cannon, "Korea Was Like a Good-Looking Woman with Gonorrhea," *Saga*, August 1963, 57. On sexual violence in wartime being linked to gender-based violence in daily life before conflict, see Kerry F. Crawford, *Wartime Sexual Violence: From Silence to Condemnation of a Weapon of War* (Washington, DC: Georgetown University Press, 2017), 163. Language as a vehicle to assumptions about gender roles in relation to war in "Preface," in *Gendering War Talk*, eds. Miriam Cooke and Angela Woollacott (Princeton, NJ: Princeton University Press, 1993), xii. See also Susan Jeffords, *The Remasculinization of America: Gender and the Vietnam War* (Bloomington, IN: Indiana University Press, 1989), xi. On the role of military indoctrination, see William Arkin and Lynne R. Dobrofsky, "Military Socialization and Masculinity," *Journal of Social Issues* Vol. 34, No. 1 (1978): 151–168.

39 *Men in Adventure*, April 1966. Kaylin quoted in Bruce Jay Friedman, "Seamless, Outrageous, and Wonderful," in *He-Man, Bag Men & Nymphos*, eds. Robert Deis and Wyatt Doyle (Philadelphia, PA: New Texture, 2013), 9.

40 John C. Bahnsen, Jr., *American Warrior: A Combat Memoir of Vietnam* (New York, NY: Citadel Press, 2007), 460. On earlier notions that World War II had "reinvigorated and masculinized the nation," see Christina S. Jarvis, *The Male Body at War: American Masculinity during World War II* (DeKalb, IL: Northern Illinois University Press, 2004), 186.

41 Quoted in Lifton, *Home from the War*, 121.

42 Barrow quoted in Madeline Morris, "In War and Peace: Rape, War, and Military Culture," in *War's Dirty Secret: Rape, Prostitution, and Other Crimes against Women*, ed. Anne Llewellyn Barstow (Cleveland, OH: The Pilgrim Press, 2000), 183. Jesse Kelley, "Why the Trump Administration Needs to Keep Women Out of Combat," *The Federalist*, 25 September 2018.

43 Philip Marnais, *Saigon after Dark* (New York, NY: McFadden, 1967), 29. "Out of the Stag Bag," *Stag*, April 1952, 80. "Letters to the Editor," *Man's Magazine*, October 1960, 6. On rechanneling rage and powerlessness into more nondestructive patterns, see Cynthia Grguric, "War Rape: Unveiling the Complexities of Motivation and Reparation in Order to Create Lines of Peace and Empowerment," in *Terrorism, Political Violence, and Extremism: New Psychology to Understand, Face, and Defuse the Threat*, ed. Chris E. Stout (Santa

Barbara, CA: Praeger, 2017), 141. On constructions of sexual violence in conflict as a larger social problem, see Eve Ayiera, "Sexual Violence in Conflict: A Problematic International Discourse," *Feminist Africa* Vol. 14, No. 1 (2010): 8–14.

44 Rite of passage in Elshtain, *Women and War*, 223. Gender inequalities in Ann-Kathrin Kreft, "Fighting Sexual Violence in War: Context Matters," U.S. Army War College War Room (on-line blog), 5 December 2018. On the nature of women disqualifying them from war, from testimony by Marine Corps Commandant Barrow, see Lucinda Joy Peach, "Gender Ideology in the Ethics of Women in Combat," in Stiehm, 161. For an example of a female sniper, see Gustav Hasford, *The Short-Timers* (New York, NY: Harper & Row, 1979), 98–103. Finally, on rethinking masculinities, see Cynthia Cockburn, "Militarism, Masculinity, and Men," in *Together for Transformation: Men, Masculinities, and Peacebuilding*, ed. José de Vries and Isabelle Geuskens (Alkmaar: Women Peacemakers Program, 2010), 19.

45 On alternatives, see Claire Duncanson, "Hegemonic Masculinity and the Possibility of Change in Gender Relations," *Men and Masculinities* Vol. 18, No. 2 (2105): 231–248. On the problems of being vulnerable without feeling emasculated continuing today, see Frank Bruni, "Donald Trump, Manly He-Man," *New York Times*, 27 February 2018.

46 On the psychological impact of harming civilians, see Bruce P. Dohrenwend, Nick Turse, Thomas J. Yager, and Melanie M. Wall, *Surviving Vietnam: Psychological Consequences of the War for U.S. Veterans* (New York, NY: Oxford University Press, 2019), 127, 161–178. For a contemporary example of the war's nonmilitary aspects, see John C. Donnell, "Expanding Political Participation – the Long Haul from Villagism to Nationalism," *Asian Survey* Vol. 10, No. 8 (August 1970): 688–704.

47 Kevin Draper, "Video Games Aren't Why Shootings Happen. Politicians Still Blame Them." *New York Times*, 5 August 2019. For an additional view, see Julie Bosman, Kate Taylor and Tim Arango, "A Common Trait among Mass Killers: Hatred toward Women," *New York Times*, 10 August 2019. On exposure to pornography and men's magazines leading men to perceive women as objects, see Paul J. Wright and Robert S. Tokunaga, "Men's Objectifying Media Consumption, Objectification of Women, and Attitudes Supportive of Violence against Women," *Archives of Sexual Behavior* Vol. 45, No. 4 (May 2016): 961.

48 On love of violence being associated with male patriotism, see Myron Brenton, *The American Male* (New York, NY: Coward-McCann, 1966), 66. On military socialization processes creating the potential for atrocities, see Peter G. Bourne, "From Boot Camp to My Lai," in Falk, Kolko, and Lifton, 468. See also Cynthia Cockburn, "Gender Relations as Causal in Militarization and War: A Feminist Perspective," in *Making Gender, Making War: Violence, Military and Peacekeeping Practices*, eds. Annica Kronsell and Erika Svedberg (New York, NY: Routledge, 2012), 19, 23.

49 Jack Raymond, "3,500 U.S. Marines Going to Vietnam to Bolster Base," *New York Times*, 7 March 1965. For table of contents taglines, see *Male*, March 1965, 4.

50 Of note, the June 2017 issue of *Men's Health* ran a story on adventure magazines and claimed that they could "still inspire men of today." Mike LaFavore, "War! Women! Weasels!" 102–125. On the disparity between idealized views of war and reality, see Hugh McManners, *The Scars of War* (New York, NY: HarperCollins, 1993), 356.

Index

Printed in the United States
by Baker & Taylor Publisher Services